Strategic
Occidentalism

Strategic Occidentalism

*On Mexican Fiction, the Neoliberal Book Market,
and the Question of World Literature*

✦

Ignacio M. Sánchez Prado

NORTHWESTERN UNIVERSITY PRESS
EVANSTON, ILLINOIS

Northwestern University Press
www.nupress.northwestern.edu

Printed in the United States of America

10 9 8 7 6 5 4 3 2 1

Library of Congress Cataloging-in-Publication Data

Names: Sanchez Prado, Ignacio M., 1979– author.
Title: Strategic occidentalism : on Mexican fiction, the neoliberal book market,
    and the question of world literature / Ignacio M. Sanchez Prado.
Description: Evanston, Illinois : Northwestern University Press, 2018. | Includes
    bibliographical references and index.
Identifiers: LCCN 2018019339 | ISBN 9780810137554 (pbk. : alk. paper) | ISBN
    9780810137561 (cloth : alk. paper) | ISBN 9780810137578 (ebook)
Subjects: LCSH: Mexican fiction—20th century—History and criticism. | Mexican
    fiction—21st century—History and criticism. | Cosmopolitanism in literature.
Classification: LCC PQ7155 .S266 2018 | DDC 863.64—dc23
LC record available at https://lccn.loc.gov/2018019339

CONTENTS

ACKNOWLEDGMENTS

The idea of this book has been in my mind for over a decade. Back in 2006, when I edited the book *América Latina en la "literatura mundial"* and defended the dissertation that would be the base of my 2009 monograph *Naciones intelectuales*, I believed there was a potential study connecting the concerns of both projects: understanding the substantial limits of world literature theories to account for the ways in which Latin American literary cosmopolitanism actually works, as well as reflecting on the ways in which Mexican writers develop strategies to work within shifting social processes and literary institutions. Recognizing every single conversation and person that contributed something to the slow development of the original idea and its conversion into this book is too much of a challenge for both the length of an acknowledgments section and the capacity of my memory. But I am a firm believer in academic scholarship as a primarily collective endeavor, so I do have to say that this book owes a great debt to the communities of scholars in which I participate and I find enriching.

As it happens with many of my endeavors, the work here has some roots in my work with my mentors. Mabel Moraña gave me the first opportunity to publish on the subject, by inviting me to edit the 2006 collection for the Instituto Internacional de Literatura Iberoamericana, and has been, as my colleague and program director at Washington University, a consistent interlocutor of my work on world literature. Adela Pineda Franco taught me my first undergraduate classes on the question of cosmopolitanism in Latin America, and her work on modernism resonates implicitly in my understanding of world literature. Pedro Ángel Palou, asides from being an author studied in this work, always instilled in me the importance of being attentive to the material workings of literature and never losing sight of the perspective of writers. I have considerable debts to all three of them, and my work, even over a decade after completing my education, would not be possible without their example and inspiration.

This project has grown out of dialogues with interlocutors in different communities. Within Mexican studies, Oswaldo Zavala, José Ramón Ruisánchez, and Oswaldo Estrada always challenge me to question and reformulate my own ideas. I have presented the material in this book many times in the conferences organized by UC Mexicanistas in Santa Barbara, Mérida, and Irvine, and I am always grateful to Sara Poot-Herrera and Jacobo Sefamí for their generosity in opening their institutions and their hearts to me and to many other colleagues. In the past years, Manuel Gutiérrez-Silva, Carolyn Fornoff, Brian L. Price, Emily Hind, Cheyla Samuelson, Sam Steinberg, Sara Potter, Sergio Gutiérrez Negrón, Bruno Bosteels, Ivonne del Valle, Viviane Mahieux, Ericka Beckman, Jorge Téllez, Ilana Luna, Rebecca Janzen, Rafael Acosta, Anna Nogar, Irma Cantú, Cristina Carrasco, Sarah Pollack, and many others have formed a community that constantly nurtures my own research in literature. The study of world literature in Latin America has developed considerably since I edited the 2006 collection. Writing this book entails dialogues and debates, implicit or explicit, with dear friends like Gustavo Guerrero, Héctor Hoyos, Mariano Siskind, Juan de Castro, and, more recently, the research group at the University of Köln in Germany: Gesine Müller, Benjamin Loy, and Jorge Locane. I hope that this book continues our ongoing polemic. Finally, this book has significant debts to scholars outside Latin American studies who are energizing the field of contemporary literary studies and who have provided references, ideas, and critiques in terms distinct form the ones within my fields. I want to recognize Sarah Brouillette in particular. I have found her work, her intelligent approach to literature, and my conversations with her to be essential when thinking through the questions in this book. In addition, I want to thank Andrew Hoberek for bringing me into spaces like ACLA and ASAP, which productively remove me from my Latin Americanist comfort zone. In these spaces, I have met scholars whose work has been inspiring in this project: Sheri-Marie Harrison, Joseph Jeon, Gloria Fisk, Jonathan Eburne, Amy Elias, Viet Nguyen, Mrinali Chakravorty, and Matthew Hart, among others.

It is not my style to work too closely with living authors whom I study, but in this book some dialogues were helpful. Pedro Ángel Palou, Ignacio Padilla, and Jorge Volpi graciously agreed to answer some of my questions for chapter 2, clarifying the challenges they faced as young writers during the period of the Crack manifesto. Cristina Rivera Garza and I have discussed her work in many occasions. And Ana García Bergua clarified a few points that I was unable to discern by myself.

The material process of writing was, as usual, supported by Washington University in St. Louis, where I have been able to work with comfort and freedom. I am grateful to my two academic homes, the Department of Romance Languages and Literature and the Latin American Studies Program, and my colleagues in both, for their constant support. This book was written in part with the backing of generous research and travel funds provided by the School of Arts and Sciences. I was also a recipient of a residential faculty fellowship at the university's Center for the Humanities, which afforded me time and resources to do a significant amount of archival and library work, and a community to debate my ideas intensely and productively. I am grateful to Jean Allman and Rebecca Wanzo for the community they have created, and to the staff at the center, particularly Barb Liebmann, for their support. I am also grateful to my fellow faculty fellows, Corinna Treitel, Robert Henke, and Erin McGothlin, and the graduate student fellows Courtney Andree, Jenny Westrick, and Sara Jay for their engagement with my work and their productive suggestions. Parts of this book evolved thanks to my graduate and undergraduate seminars on Mexican literature. I am grateful to the students in those seminars for providing yet another venue of conversation. The University Libraries at Washington University also provided outstanding services in locating very rare books, including original editions of Sergio Pitol's translations. I want to thank Daria Carson-Dussán, Katherine Van Arsdale, and the staff at Interlibrary Loan Services for going out of their way in assist in my research.

Last but not least, the editorial process that leads to the final version of this book has been carried out by wonderful people. Gianna Moser at Northwestern University Press is the type of editor that authors like me always aspire to have. She has been very supportive of this project since I approached her with a vague idea at an MLA conference a few years ago. Besides her rigor and professionalism as an editor, and the pleasure of talking to her about books and other things every time we meet at a conference, I am deeply grateful to her for supporting this book and being patient with me, as I was attempting to finish it in the middle of a challenging time in my life. The two anonymous readers provided very valuable comments that led to substantial changes and to a final version of this book that is definitely better than the original I submitted. Robin Myers, my proofreader extraordinaire, did a wonderful job in proofreading this book and helping me in dealing with the problems that arise from writing a book in one's second language. The cover image appears thanks to the generosity of Mr. Andrés Blaisten, an exceptional art collector who has been crucial in preserving modern Mexican art. I also want to thank Claudia Barragán and Andrea Chávez for their assistance in securing the image.

Like everything in my life, this book owes a lot to the support of my wife, Abby Hathaway, who is there with me as I do all kinds of conference and research travel and I spend late nights at the computer. Remarkably, she has agreed to live in an apartment with floor-to-ceiling bookshelves and not much furniture. Without her company and support, none of my projects would ever come to fruition.

A book can also be defined by loss: the passing of three people marked the writing of *Strategic Occidentalism*. My friend Ricardo Gutiérrez Mouat was one of the first scholars to recognize my work when I was a graduate student, and he was one of the most intelligent and generous interlocutors I ever had in academia. His commitment to literature, his erudition, and his passionate engagements for contemporary writers were definitive models for this book, in the happy occasions in which I discussed my research with him. I hope this book lives up to the standards of rigor and critical commitment that they always practiced.

As I was completing this book, Ignacio Padilla, one of the authors studied here and a dear professor from my undergraduate years, passed away at the peak of his career. After a few years of not talking to him, we had reconnected through my questions for this project, and I had the opportunity to talk to him about the book and about his literary passions in Mexico City just a few days before his passing. I still remember his wonderful classes on topics like Cervantes, essay writing, and modern Iberian literature, which were always modeled by reminding young aspiring scholars to never lose sight of the love of literature. He was one of the most intelligent, passionate, and enthusiastic people I have ever met, and he is dearly missed. It is my hope that my study of his work in this book helps to overcome the critical neglect of his fiction, and to recognize the richness of his literary writing, one of the most elegant in the Spanish language.

The third loss was the deepest and the most personal. In the process of writing this book my mother, María del Carmen Prado, passed away. She would have disapproved a detailed personal remembrance in print, because she was a private person. I will simply say that she was always deeply supportive, personally and materially, to my research. She had an uncanny ability to find the most difficult of books in the unlikeliest of places, and, being a woman of dazzling ingenuity, could go as far as to track the authors' homes and knock on their doors to find a rare volume. Many of my projects would not have been possible without her talents. She, of course, was always an anchor of support and, strong-willed as she was, an important counterbalance to the vanities of intellectual life and a reminder of the things that truly matter when, absorbed by research, I could often forget. This book is dedicated to her memory, imperfectly, since she found academic books unimpressive, although she was an underground contributor to what follows and to all of my work.

Strategic
Occidentalism

Introduction

✦

Mexican World Literature

On occasion, a book of literary criticism that one has been researching and writing for years will suddenly coincide with a small boom in attention to its objects of study. To my surprise, this seems to be the case with *Strategic Occidentalism*, a study of key authors of post-1968 Mexican fiction viewed through the lens of world literature theory. As a scholar of Mexican literature working in a university in Missouri, and as a Mexican reader living in the United States, I decided to embark on this project a few years ago, and to do so in English, partly as a reaction to a couple of frustrations: for one thing, the scarcity of English-language translations of even the most important Mexican writers from the 1970s onward (not to mention the scarcity of scholarly criticism on their work); and for another, the reductionist accounts of Mexican and Latin American literature in most Anglophone critical paradigms of comparative, transnational, and global literature—including postcolonial theory and world literature theory. To my surprise, during the process of writing this book, Mexican literature has slowly but surely broken through some of the barriers separating it from the U.S. publishing world as works by a handful of Mexican writers have begun to make their way into U.S. publishing catalogs and bookstores. A first bit of good news came in 2015, when I learned with great joy that Deep Vellum Publishing, a Dallas-based nonprofit startup press, had begun to translate the work of one of Mexico's most revered living writers, Sergio Pitol, the subject of chapter 1. Thanks to the efforts of editor Will Evans and translator George Henson (as well as the support of other figures like Mexican writer Álvaro Enrigue), an author with a distinguished, decades-long trajectory would finally be translated into English. This belatedness is particularly incongruous when one considers that Pitol himself is the translator of dozens of books, including numerous works by English-language writers. The fact that one of the most important translators of literature into Spanish had failed to get his own canonical writings published in English certainly exemplifies the disparities that govern world literary institutions.

Although Pitol is the most directly relevant author for *Strategic Occidentalism* in this recent (and still very partial) boom, there are other important cases as well. While this introduction was being written, Mexican and U.S. readers received the surprising news that the English translation of Mexican writer Valeria Luiselli's book *La historia de mis dientes* (*The Story of My Teeth*, 2015) was selected as one of the *New York Times*' 100 Notable Books of the Year and as a National Book Critics Circle Award Finalist in fiction.[1] This is a remarkable event in itself, as Luiselli is the first Mexican writer to ever achieve such a nomination and only the second Latin American author to do so (Roberto Bolaño's *2666* was posthumously recognized with the award in 2008). Indeed, one could argue (as Aaron Bady recently did) that Luiselli's triumph is riding a wave of interest generated by Bolaño's colossal renown.[2] Yet we must be attentive to the ways in which Luiselli's work has emerged from an ecosystem of Mexican literature that remains invisible to English-language readers and critics. Her success is among the latest iterations of large-scale developments, both in literary institutions and fiction aesthetics, that have been brewing since the late 1960s. Just as the recent success of Mexican film directors like Alejandro González Iñárritu and Alfonso Cuarón ensued, as I argue in my previous book, from the decades-long rise of a film industry that is inextricably intertwined with neoliberalism, it is impossible to account for Luiselli's achievements without understanding its conditions of possibility within Mexican literature.[3]

Even if I confined myself to the authors I study in this book, the extent of her rootedness in the ground of Mexico's world literature would still be apparent. Luiselli's first book, *Papeles falsos* (*Sidewalks*, 2010), is a collection of narrative essays based on urban wandering, travel, and cosmopolitan culture.[4] It belongs to a genre of cosmopolitan writing that Pitol established as canonical in Mexican literature, particularly after the publication of his landmark collection *El arte de la fuga* (*The Art of Flight*, 1996).[5] In fact, Luiselli wrote a piece on Pitol for *Granta*'s online series Best Untranslated Writers, where she acknowledges having read his work since her teenage years.[6] Her second book, the novel *Los ingrávidos* (*Faces in the Crowd*, 2011), intertwines the story of a young pregnant woman—a possible alter ego of the author—and that of Mexican poet Gilberto Owen, a cult figure who was part of the group known as Los Contemporáneos.[7] The connection between a member of this group and a contemporary writer is hardly new in Mexican fiction. Two writers from the Crack group, the subject of chapter 2, wrote analogous novels in the early 1990s. Jorge Volpi connected his fictional self to *contemporáneo* Jorge Cuesta in *A pesar del oscuro silencio* (*In Spite of the Dark Silence*, 1992). Meanwhile, Pedro Ángel Palou wrote a novel with many similarities to Luiselli's representation of documents from the past and their silences in his own portrayal of another *contemporáneo*, Xavier Villaurrutia: *En la alcoba de un mundo* (*In the Bedchamber of a World*, 1992).[8] I am not sure that Luiselli would claim a direct connection to the Crack group, given her divergent style and the group's divided reception in Mexican literature. That said, her own treatment of Owen unquestionably traces a possible connection. Both Luiselli and the Crack writers model themselves on a group of writers known for resisting the imperatives of nationalist literature. It is also true that the Crack group's role in redefining mainstream Mexican literature internationally, far from the types of magical realist narratives popularized by writers like Laura Esquivel, is among the factors that exempt a writer like Luiselli from serving as a native informant of stereotypical Mexicanness. Finally, we could not understand Luiselli's success without acknowledging the long struggle waged by Mexican women writers to attain cultural and editorial recognition in Mexico—a country that once declared, back in the 1920s, that its national literature was meant to be "virile," and where women writers, even major ones, generally occupied secondary places in literary criticism and historiography well into the 1990s.[9] As chapter 3 will discuss in greater depth, Luiselli certainly had important precursors in writers from the 1950s and 1960s, like Elena Garro and Josefina Vicens, who challenged the *doxa* exercised by male authors in Mexican fiction. Yet Luiselli was also preceded by the women authors who built what Jane Lavery and Nuala Finnegan aptly call a "Boom femenino," fostered by the women writers in the late 1980s and early 1990s who took over the bestseller world (with notable blockbuster novels such as Laura Esquivel's *Como agua para chocolate*) and opened important doors in the institutions of literary fiction (even if some of them, like María Luisa Puga, remain woefully understudied).[10] Indeed, Luiselli's success in Mexico and beyond is only possible thanks to the trailblazing work of women writers like the ones I will study in chapter 3—Carmen Boullosa, Cristina Rivera Garza, and Ana García Bergua—who challenged not only the concept of what a woman could write in Mexican literature, but also the aesthetics of Mexican fiction at large.

My point is not to claim that Luiselli's work is derivative. On the contrary, she is indisputably a writer of great talent and intelligence. Rather, just like Bolaño has become a representative of Latin American literature as a whole, the fact that Luiselli may come to play such a role for Mexican fiction (it is too early to tell, but not unthinkable) creates an imperative for critics and scholars to remain attentive to the larger dynamics of literary fiction in Mexico. If anything, Luiselli's success and the growing access of other writers to English-language translation has made *Strategic Occidentalism* (unbeknownst to me as I wrote it) into a critical history of a cosmopolitan paradigm of Mexican fiction and its recent ascent, as well as of the establishment of various literary institutions that would facilitate twentieth-century literary ventures. Indeed, as we can see now, the type of world literature studied in this book is currently replacing the magical realist conception of Mexican literature that was inherited from the Latin American Boom and consecrated by authors such as Carlos Fuentes and Laura Esquivel. When Mexico and the United Kingdom declared 2015 a shared cultural year, three other established writers (Cristina Rivera Garza, Juan Villoro, and Guadalupe

Nettel, just breaking into English translation themselves) were responsible for selecting twenty Mexican writers under the age of forty for an anthology entitled *México20: New Voices, Old Traditions* that would showcase Mexican literature for British readers.[11] Among the anthology's most striking features is the absence of Mexico as a topic in many of the selected works: it is clear that the committee sought to avoid representing national literature through stereotypes. At the same time, it is also clear that most of the twenty writers (Luiselli among them) sought to avoid the idea of the Mexican writer as representative of Mexicanness itself.

I decided to rewrite part of my original introduction to *Strategic Occidentalism* so that it would mention these very recent developments, which palpably illustrate the concrete points this book seeks to put forward. The boom in English translations of Mexican literature over the past two or three years is surprising, given how many of the country's major writers have yet to be translated or are translated very belatedly—not to mention the fact that many important translations have been out of print for years. Of course, the legendary disinterest of the U.S. publishing world, together with the public's equally fabled reluctance to read translations of foreign literature, is the larger problem here. Indeed, we should note that nearly all works of Mexican literature in recent translation are available thanks to the heroic work of small nonprofit presses (like Deep Vellum Publishing, Coffee House Press, And Other Stories Publishing) and a small group of translators (like Christina MacSweeney for Luiselli or George Henson for Pitol). In the United States, this is by no means a trivial concern. Given that Mexico neighbors the southern U.S. and constitutes the country's largest community of migrants, the overall indifference to Mexican literature is not only disheartening but also troubling. It implies a refusal to understand dimensions of Mexican culture that challenge stereotypes and depict the country in all its cultural complexity, enabling negative pigeonholing of both Mexico and Mexicans. Although the impact of scholarly criticism on publication trends often amounts to little more than wishful thinking, I hope to bring interested readers into contact with writers who are very well known to Mexican readers and researchers but remain almost entirely unrecognized in the English-language world—even when two of them (Pedro Ángel Palou and Cristina Rivera Garza) actually live in the U.S. and work in the academy. The book, of course, is also directed toward my fellow scholars in Mexican and Latin American literature, for whom some of the points made in this introduction may be obvious; after all, we share the same struggles. But my hope here is that *Strategic Occidentalism* will foster engagement with its case studies by carefully and thoroughly analyzing the work of important writers from the perspective of their worldly engagement—a topic that is sometimes sidelined by our Latin Americanist concern with cultural specificity.

Part of the impetus in writing this book involves another variety of the problems outlined so far: the misrepresentation (or nonrepresentation) of

Mexican literature in academic fields engaged with literary transnationalism. One could certainly reproach the field of comparative literature at large for the fact that, beyond the work of a handful of critics such as Djelal Kadir or Lois Parkinson-Zamora, Latin America occupies a place far less prominent than its rich production and transnational bonds would suggest. But it is a reality of the field that comparatists are more likely to read German or French than Spanish; moreover, compounded with the scant translation of Mexican and Latin American literature, it is not at all uncommon for Hispanophone authors to be confined to one-dimensional roles in the larger cartographies of transnational literature as established by the field. Paradoxically—and it is a paradox in which this book participates—there are perhaps more scholarly books on Mexican literature written in English than actual works of literature translated into the language.

To be fair, this phenomenon also results from the politics of disciplinary division and the cultural hierarchies at work in the academic humanities. Today, Spanish departments and programs constitute the second-largest field for studying literature in universities, and they are often subsumed into larger departments of Romance or Modern languages. In many quarters, however, Spanish still lacks the cultural capital of French and German; in recent years, it has also been displaced as a consequence of the geopolitical centrality acquired by Arabic and Chinese. Spanish is still regarded as a service field by many university administrations—and, unfortunately, as a lesser intellectual field within the realm of the humanities, which contributes to the invisibility of literary production and critical thinking in the language beyond our field. There is a fundamental disconnect between the relative intellectual strength of this area and its visibility in the literary humanities at large. The field of Spanish enjoys a steady number of students, both undergraduate and graduate, as compared to the dwindling numbers who study languages like French and German. European languages have also suffered from the precarization of the humanities and the subsequent closure and reduction of language departments, a situation that has yet to affect Spanish programs with full force. Accordingly, scholars specialized in those languages are more likely to participate in comparative and interdisciplinary programs, while it is fairly easy for scholars in Iberian and Latin American culture to remain within the bounds of their departments, at least as long as Spanish continues to sustain a viable (albeit increasingly fragile) academic job market. Further, given the large number of graduate and undergraduate students in Spanish, a considerable number of Spanish speakers in the U.S. and Europe, and a thriving academy in Spanish-speaking countries, many of us write much of our research in the language (or even in Portuguese), which many of our comparatist colleagues do not read or speak. What's more, such logics can lead us to mistrust other approaches and feel protective of the specificity of our field, and we sometimes respond to its marginalization with a regrettable self-isolation from debates in neighboring disciplines.

We could add yet another factor: the rise of the idea of "global English" in literature classes, which provides undergraduate and graduate students with the ability to read certain works of Latin American fiction alongside other texts. This is undeniably salutary in many ways, including its participation in efforts against Eurocentrism. But an unintended effect of the trend is that it weakens my field's ability to provide a site for teaching literature and culture, rather than merely the site for acquiring language skills. To be fair, this problem is not exclusive to postcolonial theory or comparative literature, but it does fit a pattern of marginalization that speaks to the low symbolic capital ascribed to Latin American culture by non–Latin Americanist humanists across the board. In many fields, for instance, one can find concepts of the transatlantic that solely focus on Britain and its former colonies, or concepts of the transpacific that are exclusively concerned with the relationship between China and the U.S.—even though Latin American countries constitute the majority of the hemisphere's shores on both oceans. We cannot ignore the pervasiveness of a politics of knowledge in the humanities that frequently allows Latin America to be erased altogether. For one thing, then, all of these factors contribute (in most cases unwittingly) to an ecosystem in which Latin American literature in general, and Mexican literature in particular, is unable to claim a place in literary conversations that would befit the size of the population of Latin American descent in the country. For another, the cultural hierarchy that grants a marginalized role to the Spanish language as a site of production of literature and critical thinking also results in a systematic conceptual problem: the inability to treat Latin American literature as a complex field, rather than as a simple machine that produces some kind of cultural authenticity serving simplistic notions of political or cultural resistance.

This discussion constitutes the book's implicit background and animates my engagement with the concept of "world literature." In its many iterations, world literature theory responds to a network of conceptual and institutional issues regarding the role of literary studies in the neoliberal era and the partial (though by no means complete) decline of the hegemonic role held by postcolonial studies and critical theory in the field. I am not interested in providing a detailed history of this process, in part because I myself am not an institutional participant in the field of comparative literature and have no particular investment in the challenges of that discipline as such. Rather, my interest is a methodological one: world literature theory is indeed a compelling critical paradigm for Latin Americanists, insofar as it provides critical tools to account for the region's complex cultural history of cosmopolitanism, as well as its paradoxical status as belonging both to the Global South (or the Third World, or the postcolonial world) and to Western culture. Both legacies exist in a history of dialectical conflict and engagement with each other, and their balance remains very much alive as a concern in Latin American studies. As Mabel Moraña has most recently discussed, the persistence of notions of identity and specificity in Latin America involves the undeniable role of humanism and universalism in the consolidation of *criollo* elites' cultural authority and in Latin America's problematic location within systems of colonial domination and the circulation of capital.[12] By contrast, cultural specificity and nationalism have also historically manifested complicity with systems of cultural domination and political hegemony in the region, particularly with the formation of modern nation-states following processes such as the Mexican Revolution. As Charles Hatfield contends in a recent book, Latin Americanism has an antiuniversalist core to which we must stay attuned.[13]

In the particular case of Mexican literature, we must keep both warnings in mind. It is true that Mexico has a highly institutionalized field in which most of its practitioners belong to an elite stratum. But relations between metropolitan and peripheral elites can be quite paradoxical. One key factor in this study is that the Mexican literature discussed here has been crucial in redefining the predominant currents of fiction writing in the country—while simultaneously remaining invisible in transnational discussions and literary fields that frequently deny Latin American countries full-fledged literary representation or significant participation in circuits of literary transnationalism. This is why, as I extensively discuss elsewhere, Mexican and Latin American intellectuals throughout the twentieth century developed an ideal of Western culture as decolonization, before such a term was defined by current postcolonial theories.[14] Insofar as Latin America does have substantial ties to the West, horizontal participation in Western culture has been theorized in the region as a way of countering Eurocentric cultural ideologies. There is a time-honored tradition of Mexican and Latin American cultural thinkers devoted to challenging the notion that universalism is solely the province of European and U.S. culture, or that the region can only be a permanent source of foreignness and otherness. This is not to say that many Latin Americans are not also excluded from participation in the elite cultural sphere. Nonetheless, invalidating the existence of humanist and universalist traditions such as the ones discussed by Moraña and Hatfield is not merely a falsification. It also performs a persistent discourse of coloniality, intensely present in the field of comparative literature's dominant theories, that makes it impossible to read the literature of Latin America on its own complex terms. We could say that even postcolonial theory's engagement with Latin American literature has consistently suffered from this fatal flaw. It is true that, in most canonical theorizations of academic postcolonialism, Latin America appears very much as an afterthought, which has to do with the fact that the core of this theory was produced in relation to Anglophone and Francophone cultural production.[15] However, the problem of colonialism and coloniality is evidently central to Latin America, a region with two centuries of its own postcolonial history, not to mention its own body of postcolonial theory—which is only minimally read by non–Latin Americanists. For my purposes, though, the few Latin American authors enshrined by postcolonial theory (primarily Boom writers or second-generation magical realists) have not represented the predominant trends in literary writing and reading in Latin America since at least the late 1980s. We could even say, a bit more harshly, that these theorizations ignore entire lineages of regional cultural production dating back at least to the independence period.

World literature theory has recently emerged and established itself as a new, presumably more inclusive paradigm, one that supposedly accommodates a more diverse and international view. Derived from Goethe's discussion of *Weltliteratur* and different historical iterations of the notion in figures such as Georg Brandes and Karl Marx, the concept of "world literature" has come to account for seismic changes in our ways of reading literature beyond national and linguistic realms. Such changes are affiliated with the de-Europeanization of comparative literature as enacted by postcolonial studies and the diversification of the literary corpus by the communicative technologies characteristic of neoliberal globalizations. Perhaps the most ecumenical definition is the one provided by David Damrosch in his seminal book on the matter. According to Damrosch, "The idea of world literature can usefully continue to mean a subset of the plenum of literature. I take world literature to encompass all literary works that circulate beyond their culture of origin, either in translation or in their original language."[16] Damrosch's definition coincides with the formulation of other concepts referring less to an aggregate of works than to systems that replicate global political and economical power structures in the realm of cultural power. Of these systems, the most widely discussed are Franco Moretti's idea of "world literature" as a world system, following Immanuel Wallerstein's conception, and Pascale Casanova's "World Republic of Letters," which she defines more or less in connection with Fernand Braudel's spatial theories and a Bourdieusian notion of autonomy and symbolic capital.[17] These are not the only approaches, of course, but they inspired what can be described as a boom of metatheoretical publications on the subject—a boom that encompasses readers, companions, introductions, debates, ongoing conversations, an academic journal exclusively devoted to the topic, and even an "against" book.[18]

Of course, the proliferation of writing on world literature theory has to do with the promise it allegedly conveys; namely, the methodological ideal of accounting for a large system and an inapprehensible body of literary works that function transnationally, but which we have only seen constrained by linguistic or national boundaries, or by approaches inordinately focused on intra-European or North Atlantic circuits. World literature is the result of the "death of a discipline": twentieth-century comparative literature. This field grew woefully outdated, according to Gayatri Spivak's diagnosis, due to the fact that "comparison in favor of the European tradition has remained in place" in all comparative approaches.[19] The prospect of writing a book that offers a Mexican or Latin American perspective on these disciplinary matters is most alluring, but *Strategic Occidentalism* resists such a temptation for three reasons. First, and most simply, I have already personally contributed to the theoretical industry described above; I edited a collection, published in 2006, in which various Latin Americanists extensively discussed both Moretti and Casanova. I wrote an extensive introduction to the collection, which was the first book-length engagement of the field of Latin American literary studies with world literature theory in its current iteration.[20] While I did not comment on Damrosch (since his book had not achieved the same level of notoriety in the Spanish field), I did write a short history of the notion for Spanish-language readers at the time, and I commented extensively on what I saw as the advantages and pitfalls of Moretti and Casanova's methods. Anyone who reads the piece will note the evolution of my views in this current book: I am less critical of Moretti's idea of "distant reading," which is one of my methods here, and my understanding of Casanova's work is both more nuanced and more skeptical than before. But I think the fundamental thrust of my interest in world literature theory remains unchanged. My analysis emerges from the need to rethink the concept to account for Latin America's worldly engagements, as well as from the possibility of appropriating those approaches without validating either the diffusionist account of Moretti's theories of center and periphery (which often overlook literary exchanges that do not mirror economic ones) or Casanova's infuriating Francocentrism (an axiomatic flaw that weakens an otherwise-compelling theory based on a persuasive account of literary power and capital).

Second, since I edited the aforementioned collection, a few colleagues in the field have published book-length monographs that have taken up the problem of world literature theory from different angles and in great depth. The most notable of these are Juan de Castro's *The Spaces of Latin American Literature* (2008), Mariano Siskind's *Cosmopolitan Desires* (2014), and Héctor Hoyos's *The Global Latin American Novel* (2015).[21] In addition, recent collective volumes in Spanish scholars have emerged, updating and expanding the conversation I sought to start in my 2006 book. I would especially emphasize the dossier edited by Guillermina Ferrari in the 2012 issue of *1616: Anuario de literatura comparada*, and the book *América Latina y la literatura mundial* (2015), edited by Gesine Müller and Dunia Gras.[22] All of this excellent work, which is incorporated into the arguments developed by *Strategic Occidentalism*, shows a decade-long engagement with the concept that is based on three concerns (concerns I also share in this current book): the persistently reductive representation of Latin America in world literature cartographies and theories, the sidestepping of Latin American writers' important contributions to world literature, and the need to more strongly substantiate the role that worldliness and cosmopolitanism has played in the development of Latin American literature. Since 2006, the conversation on theories of world literature in the Latin Americanist field has evolved in its focus, too. As De Ferrari points out, early discussions centered more on the question of who had the right to speak for and represent Latin American literature, and they were fairly resistant to the value of "world literature" as a concept; in some cases, it was seen as a reassertion of the epistemological privilege of Europe over Latin America. This was indeed the main concern held by the authors I invited to take part in my collection, and I would say that it still is. That being said, I am also attentive to De Ferrari's identification of a "turn" in Latin American world literature theory, which no longer focuses on questioning its legitimacy and applicability; rather, it more proactively seeks to intervene in its formulation.[23]

Strategic Occidentalism operates on the basis of the two concerns. Rather than describing a turn between the former and the latter, I ground my analysis on the idea that Latin Americanists have a duty to account for our field, our literature, and our theoretical approaches in a discussion in which we often have been misrepresented—and on the belief in this role as a necessary means of conceptual intervention in the field. But I also think that if we replicate these theories without questioning the politics of their locus of enunciation, not to mention their ensuing methodological and ideological limitations or deficiencies vis-à-vis Latin American literature, we risk producing critical work already demarcated by preexisting notions of the world rather than helping to construct them. To this end, *Strategic Occidentalism* will often cite, affirm, refute, and/or correct different theories of world literature, including those posited by my Latin Americanist colleagues, but the book refuses to consistently apply a single model or advance a unified theory. As someone who considers himself primarily a Mexicanist and Latin Americanist, and whose comparatist vocation is more methodological than field-oriented, my book is less concerned with defining a paradigm within world literature theory and more interested in extensively laying out the way in which Mexican literature challenges world literature paradigms as an object of study.

This leads me to my third motivation. In reading world literature theory (and essentially any other Anglophone comparative theory), I have become convinced that one factor behind the flattening of Latin America is the pervasive inattention to the specificities of each national literary and cultural field. As a Latin Americanist, I say this with a certain degree of hesitation; after all, the commonalities of history and language shared by most Latin American cultural traditions are of great political and cultural importance, and I want to stress that a focus on individual countries and subregions is not meant to detract from the continental approach and its importance. However, comparatist approaches often follow the metonymical representation of entire linguistic traditions by one or two illustrative cases. In the case of Latin America, these are typically Machado de Assis (due to the influence of Roberto Schwarz in Anglophone scholarship), Rubén Darío, Gabriel García Márquez, Jorge Luis Borges, and Roberto Bolaño. Such figures are sometimes accompanied by various writers with a certain level of name recognition in English-language criticism: Carlos Fuentes, Mario de Andrade, Octavio Paz, and a few others. But, perhaps with the exception of Brazilian writers, whose national specificity is protected by their linguistic difference, these writers are typically read as globally Latin American rather than as Mexican, Argentine, or Colombian. My point is that, beyond the regional literary field, there are crucial differences between the literary fields of each tradition, the materiality of their institutions, and their means of positioning themselves in world literature. A country like Mexico, strongly marked by state-sponsored cultural nationalism throughout the twentieth century, addresses cosmopolitanism differently than, say, Argentina—a country whose lettered class prides itself on its worldliness and whose literary culture had a more antagonistic relationship with its national populist tradition. In addition, the literary institutions typical of a large country like Mexico often produce a much different world literature than a midsize country like Colombia or a small nation like Panama. This in itself is one reason I have chosen not to write yet another work with a general Latin American focus (as has already been done by the books mentioned above). Instead, I have sought to introduce a new layer to the debate: the construction of a national world literature.

My focus on a single country, Mexico, may seem counterintuitive: one of the most important motives for conducting comparative work in general, and world literature theory in particular, is to transcend the constraints imposed by national and linguistic traditions of study. But my approach is not unusual. In fact, Wai Chee Dimock and Lawrence Buell coordinated a collection based on the idea of U.S. literature as world literature, their goal being to disrupt the insularity of the field of American literary studies, and the Bloomsbury series Literatures as World Literature has already produced volumes on individual countries like Denmark and Germany.[24] I feel that reading world literature from the perspective of a single Latin American country provides a series of methodological advantages addressing some of the concerns and problems mentioned above. For one thing, it helps decenter narratives on the circulation of literary aesthetics that are naturalized by global approaches. In general, world literature tends to emphasize either the spread of the modernist novel form (e.g., Moretti) or the literature circulating in a space seen as the literary center (e.g., Casanova's contentions regarding Paris). By focusing on a country that Moretti's terminology would see as semiperipheral, it becomes clearer that world literature is enunciated from concrete sites. Not only metropolitan centers have a view of world literature; so do regions all over the globe that are home to cultural practitioners engaged in cosmopolitanism. Second, due to the high level of literary institutionalization in Mexico, as well as its extensive connections to both material and symbolic spheres of world literature, my case study provides a change in perspective that allows me to illustrate a variety of processes, such as representations of the Anglophone writers different from those paradigmatically canonized by critics in the British and American traditions. In addition, by strategically sidestepping the French influence, which has considerably decreased in importance in Mexico since the 1970s, I seek to circumvent Francocentric accounts of

Latin American cosmopolitanism and analyze connections to other European traditions. Finally, I endeavor to shed light on the theorization of connections that remain invisible in world literature theories today (such as Mexico's engagement with Central and Eastern European literatures), and to expose the limits of their conception of that "world" (Mexican world literature does not encompass "the whole world" because it does not have the necessary access to cultural networks and capital to do so).

By privileging the world literature that circulates in Mexico and the Mexican writers who engage with it, we come to discern a much richer network of connections that is otherwise occluded by large-scale approaches. I discuss authors for whom French literature is largely irrelevant, who would much rather engage with Austro-Hungarian or Polish literature, and who have different taste in authors from the prevalent preferences in their original countries of reference. Another of my methodological claims is that Mexican literature—and other national literatures studied in this way—reveals an important deficiency in Damrosch's definition of world literature as literature that circulates outside its country of origin. Most of the writers studied here are part of world literature, due to their complex and sophisticated engagement with currents from around the world, but their work lacks meaningful circulation (or sometimes any circulation at all) outside the realm of the Spanish language. There is a very important reason for proceeding in this way. Although Damrosch's formulation does not necessarily imply as much, many studies of world literature focus on literature from the Global South that makes it to the Global North (or that travels from one Global North country to the next); the global expansion of well-known authors like James Joyce; or, even more narrowly, the literature translated into English or French. My change in perspective suggests that, when writers cannot assume they will be translated into other languages, they can still be writing works of world literature, because a worldwide circulation of form exists that is far more complex than the one derived from mainstream editorial and translation practices and ideologies.

Finally, focusing on a specific national literary field tells us two essential things about world literature. First, the "world" in world literature is not a self-evident category, but a cultural construct enunciated from a specific perspective. It never covers the whole world; in fact, its world can be very limited. In the case of my authors, the "world" is basically Europe at large and the U.S., with some intermittent influences from East Asia, Australia, and North Africa. The literature of sub-Saharan Africa is widely unknown in Mexico because there are few networks of circulation that allow it to appear. This is not to say that a hegemonic world literature does not exist. That is the object described when one follows Moretti or Casanova or even Damrosch's route: a global literature that corresponds to hegemonic cultural flows and existing dynamics of cultural power. But world literature can be constructed in countless ways, so one can indeed speak of "World Literature," capitalized, in designating the hegemonic system, or of a world literature as something read from a specific national or local site, or even of a world literature as constructed and practiced by an individual writer. In this sense, I find Peter Hallward's Deleuzian approach to postcolonial literature particularly instructive. He contends that a writer can be read not only as an articulator of specificities, but also as a nodal point that constitutes a singularity for the confluence of diverse flows.[25] This approach will be an implied methodological premise in the chapters that follow, as I will discuss the way in which a single writer or a literary group can produce a world literature of their own.

A key contention in this book is that the worldliness of world literature is neither a self-evident ideal nor a utopian pursuit. It is, rather, a concretely existing category related to specific cultural locations and material practices. *Strategic Occidentalism* focuses particularly on what a recent collection calls the "institutions of world literature," namely translations, the publishing industry, and the market.[26] If the limits of one's world literature are the limits of one's material access to the world, then no study of world literature can reasonably overlook this question. World literature requires us to be conscious of the materiality of its production. It is the product of concrete cultural labor—including material practices of translation, cultural contact, and publishing—that must be accounted for in their full historicity. Defining something as world literature because it happens to be somehow invested with worldliness, or because some author happened to read texts written in other countries, can be very uninteresting. One would be hard-pressed to find a writer from any literary field who lacks a meaningful aesthetic or ideological connection beyond his or her national or linguistic ecosystem. This is the drift of Damrosch's warning, of course, when he asserts that world literature is not the totality of all literary works. Nonetheless, what defines world literature as such is not the transnational circulation of works, but the material networks and practices that construct its archives and repertoire and determine the condition of possibility of world literature as a practice. As I hope to show over the course of the book, the reasons why a specific literary tradition is engaged, the political contexts that make said engagement meaningful, the transformations in the publishing world during each time period, the practice of translation and the material conditions that make it possible, and the influence of those practices on both a national tradition and the tradition's engagements with other literatures are more powerful forces in determining world literature than the mere fact of a given work circulating in space. On this subject, my contentions are particularly influenced by scholars like Sarah Brouillette, whose work illustrates the need to understand world literature as "a moment of purportedly global circulation that is really a moment of uneven distribution of the agency and ability to be an author and of uneven access to reading materials and to the means of publication."[27] This idea is particularly crucial for my project, because uneven distribution is what makes Mexican world literature possible in its specific form.

From this starting point, *Strategic Occidentalism* proposes an engagement with the concept of world literature from the perspective of the post-1968 Mexican novel. In doing so, it implicitly challenges the concepts of "world literature" as developed in diverse literary fields over the past two decades by studying the work of one of the most influential writers in contemporary Mexican literature (Sergio Pitol); the cultural politics of a landmark literary movement (the Crack group); and the gender dynamics that characterize the rise of three profoundly important women writers in contemporary fiction (Carmen Boullosa, Cristina Rivera Garza, and Ana García Bergua). *Strategic Occidentalism* advances a critical appraisal of concepts such as cosmopolitanism, the center-periphery binary, worldliness, and other keywords deployed and canonized by "world literature" theory. By understanding each author and work of fiction as a site where a particular "world literature" has emerged in relation to diverse social and cultural fields (the world, the nation, the political, diverse national and transnational fields of cultural production, etc.), *Strategic Occidentalism* redirects the concept of "world literature" toward critical practice at three levels of study: the formal reading of literary texts; the analysis of material institutions in the literary field and concrete networks of literary circulation, such as translations, publishers, and magazines; and a redefinition of the idea of world literature as a concrete practice performed by authors through writing and institutional engagement rather than as a unified field. For the purposes of my argument, I have devoted each chapter to a topic associated with a paradigmatic change in Mexican literary institutions and in the consequent formulation of hegemonic forms of literary writing. One could study many possible examples of literature at the margins of the Mexican literary field, but one of the phenomena described here is how a peripheral stance vis-à-vis world literature can help construct symbolic power and capital in a national sphere.

The approach developed by *Strategic Occidentalism*, while less engaged with in-depth philosophical or conceptual analysis, is a means of involvement with the category of world literature that seeks to pay more attention to the historicity and the constructed nature of the "world" part of the term—as opposed to the definition, naturalized in Moretti and Casanova's respective works, of a single world describable as a positively existing entity mirroring either the economic world system or a self-regulating transnational "Republic of Letters" that possesses a single centralized system of symbolic-capital construction. As I was completing this work, two books expressing a version of these concerns were published, and I mention them here because they confirm that my own frustrations with the existing terminologies are not exclusive to my engagement with Mexican and Latin American literature. In *What Is a World?*, Pheng Cheah provides a brilliant theoretical account of how world literature has been identified with the process of economic globalization; a rebuttal of that identification, due to its commitment to a purely spatial notion of world literature; and a complex philosophical model based on world literature as temporality and on worldliness and world making as categories that critique capital.[28] Cheah's model is less directly relevant to my purposes, since the book is heavily invested in recovering certain mainstream modes of postcolonial literature from which my own account seeks to establish some distance (as will become particularly clear in chapter 2). Also, although Cheah briefly and richly engages Néstor García Canclini's notion of modernity, his book does not contain a substantive account of Latin American literature—which is unfortunate, as his arguments might provide some necessary oxygen to the reassessment of still-existing magical realist traditions in the region. Nonetheless, I wholly share Cheah's interest in tracing "literary cartographies of social space [that] are themselves active transactions and negotiations with representational space that can critique, challenge and contest existing material space."[29] As I think will be clear in my case studies, this is precisely the reason for studying world literature from the perch of a national tradition. It provides a concrete space of enunciation for literary cartography as both imaginary and practice. My intent is to examine world literature not as a structure of cultural power and dependency that writers from the Global South are always unambiguously contesting. Rather, I wish to study it as a layered and multidimensional structure of different critiques and challenges to hegemonic world literature systems based on the creation of alternative world literatures, and of systems of cultural power and prestige that work in semiperipheral areas.

The second noteworthy book is Aamir R. Mufti's *Forget English!*, which develops a compelling argument—central, in fact, to concerns underlying my own notion of strategic Occidentalism.[30] For Mufti, Orientalism, as defined by Edward Said, remains an organizing principle of world literature. To be sure, this point resonates strongly with me as a Latin Americanist; I have read an astonishing amount of critical literature in which the production of nineteen countries is reduced either to a repository of progressive politics or to a machine that fabricates difference and otherness. Mufti's cogent and meticulous debate with existing ideas of world literature is too extensive to summarize here in a way that would do it justice. I must mention, though, that he articulates similar ideas to the ones encompassed by my own approach. He criticizes Moretti and Casanova's models because "each of them fails to understand the nature of the social and cultural processes that assign societies, languages and practices of writing either to the center and the periphery."[31] Even in coming from a different methodological position, this qualm is the very same one expressed by Brouillette in the above-cited passage—and the same one present in my own perspective. The type of literature I study here is not directly concerned with the questions of Orientalism raised by Mufti's book, or with his interest in the realignments of literature and institutional humanities. And I partly disagree with his contention that "the history of world literature is inseparable from the rise of English as a global literary vernacular and is in fact to some extent predicated on the latter," a hyperbolic assertion that makes little sense from the perspective of a Latin Americanist.[32] Nonetheless, my project and Mufti's share various crucial conceptions of the problem. I would particularly underscore his idea that one should counter "the blissful serenity of the supposed perceptions that the age of the worldwide has indeed arrived" by asking "at which locations in the world exactly such perceptions of the worldwide acquire their aura of transparency."[33] My focus on Mexico, a site in which the "worldwide" is not a self-evident category, takes this question further, as it sheds even more light on the ideologies that produce that transparency and the pushback by authors who do not participate in it.

As a result, by studying it from the perspective of a specific national tradition, the book seeks to recast the category of "world literature" as a practice, recognizing the uneven power dynamics at work between literary traditions. Mexico provides an especially appropriate case study because its literature, particularly its fiction, has established unique and substantial connections with world literary production in the context of highly developed national cultural institutions. Thus, many of Mexico's canonical fiction writers, including Pitol, negotiate personal versions of "world literature" in dialogue with a strong national tradition and multidimensional encounters with diverse transnational flows. The book does not seek to address two questions that have already been comprehensively explored in prior works: first, the process of canonization of Mexican or Latin American authors in the global literary market; and, second, the study of cosmopolitanism as a desire (to use Siskind's formulation) or as the aspiration of writers in semiperipheral or peripheral contexts. Rather, even as it bears these existing discussions in mind, *Strategic Occidentalism* is concerned with a different type of case study—worldly fiction authors canonized as such within, mostly, the national tradition—and a theoretical question yet to be properly discussed in the Latin Americanist field: "world literature" as a set of contingent networks materialized in the literary forms and ideologies of specific writers. It takes previous works on world literature as a "space" and as an "ideal," and it adds a still-understudied conception of world literature as a set of material practices and institutions. Ultimately, moving past its reading of specific Mexican authors, *Strategic Occidentalism* provides a practical reading of "world literature" beyond the Francophone and Anglophone traditions that have defined most interventions in the concept, and without elevating any other particular configuration of the world (transatlantic, transpacific, hemispheric, etc.). In fact, my point is that all of these categories can be described in terms similar to the ones I use for "world literature."

This book's title is its key concept: "strategic Occidentalism." The notion plays on Gayatri Spivak's idea of "strategic essentialism," which refers to subaltern groups' embracing of stereotypical ideas in their self-representation to achieve specific goals in political and cultural engagement.[34] I argue that "strategic Occidentalism" is understood as the way in which specific writers, particularly from a "semiperipheral" tradition like Mexico's, adopt a cosmopolitan stance to acquire cultural capital within their national tradition. This cosmopolitan stance is "Occidentalist" because it focuses fundamentally on the appropriation of Western literature, but always in a strategic form: through the translation and vindication of marginal traditions and authors and the formulation of literary aesthetics, poetics, and politics that do not replicate hegemonic waves of influence, but instead seek to reconstruct networks of cosmopolitan works through practice. In short, the idea of "strategic Occidentalism" allows us to achieve a critical study of the literary genealogies constructed by each writer, in order to understand how she builds a "world literature" that embraces and contests, to different degrees, the "world literatures" constructed by literary institutions: presses, academies, translation networks, and so on. I have used this term in my previous work on Mexican literature, most concretely in reference to Mexican humanist Alfonso Reyes. In my book *Naciones intelectuales*, I use the term to describe a desire of modernity, or a modernity discourse, based on the creation of a relatively autonomous literary field (in Bourdieu's sense of the term) and the deployment of a critical use of Western cultural archives.[35] This notion was developed in dialogue with postcolonial understandings of the concept, such as Couze Venn's idea of Occidentalism as part of "a genealogy of the present which reconstructs a particular trajectory of modernity, inflicted by the fact of colonialism and capitalism," and the discussions of the terms "Occidentalism" and "post-Occidentalism" in Latin American postcolonial studies, which focus on the construction of the Occident as a center of imperial power and, in the words of Walter Mignolo, "the overarching political imaginary of the modern/colonial world system."[36] My point in this particular argument was to show how the same archives of this "overarching political imaginary" could be appropriated and performed back at Western culture as a form of intellectual decolonization, and that this appropriation was crucial for understanding the nature of the configuration of Mexico's modern literary field.

In this book, I advance the discussion by moving into a chronologically later part of the process in the Mexican literary field. Alfonso Reyes was a world literature unto himself—corresponding extensively with intellectuals in Europe, the U.S., and Latin America, and keeping in close contact with emerging notions of world history in the work of authors such as Arnold Toynbee. He became a model in Mexican literature—like the Contemporáneos poets, another object of study in my previous book—on how to use world literature in the context of the Mexican literary field. In this book, I maintain the idea of "strategic Occidentalism" to describe the fundamental cultural device that organizes Mexican world literature, its aesthetics, and its institutions. Precisely because, as Mufti shows, Orientalism plays such a crucial role in structuring the cognitive maps of world literature theory, Occidentalism is a necessary counter to the pigeonholing of regions like Latin

America as mere sites of identity-production. Indeed, my case studies convey the enormous importance of Occidentalism in making sense of contemporary literary production in Mexico, since the fundamental aim behind Mexican writers' participation in world literature is to avoid being pegged as merchants of authenticity. One could object—accurately, in fact—that Mexican world literature is in itself Eurocentric, but this would be a simplistic way of looking at it. What characterizes all of the authors studied in this book, as well as many other major figures in Mexican literary history, is that the idiosyncratic nature of literary reading allows for involvement with canons that are suppressed, in turn, by the hegemonic structures of world literature. Bound by the structural limits of uneven literary distribution through the publishing market, Latin American writers have nonetheless pushed back by creating their own circuits of reading and translation, which thus enable them to critically engage their national literary realities. Mexican world literature, like any other national literature in Latin America, is studied here in its concrete workings: its tense negotiations with existing global literary canons, and the use of those negotiations to redefine aesthetics of writing within the national literary field.

Drawing from these initial considerations, *Strategic Occidentalism* reflects on the usefulness of categories related to world literature theory by examining three case studies: the work of Sergio Pitol as translator, critic, and fiction writer; three authors (Jorge Volpi, Ignacio Padilla, and Pedro Ángel Palou) belonging to the Crack group, a loosely formed collective; and three women writers (Cristina Rivera Garza, Carmen Boullosa, and Ana García Bergua) who represent a larger change in the gender dynamics of Mexican fiction. Since, as I suggested before, a potentially endless number of writers could be studied under the categories deployed here, I do not intend to provide an exhaustive account of world literature in Mexico. Rather, I have structured my discussion around a set of criteria that allows each of these cases to illustrate symptomatic processes that have unfolded in Mexican literature since the Tlatelolco massacre of October 1968—a watershed moment not only in politics, but also in the relationship between culture and the state. World literature played a role in dislodging the cultural nationalism that underpinned Mexico's cultural politics, and it was crucial in the development of literary discourses surrounding Mexico's slow transition from a one-party regime to an electoral democracy. Therefore, this book tells the story of how Mexican literary institutions used Occidentalism to realign themselves with the social and cultural logics of Mexico's democratic transition, extending between the reactions to the 1968 student movement and the election of the first non-PRI president, Vicente Fox, in 2000. That said, I have chosen authors who address key Mexican sociopolitical processes as part of their intellectual experience, but not in a realist (or magical realist) tone, to avoid falling into familiar narratives of the native informant and the like. Of course, many other logics of cultural resistance exist beyond the bounds of this book, so it is not in any sense a comprehensive account of the subject. Rather, *Strategic Occidentalism* offers a reading of a very precise phenomenon and its concrete effects: the gradual dislodging of the Mexican writers' categorical imperative to be essentially Mexican, and the establishment of a transnational circuit of literary publishing that would better suit both cosmopolitanism and the demands of the neoliberal cultural market.

The commonalities between the authors studied in the following chapters are determined by a few key factors. First, each case study is connected to paradigmatic changes in the structure of literary publication in Mexico. In this regard, I follow recent work in materialist lines of literary sociology, from Bourdieu's theories on the literary field to Brouillette's compelling work on literary circulation and the marketplace. Thus, Pitol illustrates the emergence of independent presses contesting canonical notions of literature (such as Tusquets in the 1970s and Anagrama in the 1980s); the Crack group constitutes a reaction to the corporate vertical integration of publication in early neoliberalism; and writers like Boullosa, García Bergua, and Rivera Garza exemplify the market's impact on the realignment of structures of symbolic capital as related to gender. Second, all of the authors are among the most widely read and discussed in the country. While their visibility may vary, it is important to my argument that they represent important moments in literary writing in Mexico at formal and thematic levels. One could study scores of writers who construct alternative and underground traditions in Mexico, but, for the purposes of *Strategic Occidentalism*, it is essential that their engagements with world literature ultimately change the definition of literary writing in the country. A related third point is that I deliberately chose authors who have failed to garner major attention outside the Spanish language. This is not terribly difficult, of course; indeed, besides Carlos Fuentes and Octavio Paz, Mexican writers have been largely ignored both by literary publishers and world literature theorists all along. But in order to make my case regarding the limits of spatial and diffusionist paradigms (and to complement other studies focused on the "global Latin American novel"), there is a point to be made about writers with substantial intellectual connections to world literature but little symbolic capital in the world system. In particular, given that I have written this book as part of a sustained encounter with Anglophone academic conversations, the absence of timely and successful English translations is an important criterion. In fact, regardless of their iconicity, Pitol has been translated decades after writing his key works; Volpi and Padilla, despite an ephemeral flash of interest following major awards, remain fairly unknown in the English market; Rivera Garza has only been translated by small presses with minimal visibility; and Palou and García Bergua have never been translated in full-book form. The only exception is Boullosa, who has enjoyed a certain degree of translation through the reputable independent press Grove and who is now being translated further by Deep Vellum in Dallas (the same house that publishes Pitol). Finally, all of these writers are iconic cases of strategic Occidentalism. They are not merely cosmopolitan: the most important references to their personal canon are idiosyncratic, and that idiosyncrasy is essential in understanding their role within both Mexican literature and world literature.

Chapter 1 discusses the construction of "world literature" as concrete networks. I explore this phenomenon by studying Sergio Pitol's work between the 1960s and 1980s. Pitol is a well-known translator (of over fifty works of literature, mostly from English and Slavic traditions), an influential and well-recognized writer, and a lively literary critic. Due to the nature of his work, he provides an especially pertinent case for the study of relationships between individual writers and the institutional networks of world literature. The chapter focuses on how Pitol constructs a personal and idiosyncratic version of world literature, then projects it both onto his writing and onto the reception of certain literary traditions in the Spanish-speaking world (via his translations and the presses that publish them). Pitol is also relevant in conveying how a particular brand of cosmopolitanism (evident in his essays) is rendered—one that does not correspond to predominant modes of world, transatlantic, global, or modernist literature. I explore, in two steps, how this cosmopolitanism leads to a major transformation of the Mexican literary canon through the ways Pitols embeds his world literature. First, I study his work as a translator and editor of diverse literary traditions, including Eastern European and Anglophone modernism, in the context of Mexico's post-1968 society and the emergence of the contemporary Hispanophone literary market in Spain during the final days of the Franco dictatorship and the first decade of democracy. From this canon, I read two key works by Pitol, the short story "Nocturno de Bujara" ("Bukhara's Nocturne," 1980) and the novel *El desfile del amor* (*The Love Parade*, 1984), to discuss the impact of traditions on his own poetics.

Chapter 2 takes the discussion to the 1990s and 2000s in general and to the emergence of the Crack literary group in particular. The Crack group appeared in the 1990s as an attempt to reframe the role of the Mexican and Latin American writer in relation to both national literature and emerging trends of globalization in the publishing industry and literary aesthetics. They claimed a practice of cosmopolitanism and worldliness for Latin American writing in order to combat nationalist and regionalist imperatives (such as the obligation to write solely about Mexico or about identity) and to achieve a wider readership in an increasingly corporate publishing world. The chapter reads the work of three Crack authors: Jorge Volpi, Ignacio Padilla, and Pedro Ángel Palou. The chapter starts by discussing how the group established itself both in Mexico (through a manifesto and a set of apocalyptic novels released in the mid-1990s) and in the Spanish-language world (thanks to the back-to-back transnational awards granted to Volpi and Padilla). But the main focus is to discuss three books that actually resist, through cosmopolitanism and worldliness, the institutional structures that the work of the

Crack group helped construct. This part of the chapter first contrasts Jorge Volpi's best-known book, *En busca de Klingsor* (*In Search of Klingsor*, 1999) with *El jardín devastado* (*The Devastated Garden*, 2008). Volpi's work poses a tension between a notion of "world literature" apt for the realm of the international bestseller (*Klingsor* is an erudite thriller set in Nazi Germany) and an alternative conception of the world that claims a geopolitical site (in this case, the Iraq War) for a novel that seeks, in its minimalist poetics, to undermine the premises of the contemporary transnational novel. Second, I will discuss Padilla's *Amphytrion* (*Shadow without a Name*, 2000), a novel about a project to supplant Nazi leaders with doubles, and *La Gruta del Toscano* (*The Tuscan's Grotto*, 2006), a fictionalized historical adventure novel based on the premise that the ruins of Dante's *Inferno* are found in the Himalayas. This reading examines another double ideology: the appropriation of genres marked as commercial (adventure, travelogue, the thriller) to advance a cosmopolitan understanding of high literature. The chapter concludes with a discussion of Palou's *Paraíso clausurado* (*Foreclosed Paradise*, 2000), a learned elegy on the decline of modern literary practices, to show how cosmopolitanism functions as a double ideology in the context of the neoliberal economic market: as a site of resistance and as a commodity.

Chapter 3 is concerned with the ways in which world literature intersected with the rise of literature written by women, which intensified in the late 1980s. Many of the first wave of women writers' most visible works were either engaged with a bestselling version of second-generation magical realism (represented by Laura Esquivel in particular, but also by authors such as Ángeles Mastretta), penned by women writers who intervened into mainstream forms of fiction like the historical novel or the romance (Rosa Beltrán is a notable example of both), or written by authors who developed more experimental poetics but lacked widespread recognition beyond small literary and critical circles (like María Luisa Puga or Angelina Muñiz-Huberman). The three authors discussed in the chapter exemplify two specific phenomena: a harnessing of the changes in literary institutions toward the development of their particular brand of literary fiction, and a redefinition of the poetics of writing in Mexico. While I could have chosen a wider-ranging study to encompass the many women writers who flourished in the 1990s (indeed, readers may think of Aline Petterson, Ana Clavel, or Mónica Lavín), the focus on these three writers allows for more effective contrasts and comparisons with the concurrent experiences of the (male) Crack writers, as well as a more precise description of a series of editorial processes that took place between the publication of Boullosa's *Son vacas, somos puercos* (*They're Cows, We're Pigs*) in 1992, García Bergua's *El umbral* (*The Threshold*) in 1993, and Rivera Garza's *La muerte me da* (*Death Hits Me*) in 2007.

It is my hope that my three case studies, examined from the modest perspective of a national tradition, will foster richer ways of theorizing world literature. As I see it, the mode of analysis employed here demonstrates the importance of not falsifying the logics at work in specific literary fields in the Global South for the sake of theoretical systematization. I find it important to focus on how literary fields work in different places, in the interests of better representing them in planetary and comparative models. Further, this book argues for the need to understand the historicity of the world in world literature—and, therefore, its unlimited multiplicity, which can be studied as the world literature of a nation, a region, or even a single author. In my view, this is necessary for world literature theories to refrain from presenting unevenness as a self-evident fact, and for them to see that the flows of cultural power and capital can have complex and distinct materialities that may or may not coincide with economic ones.

Chapter 1

✦

The Networks of a Personal World

Sergio Pitol's Heterodox Cosmopolitanism

Sergio Pitol is undoubtedly Mexican literature's leading cosmopolitan. An influential writer and respected diplomat, Pitol's literary and physical travels have occurred across one of the most extensive literary cartographies in Latin American fiction. Defined in particular by his experiences in Eastern Europe and the former Soviet Union, and by his love of heterodox writers in all Western traditions, Pitol embodies an ethos that proved decisive to the reshuffling of Mexican literature's transnational involvements between the 1960s and 1980s. Pitol has written in detail about his literary ideas and cosmopolitan engagements. In *El viaje* (*The Journey*, 2000), an essay/travelogue in which Pitol recounts his 1986 trip to Russia and the Republic of Georgia, he pens a confession that serves as a fine entryway to his work: "En ningún lugar he soñado tanto como en Rusia" (Nowhere else have I dreamt as much as in Russia).[1] This can be interpreted not only in the literal sense mentioned in *El viaje*, but also as the many ways in which Russia appears in his work: his constant reference to writers like Nikolai Gogol, Anton Chekhov, and Boris Pilniak; his famed translations from the Russian language; the deep influence that Mikhail Bakhtin and the Russian avant-garde have on his work; and the considerable number of Russian cities and writers that crop up over the course of his nearly five-decade literary career. Russia, however, is only one of his places.[2] He spent substantial amounts of time living and reading in Eastern Europe, particularly Prague, Budapest, and Warsaw; traveled deep into the Soviet Union (to places like Tbilisi in Georgia and Bukhara in Uzbekistan); developed what he himself calls an "addiction to English writers"; and became a devoted translator of modernist Italian authors (Malerba, Bassani, Vittorini) and of Chinese dissident Lu Hsun.[3] He shares the genealogy of fellow Latin American cosmopolitans like Pedro Henríquez Ureña and Jorge Luis Borges. Of course, Pitol's cartography is far from truly planetary (Africa and most of Asia are nonexistent in his work), but his forays into peculiar representations of Western European literatures, as well as in introducing an army of Eastern European, Russian, and Italian writers for the benefit of

Hispanophone readers, were crucial for the reconstitution of world literature as read in Latin America and Spain between the late 1960s and mid-1980s. In turn, his own literary style became revolutionary in the context of Mexican fiction, and his worldliness decisively shaped the history of the novel and short story genres in contemporary national literature.

In providing a particularly useful illustration of how a world literature can be constructed with a specific author as the nodal point, Pitol offers a uniquely relevant case study for the notion of world literature as developed in this book. His literary trajectory is well developed in four fields, which, in turn, shed light on the operations of world literature within a multilevel system that ranges from concrete material practices to symbolic and ideological performances of worldliness and cosmopolitanism. First, Pitol has translated into Spanish over fifty books of fiction from diverse traditions—particularly Anglophone modernism, the Eastern European avant-garde, and midcentury Italian literature. His translations have appeared in diverse editorial sites, most notably Spain, Argentina, and, of course, Mexico, thus helping to transform transnational fiction canons in the Hispanophone literary world during the second half of the twentieth century. He also curated two influential series (Heterodoxos in Tusquets in the late 1960s and Panorama de Narrativas in Anagrama in the early 1980s) that were crucial for the reconfiguration of the Hispanophone literary world. Second, Pitol has written a large corpus of critical essays and prologues, both on the authors he has translated and on the works and writers that have influenced his fiction and conception of literature. Unlike many translators in the Spanish-language world, Pitol's work makes explicit the poetics and ideologies that underlie his affinities and the results of his reading processes behind the translations themselves. Third, Pitol's renowned autobiographical writings (his early memoir from the 1960s and the books in the *Memory Trilogy*, published in the 1990s and 2000s) interweave literary criticism with his personal experiences across the world, particularly during his time in the diplomatic service in Europe. The availability of these texts elucidates the material ways in which literary contact among traditions can transpire at the microlevel of the author-translator. Finally, his fiction, most notably his *Carnival Trilogy* from the 1980s and his short stories from the same period, provides a canonical example of Mexican work transformed by its author's rendering of a world literature.

An exhaustive account of Pitol's world literature would require a multivolume study, and the level of necessary detail would certainly exceed the aims of this book. Instead, chapter 1 will focus on key moments of Pitol's work as an editor and translator and the links between this work and his key innovations in the context of Mexican fiction. This approach seeks to accomplish a series of analytical goals. First, in discussing Pitol's heterodox engagements with non-Hispanophone literatures, it will serve as a starting point for the book's discussion of world literature and strategic Occidentalism. By constructing a quadrant of literary ideologies and references enabled by the concrete, material nature of his editorial work and diplomatic role, I develop the question of world literature in its radical contingency, examining a variety that goes against the grain of the transnational flows of symbolic capital as described by spatial theories (Casanova, Moretti, and the like). In addition, the chapter remarks on recent ideas on the concept of "regional world literature" (developed by Alexander Beecroft) to argue for the importance of national, regional, and linguistic spaces as components, not as antagonists, of world literature at multiple levels.[4] In fact, the documentation of Pitol's work as an editor and translator, and his relationship to key publishing houses in the Spanish-language world, will constitute the first part of a topic to be further developed in chapters 2 and 3: the question of editorial labor and economics in both the pre-neoliberal and neoliberal eras. As I hope to illustrate, Pitol's core activity in this area takes place during a two-decade interregnum between the thawing of authoritarian restrictions on Spanish-language publishing in the 1970s and 1980s (in the context of Spain's late Franquismo, the slow decline of Mexico's postrevolutionary one-party system, and the eventual collapse of Southern Cone dictatorial regimes) and the emergence of Planeta, Penguin Random House Mondadori, and other corporate publishing juggernauts from the 1990s onward. Finally, the chapter will advance the book's argument on Mexican literature, illustrating the important transformations that Pitol's networks catalyzed within his own literary style—which, in turn, goes on to inform Mexican fiction in the subsequent decades.

The focus of the chapter will be unfolded in four sections. I will begin by describing Pitol's relationship to the literature of the Eastern Bloc, particularly China, Poland, and Russia, to discuss how world literature operates as a practice. Second, I will elaborate on these references, as well as on Pitol's ties to Russian formalism and English modernism, to discuss the ways in which his work challenged the norm of the "total novel" in the Mexican literary context, while explaining his shift from canonical to noncanonical authors in the English traditions. The third section of the chapter focuses on a reading of "Nocturno de Bujara" (1979), one of the four short stories Pitol wrote in Moscow in 1979, to illustrate the formal consequences of his world literature labors. Finally, the chapter will conclude by pointing to some crucial elements in his career-defining novel *El desfile del amor* (*The Love Parade*, 1984), which provides the most compelling example of Pitol's impact on the primary trends of narrative fiction in Mexico. The chapter thus proceeds along a series of steps that delineate Pitol's strategic Occidentalism as a concrete practice: the construction of a personal modernist canon, chiefly based on his translations of Chinese, Polish, and English writers; his development of a poetics of humor and the banal through Anglophone modernism; and the way in which these two elements are intertwined in developing his fiction. I will spend a significant amount of time documenting Pitol's worldly forays rather than dedicating myself to close readings of Pitol's texts; critics have not attempted the former with any real consistency, while they have carried out the latter to the point of near exhaustion, due to the enormous interest that structuralist and philological scholars have demonstrated in Pitol's fiction.[5] While Pitol's worldliness is a well-known fact, the literary and formal consequences of his Occidentalist efforts are rarely engaged in a systematic way. As the chapter claims, this blind spot in the existing criticism is actually the most fundamental element in accounting for both Pitol's importance within Mexican narrative and his standing as a crucial author, from Boom paradigms to the new Bolaño-centered forms of Latin American fiction.

Pitol is widely recognized as one of the most important living writers in Mexico, so it is unsurprising that numerous books have been published on his fiction. However, most focus on a rather narrow set of concerns. Pitol's reading of Mikhail Bakhtin and the use of the word "carnival" to designate his 1980s trilogy have elicited various in-depth considerations of the role that dialogism, humor, and subversiveness play in his oeuvre. Notable works in this regard are Luz Fernández de Alba's *Del tañido al arte de la fuga* (1998); Jesús Salas-Elorza's *La narrativa dialógica de Sergio Pitol* (1999); and, attesting to the continued interest in the subject, Genaro Pérez's recent *Rabelais, Bajtin y formalismo en la narrativa de Sergio Pitol* (2011).[6] Scholarly interest in Pitol's work intensified after the successful publication of his hybrid essay-memoir-fiction book *El arte de la fuga* (*The Art of Flight*, 1996), which made him one of the most celebrated and influential writers in Mexican literature. As a result, many strong critical appraisals have been written on Pitol's work overall, or on his works from the 1980s and 1990s. These include Alfonso Montelongo's *Vientres troqueles* (1998), Teresa García Díaz's *Del Tajín a Venecia* (2002), Laura Cázares Hérnandez's *El caldero fáustico* (2006), Karim Benmiloud's *Sergio Pitol ou le carnaval des vanités* (2012), Alejandro Hermosilla's *Sergio Pitol: La máscara del viajero* (2012), and Elizabeth Corral's *La escritura insumisa* (2013), as well as books devoted more specifically to his essays and short stories.[7] Finally, as his reputation grew, numerous collective volumes and journal dossiers were dedicated to his work and life.[8] Strikingly, this abundant bibliography has paid hardly any attention to Pitol's translations and editorial work, let alone to the nature of the world literature constructed in Pitol's work as a whole. Most of the existing bibliography focuses on formal and structural analyses and close readings of his fiction, on his relationship to Bakhtin, or on general accounts of his contributions to genre and humor, but little work has been undertaken on Pitol's cosmopolitanism beyond superficial and rhetorical remarks. Given this panorama, I rely on the close readings put forth in many of the abovementioned books, which relieves me of redundantly reconducting this kind of detailed work myself. Instead, my goal is to expand existing readings of Pitol to account for his world literature and its impact, both on his work and on Mexican and Latin American literature in general.

Pitol's cosmopolitanism is fascinating as an object of study because it immediately precedes the process of neoliberal globalization that would change the terms of planetary cultural engagement. He belongs to a generation of Mexican writers who saw cosmopolitanism as a way to resist the nationalist imperatives of the culture fostered by the postrevolutionary regime. Nonetheless, it is important to note that Pitol's cosmopolitanism is not the antithesis of nationalism within a clean binary distinction. Rather, it exists as a repository of cultural ideas and freedoms that resist diverse forms of political repression and power. In a recent essay titled "Confusión de los lenguajes," Pitol asserts:

> No detecto en Hispanoamérica ningún elemento de desasosiego en nuestra cultura surgido por el nacionalismo de este milenio. Por el contrario, la amenaza para la literatura, para la cultura por entero, la encuentro en concepciones mercantiles totalitarias desprendidas del modelo globalista que con una energía titánica son apoyadas por entidades gubernativas y, sobre todo, financieras. Las tensiones entre globalización y cultura nacional, metrópoli y periferias, imaginario colectivo e imaginación individual nos tocan de cerca tanto a quienes se expresan en lenguas minoritarias, a veces asediadas, como a quienes pertenecemos a las zonas periféricas.

> I do not detect in Spanish America any element of disquiet in our culture, which was born of this millennium's nationalism. On the contrary, the threat to literature, to culture at large, is found in totalitarian mercantile conceptions resulting from a globalist model supported with titanic energy by both governmental and especially financial entities. Tensions between globalization and national culture, the metropolis and the peripheries, the collective imaginary and individual imagination, make close contact both with those who write in minority, sometimes besieged, languages, and with those of us who belong to peripheral areas.[9]

This paragraph implicitly defends the type of nationalism observed in the contemporary Latin American left (as represented in Mexico by Andrés Manuel López Obrador, a man Pitol has frequently supported in his presidential campaigns, and his recently created political party, Morena) against the accusation of authoritarianism, by arguing that transnational capitalism is the true threat to literary and cultural freedom. Part of the debate here is positioned against the corporate consolidation of the publishing world, a phenomenon I will address in depth in chapter 3. For the time being, this text speaks volumes about how Pitol understands the ethos of literary cosmopolitanism: not as a mere resistance to "the national" and its pitfalls, but as something that counters the geopolitical arrangements underlying totalitarian and exclusionary forms of culture. In his very first autobiographical book, *Autobiografía precoz* (*Precocious Autobiography*), written during his time in

Warsaw in 1966, one can trace Pitol's interest in the tension between the cosmopolitan writer's freedom and the diverse political and social imperatives of revolutionary and authoritarian societies.[10] Pitol has always been a passionate leftist, and his early cosmopolitan forays took him to diverse socialist and communist countries: Cuba, China, the Soviet Union, and Czechoslovakia, among others. He directly experienced the intellectual excitement of societies in periods of revolutionary and social transition, as well as the attempts of both government and dogmatic actors to regulate that excitement. In a remarkable moment of his memoir, he tells the story of a residency in China, where he was recruited as an English-Spanish translator for the Beijing Foreign Language Publishers. Pitol describes his experience in the *Yoi Ping-yuan* (or *Yuoyi Binguan*, as it is more commonly spelled in English), a "friendship hotel" dating back to the Soviet-Chinese collaborations of the 1950s. Diana Lary describes them as "large compounds of luxury apartments . . . built to house experts" who "lived hermetically sealed off from the Chinese population."[11] Pitol's account is similar; he depicts it as a deserted city of three hundred inhabitants who were not allowed to have outside contacts, mostly due to the climate of heightened conflict after the Soviet Union and China severed ties.[12]

According to Pitol, his Chinese hosts were very emphatic about the superiority of Chinese communism for Third World peoples. In these terms, Pitol's experience in China was marked by the importance of Maoism in Latin America as a revolutionary ideology more attuned to the colonial experience, since the "Chinese reminded potential allies in the Third World of their special knowledge of colonialism, inequality, resource exploitation, cultural chauvinism."[13] Some Mexican intellectuals and political leaders were indeed swept up in the enthusiasm surrounding the Chinese Revolution, and trips to the country by union leaders and other figures influenced both official institutions and the emergence of a radical left in 1960s Mexico.[14] Pitol's trip preceded the heyday of Mexican Maoism that would materialize as guerrilla movements in the early 1970s. His visit was in fact motivated by an attempt to normalize diplomatic relations between both countries. According to Pilar Jiménez, Pitol originally traveled there at the request of Max Aub, a Spanish exile in Mexico, who tasked him with interviewing Chinese intellectuals. Despite Mexico's good trade relations with China, U.S. pressure doomed the normalization initiative to failure. Once in China, the magazine *China Reconstructs* hired Pitol to revise translations of Chinese writers into French and English.[15] Tellingly, he tells a slightly different story in his memoir: he does not mention Aub or the political aspect of the mission (he does refer to a friend at the university in Mexico, presumably Aub), and says that he had responded to a publishing house's call for translators.[16]

The point, in any case, is that Pitol was not necessarily a participant in the ideological enthusiasm surrounding Maoism, but rather a leftist cosmopolitan who was drawn to China's promise as a new political and intellectual mecca. In *Autobiografía precoz*, Pitol recognizes his attraction to the idea of a "libertad del arte y la literatura mucho más abierta, inteligente y flexible que en la Union Soviética" (freedom of art and a much more open, intelligent, and flexible literature than that of the Soviet Union), praised in early paeans to the Chinese Revolution by authors such as Simone de Beauvoir, Vercors, and Claude Roy.[17] Pitol reminisces about this period in an essay on Nobel Prize winner Gao Xingjian, included in *El mago de Viena* (*The Magician of Vienna*, 2005); he states that the utopian culture he witnessed was "a punto de extinguirse" (on the verge of extinction), giving way to the Cultural Revolution.[18] Pitol's elective affinities in China were related not to the cultural *doxa* of Maoism, but rather to the writers whose work flourished or gained recognition in the brief period of cultural enthusiasm. Among those writers was Lao She, a playwright whom Pitol deeply admired, and who ultimately committed suicide in 1966 after his persecution during the early Cultural Revolution.[19]

More relevant to my current discussion is Lu Hsun, as his name is typically transliterated in Spanish.[20] Pitol translated three of his stories from the 1920s, one of which lent its title to the whole selection: *Diario de un loco* (*Diary of a Madman*).[21] Lu Hsun occupied the kind of paradoxical place in Chinese literature that typically attracted Pitol's attention: he was a heterodox writer to which his national tradition laid claim, but his writings resisted the credo put forward by orthodox sectors of the Chinese Revolution. In a 1957 book, Chinese critic Huang Sung-K'uang earnestly locates Lu Hsun's writings and historical moment as a precursor to the ideals of the revolution, but he repeatedly works to justify the latter's noncompliance with Marxist precepts. For instance, he attributes Lu Hsun's "extreme individualism" to the "Chinese intellectual atmosphere."[22] Yet Sung-K'uang ultimately praises the writer's "realistic patriotism" and "his ardent desire for social reform as the basis of national revolution," which, in this rendering, was "the driving force behind his literary work."[23]

Pitol's conception of Lu Hsun significantly departs from this kind of interpretation. In his 1971 introduction to his own translation, written as the complex cultural oasis he had experienced was swept away by the Cultural Revolution, Pitol seeks to redefine Lu Hsun's work as that of someone who resisted political agendas. His introduction begins by pointing out that, for many years, Lu Hsun was known only by "sinólogos, miembros de las Asociaciones de Amistad con la China Popular y teóricos del realismo socialista: a todos debe haberles resultado difícil de ubicar" (sinologists, members of Friendship Associations with Popular China, and theorists of socialist realism: all of them must have found him hard to place).[24] He then proceeds to mock the easy comparisons that Lu Hsun's work elicited among his enthusiasts ("el Chéjov chino, el Gorki chino, el Nietzsche chino")—in Pitol's words, "tres personalidades difíciles de hermanar" (three difficult personalities to link together).[25] Pitol also dismisses both the Cultural Revolution's portrayal of him (which made him appear "de pronto revestido de todos los atributos de un guardia rojo" [suddenly sporting all the attributes of a red guard]) and his presentation as an apolitical writer by some antirevolutionary critics, a depiction he deems "absurd."[26] Pitol then devotes the rest of his introduction to describing a writer who was attacked from all quarters of the literary world ("tradicionalistas, vanguardistas y proletarios"); who clearly distinguished between propaganda and literature; and who mostly contended not with the certainties of a revolutionary mind but with the oscillation "entre un pasado inerte y un futuro incierto" (an inert past and an uncertain future).[27]

Pitol remained a committed leftist writer, but he refused to follow the injunction of socialist realism. Furthermore, he also refused the anticommunist use of aesthetics as a realm devoid of politics—or representative of so-called Western freedoms. Instead, he opted for a politics of literature very much engaged in the interregnum produced by revolutionary and transitional processes. In other words, the function of cosmopolitanism in Pitol's literature is not to create an apolitical subterfuge for a writer seeking to evade national politics. His concept and exercise of world literature is thoroughly defined by this ethos. World literature is, in Pitol's practice, an archive of heterodoxies that provide a source language for literature in general, and fiction in particular, toward fulfilling the political role not of propaganda or indoctrination, but rather of the uncertainties produced by historical turmoil. As I will show in the rest of this chapter, this is the core of Pitol's literary work vis-à-vis both Mexico and the Spanish-speaking world.

Pitol's early experience as a young cosmopolitan leftist traveling through different countries of the communist world (including his perception of the tension between revolutionary vanguardism and political authoritarianism), as well as his assertion of cosmopolitanism as a tool to resist the cultural flattening of late capitalism, bookend the trajectory of his world literature project. In a perceptive essay on *El arte de la fuga*, Oswaldo Zavala argues that Pitol undoes the binary distinction between nationalism and cosmopolitanism that governed most of Mexico's twentieth-century fiction and that his unique approach to literary tradition renders traditional Occidentalism "unrecognizable."[28] Zavala's point is that Pitol undermines structures of cultural capital in the Mexican literary field, which he terms the "end of Occidentalism" to emphasize the termination of a relationship between cultural cosmopolitanism and cultural power in Mexico. I would say that Pitol's world literature not only dislodges the canonical uses of cosmopolitanism in his home country, but also (and from his earliest work onward) challenges the specific notions of cosmopolitanism and worldliness that were central to Latin America's modernist and postmodernist traditions by developing forms of strategic Occidentalism (rather than an end to Occidentalism as such) that redefine the "world" in other terms. In the next section, I will discuss the specific procedures by which he constructs different notions of this world—and thus puts forward a different canon.

The Translator in the Age of Cultural Springs:
Pitol's World Making in Theory and Practice

In his "ecology of world-literature," Alexander Beecroft locates Spanish in the category of a "regional world-language," by which he means that "their role is less languages *of* the world, in the way that English and French cover the planet, than languages *that constitute* worlds."[29] Although he does not directly cite such debates, Beecroft's understanding of Spanish is far more sophisticated than the role typically ascribed to it in other world literature theories. Here we should remember that most substantial discussions of Spanish in Pascale Casanova's *The World Republic of Letters* focus on the *modernistas*, and they simply assert the idea that French (the "mental Gallicism" celebrated by Rubén Darío) allowed Latin Americans to supersede the "colonial subjugation" of Spain.[30] In Franco Moretti's case, while he defers more to experts on Latin American literature, his "laws of literary evolutions" and "waves" typically portray Latin America as a mere receptacle of canonical flows of European literature—or, in reference to periods when Spanish-language literature does influence Europe in return, as a semiperipheral space that incubates innovation in order to ship it back to the center.[31] Moretti and Casanova's models may be useful in studying phenomena like nineteenth-century fiction, where European influence was heavier and more direct. However, from *modernismo* onward, the creation of a continental and transatlantic network of Hispanophone literary relations, as well as a more sophisticated and diverse reception of world literature, make concepts like the "semiperiphery" inadequate. Beecroft breaks with this diffusionist stance by focusing on the fact that polycentric languages like Spanish (or Portuguese and Arabic, for that matter) construct "words unto themselves" and possess a "relative well-developed infrastructure for supporting transnational exchange." More crucially, the position of the Spanish language within this cartography allows it to "participate in the Eurocentric literary ecology of our time"—but also to have internal and external dynamics of its own, given the strength and diversity of its internal market and reader community.[32]

Beecroft's depiction of Spanish in the context of world literature is particularly useful for this chapter. Indeed, the institutional context that fostered Pitol's rise as a cosmopolitan writer functioned within a system that participated in the ecology of Eurocentric world literature, while paradoxically resisting that ecology through the construction of a Spanish-language world literature with a dissonant relationship to the core European canon. To fully understand this point, we must consider that Pitol's translations operate at the intersection of his own personal and literary forays into authors and traditions with which Mexico and Latin America did not have major cultural ties prior to his work. In addition, a new network of literary institutions and networks emerged in this period and provided the space for Pitol to develop his labor. Many of Pitol's translations and critical engagements transpired as the corporate consolidation of literary presses began to undermine his cosmopolitanism's material conditions of possibility. Michael Cronin argues that, in the English-speaking world, the "shortened time-scale of the post-Fordist economy" profoundly affected translation due to the stress "on accessible, readable books which favour a translation strategy of least resistance and maximum naturalization."[33] Between the 1960s and 1980s, the Spanish-language world had yet to face the brunt of these changes (which were more predominant in the 1990s, as discussed in chapters 2 and 3). Nonetheless, even in the early stages of this "shortened time-scale," Pitol's translation of writers whose difficulty is at odds with any emphasis on the "accessible" can be considered the last moment of a cosmopolitan ethos that had defined Mexican literature since the 1950s. In any case, the translation of authors outside mainstream channels of transnational book circulation is exactly the kind of activity that fosters concrete tensions between world literature as a system (in the guise described by Moretti and Casanova's Braudelian-Wallersteinian model);[34] the regional world literature space of the Spanish language as described by Beecroft; and the world literature constructed by an author who is canonical within her national tradition but has no particular relevance in transnational flows. In other words, the translational "slaughterhouse of literature" (to borrow Moretti's term) established by the contemporary book market is sometimes undermined by translational traditions like the one Pitol has constructed.[35] In deploying translations of authors like Kazimierz Brandys and Ronald Firbank through the channel of private presses like Anagrama, Pitol developed both (simultaneously) a personal world literature and a world literature network that is relevant solely to Spanish-language readers. These two levels of world literature establish meaningful frictions with the world literature system as theorized by most scholars. In many cases, too, world culture as experienced by a specific writer, country, or language-world trumps the one favored by the impersonal networks of Eurocentric, postcolonial, and post-Fordist literary diffusionisms.

For these reasons, Casanova's contention that "the internal configuration of each national space precisely mirrors the structure of the international literary world as a whole" becomes imprecise when applied to someone like Pitol.[36] While it is true that "the world of letters must be conceived as a composite of the various national literary spaces," Pitol represents, within a national literature, a form of cosmopolitanism and worldliness that antagonizes the world system without antagonizing the national space in any particular way. I would suggest that the homology identified by Casanova becomes less of a question when the fundamental dynamics of world literature do not serve to consecrate a writer in the world space. Pitol's translations and essays do not "consecrate" rare authors like Ronald Firbank or Luigi Malerba in the Spanish-speaking world, and his cosmopolitan writing has not really turned him into a consecrated "rebel," which is how the international literary market has come to define authors like Roberto Bolaño. Rather,

Pitol's importance rests more specifically on an ability to influence the literary languages of Mexican and Latin American literature, and the practices of readers who access these translations, toward a type of world literature that goes against the grain of the type advanced by the centralized international consolidation systems that Casanova has described—a type with more solid foundations in either the Eurocentric or hegemonic cultural markets.

Pitol had been translating literary fiction regularly since the 1960s, but the first major moment in his literary career as a mediator between world literature and the Spanish language came with his position as director of the collection called Heterodoxos at the Barcelona-based press Tusquets. Spearheaded by editor Beatriz de Moura, Tusquets became a unique publisher in the landscape of late-Franquista Spain, mostly in publishing books that resisted the left/right divide that defined Cold War literary culture. Heterodoxos was part of the series Cuadernos Ínfimos, which, along with the sister series Cuadernos Marginales, established Tusquets as a house that specialized in short, unique literary texts. Tusquets was part of a thriving Spanish publishing world led by Seix Barral in the 1960s. As literary historians of this period have shown, the change in publishing trends was enabled by major shifts in the censorship policies of the Franco regime; Spain's need to compete with emerging presses from Havana, Buenos Aires, and Mexico; and, of course, the astounding success of the Spanish American Boom.[37] It is particularly notable that the number of translations in Spain grew steadily from 589 literary titles in 1959 to nearly 1,200 in 1972 and over 2,000 in 1976—which explains, among other things, why a translator like Pitol would have found substantial opportunities to work in the country despite the dictatorial regime.[38] Pitol lived in Barcelona between 1969 and 1971. He was a unique figure among the many Latin American writers and intellectuals circulating through Spain in those years, mostly because of his resistance to the militant politics of the Cold War. De Moura provides an excellent description of Pitol at the time:

> En los años 71 y 72 residían en Barcelona muchos hispanoamericanos, muchos rebotados de todos los enfrentamientos ideológicos y guerrilleros de Hispanoamérica. La única excepción fue la del mexicano Sergio Pitol, entonces todavía un escritor desconocido, de quien Tusquets publicó un primer libro de cuentos. Hombre ilustrado, de gran sabiduría, que viajaba un poco al azar, buscando quién sabe qué y que quedó varado unos pocos años en Barcelona donde dejó no sólo la Serie Heterodoxos en nuestra colección Cuadernos Ínfimos, sino grandes amigos duraderos, como el editor de toda su obra posterior, Jorge Herralde.

> In '71 and '72, many Spanish Americans lived in Barcelona, many of them having bounced out of all the ideological and guerrilla clashes in Spanish America. The only exception was Mexican Sergio Pitol,

still an unknown writer in those days; Tusquets published a first book
of his short stories. A highly cultured man, enormously wise, who
traveled a bit randomly, looking for who knows what, and who was
left stranded in Barcelona, where he left not only the Heterodoxos
series in our collection Cuadernos Ínfimos, but also lasting friends,
like the editor of all of his subsequent work, Jorge Herralde.[39]

It is significant that, in De Moura's estimation, Pitol's notable features were
"wisdom" and "enlightenment," both derived from being a Latin American
who wasn't enmeshed in the ideological struggles of the day. Such traits,
also illustrated in his aforementioned approach to Lu Hsun, allowed him to
redefine the canon of translations in Latin American fiction. Heterodoxos is
a series that published, in De Moura's words, "esos magníficos personajes
que no se dejaron manipular por las corrientes ideológicas de las posguer-
ras europeas" (those magnificent characters who did not let themselves
be manipulated by the ideological currents of European postwars).[40] This
in-between ideological position permitted series like Heterodoxos, and translators like Pitol, to successfully navigate the censorship that still prevailed
under the Franco regime, while simultaneously opening up the aesthetic and
ideological canons of the Spanish publishing world. As Alejandro Herrero-
Olaizola points out with respect to Seix Barral, publishers faced the dilemma
of how to promote prodemocracy Latin American writers (or Eastern European writers, for that matter) without alienating censors or participating in
Franquista aspirations to turn the book trade into a vehicle of neo-imperial
engagement with Latin America.[41] In response, Tusquets did not aggressively
promote Latin American Boom writers; rather, it deployed high literature,
ideologically heterodox in nature, as a refusal to partake in predominant
ideological clashes.

In his own account of the period, Pitol underscores the uniqueness of the
writers published in the series and provides a list of their works. The series
includes Pitol's previously mentioned translation of Lu Hsun; his first foray
into the translation of Witold Gombrowicz; Karl Marx's satirical novel Scor-
pion and Felix; and James Joyce's Giacomo Joyce, among other works.[42]
Although Pitol does not make the pointed political judgments found in De
Moura's version of this time, he does describe his work on the series as an
experience of unprecedented freedom in Barcelona, both personal and political, and he remarks on intensity of the literary world that made Heterodoxos
possible. Pitol's list is notable because it would set the tone for the work
that ultimately defined him as a translator and editor over the following
decades. One of the authors published by Heterodoxos include Polish playwright Jerzy Grotowski, whose Teatro Laboratorio represents an unusually
experimental form of theater developed in Poland in the 1960s.[43] In this way,
Pitol continues his relationship with Polish culture, cultivated during his time
in Warsaw between 1963 and 1966. In fact, the publication of Grotowski

in Tusquets continues Pitol's editorial work as director of the Universidad Veracruzana's press from 1966 to 1968. At the Universidad Veracruzana, Pitol was responsible for a landmark collection, *Cuatro dramaturgos polacos* (*Four Polish Playwrights*, 1967), which included works by Jerzy Andrzejewski (translated by Pitol himself), Jerzy Broszkiewicz, Tadeusz Rozewicz, and Slawomir Mrozek.[44] Grotowski's selection for the series—in addition to Pitol's overall work with Polish literature (including the publication of a few of Gombrowicz's short stories under the title *La virginidad* in Heterodoxos) and his inclusion of Marx's fiction, Lu Hsun's *Diario*, and even authors such as Antonin Artaud, Tristan Tzara, and Raymond Roussel as part of the series—reveals a clear strategy behind the tenor of Pitol's world literature: the development of literary canons that go against the grain of ideological and aesthetic *doxa*. As a result, the world literature that emerged early in Pitol's work always swam against the mainstream currents of global world literature—be it Cold War modernism, Soviet socialist realism, or, later on, market-inflected transnationalism. Heterodoxos, and Pitol's translations of authors such as Lu Hsun and Gombrowicz in the context of both Franquismo and Latin America's contradictory engagements with the Cold War, operated on the premise that the politics of literature was defined not by ideological alignment, but by an attempt to undermine the imperative to participate in the period's ideological quarrels.[45]

To qualify this last statement, we should recall that it would be erroneous to read Pitol's work and stance as "apolitical." His contributions to Heterodoxos, in fact, are framed by concrete political experiences that generally shape his practice of world literature and the strategies through which he engages with diverse Western traditions. In addition to his aforementioned experience in China, right before the Cultural Revolution, his experience in Poland provides other important elements. Poland, like many Eastern European countries, went through an ephemeral period of cultural liberalization in the mid-1960s. Under the leadership of Wladislaw Gomulka, between 1956 and 1970, Poland underwent a thaw that made the country into what historians characterize as "effectively the most liberal country of the Soviet bloc."[46] The period, which fostered the Polish Film School and a remarkable generation of writers (among other results), had a strong impact on Pitol, inspiring him to begin dutifully translating Polish writers in the mid-1960s. As in his experience in China, Pitol's account of his years in Warsaw expresses a profound fascination with the type of art and literature produced in such this kind of thaw—and grows deeply troubled by witnessing its gradual expiration. Pitol recognizes that the importance of Poland in his work is unusual; after all, he has stronger personal and family connections to countries like Spain and Italy, neither of which marks his work so directly.[47] Pitol explains that his relationship with Poland is a fundamentally volitional one, and he expresses great interest in the tension between the realities of a socialist country and the imaginative artistic work being produced at the time:

Los tres años de estancia en el país se encargaron de ir destro-
zando aquellas primeras nociones, ofreciéndome día con día nuevas
sorpresas, en contacto con una realidad cotidiana en apariencia
absolutamente estática, pero cargada, por debajo de la superficie,
de dinamismo, de presagios, de enigmas, de anhelos frustrados,
realizaciones y esperanzas. Cualquier concepto fácilmente podría
fácilmente podía desvanecerse días más tarde ante una nueva visión.

My three-year stay in the country set out to gradually destroy my earliest notions of the place, offering new surprises day after day, bringing
me in contact with a daily reality that seemed absolutely static, but
which was charged, under the surface, with dynamism, omens, enigmas, frustrated aspirations, realizations, and hopes. Any concept could
easily vanish in a few days when confronted with a new vision.[48]

In this particular essay, "Conferencia de Varsovia," Pitol describes the role
that three writers of the period (Bruno Schulz, Witold Gombrowicz, and
Andrzej Kusniewicz) played in his own literature and style. However, his
choice of specific authors to edit and translate exceeds mere influence. He
selected writers who flourished in the tension between a thawing authoritarian regime and a form of writing that refused to participate in the ideological
limits established by their historical context. This stance is evident in, for
instance, his 1965 translation of Jerzy Andrzejewki's *Las puertas del paraíso*,
published both by Joaquín Mortiz, the landmark press where many writers
of his generation were publishing their first novels, and by the Universidad
Veracruzana.[49] In his introduction to *Las puertas*, Pitol establishes a contrast between Andrzejewski's enthusiasts and detractors, explaining that the
former considered him "la moral de la nación" (the moral of the nation)
while the latter denounced him as "el peor ejemplo que podía darse a la
juventud polaca" (the worst example one could give to the Polish youth).[50]
In these terms, Pitol's choice to translate *Las puertas del paraíso* (*The Doors
of Paradise*) for Mexican readers—and, later on, to publish Lu Hsun and
Jerzy Grotowski in Spain—was not informed by the Latin American "cosmopolitan desire" for emancipation "from a cultural particularity that bears
the mark of exclusion" (as Mariano Siskind puts it), or by the semiperipheral
writer's will to "achieve literary existence" or "to create the conditions under
which they can be seen" (as Casanova describes it).[51] Rather, it responded to
a literary politics that sought to deploy the literary in circumventing the Cold
War's cultural imperatives. Writers like Lu Hsun or Andrzejewski provided
models of how to use literary aesthetics in nations where cultural expression
and political authoritarianism had a problematic and mobile relationship.
This was the kind of situation relevant both to an intellectual living during
the Franquista thaw of the late 1960s and, of course, to a Mexican writer
working during the formation of the student movement in the same decade.

In this light, we should remember that Pitol's career developed at the epicenter of turmoil in Mexico. When he returned to Mexico from Warsaw, he worked as an editor at the Universidad Veracruzana, a period that coincided with the escalation of the student movement that would be violently suppressed in 1968. While, indeed, the level of censorship in Mexico was not equal to that exercised by regimes in the Eastern Bloc, the authoritarian crackdown in Mexico did allow for some parallels between the two situations in the context of the global 1968. His own translation of Andrzejewski overlapped with the rise of a generation of Mexican writers, also promoted by Joaquín Mortiz, who would be very much inscribed in diverse aspects of the counterculture—from the Beat-influenced Onda writers José Agustín and Gustavo Sáinz to the cosmopolitan eroticism of Salvador Elizondo and Juan García Ponce. Pitol himself published his book *Los climas* (*The Climates*) in '66 as part of the movement, and *Las puertas del paraíso* came out in those same years.[52] This period of cultural opening came to an abrupt end with the student massacre of October 1968, which was as much a reference for Pitol as it was for Del Paso's writing of *Palinuro de México* (*Palinuro of Mexico*). A few months before Tlatelolco, Pitol had been named the cultural attaché of Mexico's embassy in Belgrade, where he was tasked with coordinating Yugoslavia's participation in the Olympics later that year. Like other intellectuals, he left his diplomatic job in the wake of Tlatelolco and ultimately moved to Barcelona.[53] Pitol's powerful account of the period is worth a long citation:

A finales de 1968, dejé la embajada de México en Belgrado, donde desempeñaba mi primer cargo diplomático. Me resistí a seguir colaborando con el gobierno mexicano después de Tlatelolco. Regresé a México y encontré la atmósfera irrespirable. Una amiga prometió ayudarme a obtener trabajo en Londres como traductor en *The Economist*, que estaba por iniciar su publicación en español. Era casi seguro que comenzaría a trabajar en octubre. Podría pasar el verano en Polonia invitado por Zofia Szleyen. La asistencia para un coloquio sobre Conrad, creía yo, me permitiría obtener la visa. Hice una escala en Barcelona para entregar la introducción de *Cosmos* de Gombrowicz, a la editorial Seix Barral. La llevaba casi terminada: pensé que sería cosa de trabajar sólo un par de semanas más. El 20 de junio de 1969, a media noche, llegué a Barcelona por la estación de Francia. . . . En vez de las tres semanas que preveía pasar en Barcelona me quedé tres años. El recuerdo de aquellos tiempos, de algunos espléndidos amigos, de constantes sorpresas me emociona aún hoy. Mi estancia en esa ciudad, a pesar de los tropiezos iniciales y de uno que otro de esos aparatosos sobresaltos que en su momento parecen aproximaciones del Juicio Final para acabar desvaneciéndose en el aire, constituyó un diario ejercicio de libertad.

In the final months of 1968, I left the Mexican embassy in Belgrade, where I had held my first diplomatic job. I did not want to continue collaborating with the Mexican government after Tlatelolco. I returned to Mexico and found the atmosphere unbreathable. A friend promised to help me get a job in London as a translator for *The Economist*, which was about to begin its Spanish-language edition. It was almost certain that I would start work in October. I could spend the summer in Poland, having been invited by Zofia Szleyen. My participation in a conference on Conrad, I thought, would allow me to get a visa. I had a layover in Barcelona to submit my introduction to Gombrowicz's *Cosmos* to the publishing house Seix Barral. It was almost finished: I thought it was a matter of a couple more weeks' worth of work. On June 20, 1969, at midnight, I reached Barcelona via the Francia station. . . . Instead of the three weeks I was going to spend in Barcelona, I spent three years. The memory of those times, of some splendid friends, despite the initial troubles and one of those theatrical frights that seem at the time like the advent of the Final Judgment and ultimately vanish into thin air, was a daily exercise of freedom.[54]

Clearly, the "freedom" Pitol encountered in Barcelona, and the type of heterodox authors he favored both as a translator and an editor, can only be related to his own experiences with diverse contexts of cultural flourishing that existed in tension with censorial, authoritarian regimes. The political continuity of his experiences with the repression of intellectuals and young people in China, Eastern Europe, and Mexico, as well as his admiration for writers resisting the ideological *doxas* of 1960s political struggles in all of those contexts (Lu Hsun, Andrzejewski, his own Mexican generation), are crucial to his work. As both theory and practice, his world literature traces a cartography of heterodoxy to resist the hegemonic waves of Cold War aesthetics and ideologies.

After Barcelona, when Pitol returned to the Mexican diplomatic service and served, during the 1970s, in Prague, Paris, Budapest, and Moscow, he continued to expand this canon—most notably following the dialectic of openings and repression that kept defining the Soviet Union and its sphere. The most salient common denominator in Pitol's canon of Russian and Eastern European writers is their particular operations of writing in the context of highly regulated literary and political worlds. His reading of Boris Pilniak, for instance, highlights "el rencor de Pilniak a Occidente" (Pilniak's rancor toward the West) and describes his Slavophile reading of the Russian Revolution as "fuerza restauradora de un equilibrio biológico que el ruso, apresado en una compleja y asfixiante red de teorías antinaturales, por ajenas, había alterado" (restorative strength of a biological balance that the Russian man, imprisoned in a complex and asphyxiating web of antinatural theories, by virtue of their alien character, had altered).[55] In Pitol's rendering,

this eccentric ideological perspective, which would result in Pilniak's exe-
cution during the Stalinist purges, allowed the Russian writer to construct
an "ejercicio por desmontar la novela" (exercise to disassemble the novel
genre) given that conventional narrative techniques could not adequately
transmit the complex social and historical layering required to express the
primal nature of Russia's interior.[56] Pitol relies here on the ideas presented in
Marc Slonim's 1977 book *Soviet Russian Literature: Writers and Problems
1917–1977*.[57] Slonim portrays Pilniak as a "social emotionalist [who] had no
precise political credo."[58] In his account, Pilniak was an advocate for irrationalism and of the peasant class's triumph over the perceived rationality of the
city. It is absolutely clear, however, that Pitol is far more celebratory of Pilniak's spirit and work than Slonim or other scholars were. Slonim describes
Pilniak as someone who "lacked backbone in life as in literature."[59] Another
critic, Robert A. Maguire, only reluctantly recognizes Pilniak's importance,
characterizing him as "one of those writers who miss greatness but who alter
the literary history of their country," who "lacked a real gift for fiction" but
was a "borrower, an eclectic"—a writer whose mixture of previously existing
themes lent certain topics and techniques "a respectability that they could no
longer command by themselves."[60] Pitol portrays Pilniak more generously:
as a tragic figure who saw the revolution as a way for Russia to redeem
its excessive closeness to the West and for a young intellectual to "save his
life" through his own incorporation into the revolution (in the form of a
commune and peasant labor) and the union of Russia's past and future.[61] In
reading Slonim, Pitol certainly became aware of the Russian writer's ideological and stylistic imitations. Yet he clearly underplays them in such a way that
the Spanish-language reader encountering with Pilniak through Pitol would
see, first and foremost, a unique writer whose stylistic innovations allowed
him to narrate a complex tableau of the Russian Revolution.

A careful reading of Pitol's portrayal shows that his interest in Pilniak
is unconcerned with the peculiarity of his ideological stances. His essay
clearly overlooks, and even forgives, the politics of Pilniak's irrationalism.
Instead, he focuses on exploring the translatability of Pilniak's exercises
in the novel genre. Despite Slonim and Maguire's readings, Pitol's version
of Pilniak portrays him as notably self-aware in the art of fiction, a quality that Pitol was seeking to secure in his own work. Pitol wrote his essay
in Moscow in June 1980, in the wake of the 1978 publication of Pilniak's
work in the Soviet Union—its first edition in the post-Stalinist era. Pilniak's
writing in the 1920s and the publication of his works in the 1970s roughly
coincide with moments of cultural thawing in Russia, which allowed for the
emergence and vindication of such a heterodox figure.[62] The possibility of
questioning standard novelistic practices appears to be tied, in Pitol's reading
of Slavic literatures, to the ability of radical literary forms to resist aesthetic
and ideological imperatives in the context of ephemeral interregna within
authoritarian states. As T. R. N. Edwards argues, "Pil'nyak's excursions into

the realm of the irrational and the fantastic are in part an attempt to escape from an excessively prosaic work which bids fair to become even more prosaic; this assertion of freedom is supported formally and stylistically by his rejection of the developing, logically sequential narrative of the nineteenth-century novel."[63] Pitol views Pilniak's rejection not as a plea to the irrational, as Edwards does, but as the kernel of his becoming "el cronista épico de una epopeya inmensa y su envilecimiento" (the epic chronicler of an immense saga and its debasement).[64] In other words, Pitol appropriates the undermining of the classic literary form in Pilniak as part of a repertoire of literary techniques used to narrate the degradation and carnivalization of epic projects of modernity, like the Russian (or the Mexican) Revolution.

Tellingly, Pitol's critical engagement with Pilniak, as well as his efforts in translating him into Spanish, was simultaneous with his writing of the *Carnival Trilogy*. Pitol's translations of Pilniak's stories first appeared in 1980 in an edition of the series Textos de Humanidades published by UNAM; they were later republished in Anagrama in 1987, as part of Pitol's work for the Panorama de Narrativas.[65] I would claim that his reading of Pilniak foreshadows the important changes in narrative tone and style that *El desfile del amor* later introduces to Pitol's oeuvre. Before delving into this discussion, however, I will conclude the section with a few words about Anagrama. Pilniak's *Caoba* (*Mahogany*) was only one of the books that Pitol translated for Anagrama in the 1980s. Anagrama was founded in 1969 by editor Jorge Herralde in Barcelona, and Pitol became acquainted with him during this process. Early Anagrama books shared the heterodox spirit supported by Tusquets; indeed, Anagrama was transgressing the borders of Franquista censorship more boldly at this time. Its founding collections, Argumentos (which still exists) and Documentos (which published its last book in 1980), were fundamentally dedicated to political and cultural essays, and the early catalog contained provocative books such as Hans Magnus Enzensberger's profiles of Marx and Engels, Mao's writings, and Mary McCarthy's chronicle of the Watergate scandal.

A full-fledged history of Anagrama in this period would exceed my present purposes and remains a pending task for literary historians. The key facts here are that Herralde and Pitol's friendship grew throughout the 1970s and that Pitol became a key figure in the reinvention of the press in the 1980s, when it inaugurated its two landmark collections of fiction: Panorama de Narrativas, devoted to translation and launched in 1981, and Narrativas Hispánicas, focused on Hispanophone writers and launched in 1983, accompanied by Anagrama's prestigious literary fiction award, the Premio Herralde de Novela. Pitol played a crucial role in this endeavor. As one of the first translators in Panorama de Narrativas, he introduced the work of authors such as Brandys and Pilniak into the series, and he served as a critic and commentator of other works published, including Kusniewicz. He was also the first Latin American writer to publish in Panorama de Narrativas (his short story collection *Vals de Mefisto* [*Mephisto's Waltz*, 1984] was the second book in the collection) and the first Latin American winner of the Premio Herralde (with *El desfile del amor* in 1984). In fact, only *El héroe de las Mansardas de Mansard* (*The Hero of the Attics of Mansard*, 1983), by Spanish writer Álvaro Pombo, preceded Pitol in both ventures. His presence as a Latin American author in a series dominated in its first two decades by Iberian writers was so rare that in two years and forty books only two other Latin American writer joined Narrativas Hispánicas (Argentines Edgardo Cozarinsky and Luisa Futoransky). Moreover, no other Latin American writer would win the Herralde award until 1997, when Peruvian Jaime Bayly did so.

In his recollections of Anagrama, Pitol recognizes that Panorama de Narrativas "renovó el elenco autoral que se manejaba en España y enriqueció ampliamente las opciones narrativas" (renewed the authorial cast that was prevalent in Spain and widely enriched its narrative options) and describes it as a series that presents "un panorama complejo y colorido de formas y tramas de todo el siglo XX" (a complex and colorful panorama of forms and plots from the whole twentieth century).[66] If one revisits Jorge Herralde's many texts on the subject, it is clear that Pitol's work in Heterodoxos and his translations for Barral are viewed as a model for the canon of Panorama de Narrativas. Herralde describes him as a "joven hermano mayor, más culto y más leído que nosotros" (a young older brother, more educated and well read than the rest of us) and refers to his translations of Gombrowicz as a point of shared literary interest and a source of personal conversations—to the point that he laments being unable to publish Pitol's translation of the Polish writer's diaries due to competition from another publishing house. Pitol's translation of *Transatlántico* (*Transatlantic*) would ultimately be published in Panorama de Narrativas.[67] In fact, Herralde credits Pitol for directly recommending the publication of Pilniak's *Caoba* and Ronald Firbank's *En torno a las excentricidades del cadernal Pirelli* (*Concerning the Eccentricities of Cardinal Pirelli*), both of which he translated, as well as Ivy Compton-Burnett's *Criados y doncellas* (*Manservant and Maidservant*), translated by someone else but discussed extensively by Pitol in his essays. Pitol introduced two types of literary work into Panorama de Narrativas. The first was an alternative Anglophone modernism in which Pitol's "addiction to the English" met Herralde's affinity for British literature: Firbank, Compton-Burnett, and J. R. Ackerley are its representatives. The second was a refined canon of Russian and Eastern European writers that Pitol collected during his years in the Eastern Bloc and the Soviet Union: Pilniak, Vladimir Nabokov (whose *The Defense* Pitol translated for Anagrama), Gombrowicz, and Brandys.

In the 1980s, after Spain began its transition to democracy, Pitol's personal world literature became firmly established and found its culminating outlet in Anagrama. With Panorama de Narrativas—a series immersed not in the fight against a dictatorship or in the resistance against dogmas, but in a society's experience of cultural expansion in the early days of its postdictatorial era—Pitol was able to showcase the type of heterodox writer he had been championing as a translator, editor, and critic since the 1960s. Over the two decades I have recounted thus far, the defining authors of his literary ethos joined a series in which, as Pitol himself states, "no desentonan en ningún momento" (they are not dissonant at any point).[68] Panorama de Narrativas was crucial for Mexican and Latin American literature in the last quarter of the twentieth century to perform its world making in the sense that Beecroft describes. Anagrama, at least in its early decades, faced considerable financial pressure, but was able to nurture writers like Pitol and bring a cast of rare writers into the Spanish language right before the vertical integration of the editorial market in the 1990s. It is telling that Pitol's final contribution to Panorama de Narrativas was none other than Kazimierz Brandys's Rondó—written in the mid-1970s and published in 1982, in the middle of Poland's Solidarity demonstrations—and translated by Pitol for Anagrama in 1991, as Mexico was emerging from the turmoil of the 1988 election.[69] Brandys was one of the authors Pitol began translating during his stay in Poland, and he ultimately became one of Pitol's most frequently revisited figures: he translated one of Brandys's short stories for the Antología del cuento polaco (Anthology of Polish Short Stories), as well as the books Cartas a la señora Z (Letters to Mrs. Z) for the Universidad Veracruzana and Madre de reyes (Mother of Kings) for Era.[70] Brandys gained prominence in the early days of the communist regime due to his distance from socialist realism; his work was fundamentally focused on ideas rather than on diegetic narration.

Madre de reyes was a particularly bold work, as it described the effects of Stalinism on a family that sought to remain faithful to revolutionary values. Rondó is a complex and ambitious love story in which the protagonist, Tom, invents an anti-Nazi resistance group and gives "missions" to his love interest, Tola, so she can satisfy her desire for political engagement without jeopardizing her life.[71] The novel has an extremely complex structure: the central fable is plotted partly as a detective story and then complemented with extensive philosophical digressions. Everything is framed after the fact, as Tom writes a polemic against an article that, in his view, erroneously recounts his actions in World War II. The novel's considerable challenges made it a unique work to translate in the editorial landscape of the early 1990s, a time when presses like Anagrama were gradually pressured to publish bestsellers in the nascent neoliberal era. Most notably, however, this book offers a revealing corollary of the world in Pitol's world literature: a network of writers fighting the imperatives of history. As critic Aleksandar Flaker has noted, Brandys performed "a basic denial of history, regardless of who writes it, the victors or the vanquished," and Rondó is "a whole novel negating the concept of history as seen through the eye of the historian."[72]

The 1980s novelist, at the end of the temporal arc that began with the cultural flourishings of the 1960s and concluded with the fall of the Berlin Wall, took over the right to narrate the twentieth century—a right that had previously belonged to the historian. It is hardly surprising, then, that Pitol's *El desfile del amor* took up the same endeavor. The novel focuses on a historian, Miguel del Solar, who returns to Mexico in 1973 after working abroad to oversee the publication of his book on 1914, the most tumultuous year of the Mexican Revolution. As this happens, he stumbles into the story of a German immigrant's mysterious murder in 1942, a crime committed in the building where he lived as a child. The story gradually rereads Mexico's postrevolutionary era through some of its secrets: the way some Mexicans were seduced by Nazism, the role of European immigrants in its national culture, and the formation of the bourgeoisie that would rule the country throughout the twentieth century. Del Solar, like Brandys's Tom, is a fictional figure who denies history as seen by historians and highlights a different version of the past. Like *Rondó, El desfile del amor* traces a story that connects the wartime foundations of Mexican society (just like Brandys treats the war as foundation for Modern Poland) to the secrets of its midcentury consolidation and then to an era of political turmoil (just five years after the Tlatelolco massacre). I will return to this novel in the final section of the chapter. To understand the progressions of this history, though, one must understand yet another element of Pitol's strategic Occidentalism: the genealogy of humor, derived partly from Eastern Europe but without the gravity at work in Brandys. Indeed, Pitol was one of the writers of lightness to emerge in world literature in the 1980s.

Another Modernism: Humor, Cosmopolitanism, and the Challenge to Literary *Doxa*

Pitol's philosophy of translation displays a paradoxical stance when examined in the light of academic translation studies. In *The Translator's Invisibility*, Lawrence Venuti argues that "the aim of translation is to bring back a cultural other as the same, the recognizable, even the familiar," but with an important limitation: "Translation can be considered the communication of a foreign text, but it is always a communication limited by its address to a specific reading audience."[73] One could say that a literary translator like Pitol performs this limitation as something productive rather than exercising the "violence" that Venuti identifies in translation's subversions of target cultures. Because Pitol ultimately designs a world literature that broadens the aesthetic range of readership and the creative possibilities of his own writing, the resulting estrangement is not really a matter of a "cultural political practice" based on "constructing or critiquing ideology-stamped identities for foreign cultures," as Venuti would suggest.[74] While one could indeed claim that part of Pitol's work is defined by the distance of his writing from token Mexican nationalism, this assertion says nothing in particular about Pitol himself; after all, this general endeavor defines most major writers of his generation in different ways. In this sense, he is less critical of national identity than Salvador Elizondo or Juan García Ponce. Instead, the path taken by his work—from translation to critique to literary form—recognizes the unbridgeable distance between national and world literature as a site in which a writer may construct and perform both a particular version of world literature and the literary practice resulting from claimed genealogies. I would contend that this is a variation of what Venuti calls "foreignizing translation," that is, the act of signifying "the difference of the foreign text yet only by disrupting the cultural codes that prevail in the target language."[75] By constructing a new literary modernism that privileged the carnivalesque and lightness over gravity, Pitol's real intervention in Mexican fiction did not replay the binary of cosmopolitanism and nationalism that had plagued national literary debates throughout the postrevolutionary period. Rather, Pitol's work disrupts the underlying nature of that debate—by rendering, through his world literature, an imaginary assemblage of the national and the transnational that lurk behind both literary tradition and the fictional worlds a Mexican writer can potentially create. To understand this point, we must briefly discuss both Pitol's work in Anagrama's canon of British fiction and the 1980s debates on lightness in literature.

British literature occupies an essential place both in Pitol's oeuvre and in Anagrama's editorial work. The most canonical works in Pitol's corpus of translations and criticisms come from this tradition. He was responsible for major translations of Henry James (U.S.-born, but a participant in British modernism) for Seix Barral and Salvat in the 1960s and the 1970s—including *The Bostonians* (1966), *Washington Square* (1970), *What Maisie Knew* (1970), and *The Turn of the Screw* (1971)—and he would later publish his translations of *Daisy Miller* and *The Aspern Papers* in a 1984 volume for UNAM's series Nuestros Clásicos.[76] These translations effectively reshaped the availability and reception of James's work in Spanish. He also translated Jane Austen's *Emma* for Salvat in 1972 and Joseph Conrad's *Heart of Darkness* for Lumen in 1974.[77] Pitol's first major book of criticism, *De Jane Austen a Virginia Woolf* (*From Jane Austen to Virginia Woolf*), is the result of these undertakings, and its analysis of English fiction remains so central to its author's intellectual identity that the book is continually refashioned and republished.[78] When reading these translations and essays—which then evolved into the essays of *La casa de la tribu* (*The Tribe's House*)[79] and his interest in lesser-known modernists and postmodernists such as Compton-Burnett, Firbank, and Ackerley—it becomes patently clear that Pitol's most fundamental concern is modernism's role in the development of the novel as a form, and, more specifically, how one could undermine the contemporary novel by strategically appropriating key elements and authors from the modernist tradition.

Pitol's English canon mirrors his work in Polish modernism, as it performs the same operation evident in Pitol's translations of Gombrowicz and

Andrzejewski. Michael Goddard locates Gombrowicz in a Polish tradition defined by the "subversion of form." For Goddard, Polish modernism in general and Gombrowicz in particular "completely exploded every received notion of aesthetic form so that it encompasses all of social existence," so "through the subversion of form" fiction could "allow the expression of the profound life that is buried behind the rigidity of form: the subcultural, immature forces upon which human existence is based."[80] It is true that Polish modernism was born out of the ideological concerns discussed in the previous section, and of what Goddard calls the "fragility of Poland's existence and the sense of living on imperfect, borrowed time," but the concrete nature of literary form in such sources is essential to an understanding of Pitol.[81] If anything distinguishes *The Carnival Trilogy* as a literary endeavor in Mexican literary history, is precisely its ability to narrate the same "subcultural, immature forces upon which human existence is based" that Goddard identifies in Gombrowicz. In articulating the formal concerns of Polish and Communist Bloc narrative modernism on the one hand, and of English modernism on the other, Pitol was actually creating a tradition and a literary language so as to subvert the weighty paradigms of the Mexican novel.

Furthermore, it is important to remember, as Anita Starosta has recently argued, that Gombrowicz's formal innovations are a rigorous engagement with connections between nonhegemonic literatures similar to the ones established by Pitol in his own translations. Indeed, *Transatlántico*, the work crucial both to Pitol and to Anagrama, was based on what Starosta calls "the double location (or, rather, dislocation)" of Gombrowicz "in Poland and Argentina." This double location, in turn, "informs Gombrowicz's theory of Form—elaborated from this vantage point but not always solely, or even explicitly, concerned with cultural marginalization—and his persistent inquiry into the conditions of legibility of literature."[82] Gombrowicz clearly belongs to the same canon of Polish writers who sought an alternative to collectivization efforts in literary individuality. Starosta explains, "Even as Gombrowicz is concerned with the cultural-national forms that make collective sentiment and behavior predictable, however, he puts consistent emphasis on the individual voice, both as something always threatened to be engulfed by the collective and as a vantage point of critique."[83] In some ways, Pitol's time in Poland, and in other literary sites beyond the hegemonic circuits of world literature, mirrors Argentina's impact on Gombrowicz—and it advances an important argument, which Starosta also develops, for world literature that is not dependent on sites like Paris. Indeed, as Starosta writes: "For Casanova, the only conceivable end of achieving freedom is to be 'consecrated' by the center. Gombrowicz, in contrast, seeks absolute freedom, which requires complete autonomy from the center itself."[84] Indeed, Pitol's own ventures replicate this ethos. Like Gombrowicz, Pitol mocks the stereotypes and imperatives of his national tradition, but he also resists the impulse to exercise the kind of literature that was achieving (in Barcelona, no less) consecration in the center: magical realism, the Boom, and so on. In this way, then, Pitol blazes a trail that would be followed by writers such as the Crack group, the subject of chapter 2, and Cristina Rivera Garza and Carmen Boullosa, discussed in chapter 3. In his translations, moreover, Pitol goes further than Gombrowicz does: he not only claims the writer's individual freedom against stereotype or collectivity, but also transforms his own collectivity by creating a cartography of literary translations that resists, ideologically and stylistically, both the imperatives of national literatures and the mainstream modernist literature that informed writers like Carlos Fuentes.

A notable feature of Pitol's engagement with even the most canonical English writers is his interest in the works and moments in which figures like Conrad and James were at odds with the literary *doxas* of their times. In an essay on Jane Austen written in Belgrade in 1968, Pitol notes that, while Austen shared formal and comical qualities with her contemporaries, her "intrínseca ambigüedad" (intrinsic ambiguity) is what makes her stand out: this feature places her in a complex relationship with the mores and ideas of her time.[85] As for Conrad, he highlights the "foreignness" that unfolds—both in the literary subject submerged in an exotic setting and in the individual facing a conflict between his self and an alien system of values.[86] In this sense, his reading is analogous to Starosta's focus on Conrad's Polish origins and how he challenged the divides between Western and Eastern Europe, as well as between Empire and colonial sites.[87] Tellingly, too, he presents Henry James, as canonical a writer as there ever was, as marginal. In his reading of *The Aspern Papers*, he emphasizes James's major work in literary form and his contributions to literary perspective, while stressing the fact that his work "careció de lectores y de resonancia crítica" (lacked readers and critical resonance) and that his novels "fueron vistas con desgano" (were viewed listlessly).[88] I am not interested in debating the accuracy of Pitol's judgments; these authors are widely discussed in endless pages of criticism and scholarship. The key point to highlight in Pitol's *Adicción a los ingleses* (*Addiction to the English*) is how he aligns the authors in his genealogy with a certain kind of out-of-place-ness, defined as their exercise of highly innovative literary forms amid a conflictive relationship with existing societal dogmas and aesthetic norms. It is thus unsurprising that *La casa de la tribu*, the 1982 essay collection that gathers the readings and literary ideas surrounding his period spent working with Panorama de Narrativas and writing *El desfile del amor*, sees his English affinities lean toward far less canonical authors: there, Ivy Compton-Burnett, Ronald Firbank, and Flann O'Brien accompany writers such as Pilniak, Kusniewicz, Patricia Highsmith, and Nikolai Gogol.

For Pitol to be able to translate and publish these atypical writers, his shared affinity with editor Jorge Herralde, regarding the importance of these disruptive modernisms in the construction of contemporary narrative, was essential. This affinity fostered in both translator and editor the value of promoting noncanonical Western writers among both Spanish and

Latin American readers. Herralde has famously described his relationship to British literature as a "love story"; undoubtedly, one of Anagrama's most important contributions to the Spanish-language reading community is its vast project of translating Anglophone writers. Readers today are most familiar with writers who had reached prominence in the English-language world and whose work has mostly or fully been published in Anagrama: Ian McEwan, Julian Barnes, Hanif Kureishi, Kazuo Ishiguro, Timothy Mo, A. S. Byatt, Lawrence Norfolk, Graham Swift, John Lanchester, and Allan Hollinghurst are among the most famous subset. Nonetheless, as Herralde himself recognizes, the tradition began with authors like Firbank and Ackerley, and a central element of this "love story" is the tradition of English humor that lies at the core of the collections: Saki, P. G. Wodehouse, Evelyn Waugh, David Lodge, and Tom Sharpe are all translated in Anagrama.[89] In fact, the very first title published in Panorama de Narrativas was Jane Bowles's eccentric 1943 novel *Two Serious Ladies*, a romp of a story focused on two middle-class women and their descent into debauchery.[90] Herralde admits that he decided to inaugurate the collection with this book, even though neither Jane Bowles nor her husband Paul was a household name in Spanish, because "me encantó esta extravagante y chifladísima novela" (I adored this extravagant and extremely crazy novel), showing that the collection was born out of the same taste for out-of-place-ness favored by Pitol's own canon.[91] Minutiae aside, we must note that the confluence of Eastern European and British modernisms, both in Pitol's work and in Anagrama's formation as a fiction publisher, was crucial in opening the field—both to the world literature that Pitol would embody and to the literary fiction that he would write as a result of these engagements.

Pitol and Anagrama's penchant for the carnivalesque and the eccentric was not only a peculiar personal and editorial preference, but also part of a larger trend toward lightness in 1980s world literature. The charge against weighty fiction was led by two of the most important writers of the time: Italo Calvino, who wrote about "lightness" in his posthumously published lectures *Six Memos for the New Millennium* (1988), and Milan Kundera, in his *The Art of the Novel* (1986) and *Testaments Betrayed* (1993).[92] Pitol's relationship with humor, of course, precedes the publication of these books by many years, and he does not substantially engage with either author. Nonetheless, Calvino and Kundera are the key theorists of the turn toward humor and lightness in world fiction at the time. Although Calvino is more often cited, Kundera is much closer to Pitol for many reasons. His work and his theory of humor developed as an intellectual response to his own situation as a writer in the Eastern Bloc, and his extensive dialogue with the Spanish-language world, which resulted from his acquaintance with figures like Carlos Fuentes and García Márquez in the 1960s, expanded drastically in the 1980s, when Tusquets became his publisher.[93] Kundera's essays and fiction were very much present in the Mexican literary world, published in outlets such as Octavio

Paz's *Vuelta* (whose book-publishing arm released a Mexican edition of *The Art of the Novel* in the same translation released by Tusquets in Spain) and the *Revista de la Universidad de México* as early as 1980. *The Art of the Novel*'s famous first chapter not only declares Cervantes the founding figure of the novel, but also posits a notion of the genre that is quite compatible with Pitol's own preoccupations. Without going into too much detail, it is pertinent to mention that Kundera describes the novel as a history of formal discoveries, and names the center of these discoveries as the Russian tradition that runs from Nikolai Gogol to Andrei Bely—a tradition frequently visited by Pitol. Furthermore, Kundera also mentions Jaroslav Hašek's *The Good Soldier Schweik*, a novel Pitol translated in the early 1990s and listed, in a 1991 article, as one of the most important representatives of this tradition.[94]

Kundera also devotes numerous pages in the book to the values of lightness, irony, and humor throughout the history of the novel. Later on, in *Testaments Betrayed*, Kundera expands these insights further, establishing François Rabelais as another founder (alongside Cervantes) of the novel's tradition of humor and laughter, which he traces forward to contemporary writers such as Carlos Fuentes and Salman Rushdie.[95] This is yet another affinity with Pitol, who claims this legacy via his reading of Mikhail Bakhtin's writings on carnival. Pitol's work practices avant la lettre a considerable number of prescriptions favored by Kundera's manifestos. Strikingly, for example, Pitol connects his fiction and literary thinking to a preoccupation with form, advancing such ideas in a vast canon of writings a few years before Kundera defines "continuity," the notion that "each work contains all the previous experience of the novel" as a value to be defended against the "spirit of our time," which, in his estimation, is "firmly focused on a present that is so expansive and profuse that it shoves the past off our horizon and reduces time to the present moment only."[96] This is no mere coincidence: both Kundera and Pitol reached an erudite, worldly conception of the novel in the 1980s out of a need to redeploy literature against the grain of the political imperatives that became increasingly obvious during the last years of the Eastern Bloc and amid the early pressures that neoliberalism would gradually impose on the novel. To understand Pitol, we must also understand the value of "continuity," because his own fiction develops as a continuation of the tradition of formal discoveries that he explored as a translator and essayist.

Translating Firbank and Ackerley, and promoting the works of Compton-Burnett and Flann O'Brien through criticism, are logical actions from the perspective of the debates over lightness that were unfolding in the 1980s. Pitol's trilogy is among the first instances in the history of literary humor to attain canonical status in Mexico. As many critics have noted, Pitol was writing against the current of the weighty solemnity that characterized mainstream Mexican literature at the time.[97] This is one reason Bakhtin was such a central referent: his theories of the carnivalesque provided Pitol with a way to undermine the dominant trends in Mexican fiction of the 1970s. As the reference to Bakhtin has been extensively discussed in previous critical work, I will delve no further into the topic.[98] However, Pitol's modernist genealogies must be examined beyond humor alone, since his literary work in the 1980s subverts existing Mexican tradition in a much deeper way. One must bear in mind that it is unusual for a Mexican writer to claim such a complex genealogy derived from British modernism, given the weight of Cervantes and the French naturalist traditions on the twentieth-century Mexican novel— from Federico Gamboa's *Santa* to the works of Carlos Fuentes. Even if James Joyce did become a towering figure in his generation, Pitol's canon takes an altogether different direction, since Joyce inspired the kind of total narrative that Pitol's work sought to undermine.[99] Some British authors like James and Austen are not such a radical departure in Pitol's case: Fuentes himself was a James enthusiast, and his work *Aura* was directly informed by *The Aspern Papers*.[100]

Pitol's work raises a more direct challenge to the predominance of what Ryan Long calls "fictions of totality" in Mexican literature of the 1970s. Long persuasively demonstrates that one of the main paths of the novel in Mexico (followed, for instance, by Fernando Del Paso and Carlos Fuentes) was the creation of totalizing narratives to encompass a symbolic representation of the social in Mexico, following the disrupted hegemony of popular-revolutionary nationalism in Mexican cultural discourse, particularly in the wake of the 1968 massacre.[101] Pitol is perhaps the most important writer in the opposing vein: he produces not only the novel that resists totalization, but also a repertoire of forms affiliated with modernism in order to undermine that gesture's very possibility. This is, in my view, what accounts for Pitol's gradual transition from James and Austen to Firbank and Compton-Burnett. As a writer and intellectual whose trajectory was defined by the conflict against totality as a cultural endeavor, his canon always tends toward estrangement, banality, satire, and any other element that counters the "fictions of totality" developed not only by scores of his counterparts, but also by the Mexican state and by the different maximalist regimes under whose aegis he lived during his time abroad.

Although Bakhtin tends to protagonize studies of Pitol's work, scholars typically overlook a second important theoretical reference: Russian formalist Viktor Shklovsky. In his text "¿Un *Ars Poética*?" written in 1993 and included in *El arte de la fuga*, Pitol reminisced about personally meeting Shklovsky in Moscow, during the same stay in which he wrote his quartet of short stories and translated Pilniak. As a result of this meeting, he became interested in formalism, structuralism, and semiotics, Bakhtin included. While Pitol admits that the technicality of these writings was daunting and ultimately led him to stop reading them, he nonetheless speaks of the "indecible placer" (unspeakable pleasure) he felt when reading Shklovsky's *Theory of Prose*, and how he admired the ability to theorize on the concrete works of authors such as Cervantes, Sterne, Dickens, and Biely.[102] This theoretical reference is key for understanding Pitol's work in the 1980s, as well as his turn toward figures like Pilniak and Firbank. It is obvious that the canon studied by Shklovsky is very close to Pitol's own: Dickens and Biely are two of his most formative readings. But the most important issue here is that, along with Bakhtin's notion of the carnivalesque, the other key category informing Pitol's work in this period is "estrangement" or "defamiliarization" (*ostranenie*). Shklovsky coined the term in his 1917 essay "Art as Device," which opens *Theory of Prose*. According to Shklovsky's famous formulation, "The purpose of art . . . is to lead us to a knowledge of a thing through the organ of sight instead of recognition. By 'estranging' objects and complicating form, the device of art makes perception long and 'laborious.'"[103] Read from the perspective of a Mexican author writing at the end of a century of "national literature," this prescription provides a way to emphasize the denaturalization of categories such as identity and history—and to create a fiction in which readers can see the past rather than achieve "recognition" (which here carries the Aristotelian sense of anagnorisis). It is revealing that Jorge Ibargüengoitia, the comedic writer famous for his satires of genres like the novel of the Mexican Revolution, is among the few Mexican novelists discussed by Pitol in his criticism. According to Pitol's 2000 essay, Ibargüengoitia's main discovery as a writer was that "la risa nos desliga del poder y termina por desprestigiarlo. . . . Se trata de un movimiento inicial de desacralización que convierte al fin a los grandes en caricaturas, en fantoches grotescos, en ridículos cuadrúpedos, y nos permite contemplarlos en su íntima y colosal inepcia" (laughter unlinks us from power and ultimately undermines its prestige. . . . It is an initial movement toward desacralization that finally converts figures of greatness into caricatures, grotesque fakes, ridiculous four-legged animals, and allows us to contemplate them in their intimate and colossal ineptitude).[104] Through Shklovsky and Bakhtin's ideas, and his commitment to the modernism and world literature of his own making, Pitol transposes Ibargüengoitia's "initial movement of desacralization"—his well-known parody of modern Mexico— into a more aesthetic form of literary style.

I would claim that, in the context of Pitol's work, modernism in the larger sense provides a formal roadmap for shaping cosmopolitanism and desa-cralization into a concretely functional literary aesthetic, as well as into a literary style that allows a writer to focus on both the present and the past of her tradition without fully extricating herself from it. Pitol works analo-gously to Rebecca Walkowitz's conception of modernism as "cosmopolitan style." Walkowitz notes that "modernist narrative strategies can be adapted for various political enterprises, as can critical attitudes," which leads her to highlight "writers who have used naturalness, triviality, evasion, mix-ups, treason, and vertigo to generate specific projects of democratic individual-ism, on one hand, and of antifascism or anti-imperialism on the other."[105] She focuses both on writers from the period of historical English modernism (Conrad, Joyce, and Woolf) and on contemporary writers who inherit and further develop modernist style (Ishiguro, Rushdie, and W. G. Sebald). If we consider that Pitol is a close reader of Conrad and Joyce, and that Ishiguro and Sebald were both published in Panorama de Narrativas, then it is easy to infer that Walkowitz's formulation can be neatly applied to Pitol's fiction. *El desfile del amor*, in particular, uses all of the techniques listed by Walkowitz to expose the history of fascism in midcentury Mexico—and to develop a modernist hero, the historian Miguel del Solar, as the potentially revisionist voice that unveils the banality of power.

In fact, Pitol's work exhibits the very pattern traced by Walkowitz in the authors she studies: his, too, are novels that "approach large-scale international events, such as world war and immigration, by focusing on trivial or transient episodes of everyday life."[106] A point to keep in mind here is that Pitol's relationship to modernism does not fit the models of semiperipheral writing as typically identified by critics of Global South literature. Nicholas Brown, for instance, develops a theory of "postmodernism as a semiperipheral symptom" based on Brazilian modernism, one rooted in the country's location in the transnational circuits of culture and capital; meanwhile, in one of his classic formulations, Moretti identifies "nonsynchronism" as a feature of semiperipheral literatures.[107] I do not seek to contradict these constructions, which can be valuable in describing certain trends (magical realism, for example). But I believe that a writer like Pitol requires us to rethink Latin America's relationship to world literary systems beyond these ideas—precisely because he is part of a large group of major writers whose fiction is not particularly concerned with regional specificity, decolonization, identity, or even the lack of synchronicity vis-à-vis the hegemonic center. Pitol better fits a model like Walkowitz's, which is mostly concerned with English writers, than models such as those put forward by Brown, Moretti, and Casanova, given that his cosmopolitan circulation and aesthetic engagements belong to circuits of modernism that swim against the global currents of hegemonic symbolic and cultural capital.

Mexico's contact with fascism during World War II, the subject of *El desfile del amor*, is readable in Pitol's fiction because his involvement with different authors of the English modernist tradition expose him to narrative tools that are directly concerned with the banality of everyday life and the critique of fascism. The recourse to frivolity in his readings is important in this regard. In *Frivolity Unbound*, Robert F. Kiernan suggests that in Ivy Compton-Burnett's novels "trivial developments fatten themselves on complications real and illusory even while they are examined (à la Henry James) for ever-more-precise understandings of motive and impulse."[108] I will not take on an in-depth discussion of Pitol's connection to Compton-Burnett here, as I have done so elsewhere. What I wish to highlight now, however, is that the marginal modernists favored by Pitol in shaping Panorama de Narrativas are those writers who radicalize classic modernist techniques by introducing an element of radical estrangement.[109] Compton-Burnett's novels are characterized by settings in which numerous implications, left unsaid, ultimately manifest themselves in dialogues full of loaded words that permit the reader to suspect the situation's underlying complexity. We could describe these settings as a refined, ironic version of Jamesian style that can nonetheless be read via Bakhtin's notion of the carnivalesque and the Russian formalist preference for estrangement as a device. Therefore, what Pitol favors is not the kind of malleable modernist prose (as advanced by García Márquez) that results in what Ángel Rama calls "transculturación narrativa," the embodiment of the engagement between dominating and dominated culture as literary form.[110] Rather, his prose is mostly marked by a banal, comic style that thrives on the intensity of the unsaid, much like Compton-Burnett or Ishiguro do in their own novels. Pitol's affinities in the 1970s and 1980s point to a particular notion of modernism that can be defined as a literary style able to defamiliarize, through narrative form, the structures of cultural power embedded in history—without needing to provide the alternative narrative totality that other novelists sought to construct at the time. This understanding of modernism is the gateway in my analysis of Pitol's work: it shows us how the long genealogy I have described up to this point ultimately enables a reading of Pitol's fiction. In the final two sections, I will follow this conception of modernism in two of Pitol's fiction works.

"Nocturno de Bujara": Cosmopolitanism and the Challenge to Totalization

The recognition of Sergio Pitol's work as central to Mexican literature began in the 1980s, relatively late for a writer of his generation. Carlos Fuentes, only five years older than Pitol, had solidified his standing as one of Mexico's leading fiction writers in the late 1950s and early 1960s. Two other writers born around the same time as Pitol, Salvador Elizondo and Juan García Ponce, had already produced their most iconic work, and the rarity of their fiction, rather than posing an obstacle, was actually essential to their status as cult authors. Conversely, Pitol, while indeed recognized in literary circles and well-connected in the intellectual world, wrote within a narrow niche in the literary field. Pitol's belated recognition was due in part to the fact that he wrote sparingly and in a genre, the short story, that lacked the novel's cultural capital. As Pitol himself recounts, his work in the 1960s was largely defined by the publication of various collections, some with overlapping content: "Escribí todos esos libros en el extranjero. Enviaba los manuscritos a las editoriales en México, y un año más o menos después recibía los primeros ejemplares" (I wrote all of those books abroad. I would send the manuscripts to Mexican publishers, and I would receive the first copies about a year later).[111] Coupled with the difficulties of writing and publishing from faraway places, Pitol's affinity for the short story was somewhat anomalous in a decade in which so many of Mexico's most important novels were published: Carlos Fuentes's *La muerte de Artemio Cruz*, Salvador Elizondo's *Farabeuf*, Fernando del Paso's *José Trigo*, Elena Garro's *Los recuerdos del porvenir*, José Agustín's *De perfil*, and Rosario Castellanos's *Oficio de tinieblas*, among others. In contrast to this generation-defining wave of long-format fiction, Pitol's first novel, *El tañido de una flauta* (*A Flute's Tolling*), did not appear until 1972. *El tañido de una flauta*'s literary structure consists of short fragments and stands in stark contrast with the epic tone deployed by Fuentes, Garro, and Del Paso; the self-assured, youthful prose of José Agustín's early work; and even the obsessive, self-reflective work of Salvador Elizondo. Pitol's second novel, *Juegos florales* (*Floral Games*), was published in 1982, but by the author's account was written partially in 1967. Both novels are fundamentally about writing. Pitol writes that *El tañido*'s central topic "es la creación. La literatura, la pintura y el cine son los protagonistas centrales" (is creation. Literature, painting, and cinema are the main protagonists). Nonetheless, the key idea in Pitol's re-creation of his writing experience is the fact that the novel was not a comfortable genre for his self-analytical style: "El terror de crear un híbrido entre el relato y el tratado ensayístico me impulsó a intensificar los elementos narrativos" (The terror of creating a hybrid between the story and the treatise encouraged me to intensify the narrative elements).[112] In hindsight, Pitol's reluctance is rather paradoxical, given that this sort of hybrid would eventually cement his literary fame, following the publication of *El arte de la fuga* in the mid-1990s. *Juegos florales*, also centered on the topic of writing, bears a closer resemblance to Pitol's celebrated style; its most interesting character, Billie Upward, very much embodies the tribulations faced by a cosmopolitan creator. This novel, however, is bogged down by its heavy structure and its reluctance to embrace literary reflection *tout court*. Still, with this novel's publication, Sergio Pitol began to produce the texts that would more properly define his revolutionary style.

Significantly, Pitol is often absent from canonical accounts of Mexican narrative of this period. When we contrast his work with the novels and collections that have elicited critical attention, it becomes clear that his were incompatible with the main critical readings of cultural politics related to the decline of twentieth-century revolutionary nationalism. Cynthia Steele, who devotes a chapter of her *Politics, Gender, and the Mexican Novel* to this era, does not mention Pitol, as his work is not directly pertinent to the topics she highlights in her well-known study: the democratization of writing, increased narrative openness to politicized genres like the *crónica*, the emergence of women writers, and the weight of Tlatelolco in Mexico's cultural consciousness.[113] Similarly, in *The Fragmented Novel in Mexico*, Carol Clark D'Lugo focuses on the writers of the Onda movement and on Salvador Elizondo's *Farabeuf*, since her model is more engaged with a "politics of form" that intertwines aesthetics with the development of Mexico's postrevolutionary cultural edifice.[114] But the canonical historiography that best illustrates Pitol's uncomfortable position within the main trends of Mexican fiction is Sara Sefchovich's celebrated *México: País de ideas, país de novelas*, where Pitol is described as a "buscador de solitarios, de personajes decadentes o locos, profundamente románticos" (seeker of solitary souls, of decadent or crazy, deeply romantic characters), and ultimately dismissed in passing as an author whose work, despite being published in the 1970s and 1980s, is concerned with literary and stylistic preoccupations that "engarzan mejor con las de los años cincuenta y sesenta" (are better linked with those from the 1950s and 1960s).[115] Pitol's formal innovations are invisible in these critics' accounts because their respective frameworks ultimately define narrative form according to its engagement with either Mexican nationalism or state-sponsored culture. However, Pitol's role is different: it renewed the repertoire of narrative techniques and literary traditions in Mexico just as Mexico's predominant twentieth-century model reached its point of exhaustion. Other than Del Paso's sprawling historical novel *Noticias del imperio*, or the work of emerging women writers like María Luisa Puga or Carmen Boullosa, it is very difficult to find 1980s-era fiction that plays a predominant role in defining literary paradigms of post-1968 literature. Pitol's literary impact would not be really legible until the 1990s, when a generation of younger writers, most notably the Crack writers who will be discussed in the next chapter, established him as their precursor.

Pitol's awkward position in Mexican literary canons also indicates the way in which his cosmopolitan endeavors offer a counterpoint to the prevailing politics of literary form in the 1970s and 1980s. As I mentioned before, Ryan Long shows how totalizing novels—including the works of authors such as Carlos Fuentes, Fernando del Paso, and Héctor Aguilar Camín—develop in post-1968 Mexican fiction, constructing "fictions of totality" that account for both the massacre of Tlatelolco and the decline of the postrevolutionary state in its slow transition to the neoliberal model.[116] Long's account, which runs parallel to mine, provides a good explanation of a process that was taking place at the same time as the one I describe here. According to Long, "The totalizing novel is the product of a centralized society whose goal is coherent, self-contained autonomy." As this notion of Mexican society got undermined by the Tlatelolco massacre, Long contends, totalizing novels articulated "explicit critiques of the way in which the political power of the state based itself on an exclusive claim to the authorized ability of constructing national history as a guiding force."[117] In other words, Long explores a mechanism in fiction that used narrative strategies affiliated with the emergence of a national/popular state to undermine the symbolic efficiency of a totalizing project. These "fictions of totality" thus accompany the "fragmented novel" discussed by Clark D'Lugo and the civil society literature studied by Steele in reconfiguring the relationship between literature and the construction and imagination of the political.

Pitol's strategic Occidentalism, developed largely at a distance from these processes, provides a path for the radical deflation of twentieth-century Mexican literary strategies: it questions the symbolic authority less of the state than of literature itself. It is telling that the writers privileged by Mexicanist literary critics in accounts of this period are typically either public intellectuals *tout court* (e.g., Fuentes, Aguilar Camín, and Elena Poniatowska) or niche authors defined by their refusal or inability to connect with such a role: Juan García Ponce, Salvador Elizondo, and Jorge Aguilar Mora. Pitol's fiction is caught in a problematic space between these two stances: it develops at a point when the Mexican literary writer gradually loses the privilege of a public voice to historians and political analysts, who would become the key figures in public discourse during the neoliberal era.[118] Consequently, while Pitol does not shy away from public intervention (he was close to both the Zapatista movement and López Obrador's political campaign), he relieves literary writing both of the task of totality and from the urgency of direct engagement. Instead he constructs, as I have discussed in the previous two sections, an alternative literary genealogy through editing and translation. By means of this alternative tradition, the power of his writing helps reshape literary fiction's relationship with the imperatives of the Mexican political transition—precisely by dislodging fiction from the totalizing imperatives of both the Mexican national/popular state (described by Long) and the Latin American Boom (which was already concluding its cycle as the defining literary movement of the Latin American novel).[119] The defining elements of all traditions appropriated by Pitol in his essays and translations—the acerbic sense of humor accompanying writers in authoritarian societies, the reluctance to participate in politically organic forms of writing, the use of the banal and the quotidian to resist the impulse toward grand narrative—are not only contrary to the impulses that inform "fictions of totality" and genres such as the literary chronicle, but also conducive to a new kind of literary style tasked with exploring a present in which literary writing is no longer a privileged site of reflection.

Certainly, Pitol belongs to a literary field alongside other (younger) highly renowned Latin American novelists whose work likewise exists in the intersection between the deflation of the Latin American Boom's penchant for totality and the deployment of reading as a strategy to resignify the very notion of literary style in the national and regional present. In a book on the relationship between reading and writing, Neige Sinno groups Pitol with Ricardo Piglia and Roberto Bolaño.[120] Sinno persuasively describes these three authors in parallel, showing how the act of reading and the figure of the reader are crucial to the renewal of Latin American fiction at large. This is evident in Piglia, whose reader/detective Emilio Renzi reframes the history of Argentine fiction in response to the military dictatorship's dismantling of Argentine modernity. It is also evident in Bolaño, who mercilessly attacks the literary legacies of the Latin American Boom through a style deflated by irony.[121] In Pitol's case, Sinno argues, the readerly nature of his fiction is fundamental for understanding not only his influences, but also his main devices. For instance, Sinno points out that many of Pitol's works resist the reader, a tendency he draws from authors such as Jaroslav Hašek.[122] Pushing Sinno's arguments further, I would contend that Pitol's resistance to the reader is the result of his use of world literature as a tool to undermine affirmative forms of literary narration in the Mexican context. In other words, the strategy at work in Pitol's strategic Occidentalism not only turns to an alternative geography of the novel; it also constructs, within his own worldly map, a new territory for Mexican literature, one invested in subverting the pedagogical function of the national novel—which has belied many central currents of Mexican fiction since the nineteenth century. Cosmopolitanism in Pitol's work, then, does not merely avail itself of the foreign as a way to resist the national; it is not a simplistic binary. Instead, it reconstitutes the national in literature by reshaping the world that surrounds it and functions as its reference. In this context, the purpose of a personal world literature is not the transnationalization of Pitol's writing into global markets or planetary forms of circulation, but the imagination of a world that enables and makes viable a new kind of Mexican literature altogether. Through an act of reading based on translating and editing nonmainstream literary works, Pitol patiently constructs a cartography of literary style that lends meaning to his own writing strategies.

To examine Pitol's fiction in the terms outlined here, we find a useful juncture in the four short stories he wrote in Moscow in 1979 and 1980: "Vals de Mefisto" ("Mephisto Waltz"), "El relato veneciano de Billie Upward" ("Billie Upward's Venetian Tale"), "Asimetría" ("Asymmetry"), and "Nocturno de Bujara" ("Bukhara Nocturne"). Other than "El oscuro hermano gemelo" ("The Dark Twin"), the short story he would include in El arte de la fuga, these four texts were Pitol's last foray into short fiction before delving into the novels and hybrid books that would bring him renown. It is also his first series of texts after a seven-year spell without writing any creative fiction. Pitol himself is very fond of these five stories, which he considers "indudablemente los mejores, los que mayor felicidad me han proporcionado al escribirlos. A veces pienso que no he intentado hacer otros, porque sería inferiores a estos cinco preferidos" (undoubtedly the best, the ones that have made me happiest while writing them. Sometimes I think I haven't tried to write others because they would be inferior to these five favorite ones).[123] I will focus in particular on "Nocturno de Bujara," which in my view better illustrates the impact of Pitol's cosmopolitan endeavors on his style. I will conclude this chapter, in the following section, with some points on his novel El desfile del amor.

Pitol's Moscow stories illustrate his major departures from the style that characterized his short fiction in 1950s and 1960s. Those earlier stories were more invested in a mainstream high modernist style, focused on first-person narratives and on chronicling the decline of the regional bourgeoisie or his early travel adventures. The most celebrated of these texts, "Victorio Ferri cuenta un cuento" ("Victorio Ferri Tells a Story"), written in 1957, already contains some of Pitol's most recognizable stylistic features. Narrated from the perspective of a child, whose death is revealed to the reader only at the very end, the story compellingly describes the decline of his father, a rural cacique in a hellish community in Veracruz. As fellow writer Juan Vicente Melo points out, the narrative stance is a key element in the story's power: the child was born of an incestuous relationship, and the story is devoid of dialogue, privileging introspection.[124] While his subject was common in literature of the time (Juan Rulfo had famously described the infernal realities of a decimated rural Mexico only a few years before), Pitol's particular narrative of the collapsing rural order in the Córdoba region of Veracruz is founded on disorientation, on the narrator's ability to deauthorize himself from the start: "Sé que me llamo Victorio. Sé que creen que estoy loco. . . . Sé que soy diferente a los demás" (I know my name is Victorio. I know they think I am crazy. . . . I know I am different from the others).[125] With this stance, Pitol undermines literature's very ability to account for the breakdown of Mexico's rural order—a tactic that stands in stark contrast to the intense, layered narrative style of precursors like Rulfo and José Revueltas. Instead, Victorio Ferri provides the reader with a perspective that is always already estranged and estranging, and the relationship between his stated knowledge of reality and his perceived insanity provide a bewildering basis for a narrative that is as much about the decline of a social order as about the possibility of narrating it. Fragmentary, introspective studies of his home region, written in the early days of his transnational ventures, Pitol's 1950s stories were already symptomatic of his cosmopolitan style and ideological preoccupations, but they were still bound by many paradigmatic elements of mid-twentieth-century fiction: for one thing, the construction of an infernal heterotopia, San Rafael, which echoed Onetti's Santa María and Rulfo's Comala; for another, a penchant for costumbrist elements and characters (such as the focus on individual figures like Amelia Otero) that contradicted his reflective style. However, the story was still highly classical in certain stylistic aspects, particularly in its use of a major revelation at the end—which would mark a departure from the inconclusive style of his Moscow stories. His early stories still lack the sense of humor that would add a layer of complexity to his later work. Texts like "Victorio Ferri cuenta un cuento" do not always transcend the indictment of a declining provincial society.

Pitol's late-1970s short stories are not only the most accomplished of his ventures into the genre, but also a testament to the way in which he transcended the limits of literary representation faced by his contemporaries. As I have remarked, he wrote these stories in Moscow, during the period described earlier in this chapter. Among Pitol's models at the time was Pilniak, whose subject matter was close to his own early stories: the decline of a rural order in the wake of a revolution. But this was not the focus of Pitol's reading. Instead, Pilniak became notable in Pitol's criticism as a self-reflective writer engaged with the insufficiencies of the novel as genre. One can find further insights in the first essay of *La casa de la tribu*, which recounts Pitol's general perceptions of Russian literature after his return to Mexico in 1981. Writers in the French naturalist canon, like Honoré de Balzac, the model for Carlos Fuentes's fictional project, were a more common reference for Mexican writers. Pitol draws a distinction between this more typical literary genealogy and the Russian canon he read and translated in Moscow. For Pitol, the French create a character that "es el hombre nacido para triunfar" (is the man born for triumph) and "concibe la voluntad como un instrumento superior a la realidad" (sees will as an instrument superior to reality). By contrast, "la literatura rusa crea al personaje opuesto. El hombre que encuentra en la realidad una barrera infranqueable que le hace inaccesible una verdadera comunicación con la sociedad" (Russian literature creates the opposite character. The man who finds in reality an insurmountable barrier that makes it impossible for him to truly communicate with society).[126] I believe that this assertion is crucial for defining both Pitol's characters—this inability to communicate, as I will show below, is central in understanding Miguel del Solar in *El desfile del amor*—and his style. The inaccessibility of a "true communication with society" is not only a challenge faced by his characters, but also a fundamental tenet of Pitol's own authorial voice.

"Nocturno de Bujara," Pitol's most celebrated story from this period, keenly exemplifies how his disorienting style forms the bedrock of a story on the incommunicability of experience and the impossibility of memory. The action centers on the first-person narrator's nocturnal journey through the Central Asian city of Bukhara, Uzbekistan. Two friends, Dolores and Kyrim, who tell stories as they traverse the city, accompany the narrator. In the middle of the tale, we get a second story, focused on an Italian painter called Issa, who goes to Bukhara in an attempt to overcome her heartbreak over Roberto; she seems to become mentally ill during her journey. Finally, we encounter a third story, this one devoted to a character called Juan Manuel, who recounts an anecdote about a Hungarian painter, Feri; along with the narrator, he encourages Issa to travel to Bukhara and Samarkand. The plot is marked by the dubious reliability of what is being told, since the plot is built with conditionals and information relayed to the narrator (and the reader) by way of secondhand channels. In fact, the story begins with a tone that warns attentive readers that a coherent interpretation or holistic understanding of this text may not be possible:

> Le decíamos, por ejemplo, que al anochecer el aleteo y el graznido de los cuervos lograba enloquecer a los viajeros. Decir que esos pájaros llegaban a la ciudad por millares equivalía a no decir nada. Era necesario ver las ramas de los altos eucaliptos, de los frondosos castaños

a punto de desgajarse, donde se coagulaba aquel torvo espesor de plumas, picos y patas escamosas para descubrir lo absurdo de reducir ciertos fenómenos a cifras. ¿Significaba algo decir que una bandada de miles de cuervos revoloteaba con estrépito bajo el cielo de Samarcanda antes de posarse en sus arbolados parques y avenidas? ¡Nada! Era necesario ver aquellas turbas de azabache para que los números dejaran de contar y se abriera paso a una informe pero imperceptible noción de infinito.

We used to tell her, for instance, that at night the beating of wings and the cawing of the crows could madden travelers. To say that those birds reached the city by the thousands was equivalent to saying nothing. It was necessary to see the branches of the high eucalyptus trees, of the leafy chestnut trees about to break off, where that baleful thickness of feathers, beaks, and scaly feet coagulated, in order to grasp the absurdity of reducing certain phenomena to mere figures. Did it mean anything to say that a flock of thousands of crows swarmed noisily under Samarkand's sky before settling in its tree-covered parks and avenues? Nothing! It was necessary to see those jet-black mobs so that the numbers would stop counting and make way for a shapeless but imperceptible notion of infinity.[127]

Every aspect of this description points to uncertainty, bewilderment, and disorientation. The reader will not know until two sections later that Issa, the Italian painter, is the listener of this story (an ambiguity intensified in Spanish, since the indirect object pronoun is gender neutral), or even that there is a character here with any importance to the story. The passage contrasts a detailed, textured description of a flock of crows invading the city of Samarkand, another ancient historical city, even though the title alludes to Bukhara (a site that, incidentally, would be entirely unknown to most Spanish-language readers). In addition, the narrator immediately discards the possibility of deciphering the scene—by saying both that it would be pointless to count the birds and that the phenomenon's sensorial reality eludes any communicable interpretation. Finally, the paragraph closes by asserting that such an experience shows not only how futile meaning is when one tries to confront it, but also that its true significance is both shapeless and imperceptible.

The setup of "Nocturno de Bujara" is therefore predicated on the inability of literary writing to convey experience and allegory. As Luz Fernández de Alba has observed, Pitol's narrators and writer-characters must work hard to narrate experiences that they generally struggle to apprehend, but that nonetheless have made an impression on them.[128] Narrative tension operates in Pitol's fiction through an internal formal resistance to storytelling—a stance that depends on the reader's inability to fully grasp a plot or produce a well-constituted interpretive framework. Looking back at the different authors present in Pitol's translations and editing work, it becomes abundantly clear that some of his strategies can be traced back to both Eastern European and Anglophone modernism. Issa's section, for instance, evokes the treatment of old aristocracies in British fiction. The dialogue in the first section of the story—which is partly based on concealing the fact that Issa is its recipient—invokes authors like Ivy Compton-Burnett, whose "elision of narrative commentary" and "excising [of] any discernible, overarching ethical scheme" result in peculiar narrative effects.[129] In Pitol's essay about this writer, he emphasizes that "la descripción de los personajes es escueta hasta la avaricia" (the character descriptions are scarce to the point of miserliness).[130] The opening of "Nocturno de Bujara" also echoes various elements highlighted by Pitol in his reading of Boris Pilniak. In his commentary on *Mahogany*, Pitol points out that "Pilniak trata escenas naturalistas visualmente espeluznantes de una manera casual, como si describiera algo por entero cotidiano" (Pilniak treats visually lurid naturalist scenes in a casual manner, as if he were describing something entirely normal).[131] Although the opening passage does not necessarily convey the grisliness of Pilniak's most famous works, Pitol evidently and with great self-awareness fashions a version of similar procedures: in a genre convention-defying gesture, his quasi-Gothic description of crows overtaking a historic city is presented through the complete deconstruction of the ability to derive meaning from it. In linking these two stylistic traits in a single passage, Pitol's literary mechanism upends inherited narrative strategies and the ability of literature itself to construct the kind of totalizing fictions favored by the mainstream branches of Mexican fiction.

Pitol's world literary map is an Occidentalist geography of such procedures. It includes Russian authors who question both the naturalistic impulses of Czarist culture (like Gogol or Dostoevsky) and the Stalinist socialist realist imperatives (like Pilniak). One can also identify Eastern European writers (Hašek, Brandys, Kusniewicz, Andrzejewski) who deploy humor and estrangement to resist the kind of narrative closures aligned with the one-dimensional ideological expectations of engaged fiction. In the specific period of "Nocturno de Bujara," Pitol also develops a penchant for rare English-language modernists and postmodernists whose radical stylistic incursions challenge strategies of construction of subjectivity and psychological depth (Compton-Burnett, Ackerley, Firbank). And, finally, his canon of reading becomes framed by theorists of literature (Bakhtin, Shklovsky) who describe subversion and estrangement as core literary values. My point here is not to claim that influence is a primary issue for Pitol; that would require a philological organization of his readings with the sole purpose of simplistically accounting for his readings and style. Rather, I claim that Pitol's fiction, as early as "Victorio Ferri," has always demonstrated these types of stylistic challenges to totalizing narrative. His readings, translations, and editing work provide a global cartography of authors who conceive their literary task in analogous ways and who develop new literary styles—alienating, punctured by irony, deflated of their epic imperatives—in response to conjunctures in which totalizing fictional strategies correspond to the demands of a rising political or intellectual order. This is the crucial discovery of "Nocturno de Bujara," a sectionalized story that refuses closure. In its place, his style channels our attention toward a proliferating network of stories that, as announced by the cited first paragraph, may be infinite rather than acquiring any kind of defined significance. This is why we readers never learn exactly what happened to Issa. Nor are we privy to a clear temporality in the narrative sequence; nor do the stories offer even a straightforward chronicle of any of the trips to Bukhara, beyond a dreamy and unreliable re-creation of the bewildered narrator's nocturnal experience.

As a matter of fact, "Nocturno de Bujara" seeks to interrupt the contract between reader and author by exposing the inadequacy of both positions.[132] The story is conveyed to us while the narrator, Kyrim, and Dolores sit in an airport, framed by the contrast between the clueless tourists roaming the terminal and the magnificent historical panorama of Bukhara and Samarkand: "Un grupo de turistas alemanes llenaba el lugar. Todos eran viejos" (A group of German tourists filled the place. They were all old).[133] These characters are dissonant with the historical complexity of Bukhara as narrated a few pages prior, which leads the narrator to indict the tourists as savages unworthy of their destination's historical beauty:

> Mil quinientos años atrás, cuando ya Bujara existía como ciudad, los antepasados de aquellos intrusos desgarraban con los dientes los ciervos que contenían sus bosques. No obstante, la calidad de la ropa, las costosas cámaras fotográficas, el evidente deseo de marcar una superioridad, sus gestos y modales, comparados con los de los locales, implicaban una novedad en la historia, algo estrafalario y profundamente chillón.

> Fifteen hundred years before, when Bukhara already existed as a city, the forefathers of those intruders used their teeth to tear at the deer that its forests contained. However, the quality of their clothing, their costly photo cameras, their evident desire to show superiority, their gestures and manners, compared with those of the locals, implied a novelty in history, something lavish and profoundly gaudy.[134]

The text does not imply a direct allegory with the figure of the reader, but the dissonance between these ridiculous Samarkand-bound tourists and the place's aesthetic backdrop is among the many elements of incommunicability at work in the text. The trigger that leads the narrator to express such scorn for the tourists is, precisely, his inability to recall the previous night in Bukhara and the beauties he experienced there: "Lo que más me irritaba es que en el recuento que hacía con mis dos compañeros de viaje, Kyrim y Dolores, se me hubieran borrado datos esenciales que sólo reconstruía, y eso precisamente, al escuchar la narración que ellos hacían" (What irritated me most is that in the account that I was compiling with my two travel companions, Kyrim and Dolores, essential information would have been erased from my mind, details I could solely and precisely reconstruct while listening to their narration).[135] The incapacity to perceive or convey the experience of Bukhara, and the reliance on secondhand accounts to reconstruct it, reveals the core of Pitol's poetics. His strategic choice of a nameless narrator who is less competent than almost any other character in the story (in another section, he informs us that he wanted to write a story on Issa's ordeal but was likewise unable to do so) is telling: action is never conveyable in these poetics, and the story ultimately reflects the impossibility of using literature to construct memory or meaning.

Within the Mexican literary field in particular and the Hispanophone context at large, Pitol's world literature (and the techniques it yields) constitutes a territory that, in turn, provides a space for marginal styles and literary ideologies in the development of Latin America's core modernism and its connections to hegemonic circuits of world literature. If, for example, one considers Moretti's account of García Márquez's *One Hundred Years of Solitude* in *Modern Epic*, Latin America's main contribution to global circuits of the genre is aggregation. In a context where the novel becomes a predator of other literary genres, Moretti posits that the virtue of Latin American literature derives from the region's ability to preserve "*all the other forms that the novel would have otherwise swept away.*" While Moretti's account does include García Márquez in larger global subgenres, such as the family saga (which would tie him to authors like Thomas Mann or Joseph Roth), the specificity of the Latin American locus of enunciation lies at the core of *One Hundred Years of Solitude*'s totalizing gestures: premodernist literary form as an incorporation of the popular; family history as a device of repetition of continuity; "noncontemporaneity" as a totalization of time through the incorporation of present, past, and future; and a "rhetoric of innocence" that reinstates the totality of myth in the guise of regional and global political disillusionment.[136] Pitol represents the opposite gesture: a strictly parallel development of Latin American literature that posits narrative tradition as an anti-epic, contrasting with both the national "fiction of totality" (which in itself is a variation of narrative modes such as "foundational fiction" and "national allegory") and the transnational "modern epics."

Returning briefly to Neige Sinno's canon, we can see that Pitol spearheads the emergence of a Latin American literature that would be defined by this counterpointed tradition. Bolaño himself writes from a position that counters every single one of the novel's traits as described by Moretti. Moreover, as critic Sarah Pollack has brilliantly pointed out, Bolaño's legibility is limited because he is still being framed through the lens of paradigmatic Latin

American fiction.[137] Bolaño himself acknowledged the uniqueness of Pitol's fiction in Mexico and Latin America, as well as the value of his translations of Andrzejewski and Gombrowicz, and admitted to being a constant reader of his work.[138] Pitol, who has not attained the same level of readership as Bolaño, exemplifies the illegibility of whole swaths of Latin American fiction within existing paradigms of world literature theory. Defined by Occidentalist and worldly endeavors, his work is unreadable from the perspective of critical approaches that exclusively focus on works read beyond their particular country of production. Pitol is crucial for understanding Bolaño because the former's fiction is a precursor of many elements that would allow the latter to attain his current standing. Pitol's contribution to the expansion of Spanish-language translation catalogs was essential for writers like Bolaño to break with Boom imperatives. Furthermore, Pitol foreshadowed the type of Latin American literature that Anagrama, the press that catapulted Bolaño to fame, would privilege. Considering that the transnationalization of both Bolaño and Piglia took place in Narrativas Hispánicas, we must note the centrality of Pitol's style in defining this kind of poetics. In fact, his legacies are apparent in many of the major Mexican writers who currently inhabit the Anagrama catalog (including Juan Villoro, Álvaro Enrigue, and Guadalupe Nettel, all winners of the Herralde award).

Enrique Vila-Matas, another author launched by Anagrama, chronicles the importance of "Nocturno de Bujara" and the three other Moscow stories for Pitol's rebirth and consecration as a writer. Vila-Matas reminds us that these stories ended Pitol's seven-year creative drought and that, after obtaining the Villaurrutia award (Mexico's equivalent of the National Book Award), the book set the stage for his literary recognition. But the most important point in Vila-Matas's account is the confirmation of the trajectory described above: "Con los cuatro cuentos moscovitas logró desembarazarse de ciertas reglas y convenciones del relato clásico que él en sus primeras escaramuzas como hacedor de cuentos tanto había respetado" (With the four Moscow stories, he managed to rid himself of certain rules and conventions of the classical short stories that he, in his first forays as a story writer, had very much respected).[139] Vila-Matas, a close friend of Pitol's and the author within Iberian literature who most closely echoes his literary ideas, emphasizes that the act of narration matters more than the narrated act itself in these stories. Pitol is a crucial author for a generation of Latin American and Iberian writers who ultimately resisted the totalizing and mythologizing vocation that allowed Latin American fiction to break into transnational spaces. To use Sylvia Molloy's term, he lays the groundwork, in Mexico and in other parts of the Hispanophone world, for resistance to the "magical realist imperative" that is generally imposed on the region's fiction by editorial practices, translation politics, and theories like postcolonialism or certain variants of world literature studies.[140] He is the architect of a concrete, regional world literature that provided Latin American and Iberian writers with tools to oppose the world literature enunciated in North America and Western Europe, one that pigeonholed their own fiction in terms of the traits described by Moretti. His worldliness aimed to resist being both national and global; or, in other words, to resist the idea of totalization as the defining feature of fiction writing in Spanish. Finally, as I will explore further in the next chapter, the origins of these procedures allowed Mexican literature to ultimately resist the commoditization of magical realism in the neoliberal era. "Nocturno de Bujara," in its complex narrative structure, is one of Mexican and Latin American fiction's first forays into techniques that would define what Héctor Hoyos calls the "global Latin American novel."[141]

Early scholarly readings of Pitol were not fully aware of this process, which perhaps can only be identified in hindsight. Still, they clearly identified the importance of Pitol's formal techniques and the need to study their complexity. Pitol's work has been of great interest to Mexican formalist and structuralist critics, who wrote many books seeking to interpret the estranging effects of works like "Nocturno de Bujara."[142] In one of the most clarifying studies, Renato Prada Oropeza observes that Pitol's stories of the period are founded less on intertextuality than on "intratextuality," the existence of a multilayered set of textual references within the stories themselves, whose formal architecture is constructed through their allusions to each other.[143] Without delving into the minutiae of Prada Oropeza's structuralist analysis, I must underscore his contention that Pitol's estrangement comes with a canon of literary references embedded in the text itself, providing the reader with clues on the otherwise confounding narrative. Prada Oropeza's reading focuses on the textual and the structural, so I will not go into greater detail on those questions. That said, I feel that his argument on the intratextual has to be pushed much further, as it is crucial for understanding world literature as a generative matrix for transitional narratives like Pitol's.

Precisely because Pitol's narrative does not deliver totality or closure, intratextuality is a mechanism through which his literary cartography clues the reader into the rules of his writing. In "Nocturo de Bujara," such clues are manifested through a reference to a book, Jan Kott's "Breve tratado de erotismo" ("A Little Treatise on Eroticism"):

> En una ocasión, Juan Manuel me hizo leer un texto de Jan Kott: *Breve tratado de erotismo*. Lo busco en mi estantería de literatura polaca y encuentro en la edición inglesa la cita que pensaba al día siguiente de nuestro recorrido nocturno por Bujara cuando nos preparábamos a volar a Samarcanda. Recordaba con Kyrim y Dolores las ceremonias de la boda. Intento traducir: "En la oscuridad el cuerpo estalla en fragmentos que se convierten en objetos separados. Existen por sí mismo. Sólo el tacto logra que existan para mí. El tacto es limitado. A diferencia de la vista, no abarca la persona completa. El tacto es invariablemente fragmentario: divide las cosas. Un cuerpo conocido

a través del tacto no es nunca una entidad; es, si acaso, una suma de fragmentos."

In one occasion, Juan Manuel made me read a text by Jan Kott: *A Little Treatise on Eroticism*. I looked for it on my Polish literature shelf and found, in the English edition, the quote I'd recalled the day after our tour of Bukhara, when we were getting ready to fly to Samarkand. Kyrim and Dolores and I were remembering the wedding ceremonies. I'll attempt to translate: "In the dark, the body is split into fragments, which are separate objects. They exist *for themselves*. It is touch that makes them exist *for me*. Touch is limited. Unlike sight, it does not embrace the entire person. Touch is invariably fragmentary; it decomposes things. A body experienced through touch is never an entity; it is just a sum of fragments."[144]

This passage clearly illustrates a technique that Pitol often employs in his narrative work: the disclosure of his world literary canon as a map of reading. Such a disclosure occurs, too, in another Moscow story, "Asimetría" ("Asymmetry"), where Pitol invokes Chekhov to describe his characters.[145] Pitol also notably draws from this technique in his novel *Domar a la divina garza* (*To Tame the Divine Heron*): early on, he explains Bakhtin and Gogol to the reader in order to present the logic of the book itself.[146] In "Nocturno de Bujara," Kott's quote on the body shows the reader how the story functions logically. One could even offer that the body in Kott's passage is the story itself, split into fragments, just as the story's different subplots are "separate objects" that "exist for themselves." The act of reading is analogous to erotic touch: it becomes the sense that makes the stories exist for the reader. Just like touch, reading in Pitol's work is "invariably fragmentary" and "limited," leaving us with an experience in which the story, like Kott's body, "is never an entity" but "a sum of fragments."

Kott is the kind of figure that Pitol values most: a theater critic and writer, and a participant in Polish culture during the same period as Pitol's writers of reference, he was ultimately exiled to the U.S. to escape the intensification of his country's regime. The cited essay comes from one of the first works he published after leaving Poland: a compilation of his writings between 1947 and 1967. In bringing this particular text to "Nocturno de Bujara," Pitol activates his canon of readings within his poetics. In doing so, he grants meaning to his literary form, endowing it with historical depth, a critical and political ethos, and an intellectual trajectory that departs from other lines of Mexican fiction. In referring to Kott, we note how the Moscow stories involved a return to form. Indeed, Pitol was performing his ultimate translating act: not by rendering a Polish writer into Spanish, but by rendering the poetics of a writer caught between authoritarianism and commitment into Mexican literary form. This is the door that leads to his *Tríptico del carnaval* (*Carnival Trilogy*).

El desfile del amor: Occidentalism, the Nation, and the Novel

Of the three novels in Pitol's *Tríptico del carnaval*, the most obvious choice for concluding this chapter might have been *Domar a la divina garza*, which Pitol wrote under Bakhtin's influence. The novel involves many illustrative elements of Pitol's readings and styles, from a comedic grace that clearly derives from British satire to not-fully-narrated European travels. I have chosen to end this chapter with a reading of *El desfile del amor*, however, so as to bring Pitol's traditions and formal innovations into a discussion of the politics of the novel that stem from his strategic Occidentalism. Rather than providing clear intratextual elements to inscribe the novel in Pitol's map of world literature (as "Nocturno de Bujara" and *Domar a la divina garza* do), *El desfile del amor* territorializes all of the elements that Pitol had developed in his prior trajectory and uses them to inform his only major foray into anything resembling a political novel. Written in Prague and the Andalusian province of Mojácar in 1983 and 1984, *El desfile del amor* is partly the tale of a historian, Miguel del Solar, who is unable to piece together a series of significant events occurring in different periods of Mexican history (1914, 1942, 1973) into any kind of meaningful discourse. Even though the book is tinted with cosmopolitan referentiality (the title is appropriated from a famous Ernst Lubitsch film, characters include a German specialist in Spanish Golden Age theater, etc.), the book's true significance lies in the naturalization and territorialization of Pitol's repertoire of techniques, influences, and dialogues within a novel that counters the very idea of a Mexican novel in a decade (the 1980s) when historical fiction and politically oriented nonfiction were experiencing a boom.

The trend in historical fiction to which *El desfile del amor* partially belongs resulted from a process much like Long's "fictions of totality:" the erosion of the state's symbolic authority and the emergence of literature as a site for renarrating the nation. Brian L. Price has studied a canon that runs from 1960 to 2010, including Del Paso's *Noticias del imperio* and Ibargüengoitia's satirical novels, and claims that they construct a "cult of defeat," connecting traumatic moments of national history (mostly from the nineteenth century, in this case) to the uncertain emerging logics of denationalization, globalization, and neoliberalization.[147] In another account of the same process, Elisabeth Guerrero posits a similar canon (which also includes Ibargüengoitia and Del Paso and adds writers like Rosa Beltrán), but focuses instead on the idea of the historical novel as a space for confronting the pitfalls of modernity and as a claim to the modernization of the nation, on its own terms, as a new form of development emerging at the time.[148] Both critics note that the history narrated in their corpus contains a promise of modernity that never came to be, articulated either by acknowledging moments of defeat (Price) or by a Benjamin-esque task of reflection on the ruins of the past (Guerrero). I find that these critics, along with many others who have been concerned with the subject since the 1990s, have exhaustively covered many aspects of the historical novel in Mexico, but the conspicuous absence of *El desfile del amor* once again illustrates Pitol's challenge to what is otherwise a trend in national fiction. Most of the historical novels covered by the aforementioned authors, even those written by employing postmodernist strategies like historiographical metafiction or fragmented narrative, operate either by producing a thoroughly satirical reconstruction of historical events (as Ibargüengoitia did) or by claiming an epistemological privilege for the literary through which fiction can thus provide a more complete rendering of the past than history can (as in Del Paso's sprawling account of the Second Mexican Empire).[149] *El desfile del amor* is written against the grain of this trend, suggesting, by contrast, that both fiction and nonfiction are always already insufficient in accessing the past. Pitol's evasive and meandering narration, and his prose's unwillingness to fully capture action and meaning, raise fundamental questions about the role that Mexican fiction was trying to claim as twentieth-century postrevolutionary culture ceased to serve as a site of production of overarching narratives for the imagined community.

In a previous section, I mentioned that the only Mexican fiction writer Pitol discusses in his essays is Ibargüengoitia, citing him as a precursor for the use of laughter and humor in Mexican narrative. Pitol wrote this essay many years after *El desfile del amor*, but he certainly would have been aware of Ibargüengoitia's work in the 1970s and 1980s, particularly since interest in Ibargüengoitia's oeuvre intensified after his death in the infamous 1983 plane crash that killed various major figures of Latin American literature. Besides laughter, Pitol's essay recognizes Ibargüengoitia's appropriation of fictional reconstructions of the Mexican Revolution that, in turn, were themselves records of the historical "aberrations" accompanying the political process. Pitol believes that Ibargüengoitia makes the historical fiction genre into a farce: he posits it as a space for chronicling the incompetence and absurdity of historical figures. Formally, too, Ibargüengoitia deactivates the genre's ability to sacralize historical figures. Pitol describes Ibargüengoitia's fiction tellingly when he argues that, in the latter's first novel, *Los relámpagos de agosto* (*The Lightning of August*, 1964), "se detecta el aliento sofisticado de Evelyn Waugh en convivencia con algunas situaciones de tono carcelario y escenas del primer cine cómico norteamericano" (one can detect Evelyn Waugh's sophisticated voice coexisting with certain situations narrated in a carcelary tone and scenes from early American comic cinema).[150] This characterization could also easily apply to *El desfile del amor*, which is constructed in equal parts by elegantly executing the type of social satire developed by Waugh (to whom Pitol devotes a chapter en *El mago de Viena*), the claustrophobic environment of the intellectual elite in 1940s Mexico, and the slapstick humor that Pitol openly cites by naming his novel after Lubitsch. Pitol notes that Waugh's fiction (Waugh was a follower of Ronald Firbank) addresses a particular issue: "Para que la comedia humana pudiera seguir su curso normal era necesario que algunas instituciones peligrosas y todos los poderes estuvieran implicados en aquella mala vida. Sólo así se podría mantener la preciosa fachada" (So that human comedy could proceed along its normal course, it was necessary for some dangerous institutions and all powers to be implicated in that evil life. This was the only way for the beautiful façade to be maintained).[151] In *El desfile del amor*, Pitol becomes not the sprawling modernist who seeks to restore order through fiction, but the narrator whose job is to show that order never existed as such, and that its fiction was possible only through the complicity of "dangerous" social institutions. Pitol writes from the idea that fiction is responsible for establishing the impossibility of the historical as an attainable experience.

As in "Nocturno de Bujara," one of the key narrative devices in *El desfile del amor* is an open acknowledgment of the impossibility of telling its story. In this book, the historian Miguel del Solar becomes interested in writing a book about 1942, focused on the assassination of Erich Maria Pistauer, as a possible symptom of the pro-Nazi ideas in circulation during World War II. I will not attempt a close reading of the novel; Karim Benmiloud has already admirably taken up this task in his book on the matter.[152] Rather, I want to highlight how Del Solar serves as the culmination of Pitol's worldly journey described so far in this chapter—and, more importantly, how his literary progression from the 1950s to the 1980s takes up the main currents of twentieth-century Mexican fiction and empties them of symbolic value. On the way I must reference and unpack the three temporalities deployed by the book. Del Solar's purported recognition as a historical researcher comes from his book about the year 1914. This is significant because it refers to a neuralgic moment of the Mexican Revolution in two important senses. First, it had been a moment of political chaos, following the collapse of Victoriano Huerta's counterrevolutionary government, in which diverse revolutionary factions attempted and failed to create a political alliance. I would contend that the year also has literary importance, given that the foundational novel of the Mexican Revolution, Mariano Azuela's *Los de abajo* (*The Underdogs*, 1915), was written right afterward. In other words, Pitol constructs Del Solar as a novelist of the Mexican Revolution (although he actually pens historical nonfiction), the kind of writer who seeks to convey a sense of historical conflict through writing. Del Solar's book accounts not only for a year so complex that its events sometimes elude historical analysis, but also for the period immediately preceding the movement's discursive representation in fiction.

Early in the novel, we encounter Del Solar as he prepares to correct the proofs of his book. The narrator makes a point of describing the limits of his writing abilities: "El estilo le resultó duro y presuntuoso. A momentos deslavado y pedagógico; otros relamido en exceso. Pero lo peor es que el espíritu del libro comenzó a escapársele" (He found the style rough and presumptuous. Sometimes washed-out and didactic, sometimes overly affected).[153] Just before learning about Miguel's attempt to write a new history book, we are confronted with the failure of his previous attempt. His writing style is utterly unable to capture the revolutionary moment and its intensities. Instead, the novel will gradually make clear, the defects in Miguel's style mirror his own inability to grasp the reality that surrounds him, as his investigation of Pistauer's murder is always a step behind the actions of the shady characters who allegedly committed it. I would argue that Miguel's relationship to historical events mirrors, in Pitol's fictional world, the relationship between the writer and national history, exposing the futility of trying to mine the past for totalizing truths. Since we can presume that Miguel's book on 1914 seeks to sacralize revolutionary history, we can also conclude that Miguel represents the impossibility of writing revolutionary history after the deflating intervention of authors like Ibargüengoitia in *Los relámpagos de agosto*, which precedes the actions of *El desfile del amor* (set in 1973) by a few years.

The year 1973 offers a weighty historical framework for this novel, which is already historical, already past, by the time Pitol actually wrote the book. Within his own oeuvre, this year is embedded squarely into the period when Pitol wrote no creative fiction of his own, devoting himself mostly to translation and publishing. In terms of Mexican history, Pitol's novel takes place in the middle of the Luis Echeverría presidency, at a point when the 1968 massacre would be fresh in the Mexican mind (although the novel never mentions it). Perhaps more significantly, the action occurs in a period when the country's economic decline was becoming palpable. As Benmiloud points out, this shift is evident in the Minerva building, the space where the novel's most significant action transpires; the building appears run-down in 1973, long after its tenure as a site of political intrigue and the intellectual bourgeoisie's goings-on in 1942.[154] The novel is strategically positioned at the moment when Mexican fiction begins its open dissociation with questions of official history—and when the writing of history is itself under question.

The third temporality is the moment of the actual murder, 1942. The Minerva building and its inhabitants, members of the Mexican bourgeoisie, exist at the juncture of different historical currents. As we observe a newly constituted elite, one favored once again by capitalist expansion, Pitol delineates the consecration of the Mexican Revolution as a betrayal of the ideals that fueled it in 1914. The novel establishes the link between Miguel's interest in the revolution, on the one hand, and, on the other, the year 1942 at the point when he undertakes his research. The book's humor is constructed partly in parallel to that of Compton-Burnett, through the undernarrated dealings of a rising economic elite (represented by the villain Arnulfo Briones, a crooked political operator whose accesses privilege by manipulating power structures) and the descendants of a surviving ancien régime (represented by Defina Uribe, the gallery owner and daughter of a prominent politician who also acts as a social gatekeeper in midcentury Mexico). Both Arnulfo and Delfina are presented to us as inapprehensible to Miguel. He perceives

Delfina as a child, as "una figura más adecuada para contemplarse en el cine que en la vida real" (a figure better contemplated in a film than in real life).[155] Similarly, Miguel recalls Briones often sitting in the living room in a way that considerably underestimates his actual power: "Él, en cambio, lo registra como un hombrecillo insignificante, vestido de oscuro, con un portafolios negro bajo el brazo; marchito, distante" (He, in return, registers him as an insignificant little man, in dark apparel, with a black briefcase under his arm; withering, distant).[156] The whole novel, narrated indirectly from Miguel's point of view, is forged in the tension between Miguel's misperceptions and the complexity of a situation that we readers can detect but not discern. The historical layers of Mexican history in the novel, like Kott's body in "Nocturno de Bujara," can only be distinguished fragmentarily by the reader, who can never attain a coherent sense of either the murder plot or its underlying historical sequences. What exists for the reader, then, is a sensation of the complexity of the narrated events without ever achieving a full view of them. And regardless of its underlying structure as a detective story, El desfile del amor is, like the works of many other world authors discussed in this chapter, an exercise in the genre's inability to construct a totality.[157]

Instead, the book connects three Mexican historical moments defined by the impossibility of apprehension in narrative: 1914, aptly defined by Gareth Williams as an "interregnum" in which sovereign power was suspended, between the fall of Huerta and the consecration of the Constitutional movement; 1942, when the Ávila Camacho administration solidifies the "perfect dictatorship" of the PRI, combining capitalist modernization with self-redefinition as an ally to the U.S.; and 1973, marked by a global economic crisis that would definitively end the economic boom that had allowed for the consecration of the postrevolutionary regime since the early 1940s.[158] These three junctures work together to deflate and question Del Solar's capacities as a historian/narrator/detective—and, consequently, to deflate those three forms of constructing totality. Del Solar's inability as a child to understand the world around him mirrors his inability as a historian to make retrospective sense of 1942, as well as his inability as a detective to resolve Pistauer's case in 1973 (the apparent resolution of which is disclosed to him by Delfina Uribe). The novel concludes when Miguel, in a bookstore, finds a copy of El año 1914, the project he was able to bring to fruition, albeit in the unsatisfactory way described above. According to the narration, Miguel was no longer convinced of writing about 1942, leaning instead toward the possibility of a more straightforward account of the period. In the middle of these musings, two hitmen chase Miguel when he leaves the bookstore and beat him up. Tellingly, they do not even kill him; they just leave us with an image of Miguel on the verge of tears, running back to the bookstore for cover.[159] This conclusion cements El desfile del amor as a thorough anti-epic, a novel that undermines the ability to construct the national, to articulate an allegory, to build a hero, or even to write a novel.

One of the story's essential underpinnings is the focus on Mexico's murky participation in World War II from the perspective of upper-class flirtation with Nazism. The narrator informs us that, while researching the relationship between British economic interests and the revolution, Miguel comes across the investigation conducted by a fellow scholar and thus learns of the presence of German agents in Mexico during the war. Del Solar embarks on the 1942 project when he uncovers two personal connections with German agents: the name of a friend's father involved in clandestine activity, and, more importantly, Pistauer's murder, which took place in the Minerva building while Miguel was living there as a child. The actual date of the murder—November 14, 1942—implies underground operations carried out by German agents and Nazi sympathizers after the Mexican government sided more definitively with the U.S. earlier that year. As Friedrich Schuler has chronicled, Mexico maintained good relations with the Third Reich until 1941, due in part to the importance of mutual trade for both countries and in part to Mexico's belief that Germany would ultimately prevail in the war and become the reigning political power.[160] Although Mexico would eventually offer decisive support to the Allies, it is true that pro-Axis propaganda and anti-Semitism ran parallel to anti-U.S. feelings fueled by Mexican nationalism; indeed, Ávila Camacho himself was ambivalent about the conflict, partly because of Germany's decision to recognize his electoral victory against the wishes of the Spanish Falange. Nevertheless, the resistance to totalitarianism within his administration, and the increasing irritation at pro-Nazi propagandists' public critiques of government officials, ultimately compelled Mexico to side decisively with the U.S., with which Ávila Camacho also had a strong relationship.[161]

Pitol's narrative framing of the period conceals all of these events, which, at best, are conveyed to us in vague lists of occurrences as narrated from Del Solar's perspective. This evasive stance is a distilled version of the techniques that Pitol introduced into Spanish literature as a translator. The figure of Kazimierz Brandys is a possible model for narrating the ghosts of the national past—whether by negotiating a critique of the regime within the formal constraints of socialist realism in *Madre de Reyes*, one of Pitol's first translations, or by engaging undercurrents of the past through the novel, as he does in his translation *Rondó*, published two years before *El desfile del amor*.[162] Brandys provides a model for how to narrate history while still evading it, for insinuating major historical events through narrators and characters who are never fully in control of their actions. As mentioned earlier in the chapter, Brandys's *Madre de Reyes* melds a detective story with extensive philosophical digressions, which undermines the narrative's genre classification. This intersection offers an archetype of deflation that is also essential to Pitol, aligning him with what Vicente Alfonso calls "quasi-detective stories" in Mexican fiction. According to Alfonso, Pitol develops a form of crime fiction based solely on the one-by-one parade of witnesses in conversation with the detective figure.

This form, then, relativizes all versions (no story is reliable) and ultimately becomes a tale of impossibility: the impotence of not being able to know what happened.[163] The novel's politics depend on constructing this kind of evasive narrative in relation to Mexican history, in order to avoid the kind of formal decisions that were prevalent in Mexico in the 1980s: either the full-fledged account of history from the privileged stance of the literary (as performed by Del Paso's *Noticias del imperio* and other historical narratives) or the focus on nonfiction and on the social as a way to deal with the exhaustion of narrative (as seen both in the chronicle and in the emergence of social and political novels by authors like Aguilar Camín and Elena Poniatowska). Because it questions both, *El desfile del amor* is neither. It resists the fetishization of the literary as a superior mode of historical knowledge that is essential to Del Paso's totalization. It also problematizes the idea of an immediately political account of the recent past as favored by authors like Aguilar Camín and Carlos Montemayor, whose work seeks to counter official accounts and erasures of political events. Instead, worldliness is used as a strategy to resist political imperatives and to question literature's very ability to provide us with any kind of illumination in the political realm. As Elizabeth Corral explains, the capacity to convey historical drama through levity is a fundamental component of Pitol's poetics.[164]

In her provocative book comparing Russian and Brazilian modernisms, Sharon Lubkemann Allen posits the idea of eccentric or "marginocentric" literary traditions located in metropolitan centers of peripheral countries (she primarily studies nineteenth-century Saint Petersburg and Rio de Janeiro, focusing on authors such as Gogol, Dostoyevsky, and Machado de Assis). In Allen's argument, the major authors in these traditions carnivalize and deauthorize national symbols. A key example in Allen's book is Nikolai Gogol, who, in her analysis, performs the marginalization and undermining of the "concentric models" that sustain "an authority based on deep-rooted collective cultural memory," from historical authorities and public monuments to literary language and lyric traditions.[165] Pitol reflects on Gogol along similar lines in *La casa de la tribu*, particularly underscoring his role as "el más implacable testigo de cargo de un régimen condenado a desaparecer" (the most implacable prosecution witness of a regime sentenced to disappearance).[166] In a way, Miguel del Solar is a contemporary rendition of Gogol's characters: an unwitting witness to the deterioration of Mexico's order. His 1914 book is a testament to Mexico's rise, but his historical perspective grows useless when confronted with 1942 (when various seeds of decline are planted along with the gradual corrosion of Mexico's ruling elite) and with 1973 (when he already perceives the past as ruined). If Pitol opts for indirect and tangential referentiality in narrating Mexico's twentieth-century history, it is indeed because Miguel del Solar—himself an expat until 1973, when he returns after holding an academic position abroad—represents the inability to construct a "deep-rooted historical memory." In sum, Del Solar is the instrument through which Pitol brings to Mexican modernity the large-scale deauthorization of a declining regime—which is characteristic, as Allen argues, of eccentric literatures like Russia's or Mexico's. Here we could also recall Rafael Gutiérrez Girardot's reading of Miguel del Solar as a *Poeta doctus* whose knowledge is only the demonstration of "nonknowledge."[167] Ultimately, Pitol emphasizes an idea of literature more invested in undermining knowledge-structures than in replicating them.

Furthermore, it is evident that Pitol's use of humor and the critique of social mores in *El desfile del amor* is strongly connected to his English canon. Saikat Majumdar has recently argued that the "narrative innovations of modernism draw a kind of conscious attention to banality as a value and, often, to boredom as an affect."[168] Pitol does not fully belong to the tradition posited by Majumdar, which is concerned with issues of colonialism and empire. However, he represents another evolution of this narrative innovation, one in which banality narrates the modus operandi of a society that can only be imagined by hollowing out its historical densities. Majumdar argues that banality runs counter to literature's promise of engagement and entertainment. Although Pitol's humor departs from Majumdar's account (after all, his writing is both very entertaining and certainly literature), the larger point about banality is crucial for reading *El desfile del amor*: "The banal is precisely what thwarts the spatial transcendence of the immediate and the temporal transcendence of the everyday. It is the absolute tyranny of the immanent and the inescapable, the denial of the possibility of excess that is at the core of aesthetic pleasure."[169] In consequence, a fundamental component of Del Solar's perspective in particular, and Pitol's style in general, is the deployment of banality to undermine the novel's structures of transcendental meaning. This is why Ronald Firbank's influence becomes fundamental here. As José Eduardo Serrato discusses, *El desfile del amor* contains various references to Firbank, which the critic connects to the English author's search for a popular novel.[170] These lineages are the condition of possibility for Pitol's departure from many modes of cosmopolitan Mexican fiction: by connecting his novel to modernist modes of social satire that are absent in the Mexican tradition but fundamental to many of the writers in his personal canon.[171] In this sense, *El desfile del amor* moves away from Carlos Fuentes's totalizing gestures and penchant for national allegory. More meaningfully, though, it provides a fundamental departure from the two other great cosmopolitans of his generation, Juan García Ponce and Salvador Elizondo. García Ponce and Elizondo both use eroticism and the quotidian as building block for philosophical narratives. Sergio Pitol deflates this more sublime-oriented narrative, which is based strictly on the construction of excess (erotic in García Ponce's case, conceptual in Elizondo's) to assert aesthetic pleasure. This might explain the frequent observation by critics like Maricruz Castro Ricalde that *El desfile del amor* was revelatory in portraying oppressive social environments in strikingly light prose.[172]

Pitol's novel, like "Nocturno de Bujara," is written from a literary ethos—part of a legacy of twentieth-century fiction that had lost its meaning in the 1980s—in which totalizing excess is impossible. *El desfile del amor* represents a turning point in Mexico's strategic Occidentalism by assuming an alternative genealogy of the novel: the need to reinvent literary fiction at the juncture between a declining revolutionary nationalism and an emerging neoliberal order. As Sinno points out, Pitol's narrative beckons to a reader who requires familiarity and critical attention, inviting her into a certain kind of literary independence.[173] In the years to come, this stance would pose a challenge to Mexican writers facing the need to break with the legacies of twentieth-century national and Latin American fictions, as the metanarratives and social orders that had informed them were subject to substantial erosion and collapse. The task of constructing a new Occidentalism—one which sought to steer clear of the modernist traditions that had influenced Mexican fiction from the 1950s onward, and which sought new territorializations of the Mexican novel toward an idea of world literature—was taken up and pursued by many writers in Pitol's wake. In the next chapter, I will discuss how the Crack literary movement responded to this challenge.

Chapter 2

The Crack Group

Cosmopolitanism contra the Magical Realist Imperative

In 1996, two transformational events redefined Mexican prose, and their effects would have important ramifications both on the country's literature and on Latin American narrative at large for the years to come. The first is the publication of Sergio Pitol's acclaimed hybrid essay/chronicle/fiction book *El arte de la fuga*, which cemented his status as one of Mexico's leading writers and further canonized the world literary pursuits and aesthetics studied in chapter 1.[1] The second took place on August 7, 1996, when a group of five Mexican writers in their late twenties and early thirties launched the "Crack" group through a manifesto and the presentation of their five novels: *Memoria de los días* (*Memory of the Days*, 1995), by Pedro Ángel Palou; *El temperamento melancólico* (*The Melancholy Temperament*, 1996), by Jorge Volpi; *Si volviesen sus majestades* (*If Their Majesties Returned*, 1996), by Ignacio Padilla; *Las rémoras* (*The Obstacles*, 1996), by Eloy Urroz; and *La conspiración idiota* (*The Idiot Conspiracy*, 2003), by Ricardo Chávez Castañeda.[2] The group includes two other members who did not participate in the manifesto: Vicente Herrasti, an author known for writing more slowly than his comembers, and Alejandro Estivill, the coauthor of one of the group's early publications—although many accounts and discussions of the group do not regard him as a member. Emerging from events that date back to the late 1980s, when Padilla, Urroz, and Volpi were attending high school together, the Crack group was a bold attempt at reengaging cosmopolitanism and literature as the publishing world started to trend toward corporate consolidation and a new brand of Spain-centered transnationalization of Hispanophone literary publishing. The name "Crack" was an onomatopoeic reply to the "Boom," and it sought generational change in the presuppositions behind literary writing in Mexico and Latin America. Over twenty years after the manifesto (and after launching a new stage of the movement at the MLA Conference in Austin, Texas, in 2016), Crack writers remain leading figures in Mexican fiction in Mexico and abroad. The roots of their success, I believe, are found in a new form of strategic Occidentalism that each writer deployed, proceeding from his respective contributions to the manifesto.

With this chapter, I do not intend to write the history of the Crack group—a task that has already been performed both by group members and by critics such as Tomás Regalado López, who has documented phenomena related to the group in various publications, and Ramón Alvarado, who recently published a monograph on the subject.[3] Rather, I will begin by analyzing how the group engages with material practices of the literary field in Mexico and will then discuss how three particular Crack authors—Volpi, Padilla, and Palou—engage with world literary traditions and practices in developing concrete approaches to the world novel in the neoliberal context. The Crack writers are highly prolific, and I do not seek to read them exhaustively here. Instead, after providing a brief history of the group I will focus on selected works that illustrate precise issues relevant to their different iterations of strategic Occidentalism.

The Crack writers' individual careers have taken parallel but different paths. Their first joint encounters occurred when they were young: in 1988, Volpi, Urroz, Estivill, and Padilla wrote a collective work titled *Variaciones sobre un tema de Faulkner* (*Variations on a Theme by Faulkner*), which would later win the San Luis Potosí National Short Fiction Award in 1989, although it would remain unpublished until 2004.[4] In this early venture, it was clear that their chief concern was less the production of a concrete group aesthetic than the weight of Juan Rulfo's legacy in particular and Boom writers in general. *Variaciones* fuses fictional entries in the diary of a city-based writer, who wants to write rural short stories, with a selection of the imaginary writer's work. The point of the exercise was to take up texts that very much followed Rulfo's methods of representing the rural context and oral culture and then to turn them upside down, revealing the artifice through which a bourgeois urban writer was actually behind the reality-effect of these stories. The group definitively coalesced in 1994 after the publication of a second joint work, *Tres bosquejos del mal* (*Three Sketches of Evil*), which gathered novellas by Urroz, Volpi, and Padilla.[5] These works—three complex narratives based on the deliberate evasion of "Mexican" topics—more closely resemble the poetics that would bring Crack writers into the foreground a year later. All of the group's members convened for the book launch. Palou, a prolific and precocious writer who had already written a couple of well-regarded books, joined Estivill in the public presentation of *Tres bosquejos del mal*. Chávez Castañeda, who had won a few national awards and was in the process of publishing his first novel, and Herrasti, known for his carefully crafted fiction, were in attendance.

Over the following years, they would release the manifesto and a batch of five novels, which would be followed by a smaller set of three semisatirical romance books.[6] After making this initial splash, the Crack writers went somewhat separate ways until 1999, when Volpi won the prestigious (just-reinstated) Biblioteca Breve Award, which in the 1960s had helped launch the Latin American Boom and the careers of writers such as Mario Vargas Llosa and Guillermo Cabrera Infante.[7] After this win—and following Padilla's recognition with a similarly prestigious award, the Primavera Prize, in 2000—the Crack writers regrouped as part of the transnational marketing campaign, granting most of them access to wider distribution. Since then, the group has reunited periodically, most notably in the collective book *Crack: Instrucciones de uso*, which compiles *Variaciones sobre un tema de Faulkner*, the manifesto, a study by Regalado López, and essays on each member as part of the Crack phenomenon. In 2016, Crack members came together in different venues apropos the manifesto's twentieth anniversary.[8]

My choice of Volpi, Palou, and Padilla as subjects of this chapter involves their attachment to and identification with the Crack group (by contrast, Chávez Castañeda's literary practice has significantly departed from the group's core tenets, while two other members, Estivill and Herrasti, have not participated in the process at large), as well as the kind of novels they write. Eloy Urroz, while a very worthwhile novelist to discuss in a critical context, writes fiction that does not entirely engage the questions raised here (many of his works are more autobiographical in nature), and a discussion of his work would warrant separate consideration.[9] I will nonetheless rely on Urroz as a critic, since he has written some of the most influential analyses of his comembers. Key works by Volpi, Padilla, and Palou will allow me to study a few crucial issues affecting the changes in Mexico's relationship to world literature in the neoliberal era—and, more importantly, the ways in which worldly and Occidentalist literary poetics emerged to negotiate, in complex and ambiguous ways, with processes of literary globalization and the legacy of the Latin American Boom. In all three cases, their literary practices challenge distinctions between "high literature" and "the market," and the distinct poetics at work in their key novels provide a unique vantage point for assessing the challenges posed to the very ideas of the "Latin American writer" and "Latin American literature" that were prevalent at the end of the twentieth century. In my view, such challenges partially paved the way for the emergence of Roberto Bolaño at the transnational level (although he did begin to rise slightly before the internationalization of the Crack) and contributed to the diversification of Mexican literature in the 2000s, even if many younger writers do not see them as precursors.

This chapter also seeks to offer scholarly analysis on writers who, while they are widely read and have played a crucial role in Spanish-language literature, have nonetheless been largely ignored by English-language critics and publishers. Volpi has elicited much more critical attention in Spain than in the U.S. or even in Mexico. Padilla and Palou, meanwhile, have been discussed in only a small handful of academic studies, despite their prolific output (Palou has published over forty books) and general renown.[10] Translations have followed a similar pattern. Volpi has just three books translated into English. Even though the three books that cemented his reputation are regarded as a trilogy, the first and third novels were published by two different presses, and the second has yet to be translated. Only two of Padilla's books have appeared in English, and even a *New York Times* review of his first translated novel failed to elicit a broader readership or additional translations. Palou, by far the most productive writer of the lot, has never been published in English in book form. I maintain that this lack of attention can be explained by three factors: the backlash to their manifesto in Mexico; the fact that their work refuses to participate in discourses of Latin American specificity and identity that many critics hold dear, particularly in the U.S. academy; and the meteoric rise of Roberto Bolaño as the stand-in figure of Latin American literature in the U.S., a rise that has eclipsed the Crack writers' own importance in redefining Latin American fiction in the late 1990s. Surprisingly few scholarly readings have been published on Crack novels; of the existing studies, some reproduce misconceptions about the group and its members' poetics. Based on a sometimes-superficial reading of the manifesto and the ensuing debates, some critics overstate the distance between the Crack and the Boom, or the comparison between the Crack writers and those of the *McOndo* anthology, who were ultimately dispersed across different countries and lacked the continuity and endurance that the Crack movement has enjoyed. I will refrain from tackling most of these myths and readings, since Padilla has done so himself.[11] Instead, I will seek to discuss their position within the publishing world of the 1990s, and I will also conduct a reading of several key novels—two tasks I feel are necessary for a proper evaluation of the Crack group. Beyond what I attempt here, I feel that a carefully critical reading of individual Crack writers' bodies of work is still in order (and long overdue).

To understand the Crack movement's intervention in the Mexican and Latin American literary worlds, we must first grasp the challenges faced by Mexican writers in the early years of the neoliberal era. Ángel Rama's still unsurpassed account of the Boom describes many of the elements that allowed writers like García Márquez and Vargas Llosa to emerge and their transnational circulation to occur: the sizable increase of the reading class in Latin America, the search for a regional cultural identity, the development of presses that reconstructed both national and regional markets, the flattening of various decades of Latin American writing into a single marketable product, and so on.[12] These elements, though, not only accounted for the rise of visible trends like magical realism, but also provided the conditions of possibility that fostered the emergence of heterodox writers like Fernando del Paso and Sergio Pitol. It is worth remembering, for instance, that the first three editions of *Palinuro of Mexico*, Del Paso's complex 1977 novel, were published within the editorial bounds inherited by the Boom. In Madrid, it was published by Alfaguara, which at the time was still an independent press (the Santillana conglomerate would buy it in 1980); tellingly, it also published

Javier Marías's famed translation of *Tristram Shandy*, a book of great importance for Del Paso's bold experiments.[13] *Palinuro* also had a Cuban edition in Casa de las Américas (always a significant step in a novel's consecration as a Latin American book), while the first Mexican edition was published in 1980 by Joaquín Mortiz, a crucial press in the development of at least three generations of Mexican fiction writers. This Mexican edition integrated Del Paso's book into the catalog of a press that published the early works of authors like Salvador Elizondo, José Emilio Pacheco, Juan García Ponce, and José Agustín.[14] If a novel as complex and unorthodox as *Palinuro of Mexico* managed to enter the Mexican literary canon and become available to Latin American and Iberian readers over time, it was due to this editorial infrastructure, which regularly invested in works that had no immediate commercial appeal. By the late 1980s, the Boom's cultural efficiency and the spaces available for independent publishing began to erode, particularly as a result of the publishing world's corporate consolidation. The publishing juggernaut Grupo Planeta bought Seix Barral, the press most responsible for the expansion of the Boom in Spain, in 1982, and Joaquín Mortiz in 1985. Both presses remain active (and, as I will discuss below, were central to the Crack's success), but their absorption into a corporate structure irreversibly affected their role as publishers of innovative fiction.

While the complexities of this editorial process merit a book-length study of their own, the fundamental point is that, as young Mexican writers in the 1990s, the Crack authors faced a transitional period in which three overlapping phenomena transpired. First, transnational presses were showing reduced interest in fostering a regional Latin American market—a retreat related both to the end of Franquismo and to the shift in focus toward publishing a new generation of Iberian writers. A still-common practice by houses like Alfaguara or Random House consists of publishing writers solely in their respective home countries, through the local branch of the press, while providing transnational distribution to a mere handful of authors perceived to be the most profitable. This tactic is exacerbated by the fact that writers sometimes must cede the transnational rights to their works even if those works are only released in one country—a stipulation that effectively bans different national presses from publishing the book (a common practice in the Boom years). What this meant is that only well-established authors (like Fuentes or Vargas Llosa) or writers pursuing literary forms closer to the Boom and magical realism (like Luis Sepúlveda or Laura Esquivel) would secure transnational distribution. Meanwhile, the most interesting, most innovative literature being written in each country would rarely be available on other markets. Second, some of the national presses that fostered literary risk and had established distribution networks were either undermined by military dictatorships (Eudeba) or absorbed into corporate structures (Joaquín Mortiz). Finally, some of the presses that would ultimately help rebuild a transnational Spanish-language market for literary fiction, like Anagrama (which generally distributes all of its books in every country) or Tusquets (whose local branches were more proactive in developing talent) were not yet as engaged with Latin American fiction as they would become in later years.[15] But even they seem to be fading. Anagrama was purchased by Italian house Feltrinelli and Tusquets is now part of Grupo Planeta.

For Mexican writers younger than Boom authors, it became increasingly difficult to attain the same level of editorial distribution and visibility.[16] As the Crack editor Sandro Cohen told me in a recent conversation, the group came into being in the wake of the 1994 economic crisis, when many lines of Planeta's income—fundamentally based at the time on encyclopedia installment-sales—disappeared, due both to the downturn and to the emergence of computer software and the internet. Thus, when Cohen was hired to direct Joaquín Mortiz, its literary imprints called for a major overhaul. Cohen first achieved this reconfiguration by launching the writer Enrique Serna (now a major figure) and then the Crack group, although only Palou's novel was published under Mortiz. Ultimately, Cohen would migrate to another company, Grupo Patria, where the Crack would become a signature brand of their literary imprint Nueva Imagen. Nonetheless, it is worth remembering that Grupo Patria's core business is school textbooks.[17] Clearly, literary writers in Mexico often had to publish in presses for which literature was either considered a side business or a minor component of their overall revenue.

The Crack movement and its contemporaries not only faced questions related to publishers and the market. The global literary circuit, partly a consequence of the success of books like *One Hundred Years of Solitude*, developed a taste for fiction from Global South and ethnic minority authors, a trend that emerged from the transformation of magical realism into clichés: exoticist discourses of cultural authenticity, family sagas, and so forth. In an essential book on the matter, Graham Huggan uses the term "postcolonial exotic" to describe the ways in which Global South literatures and authors (in his case, African and Asian writers) have utilized strategies such as "staged marginalities," granting major prizes to "otherness," and the "cult of authenticity" to locate themselves in "global commodity culture."[18] Although, from my perspective, Huggan could have further developed the role of Latin American fiction in this process, he nonetheless points out that magical realism and the Latin American Boom novel had reached a "hypercommodified status," constructing a "blatantly commercial alterity industry" based on "exoticist spectacle, commodity fetishism and the aesthetics of decontextualization."[19] While analyzing *Midnight's Children* by Salman Rushdie, Huggan describes magical realism as "a commodified, increasingly formulaic aesthetic through which the histories of diverse cultures are effectively levelled out."[20] Critics in the English field like Huggan generally sidestep the lineage running from Anglophone and Francophone postcolonial production to the Latin American Boom—even though they are interwoven.[21] To be fair, it must be said that this commodification has to do, as Mariano Siskind has argued, "with the narrative and interpretative horizon that García Márquez opened up by making visible the relation between the universality of (colonial, postcolonial, capitalist) modern history and the particularity of local forms of oppression."[22] It is true that his depiction of shared relations between "local forms of oppression" and global capitalism through literary form—which is what Latin Americanist critics like Ángel Rama sought to account for with the notion of "narrative transculturation"—describes why magical realism was so intensely globalized. However, Latin American writers increasingly felt the burden of playing the Third World author in a sense that contradicted the more cosmopolitan cultural practices of concrete literary fields. As Siskind also illustrates, writers like Juan José Saer and literary movements like McOndo (or the Crack group, which he fails to mention) began to resist the "hegemonic demand [for] the Latin American performance of a magical realist cultural identity."[23]

Ultimately, Crack writers in particular and Latin American writers in general were trapped in a form of the international division of intellectual labor. The "world literature" distributed by transnational conglomerates is not the "truly general literature" of René Etiemble, nor the literature that encompasses "all literary works that circulate beyond their culture of origin," as defined by David Damrosch. Rather, following the argument of the Warwick Research Collective, we must understand that the marginalization of Latin American writers occurs within a world literature that replicates the capitalist world system.[24] Reading the Crack writers obliges us to consider the "irrealist aesthetics of (semi)peripheral literatures," but with a twist.[25] The point is not so much to account for the "combined unevenness" of the system—which leads the Warwick critics to privilege either realism or writers who fit some version of leftist politics—as to understand its underlying strategies of short-circuiting the international division of intellectual labor.

In any account of Latin American engagement with world literature, the region's writers are generally made to serve some function related to postcolonial and world literature theories' conception of how to resist the processes of combined and uneven development as described by the Warwick Research Collective. This tendency creates a double blind spot that must be overcome in order to read the Crack writers. First, world literature theories frequently replicate the very logics of the global market that they critique, prioritizing some direct or indirect notion of cultural or political authenticity. For instance, the Warwick Research Collective, despite admitting that they should not be advocating for yet another world literature focused on realism or modernism, ultimately provides an account of Latin American literature that does exactly this. In other words, they describe a fusion of peripheral realism with an avant-garde (which they mention but do not define) that produces a modernism "capable of capturing more adequately the experience and temper of social life in the (semi-)peripheries and of articulating more

sharply the skepticism of intellectuals towards their distorted state forma-
tions and their sense that early revolutionary aspirations have been betrayed
or incorporated."[26] Of course, my intention is not to contradict this analysis,
which is a largely accurate depiction of certain modes of Latin American fiction. Rather, the evaluation is reductionist, because it misses the same very
same point missed by nearly every other world literature theory: it overlooks
the writers who do not want to "capture the experience and temper of social
life," but who seek instead to escape that injunction through new explorations of literary form. The Crack group comprises exactly this kind of writer:
novelists who sought the right to participate in world literature without the
imperatives that world literature in its different varieties (including postcolonialism and, paradoxically, transnational corporate publishers) imposes on
them as default responsibilities of a Mexican artist.

     The subsumption of Latin American literary production into the expecta-
tions of the global literary market, as well as academic versions of postcolonial
theory, made the Crack writers distinctly frustrated with the commercial fiction output at a transitional moment for literary publishing in the region.
Sylvia Molloy has described the existence of a "magical realist imperative"
for Latin American writers and urges them to resist the definition of Latin
American literature based on metropolitan demands. Molloy also insists on
the recognition of both the full multiplicity of representational practices and
the theoretical and critical agency of Latin American literature in criticism.[27]
These ideas describe how Crack writers defined their literary practice: by
acknowledging their position in this market and proactively deploying it to
change the framework of Mexico and Latin America vis-à-vis hegemonic circuits of world literature. Critical readers of the Crack group commonly and
mistakenly believe that the movement stood in opposition to the Boom. In
fact, as Gesine Müller and Tomás Regalado López both discuss, they were
attentive readers of Carlos Fuentes and García Márquez; consequently, they
resisted the way in which forms of magical realist writing, promoted by Hispanophone and global literary markets at the time, were trivializing the work
of these writers.[28] A clear example of the trends against which the Crack
group defined itself was the juggernaut success of Laura Esquivel's *Como
agua para chocolate* (*Like Water for Chocolate*, 1989), which, along with
the fiction of writers like Isabel Allende and Luis Sepúlveda, became a prime
example of commercial Latin American fiction that derived in many ways
from the literary Boom. I acknowledge, of course, that one must tread carefully when criticizing a writer like Esquivel; undeniably, as Claire Taylor has
documented, she was a leading figure of a "feminine Boom" in 1990s Mexican fiction, which, in Mexico's male-centered literary world, is an important
event in itself.[29] I will discuss this question further in chapter 3. I should
also recognize here that Esquivel's book represented the forefront of literary
neoliberalization in Mexico at the time: a book that deftly used the most
hypercommodified elements of the magical realist style while presenting a

schematic reading of Mexican history that, as Victoria Martínez perceptively analyzed, was thoroughly aligned with the emergence of hegemonic ideologies of economic liberalization and free trade.[30]

In this light, we can read some of the Crack manifesto's contentions as a point of reference for reading works by Volpi, Padilla, and Palou. The first notable feature for my purposes is their different declarations of intent to recover and redeploy a sense of literary density and complexity (in other words, literary difficulty, so as to compensate for the perception of lightness in commercial fiction) in the Latin American novel—a density and complexity that, in their view, had been lost to the pressures of the market. Palou structures the opening text by following the prescriptions that the Italian writer Italo Calvino sets forth in his celebrated *Six Memos for the New Millennium*.[31] Palou's fundamental assertion is that because the then-ascendant culture of media and information was flattening narrative possibilities, the novel, instead of playing along with new communication technologies, should reclaim its penchant for "multiplicity":

> El *Quijote* es quizá la obra múltiple por excelencia en la historia de la literatura. *Gargantúa* le pisa los talones y el *Tristram Shandy* les lleva la maleta. Hoy, es ocioso apuntarlo, la propia realidad se nos antoja múltiple, se nos revela multifacética, eterna. Se necesitan libros en los cuales un mundo total se abra ante el lector, y lo atrape.[32]

> *Don Quixote* is perhaps the multiple work par excellence in the history of literature. *Gargantúa* steps on its heels and *Tristram Shandy* carries their luggage. Today, it is unnecessary to point it out; reality itself strikes us as multiple, revealing itself to us as multifaceted, eternal. There is a need for books in which the total world opens itself to the reader and entraps him.

Palou states that "la multiplicación de las voces y la creación de mundos autónomos" (the multiplication of voices and the creation of autonomous worlds) was the antidote to the increasingly "light" and "disposable" nature of fiction, and he proposes a purely imagination-based literature that would openly resist autobiography (a jab at the post-Boom prevalence of the family saga and the growing role of memoirs in commercial literature) and what Palou calls "optimism," a word he uses as code for exuberance and exoticism.[33] The elevation of Sterne, Rabelais, and Cervantes as the novel's top references coincides with the ethos cited through the work of Milan Kundera in the previous chapter, an ethos Pitol himself endorsed. Furthermore, the concept of multiplicity, drawn from Calvino, is complemented by the creation of "literary worlds," which echoes avant la lettre the concept developed by Eric Hayot. Strikingly, Palou concurs with Hayot's analysis, published a decade and a half later, in many respects. Apropos of Cervantes, Hayot points out that "the novel as a whole opens up a realm of self-conscious thematization of the modern world-view," which entails "an affirmation of the ontologies of the modern present that nonetheless recognizes the imposition of that present as a product of a necessary struggle."[34] In Palou's version of this notion, the novel's commitment to multiplicity and the imagination is crucial for its in-depth engagement with the contemporary and its resistance to the trend of more superficial imagination—the kind produced by what he calls "ese nuevo esperanto que es el idioma estandarizado por la televisión" (that new Esperanto, the language standardized by television), a reference to the rising forms of standard Spanish fostered by transnational television, both from Mexico and from Miami.[35] As I will discuss in the last section of this chapter, Palou's novel *Paraíso clausurado* (*Foreclosed Paradise*, 2000) provides a compelling performance of these principles.[36]

These ideas of complexity as an antidote to the "disposable" novel appear in the Crack writers' interventions. Urroz recovers John S. Brushwood's idea of the "deep novel" in Mexico, understood as a tradition of novels and novelists who "entendieron 'profundamente' el trabajo creativo como la más genuina expresión de un artista comprometido con su obra" ("deeply" understood creative work as the most genuine expression of an artist committed to his work).[37] Urroz's text is crucial for contextualizing the Crack movement, because he finds precursors in well-known works of both Mexican fiction (including Del Paso's *José Trigo*, Elizondo's *Farabeuf*, and Fuentes's *La nuerte de Artemio Cruz*) and the Latin American Boom; he argues that the editorial and commercial trivialization of Latin American literature deactivates the literary exigencies that books like *One Hundred Years of Solitude* or *Rayuela* made of their readers. Padilla puts forth an analogous point; once again, he reclaims a tradition similar to the one deployed by *Palinuro de México* (Sterne, Cervantes, Rabelais, and Dante), and associates the original five novels' apocalyptic tropes with the attempt to construct "historias cuyo cronotopo, en términos bajtinianos, sea cero: el no lugar y el no tiempo, todos los tiempos y lugares y ninguno" (stories whose chronotope, in Bakhtinian terms, would be zero: the nonplace and nontime, all times and places and none).[38] The intended result, continues Padilla, is a literature able to imitate "una realidad alocada y dislocada, producto de un mundo cuya massmediatización lo lleva a un fin de siglo trunco en tiempos y lugares, roto por exceso de ligamentos" (a crazed and dislocated reality, product of a world whose mass mediatization takes it to an end-of-century truncated in times and places, broken by the excess of ligaments).[39] The manifesto is crucial for understanding the Crack group's diverse poetics, as they clearly identify the same cultural malaise (a literature increasingly trivialized by commercialization and the shallowing influence of mass media), claim a similar tradition (writers of great density whose legacy is betrayed by their epigonal followers), and take up a shared task: redefining the novel in such a way that it can capture and respond to the terms set by the contemporary. However—and this is a crucial point—the

Crack writers attain this contemporary focus in drastically different ways: from Padilla's radically dehistoricized and detemporalized style as a way to convey dislocation to Palou's defense of totality and multiplicity, thus allowing the novel to encompass the multifaceted nature of present-day realities. This diversity explains, as will become obvious in the analysis below, how the manifesto managed to include such dissimilar authors as Volpi, whose claim to fame is a series of novels that more strictly fit what Siskind calls the "novelization of the global"; Palou, a chameleonic author who writes novels that often share little to no stylistic traits; and Padilla, who opts for highly stylized novels built with complex language and literary genealogies, and which intensely resist engagement with a reality that remains more visible in Palou and Volpi. The manifesto did not seek out to defend concrete literary techniques; rather, it laid out a set of ground rules so as to resist the imperatives of the literary market at the time.

As Regalado has chronicled, the Crack group was initially met with unanimous negativity in the Mexican literary sphere. I will not repeat the details of this controversy here, since they are well summarized in Regalado's piece, but it is worth listing the main objections raised by their detractors (both then and still) in order to understand the nature of the Crack movement and their interventions. Some critics dismissed it as a marketing ploy to promote Nueva Imagen, the publishing house that released most of the novels. Others questioned the group's promotional efforts, perceiving them as self-aggrandizing. Another line of attack highlighted the fact that the five novels did not share a consistent or unified poetics, which led to further accusations of a marketing ploy. Unsurprisingly, too, many Mexican writers—facing the same challenges as Crack authors but advocating for radically different poetics—resented what they read as a redefinition of Mexican fiction in the manifesto.[40] For instance, Guillermo Fadanelli, a dirty realist who was then spearheading an underground urban literature movement called "literatura basura" or "garbage literature" through his press, Moho, dubbed the Crack writers "literatura del frac," comparing their writings to a tuxedo—and thus emphasizing what he perceived as an elitist literature written by authors affiliated with the upper middle class.[41]

Regalado has yet to conduct an in-depth analysis of this backlash beyond simply documenting its actors and arguments. But his account contains various points relevant to my discussion. For one thing, most objections to the Crack group were aimed at the manifesto and the public presentation of their work; the actual novels received minimal critical evaluation (with the notable exception of Christopher Domínguez Michael, who distinguished his distaste for the Crack group's marketing strategy from his recognition of Volpi and Palou's talent, which he expressed in earlier reviews). The most vitriolic interventions were motivated by three factors. First, there was resistance from authors (like Fadanelli) who practiced a literature that deviated from the Crack writers' principles and thus resented the idea that these authors (generally younger than their detractors) would be in a position to define Mexican literature as such. Second, many critics saw the group's use of literary marketing to promote their aesthetic values as inherently incompatible with the stated anticommercialism of their stance. And third, some perceived the lack of coherence in the five novels' respective styles as obscuring the point of the manifesto itself, which was meant not as a prescriptive aesthetic document but as a declaration of principles with which one could write in different ways. These critics understood one of the Crack's main purposes—to incorporate themselves into the literary market—but they still (mistakenly) base their assessments on the distinction between aesthetic and commercial literature. The Crack group always operated on the premise that such a distinction was a question of choice, not of necessity, and that it was better for writers—not publishers—to decide what commercial literature should look like.

Obviously, most of these objections preceded the transnationalization of the Crack group, and it would be pointless to rehash and take sides in a twenty-year-old discussion. That said, a brief reconstruction of these reactions helps us understand how the Crack's gesture was misread, while also highlighting dynamics of Mexican literature and the attempts to reinvent it that have had enduring effects. It is true that Crack writers are still counted among Mexico's most important authors (Volpi's books are generally released with strong press coverage; Palou publishes one novel a year with strong sales, although he is generally ignored by critics; Padilla won various literary awards in the 2000s; and Urroz has managed to publish massively long books with the support of transnational presses). At the same time, it is equally true that their detractors have left an indelible mark on their reception: other than the occasional lambasting, one would be hard-pressed to find a substantial body of reviews of any Crack work in mainstream literary publications, and even though many younger writers have benefited both from how the Crack movement opened up Spanish-language presses to other Mexican writers (the catalog of Mexican fiction at presses like Planeta, Tusquets, and Anagrama would significantly expand in the wake of the Crack) and in its expansion of literary horizons (the emergence of "literary imagination" writers like Alberto Chimal would be unthinkable without the groundwork laid by Padilla), the group still lacks self-proclaimed successors. These accompanying phenomena are also essential to an understanding of Crack poetics: indeed, while the authors enacted many important aesthetic and editorial changes in Mexican and Latin American literature, these changes challenged deep-seated assumptions about the Latin American writer's role in world literature—challenges that scholarly criticism has yet to process fully.

Sarah Brouillette's brilliant study on postcolonial writers and the literary marketplace provides us with a key to interpreting the event of the Crack manifesto. Expanding critically on Huggan's idea of the "postcolonial exotic," Brouillette emphasizes the need to understand the material practices of writers involved in such paradigms. In this spirit, Brouillette contends that "self-consciousness about socio-cultural identity and positioning has become an essential, expected feature of contemporary culture, extending well beyond the postcolonial field." Therefore, one can find works that "are exercises in self-authorization, designed to register the writer's awareness of the political uses or appropriations of his works, appropriations that are intimately related to the market function of postcolonial literature."[42] Although Brouillette's case studies (Rushdie, Coetzee, and others) differ aesthetically and culturally from the Crack group, her description of these processes is nonetheless illuminating: after all, the Mexican writers studied here needed to engage with the same market that had been constructed, domestically and transnationally, by postcolonial literatures as a continuation of magical realism and the Latin American Boom. For my purposes, Brouillette's essential corrective for models such as Casanova's "World Republic of Letters" and James English's "Economy of Prestige" derives from resisting the description of the literary system as an inherently autonomous space accessible to global writers through "the willing absenting of themselves from national imperatives, and an embrace of the aesthetics of international modernism." In Brouillette's account, by contrasting an engaged avant-garde that resists commercialization and "world-readable" works that give in to the market, both English and Casanova "offer a description of the system that is a form of resignation to its ostensible authority."[43]

As I hope was clear in my analysis of Pitol in chapter 1, I feel that the study of material writing and publishing practices is an essential way to address the blind spots in systemic accounts of world literature—which, as Brouillette observes, excessively naturalize cultural power relationships, and which also inordinately privilege dominant modes of transnational circulation as if they accounted for all possible forms of global literature. In postcolonial literature, Brouillette identifies an element that emerged in literary practices around the 1980s and is crucial for understanding Crack writers: the writer's self-awareness of his position within the system, the system's overall means of operation, and writers' proactive efforts based on their understanding of the literary system in which they operate. Further, Brouillette's work shows how the binary opposition of aesthetics versus market is no longer operative in neoliberalism because—without fully denying the potential for resistance in literary work—many of its premises have become commodified themselves.[44] In fact, as Brouillette and Christopher Doody describe in a more recent piece, one can identify "a conception of the literary and the broader cultural economy as involved in close and contradictory relation, as literature's aura of distinction from commerce is thoroughly branded and marketed, is more pressing now than ever."[45] My contention here is that the Crack group's most consequential legacy is having been the first literary movement in Mexico (and perhaps even in Latin America) to take this new literary configuration seriously in the neoliberal era—and then to act on it.

While the manifesto still seemed to assert a distinction between "light" commercial literature and "difficult" literary works, Crack writers never shunned the editorial market. On the contrary, the Crack's literary practices thoroughly enact Brouillette and Doody's point at the moment when the Latin American editorial market was undergoing the early stages of neoliberalization: the only way for the kind of complex literature defended in the manifesto to survive was by attempting a takeover of the commercial industry. Going back to Brouillette's analysis of postcolonial writers, one could certainly claim that the Crack authors were operating within the same rules: "The 'world-readability' or universalizability of a given work is not inherent in it or essential to its position in the world system. It is instead the result of a series of actual or imagined reading practices that can also be challenged and opposed, in some cases, by the very texts that achieve global acclaim."[46] Even if, as I will discuss momentarily, Crack writers did write books classified as bestsellers, and while some of them participate deliberately in writing fiction that aspires to a certain degree of commercial distribution, the literary density they sought to define and defend in the manifesto does not contradict their material practices; rather, it is the very purpose of those practices. The type of writing advocated by the Crack authors proposed a "reading practice" that challenged existing standards for the "world readability" of Latin American literature. Those standards were based on the "magical realist imperative" and the territorialization of Latin American fiction into critical and market paradigms such as "Third World literature" (or any variation of high-modernist "world literature" at large), "postcolonial writing," or "Global South fiction"— distinctions that not only flatten historical experience, but also pigeonhole writers from nonmetropolitan countries into the role of native informants and traffickers of exoticism. If strategic Occidentalism was deployed by Pitol in the pre-neoliberal age to reconstruct canons of literary writing within the Spanish-speaking world, Crack writers attempted something even bolder: the redefinition of Latin American literary writing (even writing directed toward commercialism) against the grain of world trends.

At this point, readers of French sociologist Pierre Bourdieu will probably note that both Brouillette and I have drawn from some of his vocabulary and assertions: for one thing, the autonomy of the literary field; for another, notions of position and what Bourdieu calls "*illusio*" and "position-taking," the motivators behind agents' ability to modify the terms of the literary field.[47] Here, though, Bourdieu is not invoked for merely methodological purposes, but rather as a model openly followed by some Crack writers to construct their position within the field. Concurrent to the launch of the Crack group, Pedro Ángel Palou was writing his dissertation, later published as a book titled *La casa del silencio* (*The House of Silence*), at El Colegio de Michoacán (a social sciences think tank) on the Contemporáneos generation—a loosely coalesced group of authors in the 1920s and 1930s who formulated ideas on literature's autonomy in resisting the push toward nationalism in postrevolutionary Mexico.[48] Palou's main argument is that the Contemporá-neos group did not "resist," through aesthetics, the "pollution" of literature by the state; rather, they played a deliberate game of cultural politics and symbolic economy in order to create an autonomous literary field with its own logics of hegemony and power.[49] In a description of Palou's book, Mabel Moraña shows how he reads the Contemporáneos in terms similar to those applied by Brouillette to the postcolonial writer:

> Palou se mueve en la dirección de una socio-crítica actualizada, que ya no sólo lee, como la socio-historia, las relaciones entre cultura y sociedad, sino que materializa los intercambios el producto sim-bólico, dentro de un mercado donde la literatura circula de acuerdo a las leyes de oferta y demanda, más allá de toda idealización.[50]

> Palou moves in the direction of an updated socio-criticism, one that no longer reads, like socio-history, the relations between culture and society, but which materializes the exchanges of the symbolic product within a market where literature circulates according to laws of sup-ply and demand, beyond all idealization.

The point here is that Palou's deployment of Bourdieu does not annul questions of literary taste or aesthetics, as Moraña also underscores. Instead, he emphasizes that taste and literary value rely on "the exchanges of the sym-bolic product" and that one cannot sustain an idealized version of literature without grasping the nitty-gritty dimensions of cultural practice. Bourdieu's *Rules of Art*, published in Spanish by Anagrama and thus made available beyond academic circles, provides Palou with a language that allows him to construct, via the Contemporáneos, a literary tradition based on the cal-culated takeover of literary institutions—with the goal of affecting both the very nature of value within structures of symbolic capital and the readership practices of the reading class. In this sense, *La casa del silencio* is not just a study of the Contemporáneos; it also profoundly reconceptualizes the work-ings of the literary field in Mexico in the context of capitalist modernization. Palou provides an example of how the market is used to shift the nature of literary works from their status as commodities toward aesthetic density when outside institutions pressure writers to produce a simplified literature based either on state ideology (like the postrevolutionary push for national-ism) or on commercialism (the epigonal magical realism of the 1980s and 1990s). Indeed, insofar as Contemporáneos writers faced the same challenges in the literary field rather than creating a literary program to be followed, they provide a clear model for how the Crack group inserted itself into the Mexican literary field.

The Contemporáneos group was essential to the formation of the Crack group's cultural identity in other significant ways. A few years before the manifesto, in 1992, both Volpi and Palou published landmark novels in which they revisited and recovered a particular Contemporáneos writer. Volpi's *A pesar del oscuro silencio* (*In Spite of Dark Silence*) turns to Jorge Cuesta: departing from their shared first name, he constructs a subjective and fragmented biography based on Cuesta's famous poem "Canto a un dios mineral" ("Song to a Mineral God").[51] The novel, Volpi's first, already illustrated the concerns facing young Mexican writers in the early 1990s in two important manners. First, by joining the larger critical revival of the Contemporáneos group that was taking place in scholarship and publishing at the time, Volpi (like Palou) begins his literary career with a position-taking move, identifying himself with a writer who resisted cultural pressure to pursue literature on his own terms. Volpi describes Cuesta as an "alchemical master" and focuses particularly on the interaction between science and literature in his well-known poem.[52] In a perceptive reading, Danny J. Anderson argues that *A pesar del oscuro silencio* comes at the onset of a long-term concern, cutting across all of his books, about the "possibility of knowledge" in the novel. Anderson also points out that the novel's primary device is its failed attempt to identify with Cuesta's own perspective, although the book does generate readerly knowledge of his work and process.[53] I would argue that Volpi's appropriation of Cuesta is a melancholic effort to claim the creation of a work of "pure literature" (in Paul Valéry's sense) and to allegorize its impossibility in the contemporary world. It is, one could say, a summary of the dilemma facing a writer who is seeking the literary in its essence, but who is always already trapped in the mediations of tradition and the contemporary.

A similar concern is threaded through Palou's novel *En la alcoba de un mundo* (*In the Bedchamber of a World*, 1992), although it finds a different resolution. Rather than producing a subjective novel about the failure to rebuild his life, Palou reconstructs the figure of Contemporáneos poet Xavier Villaurrutia in fragmentary novel based on recollections and documents like letters and diary entries. The novel does not posit an identification between the narrator and the poet in reconstructing the possibility of literary knowledge; rather, it attempts to relocate the literary inside the network of discreet private and public connections with the literary world—an effort that prefigures his own scholarly Bourdieusian work on the Contemporáneos. While their procedures may function in opposite ways, both novels aim to position their authors within a precise practice of literary writing. As Domínguez Michael points out, the recovery of Cuesta and Villarrutia in these novels reactivates a myth of the young poet who is able to "create the world" without ever reaching maturity.[54] This creationist spirit is central to the Crack group, and it cuts across the whole manifesto: the young writer's claim to the freedom of writing against burdensome traditions and institutions. In an explanatory text on his own novel, Palou recalls that, despite their masterpieces, the Contemporáneos lacked recognition and were in some cases even persecuted by the political and literary establishment of their time.

Furthermore, he also indicates that he used an excerpt from Cyril Conolly as the novel's epigraph, which points to the English writer's notion of "enemies of promise" (a phrase that he coined to describe his own failure and that Palou links to the Contemporáneos).[55]

Furthermore, both Palou and Volpi also deliver an important treatment of cultural politics. As critic Tamara Williams argues, the appropriation of the avant-garde poet in contemporary Mexican fiction (which includes not only these two books, but also Juan Villoro's recovery of Ramón López Velarde and Roberto Bolaño's appropriation of the infrarrealists and the Stridentists) reinscribes marginalized figures "into the highly differentiated literary history of postrevolutionary nation-building Mexico as a specter of its negation and witness to the violence of its occlusions."[56] To be sure, this strategy is alive and well in Mexican cultural politics and was most recently deployed by a younger writer born in the early 1980s, Valeria Luiselli (mentioned in the introduction to this book), who wrote a novel based on the figure of Gilberto Owen that garnered her great recognition in Mexico and abroad.[57] Crucially, this tactic allows Crack writers to trace a lineage to the past in such a way that legitimizes their attempt to reconstitute the Mexican literary field, declaring themselves the inheritors of a writing practice that, in the 1920s, also deployed a form of strategic Occidentalism to articulate what Williams called the "specter of negation" of cultural nationalism. In fact, the Contemporáneos group also helps explain another element of the Crack movement. By no means were the Contemporáneos poets marked by a common, identifiable poetics. They did not constitute a coherent or programmatic avant-garde, as the Stridentists did; instead, they interacted through loose affiliations while pursuing literary projects that substantially diverged from each other. What the Crack recovers from Contemporáneos is this sense of the group as a literary strategy. The point of a group is not, as some of their critics admonish them, to advance a movement based on literary commonalities, but rather to transform the edifice of literary practices in Mexico and broaden the panorama for a diverse set of poetics—whose only truly shared feature is their opposition to existing forms of literary value and symbolic capital.

The Crack writers' proactive knowledge of the Mexican literary field was directly connected to the fact that in the 1990s—much like in the 1920s, when the Contemporáneos group emerged—the hegemonic positions within that field were in flux. Octavio Paz was aging (and not much concerned with fiction in general); Carlos Fuentes essentially lived abroad, and his work, while enjoying a considerable readership, lacked a visible following among young writers; and authors born in the 1950s, even those overseeing cultural institutions, had not made a strong enough cultural impact to be located in hegemonic positions. Héctor Aguilar Camín and Ángeles Mastretta were very important writers and had published major novels in the late 1980s, but they are recognized largely for their work as public intellectuals affiliated with the magazine *Nexos*; meanwhile, their fiction, though commercially successful and often relevant to the literary discussions of their day, became identified with the writing styles from which authors born in the 1960s, such as the Crack authors, were trying to distance themselves. The two writers from the previous generation who would ultimately become the most consequential in current Mexican fiction, Juan Villoro and Daniel Sada, did not reach their present level of recognition until Anagrama began publishing them in the 2000s; the one writer born in the 1950s who began to develop early success as a novelist, Carmen Boullosa, was facing challenges like those confronting the Crack writers, as I will discuss in chapter 3.

Considering this landscape, as the Crack writers developed their early fictional works and the manifesto, it is hardly surprising their work as critics and scholars was directly concerned with issues connected to their intellectual position-taking. As I mentioned earlier, Palou's study on the Contemporáneos is related to his understanding of contemporary literature in Mexico. Jorge Volpi wrote an intellectual history of Mexico in 1968, *La imaginación y el poder* (*Imagination and Power*, 1998), and then developed his dissertation, which he defended in 2003, on the cultural history of 1994, *La guerra y las palabras* (*War and Words*, 2004).[58] While both are among the finest intellectual histories of Mexico, it is also clear that both are shaped by intellectual strategy. First, both were published on landmark anniversaries of the crucial events in question (thirty years after the Tlatelolco massacre and ten years after the Zapatista uprising, respectively). More significantly, both works situate Volpi—and by extension the Crack group—as part of the paradigmatic changes prompted in Mexican culture as a result of these events. In Samuel Steinberg's controversial reading of *La imaginación y el poder*, he states that Volpi offers a "spirit of Tlatelolco" that "installs its own spirit of democracy, tolerance and justice" but sidelines the political struggle of the massacred students.[59] Even if one disagrees with Steinberg's stern assessment, it is nonetheless true that *La imaginación y el poder* defines the generation born at the time of these events (Volpi himself was born in 1968) as having inherited a political responsibility that must be conceived in terms not of the past, but of the present. I should also note, in reference to chapter 1 of this book, that Volpi succeeds where Sergio Pitol's fictional historian Miguel del Solar fails: Volpi writes fruitful intellectual histories of the neuralgic years that shaped the Mexican present. These histories provide a sense of movement between the 1980s and 1990s. In *El desfile del amor*, Pitol highlighted the meaninglessness of claiming Mexico's twentieth century as a reference for a political or cultural practice in the early democratic transition. Conversely, Volpi, who is well aware of participating in that transition as a writer and public intellectual, can firmly root himself in the history of Mexico's democratic opening-up and the collapse of twentieth-century revolutionary nationalism. It is worth mentioning that Padilla, too, wrote a book that connects his work to a landmark event: *Arte y olvido del terremoto* (*Art and Oblivion of the Earthquake*, 2010), a fascinating cultural history of the earthquake that devastated Mexico City, led to unprecedented levels of citizen organization, and ultimately undermined the authority of the Mexican state.[60]

The Crack group's position-taking was not only concerned with Mexican literary history, like Palou, or intellectual politics, like Volpi; it also produced important work on the novel genre and on the role played by Crack poetics in Mexico. Padilla, for instance, was also pursuing his Ph.D. in Salamanca, but his dissertation focused on the figure of the devil in Cervantes, tracing a core thematic interest in his own fiction back to the founder of the modern novel.[61] Eloy Urroz, who earned a Ph.D. in Latin American literature from the University of California, Los Angeles, devoted his dissertation to a detailed study of Volpi's fiction—the most complete study of his work to date.[62] Urroz's text on Volpi highlights the "heresy" represented by his work in the context of modern Mexican intellectual culture. However, the most obvious attempt at collective self-positioning came from Chávez Castañeda, who, along with Celso Santajuliana, wrote the two-volume book *La generación de los enterradores* (*The Undertakers' Generation*, 2000 and 2003); this work sought to describe, in a highly idiosyncratic approach to Bourdieusian literary sociology, the logics of Mexican narrative since the 1990s in order to predict which writers born in the 1960s would ultimately prevail.[63] The title is telling: this generation is defined by its joint burial of the twentieth century and its opening of the field to new poetics. Chávez Castañeda and Santajuliana generally validate authors (like Ana Clavel or Pablo Soler Frost, to provide examples beyond the Crack) not for the specific content of their poetics, but for the instances when their style can be said to depart from the twentieth century and to develop what would become twenty-first-century literature. It is not at all surprising that Volpi, Padilla, and Palou are among the survivors of the battle, although it is equally meaningful that some other writers—like Cristina Rivera Garza and David Toscana—are also afforded that status. Such results prove that the Crack did not necessarily seek to erase other forms of literary writing in Mexico; rather, they sought to coexist with a range of authors who shared their commitment to literature. In other words, their self-positioning strategy was focused less on annulling other writers of their generation, as some detractors complained, than on distinguishing themselves in a crowded literary field as they sought a reading public of their own.

As a testament to the diverse approaches available to emerging Mexican writers in the mid-1990s, the anthology *Dispersión multitudinaria* (*Multitudinous Dispersion*) was published in 1997, a volume that gathered over fifty writers under the age of forty who had published at least one book.[64] Instead of attempting a selection, editors Leonardo da Jandra and Roberto Max, along with then-directors of Joaquín Mortiz, opted to publish every single submitted text. Although reading the anthology cover to cover can be a grueling and cringeworthy experience, their decision nonetheless made it a truly valuable historical document; it showcases the diverse trends developing at the time, including authors whose careers never prospered. In examining the anthology and contemplating the many important writers absent from it (such as Ana Clavel and Cristina Rivera Garza), it is clear that the literary field's indeterminacy was a fundamental issue when seeking to position oneself as an emerging writer. The Crack movement was by no means the only visible literary trend. Among many others, one can identify a substantial number of female writers who would shift the gender balance in Mexican fiction (the subject of chapter 3); authors working in noir and science fiction (Alberto Chimal, José Luis Zárate, and Gerardo Horacio Porcayo, to name a few) and thus seeking to confront prejudices against genre fiction in the literary field; and the emerging wave of writers from northern Mexico who would challenge literary centralism with works engaged in a diverse variety of experimentalisms and vernacular writing (Élmer Mendoza, Rosina Conde, and Luis Humberto Crosthwaite would be a few examples). I am presenting these trends simplistically and schematically due to space constraints, but my point is that even a superficial glimpse at the corpus compiled in *Dispersión multitudinaria* shows how nearly every writer born in the 1960s and early 1970s shared a clear distance from the previous generation of Mexican literature. Thus, a self-conscious intervention in the literary field was a crucial strategy that served not only to distinguish oneself, but also to claim a potential hegemonic position that would validate one's literary traditions and writings.

All Crack writers but Urroz and Estivill were included in the anthology, which was published after the Crack manifesto. As one can see in the submitted works, some of the novels that would contribute to the Crack's transnationalization were already being developed. Palou's contribution, "El silencio de las sirenas" ("The Silence of Sirens"), was a fragment (bearing the novel's original title) of *Paraíso clausurado*, while Volpi's "La aritmética del infinito" ("The Arithmetic of Infinity") was an excerpt from the novel that would ultimately be published as *En busca de Klingsor* (*In Search of Klingsor*, 1999). Chávez Castañeda, Herrasti, and Padilla submitted short stories. A couple of years after *Dispersión multitudinaria*, Crack writers would enter transnational circuits. Volpi won the Biblioteca Breve Award and Padilla the Primavera Award; riding their coattails, Urroz, Palou, Herrasti, and Chávez Castañeda accessed transnational publication as well. Although the results were uneven (Volpi certainly reaped the greatest benefits, probably followed by Urroz and Padilla; Palou never successfully broke into markets beyond Mexico, while Chávez Castañeda has been somewhat dissociated from the movement since the mid-2000s), these publications led to the Crack group's influence on the national and transnational literary spheres. In the pages that follow, I will proceed to analyze the three selected authors. I discuss Volpi's *Klingsor* as a way to understand the consequences of the Crack's engagement with commercial literature, and I will briefly compare this book to his novella *El jardín devastado* (*The Devastated Garden*, 2002) in order to study the two regimes of strategic Occidentalism in his work.[65] Second, I will discuss two of Padilla's world novels with respect to his validation of diverse lines of literature (such as late Austro-Hungarian fiction and Victorian travel literature) and how this helps him construct dissonant perspectives on the past and the contemporary; I will also analyze his co-optation of the language of European colonial knowledge. Finally, I will read Palou's *Paraíso clausurado* as a meditation on the archives through which strategic Occidentalism interacts with literary subjectivity and the authorial enterprise.

Jorge Volpi: Contemporaneity and the World Novel in the Age of Corporate Literature

In a 2008 article titled "Narrativa hispanoamericana, Inc." ("Spanish American Narrative, Inc."), Jorge Volpi advances a series of ideas illustrating the position-taking strategies that allowed him and fellow Crack members to develop their respective literary styles.[66] Volpi's intellectual strategy is to radically hollow out the very idea of Latin American literature, an argument that cuts across most of his nonfiction work. In "Narrativa hispanoamericana, Inc.," Volpi chastises what he calls "literary globaliphobics," who, in his description, wrongly oppose cosmopolitanism in the name of a purportedly politicized Latin American literature concerned with identity and specificity. According to Volpi, this stance leads writers and critics who subscribe to this position (including many of the articulating postcolonial and world literature accounts of Latin American literature) to actually replicate the very same logic of globalist homogenization they decry:

> Al empeñarse en preservar a toda costa lo "hispanoamericano," los globalifóbicos de la literatura cancelan de un tajo la rica tradición cosmopolita de Hispanoamérica (que es, quiérase o no, otra forma de ser profundamente hispanoamericano). Dado que la literatura de Occidente ya no requiere autoafirmarse ni forjar su identidad—¿a quién se le ocurriría buscar la especificidad de la literatura italiana o la francesa?—, la literatura hispanoamericana entendida como marca sólo tiene como objetivo llenar el hueco del mercado que le corresponde, sin tener argumentos para oponerse a una de las verdaderas desventajas de la globalización: la confinación en estancos cerrados de las particularidades regionales como meros productos de exportación.[67]

> By insisting on preserving the "Spanish American" at any cost, literary globaliphobics cancel, in one fell swoop, Spanish America's rich cosmopolitan tradition (which is, whether we like it or not, another form of being profoundly Spanish American). Given that Western

literature no longer needs to self-affirm or forge its identity (who would even think to seek out the specificity of Italian or French literature?), Spanish American literature, seen as a brand, has the sole objective of filling the market niche to which it corresponds, without having any arguments against one of the true disadvantages of globalization: the restriction of regional particularities into close confines as export products.

Volpi's point here is that writers, academics, critics, and publishers all participate in making Latin American literature into a commodity by generating surplus value out of the division of intellectual labor. Since the core market is able to produce "universal literature," a Spanish American writer's only option is to adapt to this false sense of diversity—which is merely a flattening of regional literary tradition into a package useful both to the book market and to the symbolic market of theories and ideas. Evidently, one of Bourdieu's key lessons is not lost on Volpi: he argues that symbolic capital has an autonomous logic and that you cannot neatly apply face-value ideas regarding the fight against economic globalization to the cultural field. It is true that Volpi was formulating these ideas at a time when the Latin American and global left, fueled by figures like Hugo Chávez and Evo Morales, was reconstituting a concept of regional specificity to resist the homogenizing flows of capital. That said, the realms of the global reading class and global academia contain a hegemonic structure of symbolic capital that leans toward the aestheticization of these ideas. Volpi argues that cosmopolitanism (including what I call strategic Occidentalism in this book) is an essential element of the region's historical and cultural experience. Thus, the market-based confinement of Spanish-language writers to identity and specificity essentially reduces the complex ecosystem of Latin American literature into a single format guaranteed to sell books (or to satisfy political voluntarisms) in the Global North. In a parallel account, Héctor Hoyos shows how the narrative of "combativeness" that connects Fredric Jameson's essay on the national allegory with Casanova's *World Republic of Letters* is grounded in a center-periphery division; even when one recognizes, as Casanova has done, that this account may in fact reify what it criticizes, there still exists a "prevalence of assertions of national origin in combative literatures and the relative lack of those assertions in pacified, comfortably 'universal' forms."[68] If anything, Volpi's argument forcefully contradicts the established (and endemic) idea of Latin American literature operative in contexts that range from the marketing departments of global conglomerates to theoretical constructs pushing Latin American fiction into an axiomatic role. In this way, he attempts to demonstrate how the signifier "Latin American literature" has been ascribed a narrow definition, one that has not varied since Global Northern theorists and publishing houses were obliged to incorporate the Latin American Boom into their reflections and catalogs.

Although Volpi has a very positive opinion of Bolaño, emphasizing the greatness of the Chilean master's literary project and expressing the general admiration shared by writers of Volpi's age, he also defines Bolaño as "el último escritor latinoamericano" (the last of Latin American writers).[69] The crux of this assertion is that he is the last Latin American writer to thoroughly embody the idea of "Spanish American narrative, Inc." As we all know, Bolaño would indeed replace García Márquez as the stand-in for Latin American literary specificity. But the real point is that Latin American writers should embrace the refusal to occupy such a position or submit to the terms imposed on them (Bolaño may well have refused if the process had taken place during his lifetime). Volpi situates Bolaño at the end of "Latin American literature" so writers like Volpi are no longer required to feed the demand for stereotypes. In fact, for Volpi, the truly important phenomenon that has been taking place in Latin American fiction since the 1990s is the emergence of writers who no longer want to sell their nationality as a "brand" and who refuse to cede to the pressures of a global market seeking exoticism from Latin America. Crucially, Volpi asserts that such authors should not be read as if selling their books in this way "implica que renuncien a su identidad hispanoamericana o nacional ni que hayan sido presas de la globalización o del mercado" ([does not] imply that they renounce their Spanish American or national identity or that they have fallen prey to globalization and the market).[70] Critics often erroneously believe that Volpi seeks to validate only his brand of literature, particularly because he has expanded these ideas into quite a controversial argument on the dissolution of the idea of Latin America in the twenty-first century.[71] In fact, though, the core of his argument is that being Latin American should not limit writers to their supposed Latin Americanness. What Volpi and other Crack writers contend is not so much that all of Latin American literature should be cosmopolitan. Rather, they question the idea that cosmopolitanism and nationalism are mutually exclusive, or that Latin American writers must relinquish entire parts of their intellectual genealogy in order to appease market or academic demands. This notion underpins Volpi's rejection of the idea of the "Latin American writer" as someone following the imperative of specificity, or someone responsible for representing the contemporaneity of her region, in a way that resembles the previously cited statement by the Warwick Research Collective.[72] Indeed, some Crack writers offer strong examples against this phenomenon. Volpi's world novels, usually (though not always) concerned with subjects unrelated to Mexico, are the work of a writer who simultaneously is a well-known public intellectual, government official, and cultural administrator and has produced a considerable body of writing on Mexican political and social issues. Also, as I will elaborate in the final section, Palou's high-volume output includes world novels coexisting with biographical fiction on Mexico's national historical figures (like Emiliano Zapata and Porfirio Díaz), as well as aestheticist, cosmopolitan fiction being published, sometimes in the very same year, with books written in Mexican vernacular.

It is not at all coincidental that Volpi dedicates "Narrativa hispano-americana, Inc." to Sergio Pitol, who, as we saw in chapter 1, substantially contributes to paving the way, editorially and aesthetically, for the constitution of a new cosmopolitanism in the early years of neoliberalism. In an essay on Pitol, Volpi explores his trajectory from "secret writer" to a leading figure of Mexican literature, a path based on his uncompromising commitment to cosmopolitanism. This depiction makes sense if we remember that the tension between nationalism and cosmopolitanism is not only a matter of global literary markets, but also a hotly disputed construct in Mexican national literature.[73] A fundamental aspect of the Crack group's intervention in Mexican literature—the exhaustion of Mexicanness as a viable literary discourse—is directly related to the exhaustion of a cultural model tied to state projects of cultural development. Among the most influential ideas of the 1990s, in fact, was Roger Bartra's formulation of the "post-Mexican condition," understood as the social identity produced by the declining symbolic efficiency of twentieth-century nationalist culture. Paradoxically, as world literature theories continued to assert emancipation through specificity, Mexican writers and intellectuals were spotlighting the opposite, at least in part: that the decline of an oppressive nationalism and its imperatives produced a more open society. In fact, as Bartra famously (and polemically) points out, the "profound crisis of identity and legitimacy that began to ripen in 1968 has destroyed the Mexican regime"; this, in turn, would create "a bridge to democracy" and allow social sciences (and presumably also cultural production) to cease their focus on dissecting "the Mexican."[74]

Volpi's literary project emerged from this process, so it is hardly surprising that his notions of Mexican and Latin American literature's emancipation from the chains of nationalism are analogous to Bartra's account of the post-Mexican condition. In fact, they serve to indicate an astonishing omission in many world literature theories, which rarely ask what happens when specificity is an instrument thoroughly constructed by and legitimating of local political hegemonies. In one of the best scholarly readings of Volpi's work, Brian Whitener proposes a version of this point that links the Crack movement's post-Mexican aesthetics to a state and financial crisis: "What the Crack manifesto registers is that the primary threat is no longer of splits internal to the national, splits which might undo its coherence, but rather a threat from the outside that destabilizes the entire environment of the national popular state and subject."[75] Precisely because the "old technologies of fictive ethnicity" have become obsolete, Whitener suggests that Volpi and other Crack writers shift to "ontology" as a central concern of fiction. Whitener's analysis compellingly captures the fact that the exhaustion of the magical realist paradigm contributed to the decline of the symbolic efficacy of the national-popular. I would add, in the light of my analysis above, that the trivialization of global magical realism was both a cause and a consequence of phenomena like the post-Mexican condition: certainly, it participated in eroding any possibility of identity-management stemming from this kind of imaginary, but it also became unreadable, because its symbolic code no longer resonated with the social. In fact, I would radicalize Whitener's analysis by commenting that the decline of the national-popular for the Crack group (as it was for Bartra and many Mexican literary intellectuals) was less a crisis than an opportunity: a way to remove a fundamental obstacle to Mexico's participation in global culture (with world literature among its instances) and to decimate the symbolic complicity between nationalist forms of literature and local means of political hegemony. This is why it is a mistake to read the Crack authors as "depoliticized": their apparently apolitical cosmopolitanism is, as Whitener also implies, a way of doing politics in neoliberal Mexico. The fact that some Crack writers (Volpi and Palou in particular) also operate as public intellectuals, and even as authors of novels rethinking the Mexican past, is fully consistent with this point.

Pitol's centrality to the construction of the Crack genealogy is clear in reading Volpi's essay "Siete variaciones sobre temas de Sergio Pitol" ("Seven Variations on Themes by Sergio Pitol"). According to Volpi, Pitol's work offers no basis for continuing "la obsoleta disputa entre la literatura nacionalista y la que apuesta por valores universales" (the obsolete dispute between nationalist literature and literature that invests in universal values), and Volpi express his admiration for the fact that Pitol's fiction, whether it is located in Prague or Mexico City, never surrenders to realism.[76] Rather, Volpi concludes:

> La literatura verdadera no es la que se distingue por describir paisajes o rostros, sino aquella que, como la de Sergio Pitol, plantea problemas, desarrolla conflictos, se burla de sí misma, de sus personajes y, en última instancia, de sus lectores; en pocas palabras, aquella que cuestiona y duda.[77]

> True literature is not the kind distinguished by describing landscapes and faces, but the kind that, like Sergio Pitol's, raises problems, develops conflicts, and mocks itself, its characters, and ultimately its readers; in short, the kind that questions and doubts.

In chapter 1, I argued that a key consequence of Pitol's strategic Occidentalism was his ability to bring into Spanish, and to develop himself, forms of writing that question literature's totalizing capacity to construct mythologies related to national identity or teleological accounts of history. Volpi's reading of Pitol shows how he and other Crack members take advantage of the paths cleared by his fiction. Pitol's work, in Volpi's interpretation, displaces the imperative of the Mexican novel from content to form.

Although Volpi wrote his important essays in the 2000s, it is abundantly clear that the ideas he articulates there had been present in his work from his early fiction onward. *Dias de ira* (*Days of Rage*, 1994), his contribution to

Tres bosquejos del mal, is a complex novella concerned with the possibilities of the novel.[78] As Ana Pellicer López describes, this not-altogether-successful piece shows the enormous formal ambition underlying Volpi's work, represented in this case by a text structured like an opera; it is based on the confusion between the voice of the doctor-protagonist and that of the author of a fictional work, also entitled *Días de ira*, contained within the novella.[79] If we add this description to my earlier commentary on *A pesar del oscuro silencio*, we can see that Volpi's early fiction engaged Pitol's concepts of the novel and pushed them further, radicalizing the idea of representation in the genre. Danny J. Anderson's perceptive reading of Volpi's fiction as an exploration of the "possibility of knowledge" can be expanded in asserting that it also explored the possibility of the novel as a contemporary genre: a series of books in which highly complex formal architecture, estranging literary voices, and confounding narrative perspectives merge in an investigation of the novel's very limits. Perhaps the most interesting book in Volpi's early period is precisely the one he published during the Crack launch: *El temperamento melancólico*. The book concerns a German film director, Carl Gustav Gruber, and his final movie. The novel—which derives from a complex canon of representations of melancholy, from Albrecht Dürer's famous etching to an epigraph by Henri Cazalis, a little-known symbolist poet—incorporates formal procedures of cinematic experimentation into the novel (the second epigraph openly references Andrei Tarkovsky), which allow Volpi to use forms like the film script to dissolve Gruber's story into the apocalyptic setting of the film itself.

This literary exploration found its pinnacle in *En busca de Klingsor*, the 1999 novel that won the first Biblioteca Breve Award after its relaunch. With this prize, Seix Barral—a famed Boom publisher now under the umbrella of Grupo Planeta—sought to reposition the contemporary Latin American novel in the Spanish-speaking world. The novel tells the story of a young U.S. Army lieutenant, Francis P. Bacon, who is tasked with finding Klingsor, the man in charge of the Third Reich's atomic program. In Volpi's experimental fashion, the novel is narrated from the perspective of a mathematician, Gustav Links, whose life and metaliterary reflections are presented to us alongside Bacon's story. The story of Volpi's novel receiving the award has been discussed elsewhere and at length, so I will not rehash it here.[80] There are, however, two fundamental points to retrieve from that conversation. First, the novel has been strikingly divisive, both in terms of concrete opinions in response to it (some have declared it one of the key works of Latin American fiction since the Boom; others have offered virulent criticism of its commercial nature) and of its uneven distribution. In Spain, it became such a phenomenon that Carlos Fuentes himself called it the most widely read novel in the country that year; meanwhile, it raised over half a million dollars in translation rights at the 1999 Frankfurt Book Fair, securing publication in seven (and ultimately nineteen) languages.[81] Conversely, the English edition had a fairly modest commercial run, failing to prompt a paperback edition until many years later and eliciting what can only be described as a tepid reaction in the few critical outlets that reviewed it.[82] In Mexico, Volpi is a major figure and *Klingsor* was an undeniable success, but the literary world harbors an enormous ambivalence toward the book and its author, best summarized by Domínguez Michael: it rejects the editorial and commercial nature of both the Crack movement and Volpi's fiction, respects his ambition and his breaking away from nationalism, and judges his work in a way that oscillates between recognizing its importance and sometimes harshly assesses its style and structure.[83]

I believe that this contradictory reception contributes to the paradigm-changing nature of Volpi's writing. In some locations (like Spain or France, where the response was generally very positive), Volpi was essential in redefining notions of Latin American literature and changing the terms of its reception. In others (like the U.S. or some quarters of the Mexican literary field), his intervention was unreadable: the U.S. market's response to Latin American fiction would go unchanged until the arrival of Roberto Bolaño a few years later; in Mexico, women writers like Cristina Rivera Garza and writers from northern Mexico would have a greater impact. This, then, is the second point: partial setbacks and all, there is undeniably a before and after *En busca de Klingsor* in the perception of Latin American literature abroad. Moreover, one could certainly make the case that, by virtue of the new Biblioteca Breve Award's first winner being a book so fundamentally different from any previous stereotype of Latin American fiction, Volpi cleared the path for the arrival of many other writers, most notably Roberto Bolaño.

Volpi is not always given his due as this kind of pioneer. Hoyos, for instance, dedicates a chapter of his *Beyond Bolaño* to Nazism in Latin American literature, but he establishes Bolaño's *Nazi Literature in the Americas* (1996) as a precursor of Volpi, when in fact they represent completely different projects. Bolaño's is a Borges-style anthology (or, to be more precise, a ruthless parody of one) compiling Latin American Nazi writers. This approach has little to do with Volpi's book, which is a crime novel with a much more complex narrative architecture. Hoyos even faults Volpi for not problematizing the tension between the local and the global (something Volpi is clearly uninterested in doing).[84] As I see it, the flaw in Hoyos's argument is that his chapter overlooks two important problems. First, Volpi's book, contrary to Hoyos's assertion, is not the first novel related to the Holocaust by a mainstream writer. That would be José Emilio Pacheco's *Morirás lejos* (*You Will Die in a Distant Land*, 1967), an experimental work that has far more in common with Volpi's problematization of the narrator than with Bolaño's work.[85]

Second, and perhaps more crucially, Hoyos omits the fact that the two central traits of Volpi's novel—its German thematics and cinematographic resources—were already very much being developed in *El temperamento melancólico*, a book published before Bolaño's work was. I believe Sarah Pollack's account provides an accurate timeline:

> Collectively, the authors assembled around the McOndo and the Crack projects have been successful in loosening the stranglehold of magical realism on the US conception of Latin American fiction, and individual novelists such as Volpi have achieved moments of stardom. Nevertheless, neither McOndo's aesthetics of virtual realism, pop culture and globalization, nor the Crack's penchant for historical thrillers set outside of Latin America seem to have filled García Márquez's shoes.[86]

Although Volpi was indeed unable to make a strong incursion into the U.S. market, *Klingsor* still paved the way for a Latin American literature that looked different from the 1990s norm (dominated by authors like Isabel Allende and Laura Esquivel), which in turn permitted authors like Bolaño to redefine it. One must remember, for example, that *Nazi Literature in the Americas* did not appear in English until 2008, following Bolaño's first major translation into English, *The Savage Detectives*, in 2007. Conversely, *Klingsor* was issued by a major press back in 2002, when the only other Latin American blockbuster release was the translation of Padilla's *Amphytrion*. Volpi's book was critical for creating an environment in which Latin American writers could decisively depart from the conventions set by their immediate predecessors. We can find a good example of this phenomenon in the German reception of Latin American literature. Juan Manuel López de Abiada and Daniel Leuenberg have discussed how, when *Klingsor* was published, all other Latin American books entering the market were defined by derivative magical realism, Luis Sepúlveda and Isabel Allende, for instance, were being serially released in the mid-1990s. Considering how controversial the subject of Nazism remains in Germany, it is quite astonishing, as López de Abiada and Leuenberg meticulously illustrate, to see how many German media outlets debated the novel, including the fabled *Der Spiegel*.[87] This is not a novel about Latin American Nazis, as Bolaño's is. Indeed, it is a novel about Germans and Americans, and Mexico or Latin America are entirely absent from the plot. Volpi achieved an unthinkable feat: allowing for a Latin American writer to enter the German market with a (controversial) German topic and elicit substantial critical and readerly interest.

I contend, then, that the scope of Volpi's novel cannot be reduced to the (nonetheless relevant) sociological aspects developed up to this point; one must investigate the structural work that turned it into a world novel. One of the difficulties in discussing *Klingsor* is the temptation to read it entirely in terms of its content: as a novel about either the Nazis or science or the intersection of both. I will not do this myself; a sizable catalog of such studies already exists.[88] I am more interested in describing the confluence of literary traits that allowed Volpi to design, at the level of the novel as a form, an intervention in the field of world literature that was based on Crack principles. The novel operates through the tensions among four elements, each concerned with the possibility of narrating the truth, and simultaneously existing within a realm of knowledge that we may call, for lack of a better name, "universal": the detective narrative form as an insertion into the existing paradigms of world fiction, while following Pitol's disruptive work in the genre; mathematics as a theory of the (im)possibility of knowledge; Nazism (and evil) as a synecdoche for world history in a philosophical sense; and Volpi's own previous work on narrative perspective. Through these elements, *En busca de Klingsor* reformulates the idea of the Latin American world novel form: all four detach the genre from operations related to the construction of totality, identity, and the nation.

It is unsurprising that Volpi chose to structure his book as a detective story. Here, though, we must take care not to locate *Klingsor* within the genre's standard plot prescription: the individual seeking justice in modernity. First and foremost, opting for the detective places Volpi squarely within the lineage initiated by Jorge Luis Borges, whose work in detective fiction, as other critics have pointed out, is a direct precedent for Volpi's Frank Bacon.[89] However, the Borgesian detective has a peculiar genealogy in world literature: this figure moved into the commercial realm of the world novel that popularized Borgesian games, fashioning them into both cinematic and literary crime stories. In this sense, Volpi descends, as early readers of *Klingsor* had already recognized, from a tradition of erudite bestsellers that began with Umberto Eco's *The Name of the Rose*, published in 1980.[90] Eco, of course, is hardly the only author gesturing in this direction; as a matter of fact, Spanish-language presses began to push intellectual European bestsellers on the market throughout the 1980s. The Anagrama catalog, discussed in the last chapter, included encyclopedic novels by authors such as Roberto Calasso, as well as other strains of Borgesian writing, most notably the works of Paul Auster. Scandinavian crime fiction embarked on its process of translation into the Spanish market, with authors like Peter Hoeg and Henning Mankell entering the catalogs of Tusquets and other houses. Simultaneously, the detective story also accompanied a larger reconfiguration of Spanish-language fiction. Glen Close, for instance, describes *Klingsor* as a "somewhat anachronistic neo-classical mystery novel," which was among the strains of the general penchant for noir that occupied both literary writers (we should recall that both Ricardo Piglia and Fernando del Paso wrote in this genre in the 1990s) and bestseller fiction (such as authors like Manuel Vázquez Montalban).[91]

The true formal interest at work in *En busca de Klingsor* is its economy of mystery. Here, Volpi clearly pushed Pitol's trend toward the unsolvable. But instead of limiting our perspective to the detective's (who knows no more than we do), as Pitol does with Del Solar, we confront two levels of uncertainty: Gustav Links's unreliable narrative and Bacon's errant investigation. The novel sets itself up when Links puts forth three axioms of his own narrative: "Toda narración ha sido escrita por un narrador" (All narratives are written by a narrator), "Todo narrador ofrece una verdad única" (All narrators offer one singular truth), "Todo narrador tiene un motivo para narrar" (All narrators have a reason for narrating).[92] If Pitol's Del Solar is unable to resolve the crimes of the Minerva building (in *El desfile del amor*, discussed in chapter 1), and thus grant closure to an episode of national history, Volpi's narrator focuses on the impossibility of narrating not only the resolution of the crime, but also the investigation itself: we are introduced to a narrator who we sometimes believe may be Klingsor himself (which appears to be confirmed at the end, albeit with some ambiguity), and who, at the very least, has an agenda that undermines the relationship between the reader and the novel. Links is a more refined version of the narrators in his early works, as the plot's interweaving and the structural reluctance to fully disclose are more seamlessly constructed. In another of the novel's self-reflective moments, Links questions the idea of the crime by putting forth three laws that mirror Isaac Newton's laws of motion: "Todo crimen ha sido cometido por un criminal" (All crimes are committed by a criminal), "Todo crimen es un retrato del criminal" (Every crime is a portrait of a criminal), "Todo criminal tienen un motivo" (Every criminal has a motive).[93] The point of positing these laws is to remove the very notion of the crime from the story. Links states that Klingsor may not have been a real criminal, because he had no motives—which even Hitler and Stalin did. Thus, finding Klingsor was a question not of finding a criminal in order to bring him to justice but rather of finding evil itself, an evil that escapes the materiality provided by the detective story. If, as Whitener argues, Volpi's novel moves from the identitarian to the ontological, *En busca de Klingsor* builds a form from the impossibility of this move. The familiarity of the form, which inserts this novel both into the commercial space (because of erudite thrillers' role in world literature) and into the space of modern literature (through a supposed hero, Links, who would bring a transgressor to justice), bases its narrative tension on dismantling this familiarity. Volpi's world novel is not about narrating the certainty of the modern from a "Mexican perspective." Rather, it is about the inability of doing so from any perspective at all.

Volpi's original title, *La aritmética del infinito*, gestures in this direction. Volpi uses mathematics and physics both as a plot device (several famous twentieth-century scientists appear as characters, and their work is central to the mystery of Klingsor) and as a grand system of knowledge-based symbols. Oscillating between a sophisticated deployment of mathematics (in both form and content) and its necessarily pedagogical exposition in order to access the broad audience *Klingsor* seeks, Volpi imbues the crime novel with an intellectual history focused on the scientific and philosophical incorporation of uncertainty into knowledge of the contemporary world. The canon of physics and mathematics deployed in the novel comprise the main theories dedicated to the impossibility of apprehending the material world: most prominently, Werner Heisenberg's "uncertainty principle," Erwin Schrödinger's work with quantum mechanics and his cat paradox, and Kurt Gödel's incompleteness theories.[94] The novel's epigraph comes from a well-known statement by Schrödinger on the relationship between science and uncertainty. Crucially, the epigraph points to the role science will play throughout the book:

> Science is a game—but a game with reality, a game with sharpened knives. . . . In the presentation of a scientific problem, the other player is the good Lord. . . . The uncertainty is how many of the rules God himself has permanently ordained, and how many apparently are caused by your own mental inertia, while the solution generally becomes possible only through freedom from its limitations.[95]

The uncertainty regarding the "good Lord" and his role in determining the coordinates of reality poses a problematic stance both for the detective and for the scientist (or for Bacon, who is the intersection of the two). The novel arcs toward the denial of both science and crime fiction as narrative forms, the impossibility of reaching closure. This is a fundamental point in understanding *Klingsor*. Ingrid Simson has pointed out that Volpi describes paradoxes as part of the novel's content, but his pedagogical tone prevents him from incorporating those paradoxes, as Borges did, at the level of form.[96] In this way, the tone remains compatible with the larger audience sought by the novel and certainly contributes to its bestseller status. Still, this analysis does not fully honor Volpi's methodology. Félix Jiménez Ramírez argues that in bringing scientific language into literary language, Volpi undermines the communicative nature of the former through the resources of the latter.[97] The key issue here is that the book's resolution is tied to the moment when that communicative nature finally cedes and the narrator's agency dissociates from the pursuit of knowledge, both as a detective and as a scientist. The narrator tells us that Bacon had to make a decision and "esta vez ni la ciencia ni el amor podían salvarlo. La solidez de su mundo se había derrumbado porque a su alrededor todos buscaban escaper, como él, de la verdad" (This time neither science not love could save him. The pillars of his existence had come crashing down because he and everyone around him were trying so desperately to escape the truth).[98] What happens here is plain: the novel itself has been meticulously constructed as a means to escape the truth, not to attain it, and its meaning is shaped around a series of procedures in which signification is created through a full engagement with the uncertainty principle. The novel in itself does not need to be paradoxical. Rather, the gaze of Gustav Links, the observer who affects the outcome, is where the uncertainty principle is ciphered. Indeed, as Sergio Ricardo Arenas Martínez argues, one of the points of narrating the novel from Links's perspective is precisely how he delays and impedes the resolution of the narration itself—which would lead us to the conclusion that he is Klingsor. Thus, as Arenas Martínez also argues, the very fact that Links is the narrator is tied to the impossibility of justice in the story. Since Links is narrating from a mental hospital, legal prosecution of his crimes is not viable.[99]

In his acknowledgments, Volpi recognizes Douglas Hofstadter's 1979 book *Gödel, Escher, Bach* as a fundamental reference for his narrative structure.[100] This connection has formal consequences for the novel; even more importantly for my argument, this form also affects the concept of the world novel as Volpi deploys it. Brian McHale contends, apropos of Hofstadter's arguments about narrative levels: "Each change of narrative level in a recursive structure also involves a change of ontological level, a change in the world."[101] Furthermore, as McHale mentions elsewhere in his book, the closing dialogue of *Gödel, Escher, Bach*, in which a stage direction reads "Enter the Author," the book produces a significant collapse of the narrative structure itself: "The level of the fictional world and the ontological level occupied by the author as a maker of the fictional world collapse together; the result is a short-circuit of the ontological structure."[102] Following McHale, one could certainly suggest that a version of this recourse occurs in a considerable number of both modernist and postmodernist works. However, in *Klingsor*'s particular case, the book uses this collapse of ontological levels as a collapse of the genre itself. What the search in the novel, and the challenge posed to the reader, has performed all along (as we learn in the end), is a gradual diffusion of the levels described by McHale in order to challenge the reader's world. In other words, *En busca de Klingsor* delivers an alternative mechanism for the relationship between identity and the novel, radically breaking away from the multiculturalist functions of identity at work in magical realist fiction and providing, as Whitener suggests in the arguments cited above, an altogether ontological reflection.[103]

As a result, *En busca de Klingsor* challenges magical realism not only at the level of content, but also at the level of structure: the book's interplay between Volpi, Links, and Klingsor tests the politics and aesthetics of identification as developed by magical realist novels. What *Klingsor* proposes, then, is an alternative system of novel-knowledge that challenges the commodity of identity expected from Latin American fiction, providing instead a new form of calculated identity-construction that forecasts other possibilities for the region's novels in the neoliberal era. In harnessing Hofstadter, Volpi achieves a brilliant feat in terms of the Latin American world novel form: putting into narrative the structures of knowledge of a late neoliberalism that had not yet been solidified. In the mid-1990s, when the Crack group was launched, early forms of editorial neoliberalism promoted the aesthetics of late magical realism, which harmonized well with forms of identity-commoditization related to the emergence of multiculturalism. As Jodi Melamed has compellingly demonstrated, this "neoliberal multiculturalism" is associated with new forms of policing difference, a topic that Chilean novelist Alberto Fuguet has also powerfully discussed in his landmark essay "Magical Neoliberalism."[104] With keen intuition, *En busca de Klingsor* invests the novel with the type of scientific discourse that would claim for itself the epistemological privilege of literature in particular and the humanities in general. In academic discourse, we have seen this phenomenon in the rise of universalist and science-oriented practices such as cognitivism (a field to which Volpi has devoted a whole book) or the so-called digital humanities.[105] In this sense, Volpi joins a certain line of world novels—such as French writer Michel Rio's brief, dense narratives—in which science replaces the social sciences in providing the protagonists with existential meaning.[106] But *Klingsor*'s twist is that science is constitutively unable to overcome the unknowability of either historical fate or individual identity. Bacon's failure, then, is the failure of science to access the root of evil in order to achieve positive knowledge of its origins. Rather, scientifically oriented novels focus on what Henry Sussman, in a Hofstadter-influenced reading of Kafka, calls the "Prevailing Operating System, with political, economic, psychosocial, even sexual repercussions as well, [which] sets out from an interface, in machines, but also in language, at which the inchoate becomes *operable*, the random and non-sequential *calculable*."[107] While Sussman focuses on Kafka and cybernetics, Volpi's novel takes a different course: it is an archeology of the moment in which the axioms of the Prevailing Operating System were designed and a reflection on the geopolitical system—fascism—that sought to co-opt its power.

This takes us to the third element: Nazism. Volpi's notion of science in this book is historically located in the mainstream currents of Western history. Here we must take care not to read this topic within a Mexican/non-Mexican binary. As Hoyos reminds us, "The subject matter of the work *is* Mexican insofar as the legacies of the Second World War are part of an increasingly global cultural heritage, especially through the mediation of Hollywood films."[108] It is true that Volpi's novel was written during a period of landmark representations of the Nazis in cinema, most notably in the wake of Steven Spielberg's *Schindler's List* (1994). Science's role in the war enjoyed a similar cultural rebirth thanks to the success of Michael Frayn's play *Copenhagen* (1998), a dialogue between Werner Heisenberg and Niels Bohr, as well as Michael Apted's film *Enigma* (2001), which addresses mathematicians' efforts to crack the Nazis' Enigma machine.[109] In a commentary on *Copenhagen*, Volpi debates the play's representation of Heisenberg and contrasts it to his own:

> Al igual que Frayn, traté de conservar la ambigüedad—la incertidumbre, *hélas!*—que rodea a la conducta de Heisenberg pero que, a diferencia de Frayn, mi opinion sobre él se ve tamizada por el odio que el narrador de la novela—un inexistente Gustav Links—dirige contra el físico muniqués con el fin de achacarle sus propias culpas.

No obstante, debo reconocer que mi punto de vista sobre Heisenberg
es menos positivo que el de Frayn.[110]

Like Frayn, I tried to conserve the ambiguity—the uncertainty,
hélas!—surrounding Heisenberg's conduct, but, unlike Frayn, my
opinion on him is sifted through the hate that the novel's narrator (a
nonexistent Gustav Links) directs at the Münchner physicist in order
to blame him for his own wrongdoings. However, I must recognize
that my point of view on Heisenberg is less positive than Frayn's.

Indeed, this passage shows the point set forward both by Hoyos and in my
argument regarding the right to Western culture: Volpi assumes a voice that
speaks up as authoritatively as a European's might in discussing a history
that entails even so-called "peripheral societies." Klingsor performs this legitimacy with great openness. As Jorge Fornet remarks, Links writes the preface
to the novel on November 10, 1989, around the same time as the fall of the
Berlin Wall.[111] In this way, Volpi carefully enunciates the novel from a concrete point in world history, one that would affect Latin America as much as
other parts of the globe. Such was the preoccupation with 1989, in fact, that
Volpi's trilogy (which starts with *Klingsor*) closes with a sprawling novel, *No
será la tierra* (*Season of Ash*, 2006), which narrates the fall of the Berlin Wall
and the Soviet Union alongside the emergence of the genome project and the
rise of the International Monetary Fund as a guarantor of global neoliberalism.[112] It is evident that Volpi's novels, particularly those which have achieved
concrete transnational circulation, successfully build on their "novelization
of the global," to use Siskind's term. Volpi's claim to universality forges a
new link to the literary market for Latin American fiction, one that no longer
expects the Latin American writer to act as a simple cipher of Latin American authenticity. This success certainly played a part in allowing Roberto
Bolaño and other writers to enter transnational markets (even if some have
since been reconverted into Latin American stereotypes). Indeed, Volpi was
essential in paving the way for non–magical realist Latin American literature
to circulate in commercial publishing.

The use of Nazism to this end, and the Crack group's more general gesture toward this kind of cosmopolitanism, has not lacked for controversy.
Indeed, *Klingsor*'s aesthetics and commercial success have raised sticky questions regarding the cultural politics at work in Volpi's fiction. Fornet, for
instance, does not hesitate in calling the Crack writers (along with McOndo)
incarnations of neoliberal cultural logic, pointing out that the Crack group
as a literary movement is historically tied to Mexico's transnationalization
via NAFTA.[113] Lidia Santos raises this idea more subtly, arguing that Crack
writers activate a "market cosmopolitanism" that replaces the "State cosmopolitanism" of the twentieth century. Santos recognizes, as I do above,
that their cosmopolitanism's positive aspect is its tactical nature, resisting the

demand for magical realism that had colonized the market in the 1990s. On the other hand, she argues that this cosmopolitanism reaffirms Europe's cultural supremacy by desiring to engage with it.[114] However, I believe such an argument must be qualified: decolonized cultural specificity had so evolved as a commodity that this return to the European paradoxically fought against the Eurocentric assumption that world history was the property of Global Northern writers. Indeed, few people question European writers when they appropriate Latin American history, even when they do so in an odiously stereotypical way; for example, French writer Jean-Marie Le Clézio was recognized in 2008 with nothing less than the Nobel Prize for a literature awash with stereotypes of the Global South. Nonetheless, when Latin American writers invert this logic, they are often accused of either neoliberalism or Eurocentrism. While the observation is not completely without merit (in the end, of course, we are talking about literary markets), it remains a somewhat simplistic reading. The politics of the novel at play in our discussion cannot be adequately explained by their relationship to the commercial, as many of the Crack group's Mexican critics decry, as if this were a problem in itself. It is worth remembering that some of the same people who levy such criticism would not deny Salman Rushdie, Umberto Eco, or Milan Kundera (who, incidentally, was an important writer in Mexican literary circles at the time) their "high literary" status simply because they sell books.

Ultimately, it is very much the point of a novel like *En busca de Klingsor* to deploy the instruments of both "high literature" and commercial fiction in dislodging Latin American literature from market-constructed notions of Latin Americanness, which had transformed magical realism's political work into a ready-made commodity. If market cosmopolitanism is crucial to the Crack movement's bid for world literature, it is so because the market itself was in need of changing. Theirs was an essential cultural-political operation in the context of 1990s Spanish-language fiction because, as Eduardo Becerra has argued, Latin American writers faced a "distorted" notion of the region's literature as imposed by Spain, its publishing markets, and its academics and critics.[115] Santos, Fornet, and other critics assert that *En busca de Klingsor* excessively appeals to mass literature. I would argue, however, that this is exactly where the novel's merit lies. While American literary criticism has recently evolved to appreciate popular literature, including genres like noir and the romance novel (which Crack writers also practiced in the mid-1990s, as a matter of fact), literary criticism in the Spanish language in general, and in Mexico in particular, continues to police high literature so that it avoids direct engagement with the market.[116] In my view, this is among the Crack group's most important contributions to the Mexican debate, one that has yet to be fully absorbed: there is no necessary relationship between commercial success and literary quality. The Crack writers' wager was to resist becoming yet another group of exquisite subterranean writers (an identity that remains very much in place as a source of symbolic capital in Mexico), and instead to redesign the editorial market on their own terms. As Jorge Volpi himself has stated, the consolidation of commercial presses is a profoundly negative phenomenon from the authors' perspective; despite his commercial success, he has committed to publishing some of his work in independent presses such as Páginas de Espuma in Spain, Almadía in Mexico, and La Pereza in the United States.[117] Books like *En busca de Klingsor* are more the result of negotiating the Latin American writer's increasingly difficult situation in the context of neoliberal transnational publishing practices than of capitulating to it. The appeal to popular genres and the world literary form, the writing of what Rebecca Walkowitz recently called "born-translated" fiction, and the harnessing of topics such as Nazism, are all associated with the Latin American writer's ability to reach audiences and readers beyond the narrow confines of national and local literary worlds.[118]

To conclude this section, and before proceeding to my discussion of Padilla and Palou, I should mention that sprawling macrohistorical fictions are not Volpi's only form of engagement with the world novel as a genre. An excellent counterexample is his novel *El jardín devastado* (*The Devastated Garden*, 2008),[119] one of the most peculiar books in recent Latin American literature. It was originally written in 2007 as a series of blog entries for *El Boomeran(g)*, a blog run by Grupo Prisa, affiliated with the newspaper *El País*, and the publisher Alfaguara. The book comprises a series of short chapters, usually under a page long (and in a few cases as short as a single sentence), and it goes back and forth between two stories. One is the semi-autobiographical narrative of a Mexican intellectual who left Mexico in the wake of the 1988 electoral fraud and returns around the time of the 2006 fraud to face his past and his obsession with a woman, Ana. The other is the story of Laila, a woman who loses her family during Operation Desert Storm in Iraq.

There are two points to be made about this book in the context of my current discussion. The first is that the particular way in which this book was written illustrates the forms of participation in publishing structures that were made possible by Volpi's success with *Klingsor*. Anyone can start a blog, of course, but access to a blog with a wide readership and a pipeline to publication is enabled by the accrual of symbolic capital in the commercial market. The book did not employ the blog as a site of concrete literary reflection in a particularly original way. Rather, as José Enrique Navarro has argued,

> the objective of the editorial strategy that Volpi pursued was to try to restrict the dominance of the blog as a label or brand to a certain type of essayistic texts. Fiction and pseudo-fiction would fall outside this category, although they would have originally been published in the blog format. Their appearance in the blog could be interpreted also as a promotional strategy for the future work. In this way, the blog would function as an epitext for the book, in service to its future reception.[120]

But appropriating the visibility afforded by an electronic medium in order to establish a platform for a printed book (the blog entries went offline, so the book is now the only way to read the work) is only part of the point. The exercise in textual economics, fostered by the short-form entries, was fundamental for Volpi's own style; indeed, it is antithetical to the wide-ranging aesthetics of his other world novels.

As Ramón Alvarado has documented, critics did not necessarily take to this minimalistic style, and Volpi is often faulted for the novel's supposed minimization of literary resources.[121] I would contend, however, that condemning Volpi for not following his own previous aesthetics is a misreading of this book. The novel's form raises a fundamental problem in the context of the Crack movement: the possibility of Latin Americans as strict contemporaries of other experiences in world history. Rather than creating sprawling narratives and ample reflections on the problematic nature of the narrator, as he does with Gustav Links, *El jardín devastado* boils down to a least common denominator, in which the essential inability to narrate is a factor of the form more than a plot device. The narrator and Laila inhabit the same contemporaneity, but the latter's inaccessibility to the former creates, in the novel, an ethos of engagement with the present that can only be expressed fragmentarily. In a brilliant reading of the book, Sergio Gutiérrez Negrón reads cosmopolitanism in this book, following Kwame Anthony Appiah and Susan Sontag, as a particular kind of ethical act. According Gutiérrez Negrón, Volpi constructs

> un mapa de sufrimiento que no viola ni hace legible el cuerpo del otro . . . mediante un análisis de la movilización de la apropiación consciente y explíticamente representaciones exotizantes, que bien podríamos denominar "exotismo-a-pesar-de-sí," a modo de evitar una fijación que suponga cualquier entendimiento categórico del otro, consecuentemente poniendo en tela de juicio la representación realista en sí.[122]

> a map of suffering that does not violate or make the other's body legible . . . through analyzing the mobilization of consciously and explicitly exotifying representations, which we could well call "exoticism-despite-itself," so as to avoid a fixation that supposes any categorical understanding of the other, consequently questioning realist representation in itself.

I would develop Gutiérrez Negrón's point further and advocate that we read *El jardín devastado* more fully: as world literature. First, we must consider that the novel's ethics represent an unthinkable present (the simultaneity of Mexico and Iraq) through the recourse to an important and long-standing literary tradition in world literature: *A Thousand and One Nights* and neighboring traditions of Arabic poetry.[123] Laila is named after a central character in Arabic and Persian literature, from the story of Layla and Majnun, which dates back to the seventh century, and which the poet Nizami would later popularize in the twelfth century.[124] The canon from which Volpi derives the Iraqi part of his novel is important because it sustains the "exoticism-despite-itself" proposed by Gutiérrez Negrón. In naming his protagonist after a well-known literary figure, accessible to Western readers (in fact, Volpi uses a fragment of an eighth-century version of the text as an epigraph), the book does not claim either an allegorical representation that would serve as a stand-in for all Iraqis (the way a magical realist novel would) or a realist representation of the Iraq War that would offer, with no apparent mediation, a social interpretation of her experience. It is, rather, a peculiar form of South-South engagement that seeks empathy without mediation from the kind of world-historical narratives Volpi deploys in books like *Klingsor*. But the key here is that the same literary procedure that has always characterized Volpi's fiction—the inquiry into the (im)possibility of knowledge through fiction—is still at the core of the book; it has only been articulated in a new way that opts for the scarcity, rather than the proliferation, of language. The discursive mode of Volpi's chapters adheres to the economy and the parabolic nature of his source texts. *El jardín devastado* contains not an array of recognizable citations, but a culture of the past and a present-day war that haunt the novel form in its temporal interactions. Volpi's Mexican character is utterly unable to understand the contemporaneity of Laila's situation. He even wonders: "¿Por qué habría de dolerme una muchacha iraquí en el medio del desierto?" (Why should an Iraqi girl in the middle of the desert make me ache?).[125] The answer lies in the novel form, which makes Laila ever-present—existing in a similar time and intersecting with Mexico within the space of the novel itself.

Gutiérrez Negrón proposes contrasting the detached (or "false") cosmopolitanism of Volpi's well-known books with this "sensible" cosmopolitanism. For my part, I would resist that opposition. Volpi is exercising the Mexican writer's right to write world literature *tout court*, navigating its many distinct registers despite the judgment that such navigations may elicit. The affective detachment that characterizes *Klingsor* and other historical works stems from the formal work I have described above, in which the historical event (Nazism, the fall of the Berlin Wall) is in itself always already mediated by a vast array of cultural discourses, and which is distant by design. It is a history that, from Mexico, can only be experienced through media or formal education, as it plays little to no role in national narratives or cultural memory. *El jardín devastado* is indeed concerned with a new question regarding the ethicality of cosmopolitan engagement. The book inserts itself into the general question of the "deliverance of others," as David Palumbo-Liu has dubbed it, which involves representations of otherness and the weeding-out of its excesses in constructing what he calls an "ethical global community."[126] The questioning of realism as identified by Gutiérrez Negrón indicates a problem facing the novel form in world literature, a problem related to what Palumbo-Liu calls the "functionality of literary language"—which, in globalization, flattens the specificity of historical experience, or is able to deliver otherness as a way to map "the uneven impact of history."[127] Volpi's novel short-circuits this dilemma by inserting both sides of the binary into the narrative. It recognizes that an outside perspective cannot deliver the other's historical experience in all its textures, which it will always already flatten. But it does not reduce experience to mere rationality; to use Palumbo-Liu's formula, it operates instead through representational minimalism in order to undercut the transformation of otherness into reason.

A global reading of Volpi's fiction, still a pending task, must produce an account of the complex details threaded throughout his fiction—which includes not only the abovementioned books, but also novels in verse that employ other structures (Gutiérrez Negrón has discussed one of them, *Oscuro bosque oscuro*).[128] More recently, Volpi has written works radicalizing his own challenges to narrative perspective, which include publishing a book on the 2008 financial crisis, *Memorial del engaño* (*The Deceit Memorial*, 2013), with a pseudonym named after his protagonist, J. Volpi, and narrated as the autobiography of a banker.[129] Through these works, Volpi paradigmatically exemplifies the consequences of the Crack movement's aesthetic principles: he is a cosmopolitan writer whose world novels exercise the contemporaneity of Latin America with the planet itself. In the following section, I will discuss Ignacio Padilla, who provides an alternate solution to the same dilemma: historical imagination.

Ignacio Padilla: Appropriations of the World Novel Form

In his *Grammars of Creation*, George Steiner provides an apt image to describe the idea of temporality in Ignacio Padilla's work: "the timely timelessness within the web of history which situates poiesis and metaphysical questioning, which can be 'dated' but does not 'date.' "[130] Steiner refers to a feature of literature from the twentieth century onward, one in which "grammar," understood as the "articulate organization of perception, reflection and experience," must respond to the question of creation in contemporary times—as the rise of technology and science, and the secularization of the world, have disputed the possibilities of literary creation.[131] Steiner's argument, within the framework of his oeuvre, partly addresses the challenges to literary writing posed by historical experiences such as the Holocaust (which, as we know, are fundamental to writers like Volpi and Padilla). In Steiner's formulation, a fundamental element of the grammar of creation is an ambiguous temporal status. Writing in and about history requires a particular datedness, a set of coordinates engaging both the horizon of what is being narrated and the horizon of the novel's enunciation. But this datedness exists in constant tension with an aspiration to timeliness—which is essential, at least in some paradigms of writing, for the novel to grapple with the general questions of subjectivity and universality found at the core of the "worldliness" of certain world novels. My initial contention in reading Padilla is that his fiction is based on such a tension.

The two novels I will discuss this section, *Amphytrion* (*Shadow without a Name*, 2000) and *La Gruta del Toscano* (*The Tuscan's Grotto*, 2006), are notable for their "timely timelessness."[132] They tell the history of two world-historical catastrophes—Nazism and colonialism—through a narrative figuration of the atemporal metaphysics of evil, which manifests itself at the center of both works. Given their thematic and institutional similarities, it is always tempting to read *Amphytrion* and *En busca de Klingsor* together: both focus on the Nazi era, achieved recognition via transnational awards, used the figure of the detective to structure their narration, and developed parallel trajectories as Crack novels in the publishing world. One difficulty in reading Padilla's work (as well as the period of Palou's work I will address in the next section) is that Volpi's novel has attained more visibility and elicited a level of critical attention that sometimes makes *Klingsor* a metonymic proxy for Crack aesthetics in general. By contrast, Padilla has been studied in only a handful of scattered articles. In those studies, to which I will refer throughout my analysis, it is clear that Padilla's fiction has embarked on a fundamentally different project, even if his concerns stem from the same sources as those of other Crack writers. A careful reading of Padilla's *Amphytrion* shows considerable differences: Volpi's heavily researched historicity is distinct from Padilla's ambiguous use of temporality and site; Volpi's counterpunctual structure, oscillating between Links and Bacon, contrasts with Padilla's use of multiple narrators at different chronological points, building tension through deliberate inconsistencies between accounts. In recognizing the differences in both books, then, what most obviously stands out is a key feature of Padilla's aesthetics. Volpi's world novels participate in the "novelization of the global" and seek the figuration of both the geopolitical and the ideological devices that render a sense either of contemporaneity or of ascendency within the global. Padilla's work strikes a different balance between form and content: at its best, it is a profound reflection on the literary mechanisms that generate universality.

In the Crack manifesto, as cited earlier in this chapter, Padilla spoke of a "chronotope zero" that sought to detemporalize and delocalize the novel, granting it stronger temporal control in a contemporaneity that, as Steiner also describes, has lost the languages (myth, prophecy, symbol) that afforded meaning to the chaotic order of history. Padilla puts forth two meaningful examples to illustrate his point. The first one is *Amadís de Gaula*, a canonical chivalric novel that gathers, in its written form, various centuries' worth of orally transmitted stories, thus appearing to erase the historical discernibility of time and space in the story. This reference is telling because it locates

Padilla's conception of fiction at a foundational moment prior to Miguel de Cervantes and *Don Quixote*, since *Amadís* is one of the novels it parodies. Indeed, Padilla's brief remark gestures to a moment in which narrative myth evolved into time and timelessness became timeliness.[133] This tradition is not only foundational; it also carries over into the present, in genres like comic books, whose mythologies operate within the bounds of what Linda Hutcheon has called "historiographic metafiction," binding timeliness and timelessness through discourse.[134] But the truly significant example proposed by Padilla, mentioned only in passing, is a scene in Christoph Ransmayr's *The Last World* (1990), "al situar a Publio Ovidio Nasón frente a un ramillete de micrófonos" (by placing Publius Ovidius Naso before a bouquet of microphones).[135] The choice of Ransmayr's work might seem perplexing, given that, as some critics have noted, his reconstruction of the decline of the Roman Empire owes some stylistic and narrative debts to García Márquez and magical realism.[136] It is evident that Ransmayr participated, at least in part, in the same literary market as writers like Rushdie, who were writing big historical epics using resources inherited from the Latin American Boom. Yet—and if we recall the crucial point that Padilla and other Crack members oppose epigonal magical realism, not García Márquez—Ransmayr represents a use of Boom aesthetics that is not engaged with identity politics or discourses of regional specificity. Therefore, as in the best works of the Boom, magical realism is used as an estrangement mechanism—which, in Padilla's account, is fundamental in emptying literary chronotopes of the demands of identitarianism, historicity, and place as constructed by the literary market. Padilla finds in Ransmayr something similar to what Sergio Pitol, discussed in chapter 1, found in Russian Boris Pilniak: a counterintuitive recourse to myth and storytelling in resistance to the rationalities of a particular cultural authoritarianism.

Following Hans Blumenberg's concept of "absolute reality," Lynne Cooke offers a useful account of Ransmayr that helps us interpret Padilla's appropriation of his ethos:

> The Enlightenment mindset of rationality and order, in its modern form, is generally shown in its extreme manifestation in Ransmayr's work. So for Ransmayr, modernity and progress through accumulation of knowledge becomes the "absolute reality" whose threat becomes increasingly intolerable. However, the fantastical and fluid world of myth in Ransmayr's work does not enable humankind to successfully structure a less anxious space within the relationships with which it constructs its reality.[137]

The idea of myth is crucial here. The displacement of magical realism from García Márquez to authors like Laura Esquivel involves a refunctionalization of the role of myth within its aesthetics. In *One Hundred Years of Solitude*, myth does not provide an erasure of historical violence; rather, it offers a way to make sense of it whenever it exceeds the expressive possibilities of discourse. By contrast, in *Like Water for Chocolate*, myth not only mobilizes a system of romantic affects dissociated from historical violence (in this case, the preservation of tradition against the threat of the Mexican Revolution), but also yields the ability to confront the violence of the present by idealizing the remnants of the past (the family saga of a woman's emancipation that permits her female descendant to be an emancipated participant in the neoliberal order). Opposing this very acceptance of the present, Palou writes in the Crack manifesto that the group's novels are not "optimistic," as mentioned above. In a way, Ransmayr is the kind of author that Padilla strives to be: one who uses the powers of mythologization in literature to restore literary writing's capacity for engaging the contemporary. The outlet for this concern is not the ability of literature to exorcize the past in a self-referential fantasy or in the creation of established and commercially reproducible identities and specificities. Rather, it is rendered visible by pushing literary myth in the opposite direction: into a saturation of meaning that allows the reader to experience the horror of history in its atemporal (archetypal, if we consider a Jungian theme) dimension. Padilla, like Ransmayr, writes literature that seeks to capture, in imagination, the cultural experience of destruction and apocalypse underlying modern rationality.

Ransmayr appears in the Crack manifesto as representing a central European literary lineage that illustrates the ways in which Padilla deploys a form of strategic Occidentalism to situate his fiction within the aforementioned literary tasks. Following Franco Moretti's contention of the historical novel as an attempt to incorporate "the internal periphery into the larger unit of the state," Robin McKenzie locates Ransmayr's *The Last World* as an attempt by various novelists to contest the authority of the Roman Empire (a standin for the imperial West's cultural authority) through narrations located in its peripheries.[138] In relating to Ransmayr, Padilla activates legacies of the European model that are present in modernisms not necessarily connected to hegemonic structures of world literature, and which assemble narratives that resist the imperatives of totalization and optimism for the Latin American novel. Ransmayr was the latest representative of an Austrian literary tradition that epitomized, in many quarters of Mexican literature, an alternative genealogy of modern literature. This tradition became central in Mexico in the 1970s, thanks largely to the efforts of Juan García Ponce, who reflected extensively on the work of Robert Musil and Heimito von Doderer.[139] In 1991, novelist and public intellectual José María Pérez Gay published *El imperio perdido* (*The Lost Empire*), a long historical essay on Viennese culture and the end of the Austro-Hungarian Empire, with detailed analyses of the works of Musil, Hermann Broch, Karl Kraus, Joseph Roth, and Elias Cannetti.[140] In his years as a professor at the Universidad de las Américas in Puebla, Pedro Ángel Palou taught a seminar on the topic as well. And in 1998, the UNAM Press published a translation of Italian writer Claudio Magris's book on the Habsburg myth in Austrian literature, expressing the Mexican literary community's interest central European literature and discussing figures like Musil, Franz Werfel, and Stefan Zweig, among others.[141]

In this literature, Padilla locates the source of major stylistic and thematic features of *Amphytrion*:

> El entorno y la ubicación cronológica, acaso también la configuración de los personajes, está muy marcada, como bien sabes, por mis lecturas de la literatura cacania, en particular Zweig, Roth, Perutz, Von Rezzori y Broch (un poco menos Musil).[142]

> The setting and the chronological location, perhaps even the configuration of the characters, is very marked, as you well know, by my readings of Kakanian literature, especially Zweig, Roth, Perutz, Von Rezzori, and Broch (Musil a bit less).

The activation of this canon involves the cultural story behind it: the decline of an empire and the sense of enduring cultural apocalypse that resulted from it. *Amphytrion* is plotted on the idea of supplantation. Appropriating a Greek mythological character in the title, the novel begins when a deployed German soldier, Thadeus Dreyer, and a train attendant, Viktor Kretzschmar, exchange identities during a chess match. As time passes, the original Dreyer languishes in his railroad employment, while Kretzschmar scales the ranks of the German army to become, under Dreyer's name, a Nazi officer. During the war, this supplanted Dreyer is part of "Amphytrion," a project run by Hermann Goering that provides body doubles to high-ranking officials of the Nazi regime. As the war comes to an end, the novel suggests the possibility that the original Dreyer's son, Franz Kretzschmar, supplants Adolf Eichmann in his war crimes trial. I must stress, however, that it is nearly impossible to do justice to the complexity of *Amphytrion*'s plot, which packs numerous interwoven stories and historical implications into a relatively small number of pages. Focusing on the four narrators alone, we have, in addition to Franz Kretzschmar, a character like Aliosha Goliadkin (named in reference to Dostoyevsky's *The Double*), a Russian soldier who killed his twin brother in a duel and becomes a manipulator of the impostor Dreyer; or Richard Schley, a man who also challenged the original Dreyer to a duel and ultimately supplanted him—which adds the twist that Schley knew Dreyer as someone called Jacobo Efrussi. I will not attempt to untangle the novel's labyrinthine plot here, but I will emphasize that the story's concentrated complexity is part of Padilla's aim: to use literary form to counter the idea of literature as something that can somehow provide a plain allegory of history. The aggregate of impostors (related by unreliable narrators who are only partially involved in the conspiracy), and the suggestion that the event that supposedly represents justice (Eichmann's trial) may not have done so, are all directed, like Ransmayr's poetics, at creating a mythology of modernity—one that further confronts us with the depths of evil rather than providing refuge from the horrors of reality.

Given this subject matter, it is unsurprising that scholarly commentary has generally focused on questions of memory and justice. Claudia Macías Rodríguez, for instance, employs the theories of Paul Ricoeur to privilege the tension between memory and forgetting in the novel, as well as the consequences of this tension for the characters' sense of identity and history.[143] Other critics, like Marcie Paul and Ezequiel de Rosso, have focused their readings on the novel's relationship to detective fiction and on the role played by the trope of the secret in its structure.[144] Finally, in a brilliant reading of its politics, Anne Marie Stachura suggests that the novel's artificial mythological substratum "responds to continued attempts to enact justice on a transnational scale, during a time of increased communication between distant individuals due to forces of economic globalization." The result is that "the mythologizing of the Eichmann trial in Padilla's novel subverts not only the foundational myth of the Israeli Nation-State, but also the myth of the fair and equitable functioning of autonomous Nation-States in the age of globalization." Stachura concludes: "*Amphytrion* attempts to use fiction as a means to destroy mythologies of globalization processes from within, by creating an artificial myth, just as the fictional Amphytrion Project attempted to destroy the Third Reich."[145] I generally feel that Stachura provides the best assessment of justice as a question in this book; indeed, this topic is not really my concern here. But I am particularly interested in another element of her reading: her connection of transnational justice to the 1989 juncture as manifested both in the decline of the nation-state (an essential concern in the Crack group's attempt to throw off the shackles of Mexicanness) and the undermining of foundational narratives of what we may call (though Stachura does not) the neoliberal order. In this reading, then, Padilla produces a world literature that is not identifiable with the communicability of neoliberal globalization, but rather serves as a reflection on the impossibility of those connections. This is why the last narrator, a man called Daniel Sanderson, writes a novel rather than a testimonial in 1989: history is as undecipherable to him as it is to the reader.

Padilla's strategic appropriation of the history of Finis Austriae literature acquires significance in this light. In resisting the rising order of neoliberal globalization, including the epigonal magical realism complicit in that order, Padilla builds a literary genealogy for himself that is based on entropy, decadence, and the inability to derive a definitive sense of meaning out of the self or history. In a discussion on Elias Cannetti's *Auto-da-Fé*, a novel that Padilla openly acknowledges as an inspiration for *Amphytrion*, William Collins Donahue argues: "*Auto-da-Fé* breaks modernism's empathetic spell over the reader and questions the political and social implications of a fragmented protagonist by, first of all, placing the notion of a universal, ungendered self into serious doubt." Through this procedure, "Canetti challenges the (often only implicit) consensus that the modernist protagonist is the inexorable end product of a world come unhinged, a victim of the vanishing nineteenth-century certainties." Suggestively for my purposes, Donohue contends that the site of this challenge is identification: "Identification remains for Canetti a problem: both within the fictional world of the novel and at the level of reader and text, identification emerges as a vehicle for approaching and utterly distorting reality."[146] The untraceability of the protagonist's identity in *Amphytrion* constructs an updated version of Canetti's modernism. To paraphrase Donohue, Padilla questions the notion of the literary protagonist as an allegory or a stand-in for a community; in doing so, he questions a narrative technique essential to the complicity between magical realism and neoliberalism. Targeting identification is perhaps even more fundamental to Padilla than to Canetti, because, as a Mexican writer, the procedure allows him to critique not only modernity at large, but also the demands that hegemonic Mexican cultural projects make of the country's authors. By this I do not only mean that he resists national identity per se—an action so patently obvious that it requires little explanation. Rather, Padilla's aesthetic engages with something more fundamental: literature's ability to construct memory. Theodor Dreyer is precisely that: a man who can never be territorialized into a knowable past. Another Kakanian author, Hermann Broch, offers a different way of examining this phenomenon. According to Kathleen Komar, "Broch's history as constructed narrative will follow traces of power and authority as they are inscribed in the lives—and quite often on the very bodies—of his characters."[147] The demonic nature of Dreyer's nonidentity is a suspension of history: the protagonist's uncanny nature constitutes the impossibility of finding the traces of power and authority inscribed in him. Dreyer is a chronotope zero: a subjectivity with no space, time, or allegorical meaning that embodies the impossibility of any kind of testimonial memory. The consequence of this impossibility, as the novel's aesthetics and politics, is that literature ultimately becomes a record of what evades material transmission.

Significantly, in light of these procedures, Padilla does not reflect (as Volpi does) on 1968 and 1994 as central years in Mexican history. Rather, he focuses on 1985, when an earthquake in Mexico City became a catalyst for social organization in the country.[148] Padilla declares that his interest in the earthquake lies specifically in the fact that one cannot derive a clean narrative of a "Mexican democratic transition" from it: indeed, intellectual sectors of the civil society that emerged from 1985 later endorsed the Salinista regime, which was responsible for economic reforms that would unleash the brutal economic crisis of 1994 and install the reign of neoliberal economics in Mexico. Padilla devotes a book to the art made in commemoration of the earthquake, identifying it, due to the event's ambiguous status in Mexican ideologies of democratic transition, with a tension between memory and forgetting that has been decisive in recent Mexican history.[149] Invoking Canetti, Padilla addresses the need for postmemory and responsible forgetfulness in the construction of collectivity:

> No basta con que nos aferremos a un fárrago de testimonios, que, después de todo, favorecen sobre todo la discordancia de los tiempos singulares de la historia; a ellos hay que añadirles y tal vez imponerles los tiempos generalizadores del arte, que instruye al sujeto en la concordancia con las voces del pasado como un tiempo que atañe a todos los hombres.[150]

> It isn't enough for us to cling to a jumble of testimonies that, after all, mostly favor the discordance of singular times in history; we must add to them, perhaps impose on them, the generalizing times of art, instructing the subject in concordance with the voices of the past as a time that concerns all men.

Critiquing the increase of testimonial narratives in the 1980s (led by the increasing centrality of genres such as the *crónica* and the *testimonio* in Latin America), Padilla carves out a role for art in its ability to fashion the past into a *longue durée*, which is crucial for the community:

> El lenguaje del arte redime a la colectividad de la inmediatez del acontecimiento y lo vuelve en verdad communicable, es decir, *común* por encima de las barreras del tiempo y del espacio. Reescrito en una temporalidad nueva que ya no es la de la noticia o la crónica, un tiempo ampliado que privilegia lo subjetivo sobre lo objetivo, el desastre vuelve a ser enunciable, confrontable, digerible. Cuando se han terminado los testigos directos del dolor, el arte permite que las generaciones siguientes puedan también experimentarlo, quizá con mayor realismo o lucidez, pues lo experimentan a su salvo.[151]

> The language of art redeems collectivity from the immediacy of the event and makes it truly expressible, that is, *common*, over the barriers of time and space. Rewritten in a new temporality that no longer belongs to the news or the chronicle, an expanded time that privileges the subjective over the objective, the disaster becomes, again, enunciable, confrontable, digestible. When the hurt's direct witnesses are gone, art allows the next generations to experience it, too, perhaps with greater realism and lucidity, since they experience it safely.

In her book on postmemory, Marianne Hirsch develops a similar point: "Postmemory's connection to the past is thus actually mediated not by recall but by imaginative investment, projection and creation. To grow up with overwhelming inherited memories, to be dominated by narratives that preceded one's birth or one's consciousness, is to risk having one's own life stories displaced, even evacuated, by our ancestors."[152] *Amphytrion*'s deployment of Kakanian literary aesthetics in the contemporary Mexican novel becomes legible through these insights. *Amphytrion* can be read as a fictional treatise on the limitations of the witness (based on the fictional testimonies of four narrators who experienced various decades of European history first-hand and are utterly unable to account for it). It also plots the importance of historical distance as a recourse for the novel: because of his many changes in personality and the fact that the name "Dreyer" is used by many people, any contact with his body is meaningless. In other words, there is no corporal record of history: there is no way to know whether the Dreyer in one time period is the Dreyer in the previous. Only the tools of the fictional and metafictional, then, can overcome testimonial limitations. We could even say that there is a double significance in the fact of a Mexican writer performing these operations. First, he writes the story from a site in which testimonialism is impossible and the history of both world wars is always already postmemorial—there is no claim to witness. Second, following Stachura's reading, Padilla allows for an element of Nazism and memory to be read as world history: the discourses of justice and human rights are situated at the foundation of a contemporary world in a way that exceeds merely European experience. If Volpi's world novels claim the right to map modernity as if Mexico were not a peripheral site within it, Padilla's *Amphytrion* goes even further: it incorporates the universalizing gesture of fiction, devoid of identitarian claims, in renarrating that history beyond its testimonial demands.

From his early works onward, Padilla has deployed a vast archive of Occidentalist culture to construct an eschatological poetics of evil, horror, and apocalyptic images aimed to dislodge, through imagination, the duty of identity and memory. The two novels that accompanied the release of the Crack manifesto, *La catedral de los ahogados* (*The Cathedral of the Drowned*, 1995) and *Si volviesen sus majestades*, are narratives of loneliness and historical futility, constructed as careful narrative architectures.[153] The former tells the story of a man on a deserted island and is structured like the architectural spaces of a cathedral; the latter narrates the misadventures of a seneschal, pointlessly waiting for the monarch's return, in the literary prose of the Spanish Golden Age. His most recent works have expanded these reflections into the role played by animism and fantasy in contemporary life, as in the essay *La vida íntima de los encendedores* ("The Private Lives of Lighters," 2009).[154] In the final couple years of his life, he worked on the role of fear and horror as a catalyst for fiction in another essay, "El legado de los monstruos" ("The Legacy of Monsters," 2013), as well as on a short story collection, *Las fauces del abismo* (*The Mouth of the Abyss*, 2014).[155] In my opinion, however, Padilla's crucial novel, in which his poetics and literary ideas truly speak for themselves, is *La Gruta del Toscano*, to which I will devote the remainder of this section. Padilla would have resisted my focus on his novels, as he considered himself first and foremost a short story writer. Yet his novels are excellent examples of how he engaged with world literature to produce fiction that sought worldly status. Told from the perspective of a Nepalese Sherpa called Pasang Nurung, *La Gruta del Toscano* chronicles a history of explorations of a Himalayan cave—which, as the adventurers gradually discover, contains none other than Dante Alighieri's *Inferno*. The book narrates various expeditions to the cave, as well as the attempts to determine whether certain accounts of these expeditions are accurate.

La Gruta del Toscano is notable because it is founded on a form of strategic Occidentalism that targets the West's epistemological ability to narrate the world in an Orientalist fashion. The novel operates narratively by co-opting stylistic technologies with long histories of operation in the context of Orientalism and cultural colonialism, undermining them through its refusal to engage in the production of any kind of ethnographic knowledge. Its narrative discourse claims a complex legacy of adventure and exploration-based literature, particularly from the British tradition. Padilla describes his sources as follows:

> Se trata desde luego de un homenaje a la literatura que determinó mi vocación, alguna tan mala como Julio Verne y Salgari, y otra definitivamente apreciable como es la literatura pelágica de Conrad y Melville. Desde luego, toda la obra gira en torno a mi obsesión por el infierno y la literatura de Dante, así como al trabajo de Paul Bowles. Es, creo yo, o pretende ser una novela de aventuras, pero sobre todo es una paráfrasis de las crónicas de alpinismo sobre las que me volqué sobre todo después de que conocí la noticia del hallazgo del cadáver de George Mallory en el cuarto escalón del Everest. De cronistas como Baldwin y especialmente Krakauer, aunque también de los relatos de las conquistas y desastres de los ochomiles, sé que obtuve la mayor influencia. Eso, y sin duda, de manera muy explícita *El prisionero de Zenda*, de Anthony Hope, con sus guiños a Kipling (*The Man Who Would Be King*), a Beckett (*Esperando a Godot* y *Fin de partida*, que son también modelos para *Si volviesen sus majestades*), mucho *Beau Geste*, de Wren, y *Las minas del rey Salomón*, de Haggard.[156]

> It is of course a tribute to the literature that defined my vocation, some of it as bad as Jules Verne and Emilio Salgari, and some definitely significant, such as Conrad and Melville's pelagic literature. Of course, the whole work revolves around my obsession with Hell and Dante's literature, as well as Paul Bowles's work. It is, I think, or tries to be, an adventure novel, but more than anything else, it's a paraphrase of the mountaineering chronicles I threw myself into after I heard the news that George Mallory's body had been found on the Fourth

Step of Everest. I know I was especially influenced by chroniclers like Baldwin and especially Krakauer, but also by conquest stories and disasters of the 1800s. That, and certainly, in a very explicit way, Anthony Hope's *The Prisoner of Zenda*, with some winks to Kipling (*The Man Who Would be King*), Beckett (*Waiting for Godot* and *Endgame*, which are also models for *Si volviesen sus majestades*), a lot of Wren's *Beau Geste*, and Haggard's *King Solomon's Mines*.

I will not attempt to discuss the entirety of this canon; indeed, such a task would probably require a book of its own. Rather, I will limit myself to three points that, in my view, successfully encapsulate the significance of *La Gruta del Toscano* in my broader discussion of strategic Occidentalism and world literature. First, Padilla provides a compelling case for how literary canons that clearly call for postcolonial critique operate when they are deterritorialized into a literary discourse devoid of the imperial ambitions and ideologies at work in the original literary texts on which novels like Padilla's are based. While a superficial reading of the book may claim that it reproduces imperial discourse, a more careful approach shows the extent of Padilla's efforts to deactivate it. Aptly locating the book within a history of Orientalism in general, and Latin American exoticism in particular, Rosario Hubert reaches a suggestive conclusion: "In order to criticize exoticism, Padilla removes all references to any national or cultural particularity of the Oriental setting." Hubert also points to the fact that the only place meticulously re-created there is "the fictional European kingdom of Ruritania of Anthony Hope's novels." Hubert concludes by highlighting the Borgesian idea of a "universal geography available to the peripheral writer, for he transcends the global scope of the world as his patrimony and takes on literary settings."[157] However, Hubert's points have far more significant implications. Regarding the critique of exoticism, Padilla's representation of Nepal as a site with no cultural specificity explicitly renounces the core feature of Orientalist narrative technologies: the ability to name the space and identity of the other. Further, Padilla turns the exoticizing gaze back on Europe, to Ruritania—which, as Vesna Goldsworthy discusses, is in itself an imperial fantasy projected by British literature onto the Balkans.[158] *La Gruta del Toscano* performs less a provincialization of Europe, as Dipesh Chakrabarty would call it, than what may be called an Orientalization of the continent's historical legacies. It deploys the stasis necessary for imperial fantasies through a critical construction that assumes it as a literary history, not a political one.

Padilla's reference to Salgari is instructive, because the popular cosmopolitanism at work in Salgari's narratives was not informed by empire or even by travel. Instead, as Cristina Della Coletta describes it, it was a mythology that addressed "the passing of time," representing "a transitional age, still brimming with epic grandeur yet already tarnished and unable to display the ravages of time."[159] This phenomenon is very much in line with Padilla's general interest in literary traditions that narrate the crisis of modernity and the failed constitution of subjectivity. Adventure fiction of the kind invoked in *La Gruta del Toscano* is an ideal mechanism for undermining the colonial scaffolds of Western literature—not only because it is a minor tradition, obviously dated and located in imperial projects (it is hard to think of a writer more committed to such projects than Henry Rider Haggard), but also because adventure fiction has persisted within a canon of European exoticism consumed in peripheral sites like Mexico. Salgari, for instance, is extensively published in Porrúa's famed collection Sepan Cuantos, a series of widely circulated and inexpensive paperbacks used in classrooms across Mexico, while the film adaptations of works like *King Solomon's Mines, The Prisoner of Zenda,* and *Beau Geste* reached sizable audiences both in theaters and via television broadcasts. Another feature of this canon is that it shares a historical location with the sources of *Amphytrion*: Hope published *The Prisoner of Zenda* in 1894, while Salgari's Sandokan series were issued in 1895, chronicling the cultural mood in the last days of the Victorian era and the beginning of Italy's destructive colonial rule in Libya. In playfully appropriating these imaginaries, *La Gruta del Toscano* develops an aesthetics founded on the historical failures of imperial culture, deploying them through the futility of the various expeditions. Tellingly, the book was inspired by one such failure, George Mallory's death and the discovery of his body decades later; indeed, the search for a physical hell is a topic that already points toward imperial hubris.

The second element to emphasize is that *La Gruta del Toscano* not only intersects with the adventure novel's specific historical genre, but also makes implicit claims regarding the history of the novel at large. In an essay on adventure literature entitled "Ulises viudo" ("Ulysses the Widower"), Padilla recognizes that, after the urban journeys of writers like James Joyce and Robert Walser, the romantic notion of travel as embodied in the canon that inspires *La Gruta del Toscano* becomes outdated.[160] Even so, Padilla confronts this genre from the early moments of his writing career onward, particularly in relation to his own trips to Africa. These travels are marked by two notable moments. First, Padilla spent some time in Swaziland in 1987, at a time of political turmoil due to the death of a monarch, the crowning of his heir, and the ripple effect of the crisis and decline of Apartheid in South Africa. In his chronicles, published in a now-defunct cultural supplement and ultimately collected in book form, the main narrative contrasts the idyllic experience of life in a remote land with the constant and overwhelming threat of politics, racial tension, and violence pervading daily life in the country.[161] It is significant that Padilla subtitled the book *Espejismo y utopía en el reino de Swazilandia* (*Mirage and Utopia in the Kingdom of Swaziland*), openly assuming the elements of fantasy, exoticism, and romanticism in his own narrative gaze.

Another relevant experience occurred in 1996, when Padilla went to Tangier to meet an elderly Paul Bowles. Bowles is an essential presence in Padilla's personal canon. As a writer of travel literature, his role was cemented on the fictionalization of local resistance to the framings and paradigms of the imperial romance novels by writers like Haggard.[162] Padilla won a national award with an essay (never published) on Bowles's travels to Mexico. "Ulises viudo," however, patently expresses disappointment with their meeting in Tangier. In his account, he found Bowles insistent on dispelling readers' romantic conception of him and wholly consumed by his personal decline.[163] These two experiences profoundly shaped the young Padilla's perspective: he found a stark contrast between the romanticism of travel as literature and its gritty materiality. From the very start, then, the traveler-narrator of *La Gruta del Toscano* is a skeptic regarding the viability of his own story. Padilla confesses: "Lo que veo de mí en este aparente viajero es sobre todo su incredulidad, su galopante duda, su escepticismo frente a la idea romántica del viaje, una idea que acaricié en mi juventud de lector ávido y pueril aventurero" (What I see of myself in this apparent traveler is, above all, his incredulity, his intense doubt, his skepticism about the romantic idea of the journey, an idea I cherished in my youth as an avid reader and puerile adventurer).[164] Padilla is not activating the canon's romanticism; rather, he harnesses its historical void in order to expose the conflicting enterprises that the genre embodies and that represent a complex history of colonial legacies.

The third element to discuss is the goal of the expeditions chronicled in *La Gruta del Toscano*. The complex politics of racism and knowledge at work in Haggard's imperial romances was associated with the brutal logics of mineral extraction and labor exploitation in the colonies. In Laura Chrisman's analysis, Haggard's fiction responds to this phenomenon by placing the narrative focus on the emergence of British imperial capitalism and the mythologies facilitated by archeological discovery.[165] Yet the imperial romance is in itself a process of worlding that can be linked to two phenomena. First, as Elleke Boehemer has pointed out, imperial romances belonged to forms of literature that were "predicated on the 'worldlng' of both British society and its national literature."[166] They represent an instance in which the writing of "world novels" is very literally predicated on the construction of an archive of domination that would provide the British empire with epistemological tools of control and cultural imaginaries—tools with cultural lives that would extend far beyond the existence of the empire from which they were issued, as attested in the imperial nostalgia fantasies of Merchant Ivory films or the persistence of institutions such as the British Museum.[167] As technology, though, as Aaron Worth argues in a recent book, the novels also served as media sources of imperial communication, and provided a way to argue that the colonized land had "stored imperial histories" of their own.[168] If the adventure novel and the imperial romance are instruments related to resource extraction and the romanticization of enslavement (which could also be said of Salgari, writing during Italy's colonial ventures, or even Bowles, for whom the colonial background can act as a mere backdrop to the

European protagonists' romance), the task of a nonimperial author appropriating this canon of writing qua literature is to dehistoricize it from its ideological connotations in order to spotlight the material mechanisms of its narrative technique.

By constructing his Nepal as devoid of the country's actual cultural identity and specificity, Padilla subverts this archive's ideological premises and turns them onto themselves. He does so by establishing as the objective of the search not some legendary native jewel or new treasures to exploit, but a foundational cultural object of Western culture: Dante's *Inferno*. In Padilla's scholarly work, the devil is a fundamental category of Western culture that serves to illuminate haunting zones of cultural consciousness. Out of his doctoral dissertation, Padilla published a book on the widespread presence of the devil, hell, and diverse Faustian motifs in Cervantes's work.[169] In reaching even farther back to a critical moment of Western culture, Padilla sets the terms on which he performs the narrative technologies of the imperial romance: he employs a series of brigades mostly from Ruritania, a region that exists only in European fiction, who are seeking a text central to European literary modernity. The book launches its premise, then, with an imaginative paradox. When a squadron from the Ruritanian army reaches the cave, a Sherpa named Pasang Nuru takes Captain Reissen-Mileto to the entrance of the cave and proceeds to read him, in German, the verses (inscribed in Sanskrit, which the captain never learned) corresponding to those that Dante claims to have read at the gates of hell in the third canto of the *Inferno*.[170] Emboldened by the possible fame that the discovery could grant him, he copies down the symbols and tries to persuade the Sherpa to interpret them, which the latter is either unable or unwilling to do. The discovery will eventually bring disgrace to the captain: his troops disappear while he explores the cave, leading to suspicions of desertion, although the circumstances of the disappearance are unclear. Two months after discovering the cave, the captain is executed. We learn of this story from two sources: an interview with Pasang Nuru himself, an elderly man who speaks perfect English, conducted by a Western woman named Milena Giddens; and an old veteran from the Ruritanian army, Beda Plotzbach. Both accounts are unreliable, given the speakers' role in the events.

This setup, which unfolds across the novel in various ways, exposes the workings of genres associated with imperial romance and travel. It essentially parodies a variety of tropes: the native curse that affects Westerners seeking their fortune in the colonies, the purported wisdom of the native guide who facilitates the Westerners' access to local knowledge, and the construction of anthropological knowledge (via the interview) toward discerning historical events not properly recorded in the imperial archives. In gradually and persistently estranging his reader from the expectations established by the genre's cultural history, Padilla intervenes in an archive of imaginaries and techniques through which world literature has been constructed, laying bare the epistemological privilege and colonial violence exercised by metropolitan nations. We should also note that a variant of such mechanisms has operated to consecrate magical realism as the privileged mechanism of world fiction in the early neoliberal era. Pasang Nuru, ironically engaging with the ambitions of decades' worth of imperial travelers, plays an analogous role to that of the Latin American writer who is pressured to traffic stereotypes and authenticity to generations of Global Northern readers. In *La Gruta del Toscano*, one finds the most compelling example of the cultural politics underlying many crucial Crack works: a masterful use of cosmopolitanism that lobs the technology of exoticism back at Europe in the way of a retort. By Orientalizing Europe, Latin American writers can be relieved of the expectation to Orientalize themselves.

Pedro Ángel Palou: World Literature as Melancholy

Of all the Crack writers, Pedro Ángel Palou represents the most daunting challenge to critics. By far the most prolific writer in Mexico today, he has published an average of one to two books a year since 1989; at the time of this writing, he has around forty books in print. The challenge is not merely quantitative. Palou is a notably chameleonic fiction writer and his books navigate an astonishing range of registers, from dense high-literary novels to popular historical fiction. His corpus contains books written in poetic styles and in diverse forms of vernacular, biographical works on Mexico's national heroes, and erotic fictions written from the perspective of a highly subjective narrator. All of his fiction is framed by a body of books of essays concerned with the construction of the literary field in Mexico and the role played by literature and culture in designing the country's modern projects. Considering the copiousness of his work and the mainstream venues in which it has appeared (mostly in imprints of transnational publishers like Planeta, Random House, and Alfaguara), it is remarkable that he has been the subject of so few critical studies; many of his most important works have yet to be addressed by scholarly criticism. This scarcity may be due in part to the quantity of his published works and the difficulty of keeping up with them. But if Volpi exemplifies the way in which Crack aesthetics have defined Mexican and Latin American fiction transnationally, and if Padilla illustrates the operations and consequences of the group's aesthetic programs and claims, Palou's oeuvre compellingly demonstrates the diversity of works that Latin American writers may produce once they are liberated from the magical realist imperative. Palou's thematic range, from the most specifically Mexican topics imaginable (the lives of revolutionary heroes like Emiliano Zapata and Pancho Villa) to the most dilettantish cosmopolitan ones (melancholy, evil, subjectivity), follows from the premise that writers need no longer respond to pressures of the literary field—either as producers of the kind of work

that grants large-scale symbolic capital (like the magical realists) or as consecrated heretics whose work circulates among a small group of acolytes (as in
the context of Mexico's cult of the rare writer, discussed in the introduction).

Palou's defiance of these two characterizations is both the key to his success as a writer—he has an established community of readers who buy his
books in respectable numbers—and his failure to garner critical attention, as
it is nearly impossible to locate him squarely within any current in contemporary Mexican fiction. He has yet to benefit from the Crack group's visibility
as far as translation is concerned: only a few of his works are available in
languages other than Spanish, and, notwithstanding even the commercial
appeal of some of his novels, none has been published in an English edition.
A careful study of Palou's work is a still-pending task for literary criticism. In
the rest of this chapter, I will not attempt the daunting endeavor of discussing
Palou's work at large, nor will I dare to study the books that fit the parameters of this study, which would amount to a dozen novels at the very least.
Rather, I will devote my attention to *Paraíso clausurado*, the novel that most
clearly manifests the key features traversing Palou's body of work, and an
unheralded masterpiece that has lacked critical and readerly attention due to
its uneven editorial history and its eclipsing by his other more commercially
successful works.[171]

One could divide Palou's fiction into three general periods—although one
can also find works in each stage that follow the logic at work in one of the
others. Between his first book, published in 1989, and his participation in the
Crack manifesto, Palou wrote a series of novels in which he gradually defined
and refined his style; the most notable is the aforementioned *En la alcoba del
mundo*, on Contemporáneos poet Xavier Villaurrutia. The second period,
which begins with his adhesion to the Crack manifesto and his apocalyptic
novel *Memoria de los días*, is characterized by a series of books in which
he takes up some of the group's themes but pushes them different direc-
tions. For instance, his World War II novel, *Malheridos* (*Injured*, 2003), deals
with the question of evil in a more philosophical fashion; the plot involves
a love triangle and a philologist working on a biography of Ovid (a nod to
Ransmayr).[172] He also explores the topic of love and eroticism more prominently than other Crack writers, producing a series of novellas—such as
Demasiadas vidas (*Too Many Lives*, 2001), *Qliphoth* (2003), and *Casa de la
magnolia* (*The Magnolia House*, 2004)—that questions identities disjointed
by affects.[173] *Paraíso clausurado* belongs to this period. More recently, Palou
has become a writer of erudite bestsellers and historical fictions. One could
say this trend began with *Con la muerte en los puños* (*With Death in His
Fists*, 2003), a novel about a boxer by the name of Baby Cifuentes, written
in a vernacular tone unusual for Crack writers.[174] The book won Mexico's
Villaurrutia Award (the equivalent of the National Book Award), and was
central to Palou's consecration in Mexico. Given that his more cosmopolitan books failed to garner the level of transnational attention afforded to

Padilla, Volpi, and even Urroz, Palou returned to the Mexican market, writing a succession of novels on diverse historical characters, including Emiliano Zapata, Pancho Villa, and Porfirio Díaz.[175] He has also has written cosmopolitan thrillers, including one based on the life of Saint Paul (*El impostor* [*The Impostor*, 2012]), another on a series of murders in the Vatican (*El dinero del diablo* [*The Devil's Money*, 2009]), and a remarkable novel on a Holocaust survivor torn between revenge and survival (*La amante del ghetto* [*The Lover from the Ghetto*, 2013]).[176] In my view, the latter three represent one of the Crack group's most meaningful engagements with the idea of transforming the literary market. Notably, some of Palou's cosmopolitan books from this period have achieved more transnational visibility (particularly *El dinero del diablo*, which was a finalist for a major award in Spain and was translated into French) than his books on Mexican history, which are well circulated within the country (they sell in tens of thousands of copies and frequently appear on bestseller lists) but have lacked distribution beyond it.

The task of framing Palou's work is additionally complicated by the absence of the kind of critical engagements pursued by other Crack writers. His essays tend to focus more on Mexican literature and culture than on his cosmopolitan readings as a critic. It is thus much harder to make claims on Palou's readings than those of the other authors studied here. There is hardly any scholarly criticism available; what exists generally focuses on his Mexico-themed books. Due to his use of intertextuality and humor, Palou has been characterized as a "postmodern" writer, but I disagree with this characterization; indeed, the diversity of his techniques and genres resists it.[177] As my subsequent analysis will show, *Paraíso clausurado*, far from being postmodern, defends the idea of an aesthetic stance against the voiding-out of that experience by postmodern irony. More significantly, Palou's own ideas about literature, due to the wide-ranging nature of his fiction, have varied considerably over time. In a satirical 1994 essay, in which it is hard to discern whether he is being comical or expressing his actual ideas, he proposes a twenty-year ban on historical novels; ten years later, the historical novel would become a central genre in his work.[178] However, a careful reading of Palou's trajectory allows us to identify a consistent literary ethos, one that provides crucial points for the conclusion of this chapter. Volpi offers an excellent example of how Crack aesthetics challenges the transnational paradigm of magical realism, and Padilla's work, as we have seen, keenly illustrates the narrative technologies of world literature as appropriated by Mexican writers. For his part, Palou's work demonstrates the ways in which world literature allows for the reinvention of Mexican fiction at the turn of the century. *Paraíso clausurado* is a clear example of a novel articulating world literature as a matter of form and ethics in order to reframe the possibilities of literary writing in Mexico. Moreover, the invisibility of *Paraíso clausurado* within most Mexican literary criticism illustrates the importance of material structures of circulation in the consecration of world novels written in peripheral sites.

Paraíso clausurado is a scholarly novel that seeks to exorcise the twentieth century's literary legacies in order to pave the way for twenty-first-century literature. It tells the story of the last years in the life of a poet, Juan Gavito, from the perspective of his disciple, Eladio Villagrá. The novel is divided into four sections, labeled "books," constructing its plot in dialogue with Robert Burton's *Anatomy of Melancholy* by treating Gavito's life and ideas as a fictional treatise on his mental and spiritual illness. *Paraíso clausurado* is remarkably multitonal, and its different sections and chapters move across various different registers. There are moments of costumbrist comedy, long intellectual and affectionate letters between master and disciple, lyrical interludes on moments in the cultural history of melancholy, and even poems written in Gavito's voice. In many ways, the novel grows out of Palou's *En la alcoba de un mundo*, which also narrated the life of Xavier Villaurrutia as an aggregate of texts in multiple registers. In this novel, Villarrutia is a historical figure located within a clear genealogy in Mexican literature—a cosmopolitanism that resists, as the Contemporáneos did, the imperatives of nationalism. Palou writes the novel, as well as some of his most significant works of literary criticism, to identify himself as an heir of that tradition. *Paraíso clausurado* is a novel not of foundation, but of loss. Gavito embodies a notion of literature (modernist in spirit) that is no longer possible in the contemporary era—his disciple Eladio's temporality. Thus, the novel not only chronicles Gavito's descent into melancholy; it also articulates a melancholic stance toward literature. This stance is firmly grounded against the perception, expressed in the generational distance between both characters, of aesthetic experience as impossible in the neoliberal era.

To properly engage with *Paraíso clausurado*, we must consider its unfortunate publishing trajectory and its relationship to Palou's ideas on the Crack group. The novel's first edition was released as part of the batch of Crack books published by Muchnik, an independent, Barcelona-based press that shared Anagrama and Tusquets's cosmopolitan outlook. Besides *Paraíso clausurado*, Muchnik also published an edition of *Tres bosquejos del mal* and of Vicente Herrasti's *Diorama*—a clear attempt to capitalize on the enormous success attained by both Padilla and Volpi in the preceding months.[179] The decision to publish with a press like Muchnik reflected the fact that these three books lacked the broad appeal of *Klingsor* and *Amphytrion*; a high-literary press with a niche market and a carefully curated catalog seemed like a better fit. This decision ultimately damaged *Paraíso clausurado*'s search for an audience. Unlike the two other Crack books published by Muchnik, this one was not published beforehand as a Mexican edition, and Muchnik lacked the distribution necessary for the book to reach stores in Palou's home country. Thus, *Paraíso clausurado* drowned among Palou's other books, published mostly in Mexico, and became nearly impossible to find. A new edition didn't appear until 2016, when Tusquets reprinted it as part of their recent aim to republish Palou's backlist.[180] This editorial story yields two important points. First, like other examples in my analysis but in its own way, it shows how crucial it is for a novel to have material forms of transmission that will distribute it at local, national, and transnational levels. As the publisher of *Paraíso clausurado*, Muchnik failed either in preventing the book from finding a readership or in preserving it sufficiently over time so that it could acquire one, as Anagrama did for Sergio Pitol and Sandro Cohen provided at Joaquín Mortiz and Nueva Imagen in the Crack movement's early days. That one of the most significant works of a well-known author is so widely unknown truly proves how iconicity in national and world literary circuits is as much a question of aesthetics as of the book trade's material conditions. The second point is that this experience undoubtedly exemplifies Palou's (and the Crack group's) stance on not shunning commercial distribution, even when seeking to write literature that does not bend over backward to accommodate the publishing market. *Paraíso clausurado*'s intellectual investment and literary complexity does not correspond to the meager distribution it was afforded, and many other Crack novels (included some of Palou's own books) attained much wider circulation.

The book's epigraphs offer a useful guide to the nature of *Paraíso clausurado*'s protagonist, Gavito. Both point to the paralyzing nature of literary genius, a crucial image of melancholy as presented in the novel. The first epigraph comes from the poem "Astringency," published in Ted Hughes's 1998 collection *Birthday Letters,* which he famously dedicated to Sylvia Plath. The excerpt opens Palou's novel with an image of the limits of genius: "The sole metaphor that ever escaped you / In easy speech, in my company."[181] The second is from Eugenio Montale's poem "Genius," in which the Italian poet reflects on the immobilization imposed by the creative mechanism: "Regrettably genius doesn't speak / through its own mouth. / Genius leaves a few traces of footprints / like a hare in the snow. / It's the nature of genius that, when it stops / moving, every mechanism is stricken / with paralysis."[182] The poem is included in one of his late collections, *Satura*. I find the presence of this particular work by Montale particularly significant as part of the novel's setup. First, it signals to a fundamental element that Palou absorbed from the Crack group; namely, the idea of subjectivity that can never fully achieve closure. In her study of *Satura*, Rebecca West contends that Montale "subtly emphasizes the fact that by its very nature poetry is thoroughly imbued with its own estrangement from the reality of life and from the language of quotidian exchange."[183] *Paraíso clausurado*'s architecture narrativizes an analogous ethos through the abovementioned tonal range. The novel articulates a palpable contrast between Eladio's conversational voice (which expresses the quotidian elements of the novel) and Gavito's written work (present throughout the book in letters, fragments of a novel, and poetry, among other texts). The estrangement between both voices marks the distance between intellectual and material life in the neoliberal era, particularly in reference to the absurdity of academia in the early stages of the precarization of the humanities; it also conveys the disconnect between Gavito's genius and a literary world unable to identify it. Eladio's first description of Gavito stands out due to its utter triviality:

> Era un poeta importante—autor de dos libros saludados con una-
> nimidad por la crítica como imprescindibles dentro de la literatura
> mexicana—, y algunos compañeros del grupo Hypnos venían aún
> a visitarlo en jornadas de alcohol y lecturas de manuscritos que se
> prolongaban por varios días.[184]

> He was an important poet—the author of two books that critics
> unanimously declared indispensable within Mexican literature—and
> some of his peers in the Hypnos group came to visit him for sessions
> of alcohol and manuscript-readings that went on for many days.

If anything, the novel undermines this empty, blurb-like description of Eladio's first encounter with Gavito by enacting, at the core of its narrative form, the estrangement that Gavito's genius evokes in Eladio's more grounded and quotidian subjectivity. Through the language of melancholy, Gavito and Eladio's relationship suggests (especially in the figure of Gavito) the existence of a kind of transcendental knowledge whose accessibility is receding along the shores of the contemporary. As Daniel Sada said in an astute review of the book, "Lo emocional—la denodada búsqueda del amor—encuentra una empatía sugestiva con los avatares del conocimiento" (The emotional—the unflagging search for love—finds a suggestive empathy in the avatars of knowledge).[185] In the tension between Eladio's earthly presence and Gavito's saturnine temperament, we readers catch glimpses of the intersection between knowledge and emotion, but never fully or with any closure. Palou constantly points to the idea that the tradition deployed in the novel is always already lost to the present-day reader.

Paraíso clausurado is the story of Gavito's failure to write his magnum opus, a novel titled *El Grande Theatro de la Melancholia*. Palou enacts Cyril Connoly's dictum regarding the imperative to write only masterpieces. Connolly is a constant presence in Palou's poetics: the epigraph to *En la alcoba de un mundo* comes from *The Unquiet Grave*, and in "Pequeño diccionario del Crack" (his contribution to *Crack: Instrucciones de uso*), he cites Connolly in defining the novel as "la búsqueda de la obra perfecta" (the search for the perfect work).[186] Palou's crucial decision in the novel's structure is that we can actually read Gavito's writing and feel the tension between the high-literary timbre of his prose and his own inability to deliver a total novel that would fully capture the nature of literature as he conceives it. Juxtaposing Gavito's texts with Eladio's narrative voice, Palou illustrates the novel's fundamental concern through the contrast between Gavito's grand literary spirit and his disciple's inability to entirely understand him. *Paraíso clausurado*, melancholic in structure, enacts a double failure: Gavito's inability to live up to Connolly's injunction, and Gavito's incapacity to create a masterpiece on melancholy, resigning himself instead to narrating his failed attempt to write one. In dialogue with the Crack group's own attempt to recover the total novel as an instrument to restore literature's power vis-à-vis the early neoliberalization of the literary market, *Paraíso clausurado* is a complex meditation on the loss of the ability to achieve such a revival in the current era.

Hence this crucial fact: Gavito's creative endeavor is related to his attempt to reclaim what Edward W. Said calls a "late style." Said offers a compelling description: "There is therefore an inherent tension in late style that abjures mere aging and that insists on the increasing sense of apartness and exile and anachronism, which late style expresses and, more important, uses to formally sustain itself."[187] Gavito, however, embodies not the affirmative gesture at work in Said's description, but the failure to harness a late style. Even so, it is significant that Gavito can be properly defined by the terms Said presents: "apartness," "exile," "anachronism." Gavito's gradual isolation from the world, his exile from the contemporary, and the anachronism of his commitment to literature, are the terms that make his late style not the basis of a literature to come, but the signal of an irreversible loss—one symbolized by the fact that his novel only exists in isolated fragments. West's reading of Montale offers further guidance in this respect. She argues that Montale's voice in *Satura* is not "evidence of a renewed vitality, a surge of strong, youthful inspiration, but . . . instead the dilapidated, worn-out remains of a poet whose Muse is dressed in 'scarecrow's rags' . . . and who will time and time again use the past-remote tense in referring to himself." West continues with a crucial point: "This is self-deflation carried to its most extreme limits; yet the programmatic humiliation is directed not only at the poet himself but more importantly at poetry in its present context." Thus, Montale's collection denotes an argument on the status of the relationship between poetry and contemporaneity: "contemporary poetry as necessarily debased, given the fundamentally illuminated reality from which it emerges."[188] Palou's complex literary archive seeks to formulate a narrative version of this reflection. The epigraphs come from two authors who not only illustrate Said's notion of late style (which I am using extemporaneously, since Palou's book precedes it), but who also did so in a deflating rather than an affirming way. Within this paradigm, the figure of Hughes—cited from a late collection that is profoundly haunted both by his status as a poet and by Plath's ghost—is incorporated into Gavito, whose loss is also related to a love story.

Through both his framing of the novel and its encyclopedic range of literary references, Palou puts forth a rare but deeply significant version of the world novel. His book is not an attempt to "novelize the global" in Siskind's sense, as Volpi does, or to harness and co-opt a worldly style like Padilla. Rather, the worldly nature of *Paraíso clausurado* exists in the performance of world literature as affect, mapping a literary subjectivity in utter friction with the contemporary. Melancholy in *Paraíso clausurado* is present not only as writerly failure, but also as textual genealogy. Jonathan Boulter has studied this subject with admirable insightfulness in contemporary fiction (applying it to authors like Paul Auster and José Saramago). Boulter identifies a trend in the contemporary novel—to which, in my view, *Paraíso clausurado* also belongs—regarding the relationship between melancholy and the archive. He describes novels that "produce readings that must become records, traces, archives of a kind of (melancholy) failure to fully comprehend the original archive." In a Derridean key, Boulter draws a telling conclusion: "Perhaps, finally, any reading of the archive can only ever be a monument, a document, of the archive's melancholy betrayal."[189] Boulter references this idea with respect to the reader, whose melancholy failure in *Paraíso clausurado* is fictionalized through Eladio. Gavito functions as the last entry in an archive about melancholy itself (his novel would be a grand *summa melancholica*, the repository of the entire Western tradition on melancholy), and Eladio, along with the reader, stands in the position from which that archive is no longer legible.

The topic of melancholy had been present in the Crack novels since the early days of the movement. Melancholy appears as a concern in essentially all of Palou's novels between 1991 and 2006, and Volpi's *El temperamento melancólico* is both a complex novelistic reflection on the subject and another tale of creative genius facing the formidable task of late style. The protagonist of *El temperamento melancólico*, Carl Gustav Gruber, channels the spirit of German filmmakers like Werner Herzog in his obsessive quest for a film that constitutes an eschatology in itself. The novel is basically founded on pictorial traditions of melancholia, particularly the one developed by Raymond Klibansky, Erwin Panofsky, and Fritz Saxl.[190] However, Palou's approach takes a more distant perspective; here the work of art is not the culmination of a cultural crescendo, but a ghost that preoccupies the whole novel. In this way Palou enacts a tradition rooted in Robert Burton's grand treatise *The Anatomy of Melancholy*, which is the origin of the archive on which *Paraíso clausurado* is grounded.[191] As Stephanie Shirilan argues, "Burton's cento transforms melancholy from a disease, as it is represented in classical and neoteric sources, into a kind of spiritual privilege that draws on the impressionability of the melancholic imagination."[192]

In Palou's case, the "world" of his world novel is an imagined map of emotions gathered through archeological and cartographical work in the symbolic terrains of Western tradition. The novel has two interludes (one focused on Fernando Pessoa and the other re-creating the story of Andromache) that function as sites in which the reader can experience Palou's strategic Occidentalism as a cartography and archeology of melancholy and loss. As part of Gavito's failed novel, the interludes operate as locators of the emotional and aesthetic archive. The Pessoa section, for instance, deploys the Portuguese concept of *saudade*, an untranslatable term derived from the same paradigm of melancholy.[193] As Kyra Giorgi studies at length, *saudade* is a sense of mourning or loss associated with Portugal's marginal position on the map of European culture, triggered in part by its imperial losses and historical development.[194] Without delving too deeply into this point, Palou's revival of this emotion—as articulated in Pessoa's multiple selves and in the death of poet Mario de Sá Carneiro—does not yield the political implications described by Giorgi, but it does raise the peripherality of the emotion's historical location (other scenes in the book take place in Brazil, and we are even told that Gavito is friends with Paulo Leminsky, a real-life Brazilian poet).[195] Palou presents melancholy and other paradigmatic emotions not as ahistorical, but instead as painfully historical. From Burton onward, melancholy is a culturally located trope with which the peripheral writer will always have an awkward and problematic relationship. However, Palou does not elaborate on the identitarian nature of this question—a stance that would be anathema within Crack aesthetics and his own. Rather, it becomes an aggregate of cultural exile that is embedded into the withdrawn subjectivity of melancholy itself. Gavito's subjectivity is misplaced not because he is Mexican, but because he is part of a Western tradition in which estrangement is the price to pay for spiritual privilege. When the privilege is lost, as is the case in Gavito's last days, an ephemeral sense of belonging is not ultimately restored.

Thus, the last section of the novel, the fourth "book" of the melancholy treatise, is called "Apokatástasis," a Greek word that means restoration to an original position. Written mostly in Gavito's voice, it closes the novel's cycle by liberating Gavito from the weight of history so that he may confront his own loss. By locating itself at the end of the archive inaugurated by Burton, *Paraíso clausurado* (the title expresses foreclosure, cancellation) novelizes the exhaustion of the melancholic imagination's spiritual privilege. Or, to be more precise, as a novel written in Mexico, claiming this tradition through an act of strategic Occidentalism, it imagines the exhaustion of the Western tradition to which it seeks to belong. This is why the book's final scene is an enactment of original loss. In a dream, Gavito remembers the first time he glanced at the love of his youth, Alicia Tosso, whom he has failed to find again. In the dream, he touches Alicia until everything turns black and he wakes up. The last line summarizes the different losses that structure the book: "Ignoro si podré volver a verla" (I do not know if I will be able to see her again).[196] The sentence is not only about Alicia: it also alludes to the spiritual privilege at work in Gavito's temperament, the final dissolution of a memory that was always already feeble. Eloy Urroz points out that Gavito does not commit suicide because the destructive nature of melancholy seeks to prolong itself in time.[197] I would say that the novel's ethos grows clear in this decision: by assuming the loss of aesthetic experience and spiritual privilege, Gavito can return to his origins, come to terms with his loss. Palou's erudite book is an assertion of world literature not as emancipation, but as burden—a burden that goes unexorcised. The novel trades its weight for the lightness of loss, echoing the principles of Italo Calvino as invoked by Palou invoked in the Crack manifesto. Gavito does not finish his book, but he does accept his affective origins. The literary work is a casualty of the self.

This ending is the final step in Gavito's trajectory, which deals with loss by unfolding himself across texts, times, realities, and fictions. Like Padilla's Dreyer or other Crack characters, Gavito unfurls himself into diverse subjectivities (including that of a heteronym called "Gregor Brüchner") and the diverse narrative voices appearing in the excerpts from his novel, which are presented to us as interludes to the main narration. Eladio asserts that Brüchner provided a way for Gavito to "dominate his demon." As Gavito describes him, Brüchner was a fictional German poet, an emigrant who stopped writing. This voice allows Gavito to channel his failure away from his own subjectivity. It is crucial that Brüchner is German; this fact presumes a belonging, unmediated by the unevenness of world literature, to the tradition of melancholy. That Gavito, in writing his novel on melancholy, requires the erasure of his personal historicity and the creation of a fictional character whose makebelieve historicity is more meaningfully attached, grounds Palou's novel in the dilemma that has long occupied Mexican strategic Occidentalism: belonging to tradition. Pitol resolved this quandary through translation: the construction of a world literary framework that grants legibility to his own position within it. Padilla solves it through style: the ironic and masterful performance of traditions that would otherwise be alien. Palou's narrative solution is a sense of loss constructed in the tension between two poles: the intuition of the sublime that exists in the archive itself, and that archive's fundamental incompleteness and unknowability. Gavito's failure is a failure of the lines of cosmopolitanism inaugurated by Villaurrutia, his precedent in Palou's narrative corpus. It is not surprising that Palou would eventually return to writing about Mexico. The characters in his historical novels are the work of a writer who goes back to that country with an acute awareness of loss. And the loss is not a defeat: it is a politics of representation.

Chapter 3

✦

The Idea of the Mexican Woman Writer

Gender, Worldliness, and Editorial Neoliberalization

Together, the important changes in women's roles within the literary field, the irruption of major women writers in the publishing realm, the release of various landmark works by women, and the emergence of literary criticism on the phenomenon in both Mexico and the United States constitute one of the most significant event constellations in Mexican literature of the early neoliberal era. This *Boom femenino*, as it was denominated in the title of a watershed critical collection, encompasses the group of women writers, born mostly in the 1950s and 1960s, who managed to challenge the prevailing gender dynamics in the Mexican literary publishing world.[1] Yet the simultaneous rise of various significant women writers in the Mexican editorial landscape of the late 1980s and the 1990s—from bestselling novelists like Laura Esquivel and Ángeles Mastretta to experimental authors like Ana Clavel and Cristina Rivera Garza—raises important questions about the very idea of the "Mexican woman writer." In the context of my discussion in previous chapters, it is relevant to note that the *Boom femenino* roughly coincides with the process of editorial neoliberalization against which the Crack group pitted itself. Indeed, Laura Esquivel's success was among the targets of the Crack movement's strategic Occidentalism, conflating *Como agua para chocolate*'s commercial appeal with magical realism and nationalism, and the Crack writers ultimately held up her work as a representative of the "bad literature" they were trying to combat. Equally undeniable, however, is the fact that the Crack group comprised only male writers and that there is a gendered component to their performance. For instance, the "literary density" defended by the Crack writers can sometimes insinuate a dismissal of genres favored by women writers and readers—such as romance, the genre practiced by Esquivel. Similarly, their attempt to join the new editorial landscape in the neoliberal era, which was defined by transnational corporate publishing, implicitly or explicitly set them against the reality that women writers commanded an important role in the formation of that paradigm.

In this chapter, I will discuss how the idea of strategic Occidentalism can help us understand the literary practices with which some women writers navigated this landscape. The three case studies I propose in this chapter—Carmen Boullosa, Ana García Bergua, and Cristina Rivera Garza—appeal to alternative cultural archives and ambiguous forms of resistance to imperatives of the literary market in problematizing their own status as woman writers in the literary landscape of the 1990s and 2000s. To illustrate this point, I argue that the idea of the "Mexican woman writer" is a position within the Mexican literary field that, rather than defining individual female writers in an all-encompassing way, becomes a transcendental signifier in relation to which individual authors operate in tension. In this claim, I follow Nuala Finnegan's perceptive understanding of the critical traditions used to interpret Mexican women writers. As Finnegan points out, "There is a tension between the production of a woman-centered fiction in which women's concerns are foregrounded and a hostility toward gendered readings of texts."[2] I would add that the notion of the Mexican woman writer is not a self-evident category, but an institutional construction that locates literature written by women at precise coordinates of publication, circulation, marketing, and readership. Thus, what the idea of strategic Occidentalism allows us to perform is not the type of gendered readings described by Finnegan (although reading is always already gendered); instead, it permits us to present interpretations that illustrate the strategies through which women writers position themselves in the neoliberal editorial market—beyond the strategies that relate directly to gender. In this regard, the present chapter engages in dialogue with recent scholarly work on Mexican women writers that addresses their public personas and underlying gendered performances, as analyzed by Emily Hind, and the textual and intellectual strategies of dissidence that counter structural sexism, as studied by Oswaldo Estrada.[3]

What this book adds to the discussion in deploying the concept of strategic Occidentalism is that, insofar as individual women authors exist in tension with the institutional positionality implicit in the idea of the "woman writer," we must also pay attention to strategies of reading and writing that are not explicitly gendered—strategies that, in turn, are crucial to an understanding of how female novelists (the case in focus here) problematize the imperative of writing according to specific parameters. Just as Crack writers sought to combat market-constructed ideas of the Latin American writer and the obligation to write magical realist texts, authors like Boullosa, García Bergua, and Rivera Garza develop a literary praxis in which the accrual of cultural and symbolic capital is concerned not only with masculine domination, but also with the different strategies deployed by women writers that, over time, become structures of cultural power in themselves. As Pierre Bourdieu has noted in the context of social practices that sustain masculine domination: "Whatever their position in the social space, women have in common the fact that they are *separated from men by a negative symbolic coefficient* which . . . negatively affects everything that they are and do, and which is the source of a systematic set of homologous differences."[4] Yet, Bourdieu continues, "despite the specific experiences which bring them together . . . women remain *separated from each other* by economic and cultural differences which affect, among other things, their objective and subjective ways of undergoing and suffering masculine domination."[5] When translated to the Mexican literary field, this notion entails that one should focus not only on the ways in which women writers position themselves given the "negative symbolic coefficient" that affects their whole praxis, but also on the "differences" in their objective and subjective relations to cultural power. On the one hand, the *Boom femenino* created forms of legitimation of the woman writer within the field of cultural production; on the other, it also yielded diverse aesthetics and cultural practices that, inevitably, led to different ways of accruing cultural capital. Authors like those studied in this chapter must position themselves not so much in relation to masculine domination at large as in relation to an idea of the "woman writer" that was producing cultural hegemonies within this category for the first time in Mexican literary history. Their strategic Occidentalism and their different engagements with the idea of the woman writer go hand in hand.

Although, given the purposes of this book, I cannot embark here on a full-fledged history of the idea of the Mexican woman writer prior to the neoliberal era, I will mention several aspects of its development in the twentieth century as a necessary prelude to the analysis that follows. Throughout the twentieth century, women writers were essentially part of a canon of rare, underground writers: they either occupied marginalized positions during their entire careers or would reach notoriety with a specific work or period—only to see critical attention wither over time. As Sarah E. L. Bowskill shows in her excellent book on the subject, the construction of literary value in Mexico is marked by a fundamental gender disparity. This disparity has existed throughout history, to the point that one can see how reviewers and critics valued male-authored books as key to the formation of national literature, while books written by women at the very same time failed to acquire the same status, even in appealing to analogous historical and social processes.[6] Consequently, women writers who directly participated in the literary figuration of processes like the Mexican Revolution failed to garner attention; it would often take decades for their rightful place in literary history to be recognized. Here we could compare the way in which representations of the Mexican Revolution by writers like Nellie Campobello or Elena Garro lack the symbolic capital enjoyed by works of authors like Mariano Azuela or Carlos Fuentes. A more significant phenomenon for my purposes in this chapter is the long-standing tradition of cosmopolitan Mexican women writers whose literature operated outside the confines of national literature and appealed to genres and topics beyond the mainstream. One could highlight the fantastical literature of writers Guadalupe Dueñas and Ámparo Dávila (the latter is a key referent for Cristina Rivera Garza), who were precursors to trends that sought Mexican narratives in resistance to nationalist literature and who have spent decades in critical oblivion; or Inés Arredondo, who wrote short stories with a worldly bent that failed to attain the same level of visibility as contemporaries such as Salvador Elizondo and Juan García Ponce. The historical significance of the *Boom femenino* lies in the fact that, regardless of the concrete aesthetics pursued by the writers identified with this phenomenon, it allowed women writers to reach unprecedented levels of readerly and critical attention. Moreover, and unlike their predecessors, many writers in the *Boom femenino* (from Esquivel and Mastretta to the ones I discuss in this chapter) managed to maintain consistent literary careers and presences as public intellectuals in ways that previous generations were denied.

Not coincidentally, at the very same time as this boom was taking place, scholars both in Mexico and the United States were producing landmark works in the study of literature written by women. The formation in 1983 of the Programa Interdisciplinario para la Mujer (PIEM) at the Colegio de México, and of the Programa Universitario de Estudios de Género (PUEG) in UNAM in 1993, provided institutional spaces for the development of literary criticism focused on women writers. More importantly, the Taller de Teoría y Crítica Literaria Diana Morán, formed in 1984 out of the PIEM, still comprises a notable group of Mexican women critics and scholars who have produced many books devoted to women writers.[7] In English-language criticism, a new line of inquiry was opened in the early 1990s thanks to a flurry of works exploring the representation of women in Mexican literature. This increased activity not only enabled questions of gender in literature to be spotlighted; it also foregrounded women writers who were eclipsed by masculine domination in the twentieth century. Such studies include Jean Franco's *Plotting Women*, Claudia Schaefer's *Textured Lives*, Debra Castillo's *Easy Women*, and María Elena de Valdés's *The Shattered Mirror*.[8] The rising visibility of women writers at the time created new openings for scholars to write about them and to construct institutional and editorial spaces devoted to gender studies in literary criticism. Most approaches generally focused on two pursuits: the revival and assessment of women writers who had been forgotten by or marginalized in the canon (a task that entailed both publishing the writers' work and finding theoretical coordinates to read them), and the debate on whether literature written by women was characterized by specific traits, following the theorization of *écriture feminine* by Hélène Cixous and other poststructuralist thinkers.[9] Yet in using contemporary critical ideas to assess women writers from the 1990s, new approaches become necessary in order to expand and complement this pioneering analysis. Authors from the *Boom femenino* have developed individual trajectories, and critics and scholars have left us with a large and complex group of revitalized women writers and scholarship discussing those writers. Thus, this chapter sets out not to assert women writers as an end in itself, but to conduct a critical reading of how the concept of the "woman writer" was constructed in editorial and academic institutions—and how specific authors navigated this construction.

Most if not all scholarship on the *Boom feminino* ignores the fact that, far from being a phenomenon limited to Mexico and Latin America, it actually responded to global trends in world literature that placed great value on fiction written by women and on the market of women readers. Critics in the *Boom femenino* collection do recognize the important market phenomenon underlying the rise of women writers. Bowskill, for instance, follows Ángel Rama's study on the Latin American Boom to show that Mastretta benefited from similar phenomena as Boom writers (and as women writers in Latin America such as Isabel Allende): national and international awards, publishers with a strong presence in Latin America and Spain, and so on.[10] Bowskill concludes by arguing that publishing houses and marketing campaigns were essential in creating the *Boom femenino*, as represented by Mastretta and Esquivel. However, she also notes that unlike in the original Boom, critical endorsement played a lesser role here, given that "there is an on-going three way battle between the critical establishment, publishing houses and readers for the role of the privileged reader who has the authority to consecrate the text."[11] If we were reading this statement in a Bourdieusian key, we would point out that the *Boom femenino* was made possible in part because the "economy of symbolic goods," which allows literature to create value autonomously from the market, was interrupted as publishing houses began to have more power than the critical establishment in granting symbolic capital.[12] Practically speaking, this means that women writers in Mexico and elsewhere were able to overcome both the masculine domination embedded in what Bowskill calls the "critical establishment" and the stigma by which genres with women at the forefront, such as romances and fiction, were systematically excluded from the canon. It is no accident, for instance, that Isabel Allende and Laura Esquivel's rise occurred just as some female scholars, most notably Janice Radway and Tania Modleski, were revaluing the romance genre against the current of prejudice.[13] For my purposes, the point is that the neoliberalization of publishing was essential for women writers' ability to enter both Latin American and world literature in significant numbers—and to achieve success, circulation, and the symbolic and cultural capital they entail. As we saw in chapter 2, such breakthroughs have been met with resistance. The Crack writers, for instance, portrayed themselves as opposing the rise of market literature and the breakdown of the economy of symbolic goods. But, as male writers, they were partly castigating the very genres that allowed women to occupy a place in world literary circuits, such as romance.

Market-related issues must be expanded to the world scale because Mastretta and Esquivel, much like Isabel Allende before them, belong to an international boom of women writers in the world literary arena. As Debra Castillo recounts, various women have become staples of global gender studies classes and world literary contexts, including Rigoberta Menchú, Malalai Joya, Ayaan Hirshi Alí, Virginia Woolf, Leslie Marmon Silko, and Anna Akhmatova. Castillo points out that while some of these women are "associated with high art," others write testimonials and memoirs rather than "literature" in the traditional sense. Castillo concludes by noting that the last three women on the list are the only ones who appear in all major canonical anthologies of world literature (Norton, Bedford, and Longman).[14] In reviewing Castillo's rich analysis, it is worth highlighting two dynamics at work: one in which women writers enter literary canons gradually but not in adequate numbers, and another in which women's writings participate in the very expansion of the concept of literature—in this case foregrounding testimonials and memoirs, just as other writers revalidate romance. Castillo's analysis focuses on academic constructions of world literature, but we must remember that the 1980s and early 1990s were marked by a global trend of women-authored bestsellers, providing Esquivel and others with a readerly context. These novels were generally marked by second-generation magical realism, the popularity of family sagas, the rise of so-called "ethnic" fiction, and the aforementioned popularization of the romance. Limiting myself to works that had a significant editorial presence in Mexico at the time, novels like Marguerite Duras's *The Lover* (1984), Amy Tan's *The Joy Luck Club* (1989), and Kenizé Mourad's *Regards from the Dead Princess* (1987) were all part of the same sphere as Esquivel's *Como agua para chocolate*, although these books enjoyed a literary prestige in Mexico that Esquivel was denied (for instance, both Duras and Mourad were published by Tusquets).[15] The homologies between these texts, both within their national literatures (where commercialization opened up a demand for women and/or minority authors in their respective countries) and in world literary circuits (where they all served a demand for historical sagas and women-centered stories that corresponded to the global reading class at the time), locate them within the realm of various critical approaches to world literature—including Graham Huggan's contention that women-authored and ethnic fiction participate in the larger market for the "postcolonial exotic" and Rebecca Walkowitz's identification of world novels that are "born translated," given their awareness of global circulation and readership.[16]

In light of this panorama, we should note that the role of literature written by women in contemporary world literature is conspicuously absent in canonical discussions of the term: neither Moretti nor Casanova nor Damrosch nor the various books published by Routledge address it in any significant way—nor even recent interventions by Beecroft, Walkowitz, Mufti, or Cheah. What is undeniable is that contemporary world literature is constructed in part through the development of what Shu-Mei Shih calls "technologies of recognition": that is, "mechanisms in the discursive (un)conscious—with bearings on social and cultural (mis)understandings—that produce 'the West' as the agent of recognition and 'the rest' as the object of recognition, in representation."[17] We could indeed stress that many of the literary mechanisms promoted by technologies of recognition (academia and the market), as recognized by Shih ("the time lag of allegory," "the exceptional particular," and others), very much apply to fiction written by women. My point is that, insofar as the market emerged as a mechanism for recognizing minority discourse in literature in the 1980s, it is impossible to read women writers without considering their complex position vis-à-vis the paradoxical role of "feminine writing," both as a marginalized set of positions attaining recognition in the canon at the time and as a commodity that held concrete economic value in the marketplace of cultural goods. It is important to note that being promoted by corporate publishers and the market carries no value in itself; there is no necessary relationship between a book's quality or critical importance and the material aspects of its publication. We must understand, rather, that attributing symbolic value to literature produced by the corporate-oriented market means "position-taking" in Bourdieu's sense, in which individual writers seek to proactively manage their positions in relation to structures of power and value within the literary field.[18] The Crack writers did so when they defined themselves in opposition to the structures of world literature which favored authors like Esquivel and which sought from Latin American writers the type of magical realism and family sagas that had been popularized by García Márquez. In discussing women writers like the three I will study below, then, we must remember that they are obligated to establish position-takings not only regarding the expectations imposed on Latin American writers, but also regarding the expectations associated with the role of women writers in world literature. While we should not negate the importance of the romance genre as a cultural product, we must also recognize that women writers are frequently pigeonholed into genres and themes commodified by the market, thus privileging formulaic representations of women's stories that women writers often seek to problematize, confront, or even sidestep in their own work.

In an essay on Ana García Bergua for the *Boom femenino* collection, Niamh Thornton shows how problematic it was for writers not writing in the romance genre to follow the success of Esquivel and Mastretta. In an interview with Thornton, García Bergua calls *Como agua para chocolate* "a bad novel, that sort of clichéd Magical Realism vein."[19] Indeed, as Thornton demonstrates in her analysis—based not on the books I will discuss below, but on her LGBTQ-themed novel *Púrpura* (*Purple*, 1999)—the *Boom femenino* may have helped enable greater access to publication by women writers in general, but it also created struggles for authors like García Bergua, whose work does not follow the norms established by Esquivel or Mastretta's successful novels.[20] *Púrpura* is a novel that "ignores the long tradition in the melodrama of the female or gay character who is punished for transgressing social norms" and displaces this post-Boom representation to a gay male character, an unusual choice for a woman writer of the late 1990s.[21] This choice is particularly significant if one considers, as Hind argues in the same collection, that many writers of the *Boom femenino* (including Mastretta and Esquivel but also Guadalupe Loaeza, Rosa Nissán, and even Carmen Boullosa) sustain conservative views of gender and womanhood, in some cases even associating them with celebratory notions of neoliberal forms of consumption and subjectivation.[22] Hind's point—that one should be attentive to these phenomena rather than dismiss them—is well taken. Indeed, we should add that, insofar as production occupies such an important place in the literary market, it is impossible to read these women writers without considering their position-takings on the predominance of that kind of corpus (that is, Esquivel, Mastretta, and other women writers perceived as commercial). Of course, this is not to say that one should validate binaries, such as literary versus popular, or claim that they hold inherent value. But we must recognize that women writers navigate the social efficacy of such binaries in ways that must be accounted for. For instance, as I will discuss below, part of Boullosa's work may well belong to the conservative strain identified by Hind, but many of her other novels also perform notions of literariness that are absent in all other writers on the commercial end of the *Boom femenino*. Indeed, just as the Crack writers rejected the market's imperatives to take over the market itself (and some, like Volpi and Palou, indeed became commercially successful), writers like Boullosa do not operate in the axiomatic opposition between literary value and the market; rather, they seek to participate in the publishing market by setting the terms of what constitutes commercial literature. In the case of women writers, this term-setting is of the utmost importance: access to the market allows women writers to sidestep the structural sexism that so obscured the work of their precursors. Among the central concerns of my analysis is precisely the ways in which all three writers—Boullosa, García Bergua, and Rivera Garza—have managed to navigate these tensions in establishing over-twenty-year careers (at the time of this writing) with a level of visibility that exceeded the attention afforded to women writers in nearly all previous generations. In my view, their current success surpasses the one enjoyed today by 1990s commercial writers like Esquivel or Nissán (Mastretta remains an important figure, although her novels are less successful now than they were in the 1980s or 1990s).

Precisely because literature written by women is not a monolithic category, but a site of struggle in which diverse authors establish themselves through distinct aesthetic and political position-takings, I opted to study three writers with distinct poetics—Boullosa, García Bergua, and Rivera Garza—rather than write a monographic chapter on a particular author or particular group, as I have done in chapters 1 and 2. Regrettably, their differences are often erased when the three are lumped together in gender-studies approaches to literature. One criticism that should be directed at the idea of a *Boom femenino* is that it flattens substantial aesthetic and ideological differences between women writers, making gender the defining trait of their fiction—even if some of them proactively resist such a characterization. It is true of all three writers that relatively few critical works on their diverse and complex oeuvres are focused on anything other than gender in general and their status as women in particular. My point is certainly not to dismiss this critical production; rather, I intend to build on it. I believe the question of women's representation in their works has been sufficiently discussed by scholars before me, and the gender-related question that links more directly to this chapter is the one delineated above: the way in which they construct position-takings and strategies through Occidentalism and cosmopolitanism. In two of the three cases, we find authors who attained renown partly because of how they followed the script of the *Boom femenino* in order to later depart from it. Carmen Boullosa first gained recognition through two novels that narrated questions of family and identity through girls' and women's perspectives: *Mejor desaparece* (*Better Disappear,* 1987) and *Antes* (*Before,* 1989), for which she won the Xavier Villaurrutia Award, granted to the best work of literature in Mexico in any genre.[23] A few years later, historical fiction became essential to Boullosa's consecration, and her revisionist novels on the conquest and colonial Mexico, *Llanto* (*Crying,* 1992) and *Duerme* (*Sleep,* 1994), garnered considerable attention.[24] Similarly, Cristina Rivera Garza was launched to fame with her historical novel *Nadie me verá llorar* (*No One Will See Me Cry,* 1999), which narrates the story of a Mexican asylum in the late Porfirian and early revolutionary era partly from a woman's point of view.[25] However, even a superficial reading of these books shows profound aesthetic and stylistic differences when compared with the mode of writing prevalent in Esquivel and Mastretta: both Boullosa and Rivera Garza work in experimental registers, with more problematic relationships to modernist style, and in a clear departure from the allegorical mode of more commercial historical sagas.[26]

While many critics have rightly studied how Boullosa, García Bergua, and Rivera Garza represent women and how the female perspective operates in their books, my interest in this chapter is precisely how they also depart from *Boom femenino* scripts and performances. While Boullosa still returns to these topics, she has also written copious works of cosmopolitan fiction, some of which, like the ones I will address below, do not even have gender-based or a female perspective at their center. I will pay particular attention to her two pirate novels, *Son vacas, somos puercos* (*They're Cows, We're Pigs,* 1991) and *El medico de los piratas* (*The Pirates' Physician,* 1992), which offer significant counterpoints to those of her works that are framed in more mainstream conceptions of the Mexican woman writer.[27] As for Rivera Garza, her work immediately departed from historical sagas and has evolved into an experimental venture that questions not only conventional forms of narration, but also the very idea of the novel. The other writer discussed in this chapter interests me because she does not follow the script at all. Ana García Bergua's early work opts for imaginative literature and nonallegorical narrative. This is to say not that these three authors do not write gendered work, but that they resist the imperative behind institutional ideas of the "woman writer" by taking positions that are not constructed in binary opposition to those ideas. My claim here is that the concept of strategic Occidentalism, in its ability to analyze the concrete practice of cosmopolitanism embedded in their respective works, allows us to understand the three writers' double position-taking in relation to the market imperatives imposed both by Mexicanness and by womanhood.

Carmen Boullosa: Strategic Occidentalism as Position-Taking

Studying Carmen Boullosa's literature poses various challenges to scholarly criticism. She has authored one of the broadest and most thematically diverse oeuvres in all of Mexican literature. She is an accomplished poet with multiple collections, many of which preceded her fame as a novelist; while hers is among the most interesting work in the genre in the 1970s and 1980s, there is no real body of scholarship engaging it.[28] Even as a novelist, her work seems to be recognized for only a handful of her dozens of writings. A basic search in the MLA bibliography yields over two hundred studies devoted to her work, but the vast majority focus on womanhood (with a strong focus on *Antes*); her books dedicated to Mexican history (particularly *Llanto*); or, in another important subset, her incursion into science fiction with *Cielos de la tierra* (*Heavens on Earth*, 1997).[29] This extensive bibliography only rarely raises some of the questions of interest to my discussion, including her construction of literary tradition or her positioning in relation to the publishing market. I believe Boullosa perfectly embodies the way in which a Mexican woman writer can build a career which benefits from the openings made by the *Boom femenino*, but which also delivers literary writing above and beyond the narrower allegorical mode favored by 1980s bestsellers like Allende's *The House of Spirits* or Mourad's *Regards from the Dead Princess*. In my view, Boullosa's work exemplifies, better than any other case in Mexican literature, the literary transition from the high-modernist paradigm of Bourdieusian autonomy to a new regime of subsumption to capital where one can no longer presume that writing is inherently resistant to the market. Sarah Brouillette points out that one of the ways in which literature's autonomy "tends to be negotiated and expressed today is in authors' acknowledgement of and engagement with the fact that even when their work is highly critical of capitalism it is still available for consecration in the market."[30] Insofar as writers negotiate every day with publishers and the global system of agents, translators, and marketers, to act as if literature were still an autonomous pursuit is more of an ideological stance (like the one articulated by the Crack manifesto, discussed in chapter 2) than anything else.

As evidenced in several well-known interviews, Boullosa is conscious of her position in the literary field. She is clearly aware that some of her works—the ones that hew more closely to registers perceived as commercial—have alienated the critical establishment. She notes, for instance, that after some of her novels (like *Duerme*, a historical novel about a British woman who migrates to New Spain and disguises herself as various characters, echoing Woolf's *Orlando*), "la crítica en México dejó de quererme" (criticism no longer liked me).[31] She also resists the trend of feminist readings of her texts, calling it reductionist, and claims to feel little fondness for such readings because, despite the importance of feminism in everyday life, they do not account for the intricacy of her literature.[32] More importantly, she tends to emphasize the complexity of her work in nearly every interview, since interviewers often describe some of her works as "simple." In one of her longest responses to a question, she remarks that although some of her works have easier structures than others, they also contain latent challenges and depth and are highly diverse in their topics and pursuits.[33] The fundamental point of these assertions is that, on a closer reading, Boullosa is articulating a series of position-takings vis-à-vis the neoliberal literary field in Mexico and the academy as a structure that grants symbolic capital. As a writer, she resists the type of feminist readings that would place her in the same field of meaning as any other *Boom femenino* writer and would explain her consecration as a woman writer as a simple result of both increased critical and scholarly attention and her participation in the mass market opened up by Mastretta and Esquivel. At the same time, by emphasizing the diversity and complexity of her work and resisting the characterization of some of her novels as simple, she implicitly distances herself from the stereotypes that plague many women writers (such as being "formulaic"). The thematic and stylistic diversity of her work, and her chameleonic approach to theme and style, is more similar to Crack writer Pedro Ángel Palou's than to the trajectory of other women writers like Mastretta, who adheres more closely to the topics and narrative forms of her more famous books. In this sense, Boullosa clearly faced, and from early on, the same challenges that Crack writers would later articulate in their manifesto, drawn from their resistance to complying with market imperatives. But, as with the Crack writers, Boullosa's notion of literary complexity does not contradict her participation in the market.

An interesting detail in the abovementioned interviews is that Boullosa frequently eludes the question of her book sales. When an interviewer points out that *Cielos de la tierra* sold out its first Mexican edition in weeks but was ignored by critics, Boullosa describes the novel at length; when the interviewer insists, she speculates about the critics' silence but says nothing about her sales.[34] As I see it, avoiding direct engagement with the commercial question partly involves the stigma still ascribed to commercial success in the 1990s Mexican literary field (recall that Crack writers were criticized after the manifesto for trying to work within the market). In Boullosa's case, though, it also involves the fact that being identified as a bestselling author would affiliate her with writers like Esquivel. In one interview, she acknowledges

that Esquivel and Mastretta's commercial success created "una tirria gener-
alizada" (a generalized annoyance) against many women writers.[35] Aware of
the challenges facing women in acquiring symbolic capital in Mexico, variations and complexities in literary form have provided Boullosa with a way
to stay current and for her books to attain critical and readerly attention
beyond the prejudices against both women writers and the market. In fact,
Boullosa notes that Esquivel and Mastretta's successes were paradoxically
counterproductive, because the male-centered critical establishment rejected
their triumph—unlike their response to female writers back in the 1970s,
who were accepted insofar as the establishment saw them as exceptions.[36]
The *Boom femenino* therefore requires women writers to be more reflexive and strategic in their position-takings, because the opening up of visible
spaces often levies a backlash against them—whether that backlash takes the
form of ignoring books that are otherwise getting attention (like *Cielos de la
tierra*) or dismissing them for their gendered angles (like *Duerme*).

Throughout her career, Boullosa has generated symbolic capital for her
works by maintaining a presence in a diverse spectrum of editorial spaces.
However, this presence also entails certain risks; it sometimes limits rather
than expands her access to audiences. In an interview, Boullosa mentions an
example of the challenges faced in distributing her books:

> Por ejemplo, yo misma, me salí de Alfaguara, saqué un libro, el de
> Cleopatra, en Plaza y Janés y resultó que estaba cambiando el ger-
> ente, vamos, que fue un desastre. Ahora saqué la novela en El Fondo,
> que no tiene la misma distribución cultural, que es poco comercial
> y de pronto estoy desaparecida, tengo que esperar al siguiente libro
> que regreso a Alfaguara y entonces otra vez voy a estar en todas
> las librerías. También hay que tener en cuenta que en México sólo
> el dieciocho por ciento de la población lee, el promedio es un libro
> al año. Hay menos librerías per cápita en México que en Haití. Es
> trágico, así que si no tienes todo el apoyo y el aparato y todo lo
> demás . . . no hay un espacio para las novedades, los libros no llegan,
> hay demasiado desorden, es un desastre. Pero encima de eso yo sí
> creo que ahorita hay una moda enorme. . . . No quieren saber nada
> de autoras mexicanas, nada.[37]

> For example, I myself, I left Alfaguara, published a book, the one
> about Cleopatra, in Plaza y Janés, and it so happened that the man-
> agement was changing, so it was a disaster. Then I published the
> novel in El Fondo [de Cultura Económica], which doesn't have the
> same cultural distribution, which isn't very commercial, and suddenly
> I disappear; I have to wait for the next book so I can I return to
> Alfaguara, and then I'll be back in all the bookstores. We also have to
> acknowledge that in Mexico only 18 percent of the population reads,

and the average is a book per year. There are fewer bookstores per capita in Mexico than in Haiti. It's tragic, so if you don't have all the support and the apparatus and everything else . . . there's no space for new releases, the books don't arrive, there's too much of a mess, it's a disaster. But more than all of that, I believe there is a tremendous fad. . . . They don't want to hear anything about Mexican women writers, nothing at all.

This statement expresses the importance of being reflexive in one's position in the literary field with respect to Mexico's book market. From the mid-1990s onward, Boullosa published in Alfaguara, which at the time was part of the then-mighty Grupo Santillana and a leading force in the commercial market (for instance, it already owned the rights for the works of top Latin American authors like Carlos Fuentes and Mario Vargas Llosa, and would also acquire Mastretta's work). This publishing relationship had an impact on books like *Cielos de la tierra*, whose commercial success perfectly illustrates how corporate publishers could counter the silence from the critical establishment. Yet, as Boullosa recounts, when she moved away from this commercial transnational publisher, she found it challenging to reach the same levels of readership. Her 2002 book *De un salto descabalga la reina* (*Cleopatra Dismounts*) was published by Debate, an imprint of Plaza y Janés, which was changing leadership due to its 2001 merger with the Mondadori group (Mondadori, Plaza y Janés, and Grupo Santillana have merged into the corporate group currently known as Penguin Random House Mondadori).[38] *De un salto descabalga la reina* was part of a series of fiction books marked by a sober gray design and prominent cover illustrations. The same series released books by other writers discussed here, such as the reprint edition of Pedro Ángel Palou's *En la alcoba de un mundo* (discussed in chapter 2), as well as Ana García Bergua's second short story collection, *La confianza en los extraños* (*Trust in Strangers*, 2002) and an anthology of world short fiction compiled by Sergio Pitol.[39] Studying the book in relation to the whole series, Boullosa's book appeared in a context that significantly invested in Mexican writers who hadn't yet been consecrated (Palou has not fully attained the Crack group's success; García Bergua is barely known outside Mexico); it could be said that she was the single author in the series, perhaps other than Pitol, who had a strong commercial career publishing there. However, the material circulation of the novel (which tells the story of Cleopatra in prose laced with poetic tones and sober ornamentation) was in fact a commercial and critical step backward from Boullosa's Alfaguara novels (*Duerme, Cielos de la tierra*, and *Treinta años* [*Leaving Tabasco*, 1999]), books that had enjoyed significant sales, visibility, and eventual scholarly attention.[40] In other words, insofar as Boullosa's fiction from this period had attained a level of commercial success that was challenged by the critical establishment's rejection of both literature written by women and commercial literature, the ability to acquire symbolic capital was crucial for her continued presence at the forefront of Mexican literature. Relevantly, in 2002, there was a backlash in the Mexican literary field against Alfaguara because it was generally seen as responsible for a purported homogenization and flattening of literary writing in Latin America—a phenomenon called "alfaguarización" by critic Víctor Barrera Enderle.[41] Boullosa's chronological switch to another publisher, even though her Cleopatra novel was written very much in the tone of *Duerme*, made sense, because Alfaguara's overt appeal to the commercial actually reduced its cultural capital. At the time, Anagrama was quickly becoming the go-to press for literary fiction in Latin America (led by the publication of Roberto Bolaño, Ricardo Piglia, and Sergio Pitol), while the recently revived Seix Barral (with Jorge Volpi front and center) was swiftly becoming an alternative for many emerging Latin American writers. Debate's fiction series joined these new efforts to rebrand literary publishers in resisting the backlash against commercial literature. Nonetheless, her shift to this purportedly more prestigious outlet ultimately harmed Boullosa's distribution, as the commercial element acted partly as a shield against structural sexism in literary institutions. Thus, Boullosa's case patently illustrates the ways in which the position of the "woman writer," and the blurring of the lines between commercial and literary fiction that was transpiring in corporate neoliberal publishing, undermined the workings of the Bourdieusian economy of symbolic goods in which literary value was generally autonomous from commercial success. While Pitol was able to acquire significant prestige in distancing himself from trends ascribed to the commercial writer, Boullosa's early success was due in part to the way in which commercial publishers enabled a suspension of prejudices against women writers and their works in the Mexican literary field.

The second experience described by Boullosa in the interview cited above refers to her Cervantine novel *La otra mano de Lepanto* (*The Other Hand of Lepanto*, 2005), published by the Fondo de Cultura Económica.[42] The book appeared in a recently redesigned version of the Letras Mexicanas series. For decades, Fondo de Cultura Económica has published both key and collected works by canonical Mexican authors, constituting the series that most closely resembles the importance of the Bibliothèque de la Pléiade or the Library of America in their respective traditions. By the mid-2000s, the series opened up to include new works both by established writers and by emerging ones. Two of Boullosa's books were published as part of this effort: *La otra mano de Lepanto* and the poetry collection *Salto de mantarraya (y otros dos)* (*The Stingray's Leap (and Two More)*, 2004).[43] Inclusion in the series grants near-instant canonization to new works by authors writing in genres not generally canonized by the market, such as Sergio Pitol's essay-memoir *El mago de Viena* (*The Magician of Vienna*, 2006), discussed in chapter 1, and a collection of short stories by cult author Álvaro Uribe, *La linterna de los muertos* (*The Lantern of the Dead*, 2006).[44] Boullosa's books are accompanied by a notable roster of writers: consecrated cult figures like Gerardo Deniz, Esther Seligson, and Alejandro Rossi; the first sets of collected poems by Fabio Morábito and Cristina Rivera Garza; and younger authors who elude the commercial market and write high-literature fiction, like Eduardo Rojas Rebolledo. Letras Mexicanas grants cultural capital to a writer like Boullosa in a different way. In the above-cited interview, she does complain that Fondo de Cultura Económica lacks the distribution of a commercial press. In exchange, however, Boullosa was able to publish a more formally challenging novel than she had been able to do in Alfaguara, with the comparatively straightforward *Treinta años*. Full of erudite references, *La otra mano de Lepando* was written with support from grants that gave her access to scholarly research materials. She wrote the novel at the Center for Scholars and Writers at the New York Public Library and with additional backing from the Andrés Bello Professorship, granted by New York University's King Juan Carlos Center, which included the opportunity to teach.[45] The novel's baroque structure, cultured references to Spanish Golden Age culture, and its complex four-section architecture (it has eighty-five numbered chapters) mark a clear departure from the less intricate frameworks of her two prior novels, *Treinta años* and *De un salto cabalga la reina*, books in which the depth of her research is more implied than apparent and the stories' historical nature does not influence the narrative form so openly.

The symbolic capital acquired by this purportedly more literary novel broke the silence on Boullosa's work that key literary publications in Mexico had maintained. We can find a good example of this shift by examining the trajectory of Boullosa's novels in Octavio Paz's magazine *Vuelta* and its successor, Enrique Krauze's *Letras Libres*. Boullosa's early novels generally received positive reviews, particularly her two buccaneer novels—*Son vacas, somos puercos* and *El médico de los piratas*, which I will discuss below—and the other novels she published with the independent press Era, *Llanto* and *La milagrosa* (*The Miraculous Woman*, 1994).[46] However, when Boullosa switched to Alfaguara, the critical tone changed. Christopher Domínguez Michael, who had praised some of the previous novels, trashed *Duerme*. In a review titled "La civilización sin alma" ("The Soulless Civilization"), he remarks on her prolific output and states that "confía demasiado en los poderes de su imaginación y ésta carece de esa fecundidad a la que ella aspira" (she overly trusts the powers of her own imagination, which lacks the quasi-miraculous fecundity to which she aspires).[47] Domínguez Michael further notes that the book fails due to its choice of an archetypal protagonist, Claire, based on Virginia Woolf, and by trying to grant it density through stereotypes of pre-Columbian and colonial culture. He concludes:

> *Duerme* no es verdad novelesca sino artificio ontológico. La Claire de
> Boullosa es menos hija de la imaginación literaria que de la ansiedad
> por otorgar a los mexicas una inmanencia que la literatura moderna

nunca prueba. Que Boullosa—la novelista más fecunda de su generación y un escritor que no cederá su lugar—incurra en la fe que
estropea *Duerme* me parece producto de ese error sociológico que
trato de explicar. Carmen Boullosa parece creer a ciegas (postura
admisible en religión, no en literatura) en una mexicanidad prehis-
pánica cuyas maravillas no brotan con facilidad.[48]

Duerme is not novelized truth; it is ontological artifice. Boullosa's
Claire is less the daughter of literary imagination than of the desire
to grant the Aztecs an immanence that modern literature never demonstrates. That Boullosa—the most prolific novelist of her generation
and a writer who will not cede her place—incurs in the faith that ruins
Duerme seems a product of the very sociological error that I will try
to explain. Carmen Boullosa seems to blindly believe (an acceptable
stance in religion, but not in literature) in a pre-Columbian Mexicanness whose wonders do not easily blossom.

The review clearly castigates the features in *Duerme* that orient it toward a
wide readership. Although Domínguez Michael's notion of literature does
not admit the idea of a pre-Columbian culture constructed on ideas of myth
and immanence as part of modern literature, this type of narrative very much
corresponds to the commercial appeal of Boullosa's Alfaguara novels. It also
reveals a prejudice against forms of narration by women writers who seek to
revisit historical events through topics that correspond to 1990s ideologies of
multiculturalism. As Ute Seydel and Oswaldo Estrada show in their respective analyses, the historical register of *Duerme* projects various contemporary
discussions onto issues like the unrecognized social heterogeneity of Mexican
history and the subalternized role of indigenous cultures and cosmovisions
in that history—fundamental topics in Mexico's cultural discussions after the
Zapatista indigenous uprising of 1994.[49] Specifically in response to Domínguez Michael, Seydel notes that he overlooks a central literary device: the way
Claire deconstructs essentialist notions of the feminine body as a receptacle
for identity—an element of the novel's construction that directly contradicts
his reading.[50] One could even cite the fact that Domínguez Michael calls
Boullosa an "escritor," not an "escritora," as evidence that he does not see
gender as a factor, although one could certainly counterargue that his use
of this term shows that being a woman writer, at least as a positionality
within the field, carries a stigma. As Emily Hind points out, his choice of
language replicates Boullosa's own preference to not be read as a woman
writer, given that the Mexican literary field contains an implied notion of
the feminine—a notion, indeed, that even female writers assume—as unin-
tellectual and domestic.[51] But even more tellingly, as Seydel recounts in her
exhaustive reading of responses to *Duerme*, some critics identify Boullosa's
book with hypercommercial literature marked by self-help and spiritualist

tones, missing the fact that Boullosa's literary devices differ significantly from this sort of prose.[52]

The critical establishment's inability to read Boullosa's literary techniques and works when she crosses the threshold into commercial presses is symptomatic not only of the struggle between the market and the literary field described above, but also of the gendered nature of the tension between critics and authors. It is noteworthy that Boullosa would never again be reviewed in *Vuelta* (although an excerpt of *Cielos de la tierra* was published in a 1997 issue); her first review in its successor magazine *Letras Libres* is dedicated to *La otra mano de Lepanto*, the novel with which Boullosa more fully participates in traditional frameworks of literary value in Mexico.[53] The critic, Lucía Melgar, highlights "la hondura de estas reflexiones, aunada a la intensidad imaginativa de la novela" (the depth of these reflections, along with the imaginative intensity of the novel), granting Boullosa the very features that Domínguez Michael considered absent.[54] Tellingly, in a 2009 review of *El complot de los románticos* (*The Romantics' Plot*, 2009), Domínguez Michael himself squares the circle by calling this her most successful book because it breaks away from her "academic" novels and is self-critical in terms of parodying "feminine" literature.[55] I should say that, after *La otra mano de Lepanto*, Boullosa has been frequently reviewed in *Letras Libres*.

Beyond her critical reception, Boullosa has deftly navigated editorial landscapes in order to accrue cultural capital. Alfaguara continues to grant her significant visibility and distribution. She ultimately returned to the publisher with *La novela perfecta* (*The Perfect Novel*, 2006), a book that presents parallel stories between Brooklyn and Mexico City; her two latest major works were also released by Alfaguara, now under the umbrella of Penguin Random House: *Texas* (2012), a novel about a little-known 1859 invasion of Texas, and *El libro de Ana* (*Anna's Book*, 2016), which narrates the story of a book purportedly written by Anna Karenina.[56] But this is not the only press to have published her books. Many of her more recent works were issued by Siruela, a Spain-based prestige publisher known for its selective catalog. They have published editions of both *La otra mano de Lepanto* and *El libro de Ana*, as well as many of Boullosa's most cosmopolitan novels, including *El Velázquez de París* (*The Velázquez of Paris*, 2007), *La virgen y el violín* (*The Virgin and the Violin*, 2008), *El complot de los románticos* (which won the 2008 Café Gijón Award), and *Las paredes hablan* (*The Walls Speak*, 2010).[57] These books represented a second hiatus from Alfaguara before her return in 2012, but Siruela granted various valuable assets to Boullosa: for one thing, a respectable presence in Spain to compensate for the intermittent silence that has met her work in Mexico; for another, a venue where some of her erudite literary works could join other examples of high-culture world fiction. In those years, Boullosa shared the catalog with authors such as Alejandro Jodorowski, Clarice Lispector, Carmen Martín Gaite, and other writers with devoted literary followings. Similarly, Boullosa's only book of short stories,

El fantasma y el poeta (*The Ghost and the Poet*, 2007), was published in another prestige publisher, Sexto Piso, a Mexico-based cosmopolitan imprint based that only rarely publishes Mexican authors and launched the career of acclaimed younger writers like Valeria Luiselli and Emiliano Monge. Boullosa's fiction, then, is framed by her participation in two distinct structures of symbolic capital and value that exist in tension with each other: independent imprints (Era, Fondo de Cultura, Sexto Piso, Siruela) known for their high-literary pursuits and renowned for their support of authors against the current of the market, and commercial publishers (Océano, Debate, Alfaguara) that allow authors like Boullosa to short-circuit gender prejudice and reach readers. Her work is important because she successfully navigates both worlds, and her most significant and enduring works come from both ends of the spectrum: *Duerme, Cielos de la Tierra*, and *Texas* in the commercial imprints; *Son vacas, somos puercos, La otra mano de Lepanto*, and *La virgen y el violín* in the prestige imprints. The curious point to raise here is that, beyond the different orientations of the two kinds of publishing houses that have issued her work, Boullosa's books are quite consistent in their core stylistic and thematic interests. The two editorial lines rather show that a prolific woman writer like Boullosa can successfully navigate different forms of cultural capital in order to short-circuit gender prejudices in the neoliberal literary landscape. The paradox is that the same landscape grants new avenues of success, but when that success materializes, it becomes an obstacle within the literary field. Boullosa's editorial oscillations are partly a manifestation of this problem.

The formal and cultural genealogies that inform Boullosa's work are framed by her complex interaction with systems of literary value in Mexico. Hind has perceptively pointed out that Boullosa "depicts women protagonists who fail to become intellectual leaders and artists."[58] Tracking characters from *Antes, Duerme*, and *Cielos de la tierra*, Hind reproaches Boullosa for her clichéd conceptions of the Mexican intellectual woman (Sor Juana in particular); despite her daring formal exercises, her book constantly puts forth the idea of the woman who feels she must act like a "bearded lady" to command intellectual respect.[59] That said, Boullosa's point of wishing to not be read as a "woman writer" involves, as we have seen so far, the ways in which being a woman—and writing works that lend themselves to feminist readings—affect the public standing of a Mexican writer. Boullosa is frequently defined as the author of books not so much about failed women as focused on female identities that the critic Cristina Santos characterizes as "authentic." Santos uses tools from sociolinguistics to study Boullosa's narrative styles and to contend that they "achieve an expression of individuality which is not limited by time"; she reads their narratives as a "journey of self-affirmation."[60] In a similar vein, Yolanda Melgar Perías reads Boullosa alongside Mexican American writer Sandra Cisneros as an author of bildungsromans that dismantle historical paradigms of gender—works that, regardless of their deconstructive bent, open up positive spaces for new feminine *mexicani-dades*.[61] Strikingly, all of these readings emerge from the fact that the idea of what a Mexican woman writer should do creates imperatives that are alien to Boullosa's own writing. From Hind's deconstructive approach (which seeks to understand the negative traits identified with "base" femininity, as she calls it), to Santos and Melgar Pernías's methodologies (which seek to align Boullosa with forms of feminist reading that Boullosa herself disavows in nearly every interview), there is a telling friction between the vast, erudite writing in her oeuvre and the hermeneutic tools we have developed for women writers. This is not to say that the methods are invalid. In fact, they fit mainstream writers well, as in Hind's analysis of Poniatowska or Loaeza, as well as the more open engagement with Mexicanness and feminism deployed by a writer like Cisneros.

Another level of illegibility in Boullosa's fiction is the way in which her literary style is generally framed within the catchall concept of the historical novel's postmodernism. This certainly plagues the novel that I will discuss in the remainder of this section, *Son vacas, somos puercos*, a book that does not lend itself to the type of feminine reading I just described. Alessandra Luiselli, for instance, locates Boullosa's novel as part of the so-called "nueva novela histórica latinoamericana," following Seymour Menton's model, and proceeds to assert that the newness in Boullosa's historical approach comes from the "postmodern" features of her writing.[62] In a more sophisticated reading, Cynthia Tompkins places the novel within Linda Hutcheon's category of historiographic metafiction; furthermore, implicitly contradicting feminist readings, she notes that this particular book is not a bildungsroman, but rather "a nonfoundational order that results from the slippage from the narrator's subject positions."[63] While Tompkins's reading provides an illuminating perspective, the issue I want to emphasize is that Boullosa's work is generally trapped between three approaches: journalistic criticism that responds to her through stereotypical notions of literariness and dismisses some of her work as inadequately literary, given their nods to gender and to popular narrative forms; feminist readings that reduce her to the very notion of the woman writer she seeks to resist; and formalistic readings that acknowledge the aesthetic complexity of her work but still seek to constrain it into forms of taxonomical classification ("nueva novela histórica," "historiographic metafiction") that remove the specificity of her project from the analysis. To resolve this impasse, we must first recognize the uniqueness of Boullosa's work in relation to all coordinates used to make sense of it. Her public persona and the type of female characters who inhabit her works (the little girl breaking free of the bildung narrative, the cross-dressing woman facing structural violence head-on, the artist who is never able to translate her talent into recognition) are part of a larger aesthetic project of ironic intervention into the spaces of the past in order to expose the semantic gaps and structural blind spots in our narratives. However, this aesthetic must also be understood in relation to the various ways a woman writer can in fact appeal to readership communities who have never enjoyed long-term access to literary projects created by a specific woman writer. What I mean is that the complaint articulated by Domínguez Michael in his review of *El complot de los románticos*, that Boullosa is writing "the same book" over and over through a constant use of a lyric "I" and a similar engagement with historical discourse, misunderstands a fundamental challenge confronting woman writers: in the 1990s, no Mexican female author had ever been able to maintain a steady, decades-long relationship with an audience. The consistency in Boullosa's styles and thematics, her openness to both literary and commercial audiences, and her use of familiar tropes, such as the figure of Orlando, are all devices that account for the endurance of Boullosa's fiction in both the literary field and the literary market.

Son vacas, somos puercos is a unique work in the landscape of the Mexican novel. Along with its accompanying novel, *El médico de los piratas*, it retells the story of Alexander O. Exquemelin, a Frenchman who became a buccaneer in the seventeenth-century Caribbean and wrote a remarkable chronicle of his life.[64] Smeeks, as Boullosa renames the character, reaches the colonial company as an indentured servant and befriends a slave nicknamed Negro Miel. *Son vacas* unfolds in two sections: the first narrates Smeeks's arrival as the property of a surgeon, his own learning of the trade, and the killing of his master; the second part narrates his incorporation into a pirate crew. *El médico de los piratas* retells the story in a more straightforward way and was designed for a wider audience; it is part of Siruela's series Las Tres Edades, created in 1990 to attract young adult and adult readers alike. In this sense, and given young adult literature's role in influencing readers and commercial writers from the 1980s onward, *El médico de los piratas* illustrates Boullosa's interventions in shaping commercial genres without sacrificing her own aesthetics. *Son vacas* is a denser and more fragmented novel, published originally by Ediciones Era in the series Narrativa Era, where Boullosa joined a catalog of writers who were already canonical or in the process of becoming so; José Emilio Pacheco, Sergio Pitol, Elena Poniatowska, and Hugo Hiriart were among the most notable. Boullosa's short historical novels, along with *Llanto* (also published by Era), were strikingly different from mainstream Mexican novels at the time: they did not fit the trend of sprawling historical novels as represented by Fernando Del Paso's *Noticias del imperio*; they diverged in all formal aspects from the writings of Mastretta or Nissán, which were reaching prominence; she did not follow the testimonial and journalistic current headed by Elena Poniatowska; and, even if María Luisa Puga comes close in thematic diversity, she wrote with her own stylistic economy. Perhaps some similarity may be found with Hugo Hiriart's *Galaor* (1984), insofar as it re-creates the prose of the medieval chivalry novel, but the latter does not share Boullosa's level of formal experimentation; another comparison could be made with Ignacio Padilla's picaresque novel *Si volviesen sus majestades*

(1996), though it lacks Boullosa's investment in plot. The uniqueness of the buccaneer novels and the circulation of her work indicate that while some of Boullosa's books (like *Llanto*) operate in engagement with national literary and cultural traditions, *Son vacas* and *El médico de los piratas* incorporate world literary lineages that provide lines of flight from the territorrialization of her works to conceptions of the literary that were predominant both in the Mexican literary establishment and in the *Boom femenino* at the time.

In his discussion of postcolonial fiction, Peter Hallward notes that although historical novels of the late 1980s and early 1990s may all deploy postmodern questionings of narrative and technique and problematize ideas of testimony and truth, individual projects are still marked by specificities that introduce significant formal and ideological differences. In particular, Hallward compares two African American novelists, Charles Johnson and Toni Morrison, to illustrate how the former tends to move characters out of history, while Morrison returns them to history.[65] In these terms, Hallward points to a way of envisioning literature that I think can be helpfully applied to Boullosa's aesthetics: "Between the immediately singularizing pressures of contemporary commodification and the reactively specifying pressures of 'ethnic' or 'traditionalist' responses to such commodification, what goes by the name of artistic or creative writing will continue to open a fragile space of relational detachment and imaginative engagement."[66] Without unpacking the terminology in full, we can say that Hallward effectively describes the sort of trap in which a writer like Boullosa, as an author of historical fiction, faces: her style seeks to avoid both the type of self-referential and commoditized world present in ultracommercial fiction (like the exoticist worlds of authors like Luis Sepúlveda or the commercial fantasies of Gary Jennings and the late Isabel Allende) and the reactive authenticity embodied in traditions related both to gender and political engagement (as in the type of Chicana literature written by Sandra Cisneros, informed by U.S. paradigms of ethnic fiction), to claim a role for the imagination in the early neoliberal era.

In her review of *El médico de los piratas*, Adriana Díaz Enciso notes that the narrative voice is Smeeks's and not Boullosa's, not even in indirectly or in a disguised way. Díaz Enciso, herself a notable poet and novelist, contends that Boullosa's language is thus "free" and able to re-create the pirates' story on the story's own terms.[67] Díaz Enciso's judgment can be read as an implied rebuke to the idea, discussed above, of "feminine writing" inherited from poststructuralism.[68] The notion of an inherently embodied language and the consequential genderization of writing is an imperative—one very much present in feminist criticism—that both Boullosa (as author) and Díaz Enciso (as critic) question in this case. This is not to say that such notions (inherently embodied language, the genderization of writing) never apply to Boullosa; the protagonists of *Antes* or *Duerme* can indeed be read from these perspectives. But *Son vacas* and *El médico de los piratas* operate through Boullosa's attempt to decenter her writing against gender stereotypes—right at the very moment when those stereotypes were becoming mainstream. Precisely because what differentiates the two books is narrative voice, Boullosa ultimately opted to publish the second one though it told the very same story. This gesture shows the extent to which Boullosa values the construction of her narrative selves.[69] Given that *Mejor desaparece* and *Antes* precede the juggernaut success of Esquivel's *Como agua para chocolate*, it is quite telling that Boullosa switched into historical narrative modes and never returned to the subjective plots of her earlier work. I believe there is an implicit sign in her choice of a wider imaginative world rather than the type of self-referential female story that would become the norm in the context of the *Boom femenino*. In an interview, Boullosa states that writing the books was painful precisely because she discovered an interest in books with male protagonists and thus had to detach from her proclivity to write feminine worlds.[70] In retrospect, though, this intentional distance clearly enriched her historical writing, as she grew able to move in and out of the subjective in constructing narrative voices. She also moves her work away from the very idea of femininity promoted by the type of criticism she decries.

Boullosa's pirate novels operate by claiming alternative traditions of world literature—that is, drawing from a form of strategic Occidentalism—and then introducing a parallax into their narrative and technique. This is the very technique employed in *Somos vacas* and *El médico de los piratas*. Even though the narrated object is the same, the change in narrative perspective, a parallactic displacement, creates two different works: one based on a fragmented mode of re-creating historical prose, and the other on a more cinematic mode of narration. Describing her philosophy of language in an interview, Boullosa notes that she does not identify with any writers in particular, especially in prose, but she mentions a clear ethos: "I believe that words have to be alive to have meaning. I don't believe in the prose of best-sellers, which is used without giving it importance, without letting the words display their vitality and their stories their many meanings and their difficulty. I believe that prose must be alive, that books are alive, that prose must speak by itself, which doesn't mean that it has to be embellished, far from it."[71] Elsewhere, Boullosa describes the kind of encounter she wants her readers to have with her book:

> Quiero que desde la primera frase el lector se encuentre con una lengua posesionada por el alma de la historia. No un estilo correcto, elegante, adornado o bello, y no porque desprecie la belleza pero creo que la belleza también se consigue de otra manera con la lengua, contaminándola, violentándola, haciéndola cómplice y protagonista de lo que ella nos está contando que ocurre.[72]

> From the first sentence onward, I want the reader to find a language possessed by the soul of history. Not a correct, elegant, ornamented,

or beautiful style, and I say this not because I reject beauty, but I believe that beauty is also achieved with language in another way, by polluting it, distorting it, rendering it accomplice and protagonist of what it is tells us is happening.

Clearly, the linguistic interventions of the author—her interventions in language itself—are fundamental in Boullosa's literary system. It therefore matters less whether she writes about Caribbean buccaneers, historical figures of the Conquest, or characters from Cervantes or Tolstoy. The central tenet in Boullosa's strategic Occidentalism is that her sources do not forge a path toward a literary language (as was the case in Pitol and certain Crack writers); rather, they intervene retrospectively in the language of the past. Her language is "possessed" by history, but as an author she "pollutes, enacts violence and makes it an accomplice." In this way, her writing is attentive to the memory it transmits, but also proactively intervenes in the form of the past. Language, as the protagonist, becomes as necessary as the plot itself. This is how she can take Exquemelin's obscure text and deliver two distinct novels from it. Many scholars read Boullosa's pirate novels through straightforward conceptions of postcolonial literature, as if the novels had a direct stance on the represented historical period.[73] In my view, such readings miss the point: Boullosa's fiction has no direct relationship to the past's effect on the present, which is how we usually read the genre. Focusing on the content of the historical novel betrays the protagonical role of form within the narrative. Here Boullosa's work certainly marks a departure from Laura Esquivel, who traces the family genealogy of her revolutionary protagonist to a present-day woman. Boullosa's interventions occur in the past itself. As Tompkins notes, Boullosa's representation of the buccaneer brotherhood introduces an "ethics of dissensus" that "undercuts the egalitarian nature of the filibuster's Brotherhood, suggesting that their liberating communal ideology replicated the imperialistic position of the Spaniards." But the key conclusion is that she performs this action at the level of linguistic intervention, in which the "text logocentrism is undermined by the simultaneous displacement of othering(s) along axes such as gender, race and ethnicity, religion and economics."[74] The dissensus described by Tompkins operates precisely in the intersection between language and the parallactic perspective: Smeeks's peculiar subjectivity and his embodiment in the language of the narrative voice permit the gap of signification that exposes the limits of the pirates' political community.

This linguistic liveliness refuses the idea of the woman writer as the author of fiction in the allegorical and confessional modes favored by the neoliberal editorial market—Boullosa directly indicts the language of the bestseller as inert—and instead proposes, in her more gendered stories, the possibility of intervening in the past through parallactic displacements enacted by different linguistic perspectives, which may or may not be embodied in female characters. Oswaldo Estrada notes, for instance, that the fragmented narrative in *Llanto*, which intersects literal references to sources like Bernardino de Sahagún and Hernán Cortés's writings with the voices of contemporary women who find Moctezuma in a Mexico City park, activates reflection on Mexican history.[75] The concept of activation is effective in distinguishing Boullosa's fiction from the kind that understands language as a cosmopolitan legacy to be deployed in the present, as in Ignacio Padilla's approach to the adventure novel. Boullosa activates and deactivates past traditions through a language that lives and is rooted in her engagement with contemporary readers. Karim Benmiloud suggests that Boullosa deactivates the tradition of adventure novels (embodied in Robert Louis Stevenson, by example) by introducing forgotten elements, like the pirates' crimes and the forgotten female characters.[76] I would go further and suggest that Boullosa uses literary form to puncture historical fantasies and suffuse them with literary tension—a tension drawn not from those fantasies' connection to the present, but from the linguistic revision of their structural terms. This phenomenon is what, in her formal analysis of the novels, Anna Forné calls "textual amplification": it is what operates, in turn, the protagonist-narrator's subjective presence and ultimately introduces dissonances between narration and story.[77] The use of these literary devices, and the dissonance between narrative and history, account for the significant range of historical contexts in Boullosa's books: linguistic liveliness expands her frame of reference into world literature and annuls any imperative to focus on—or evade—national stories. Here we can close the circle opened at the start of this section: by writing in the tension between the market and the literary, in the intersection between language and history, Boullosa becomes the key example of a writer who, conscious of the advantages and disadvantages of writing as a woman in the context of the *Boom femenino*, develops a literary project that was launched by institutional dimensions but not defined by literary imperatives.

Ana García Bergua: Writing against Imperatives

Boullosa's mode of writing history is part of a larger trend in contemporary Mexican literature toward revising and rethinking the past. In Boullosa's case, her historical fiction has exceeded the borders of the national and her philosophy of language has opened up the panorama for her work to rethink not only Mexican history, but also world history and world literature. Yet the ways in which canons like the adventure novel ultimately manifest themselves in Mexican fiction are numerous and broad, and there are other forms of historical intervention worth noting. Among the most remarkable historical novels written in twenty-first-century Mexico may be Ana García Bergua's *Isla de bobos* (2007).[78] This novel fictionalizes the story of a company of Mexican soldiers that sought to reclaim sovereignty over Clipperton Island in the Pacific by wresting it from French control. García Bergua's story devolves into chaos as the lighthouse keeper, Saturnino, takes control of the island, and as the Mexican government forgets the expedition due to the start of the Mexican Revolution, leaving the women and children at the mercy of the new tyrant. With a unique history that helps problematize ideas of nation and sovereignty in Mexico, Clipperton has emerged as a recent obsession in literary representation. Its horrific story has been the subject of at least two other novels: the more accurately historical *Isla de la pasión* (*Island of Passion*, 1989) by Colombian writer Laura Restrepo, and, more recently, the complex palimpsest fiction *Clipperton* (2014) by Pablo Raphael.[79] García Bergua's version appropriates historical documents but fictionalizes all the characters: Saturnino is actually a historical figure called Victoriano Álvarez, who levied a regime of terror and rape over the island's women; the novel's protagonists Raúl Soulier and Luisa correspond, respectively, to Arnaud, the captain in charge of the takeover, and his wife; and even the island is only referred to as Isla de K. in the fictional account. If Boullosa intervenes in the historical story of Smeeks through linguistic displacements, García Bergua's parallactic procedure functions at the level of fictionalization and imagination, of hewing close to the historical source but not adhering to it faithfully. This tactic also appears in another historical-themed novel, *Rosas negras* (*Black Roses*, 2004), a joyful ghost story that fictionalizes the obsessions with Spiritism in 1890s Mexican pseudoscience.[80] García Bergua does not write in the baroque register that characterizes Boullosa; she employs a concentrated, economized style that presents rich images without linguistic ornamentation.

Isla de bobos is a thoroughly successful novel, certainly the best of those focused on Clipperton, because she resists the temptation to write either a sprawling allegorical saga (which Restrepo delivers through admirable efforts, but not always with successful results) or an overloaded historical fiction (which weighs down Pablo Raphael's book). In an interview with Emily Hind, García Bergua expresses her admiration for the ability to condense a saga into a few pages (she cites Christopher Domínguez Michael's novel *William Pescador* as an example) and questions the need to innovate when literary innovation adds nothing to the story.[81] Such narrative and formal economy makes for difficult reading, but it is important to note how fundamentally this economy alters the very experience of what is narrated. As Milagros Ezquerro points out in a formalist reading of the novel, García Bergua's work with fragmentation and polyphony results in a "peculiar tratamiento del tiempo" (peculiar treatment of time), which gives "al lector una impresión de caos narrative que le exige una atención y una actividad intelectual constantes, hacienda de él un cómplice y co-creador de la obra" (the reader the impression of narrative chaos that demands constant attention and intellectual effort, making him an accomplice to and co-creator of the work).[82] García Bergua resists the formation of meaning as embodied in the historical novels written by women; this is true not only of Mastretta and Esquivel, but also of some of Boullosa's characters, like Claire in *Duerme* or the protagonist of *Treinta años*. Instead, García Bergua's writing interrupts the creation of meaning in historical narrative. Of course, this interruption does not mean that her works do not allow for gendered readings. As Davy Desmas illustrates, one can indeed read *Isla de bobos* as a subtle rehabilitation of the experience of women who suffered the horrors of Victoriano Álvarez's regime.[83] Even so, García Bergua's literary procedures in *Isla de bobos* are rooted in the ability of fictionalization to convey a historical core—and in an accompanying style based on precision rather than excess—without the burdens of either formal innovation or excessive documentation. It is a performance of style in which García Bergua resists the imperatives imposed by the idea of the Mexican woman writer developed in the early 1990s; the book emerges from a trajectory of writing against the modes of woman-written fiction predominant in that decade. García Bergua's own presentation of her narrators illustrates this performance and its resistance. When Emily Hind notes that her earlier books employ masculine narrative voices, García Bergua responds: "Porque sale así, Tolstoi cuando escribió *Ana Karenina* no estaría pensando si su narrador o su personaje era mujer" (Because that's how it comes out. When Tolstoy wrote *Anna Karenina*, he wouldn't have thought about whether his narrator or his character was a woman).[84] After Hind presses the point, remarking that her choice is very uncommon, García Bergua elaborates:

> Se me hace más fácil; no sé por qué. Tiene varias respuestas. Una respuesta idealista podría ser que así se le revelan a uno los personajes. También puede haber una trampa en el hecho de elegir una voz masculina para alejarte de ella y trabajar con un objeto, algo con lo que te involucras menos. Quizá al revés es una dificultad.[85]

> I find it easier; I don't know why. There are many answers. An idealist answer would be that this is how characters reveal themselves to the writer. There can also be a sort of trap in choosing a masculine voice in order to distance yourself from it and working with an object, something you're less involved with. Maybe it's harder the other way around.

I interpret this assertion in more or less the same terms as I would interpret Boullosa's reluctance to be read in a feminist key: García Bergua is actively resisting gender predeterminations in her fiction. But she takes it a step further: by suspending the autobiographical and identitarian potentialities of writing in a female narrative voice, García Bergua displaces the mechanisms of her fiction to a realm of imagination from which her authorial voice is detached. If, as I suggested before, fictionalization is a way to understand the experience of a historical event in works like *Rosas negras* and *Isla de bobos*, a writer like García Bergua must find a starting point in the possibility of writing fiction without the autofictional devices that defined writers established by the *Boom femenino*.

Of all the authors discussed in this book, García Bergua offers the most substantial resistance to the methods I have deployed in my analysis: it is nearly impossible to document her cosmopolitan literary genealogies. Even though she majored in French literature at UNAM, she has authored little literary criticism of her own, and she makes few literary references in the major interviews on her books. This shortage of materials limits my ability to offer an extensive analysis of her work, but I decided to include a short section on her in this chapter because I see her first two works—the novel *El umbral: Travels and Adventures* (*The Threshold: Travels and Adventures*, 1993) and the short story collection *El imaginador* (*The Imaginer*, 1996)—as relevant examples in of how 1990s Mexican writers deployed cosmopolitan styles to engage both with the decline of national identity as a central concern and with the rise of neoliberal publishing systems.[86] García Bergua shares many important experiences and ideas with other authors discussed in this book. Like Boullosa, her more cosmopolitan work has been made possible by her relationship with an independent publisher, Era, which published the three books that made her a central figure in Mexican literature; in recent years, it has also either republished or reissued her novels (both *Rosas negras* and *Isla de bobos* are now available in Era editions). Moreover, she and Ignacio Padilla shared some of their formative years as colleagues and friends. In a text she read in Padilla's last public appearance (a tribute to his work by the Dirección General de Publicaciones), García Bergua recalls that they were both students of Silvia Molina and expresses particular admiration for his work in fantastic literature.[87] This is a key trend in her work: García Bergua participated in a recent revival of Efrén Hernández, one of Mexico's foremost authors of fantastical fiction.[88] In her shared experiences with Padilla and Boullosa, García Bergua is part of a generation of writers who used cosmopolitanism as a refusal to accept the terms of early corporate publishing, which reproduced the family saga and magical realism due to their market success. Unlike Boullosa or the Crack group, García Bergua does not exemplify what it means to change the nature of the literature published on the market; indeed, even her foray into Seix Barral ultimately sent her back to independent publishing. Rather, she demonstrates the possibilities of using the expansion of literary venues—the growth of independent publishing—to protect literary projects against market demands without becoming a secret or rare writer. García Bergua is well known and well recognized, and the publication of her major books has remained a noteworthy phenomenon for over two decades. That said, she did not establish herself through the proliferative approach discussed with respect to Boullosa. Instead, her early works constructed a philosophy of writing that remains at the core of her fiction.

El umbral tells the story of Julius, a young bibliophile with an active imagination who himself is writing a book called *Travels and Adventures*.

The novel is García Bergua's tribute to her brother Jordi, a cult author of fantastic literature who died in 1979 at the age of twenty-three, but who wrote one of the most significant works of the genre in Mexican literature, *Karpus Minthej* (1981).[89] Just as in *Isla de bobos*, García Bergua distances herself from self-fashioning and from memory by giving her protagonist a fictional name—Julius, in this case, which consciously or unconsciously echoes the name of the protagonist in Alfredo Bryce Echenique's novel *Un mundo para Julius*, one of the most memorable child characters in Latin American fiction. In an interview with Mauricio Carrera and Betina Keizman, García Bergua notes that her penchant for fantasy, a genre that was becoming central in the 1990s thanks to the work of authors like Padilla, Álvaro Uribe, and Javier García-Galiano, emerged from a will to be more cosmopolitan.[90] *El umbral* shows a further desire to innovate in the genre, in part because García Bergua was originally closer to the performing arts (she herself was a scenographer, and her father, Emilio García Riera, was a founding figure of film criticism in Mexico). García Bergua mentions David Lynch as one of her key influences, particularly through the notion of narrating a story through disconnected scenes.[91] A notable element in *El umbral* is precisely how, in Lynchian fashion, the fantastic operates not in a magical realist fashion, but in the naturalization of estrangement. In one passage from the novel, for instance, Julius is confronted with his possible future grave:

> Julius se sorprendió al ver, en el cementerio, que su última morada ya existía, pues Don Juan había completado todos los pagos de la cripta. Y mientras su padre descendía con rechinidos de poleas no aceitadas a la entraña de la tierra, Julius supo que jamás llegaría a estar enterrado ahí. Mientras, Don Luis abrazaba a la Abuela con una congoja tan evidente, que era difícil no imaginar el gusto que le provocaba la situación.[92]

> Julius was surprised to see, in the cemetery, that his last dwelling already existed, since Don Juan had completed all the payments for the crypt. And while his father descended with the creaking of unoiled poles into the guts of the earth, Julius knew he would never get to be buried there. In the meantime, Don Luis hugged his Grandmother with such evident grief that it was hard to not imagine the pleasure the situation was causing him.

This passage comes at the end of an uncanny succession of events triggered by Julius's father's death. In this succession, Don Juan dies in Julius's arms after a scene in a brothel that may or may not have been imagined; the emergence of a character, Luis, who sought to marry his mother; and an attempt to communicate telepathically with his sister. The scene effectively illustrates the novel's style: the burial scene is made strange by Julius's peculiar train of thought, and the whole scene, rather than being described in detail, is narrated with a minimalist form of costumbrism, represented by the creaking of the unoiled pole. The passage illustrates two essential points: the way in which the fantastic introduces parallactic displacements in Julius as a character, consistently disturbing any attempt to derive allegorical meaning from him; and the amassing of rich scenes in short phrases and descriptions. García Bergua uses the fantasy genre to counter the type of aesthetics embedded in magical realism, producing discrete estrangement instead of an exoticist conception of literature.

Surprisingly, García Bergua names the nineteenth-century European tradition as a center of gravity for the history of the novel, and she notes that the inherited value of the genre lies in "la posibilidad de estudiar el mundo que en ella se expone" (the opportunity to study the world exposed in it).[93] Because of its expository nature, García Bergua argues that the novel is in fact more impervious to formal innovation than other genres: certain fundamental aspects of the novel are still preserved even by leading contemporary novelists known for innovation, like J. M. Coetzee. Furthermore, despite constant declarations of the death of the novel, the genre has survived radical questioning by both modernism and postmodernism.[94] In these terms, García Bergua defends the notion of the novel as a total and self-referential genre that, crucially, need not make too many commercial concessions, because its resistance to radical innovation preserves its legibility. In considering these assertions, we could derive a factor that distinguishes García Bergua's early work from the type of novel written by Esquivel: she does not feel obliged to turn to formulaic structures to make her novel more legible. Interestingly, she finds an excellent model in a writer who is more closely identified with feminist topics and with subjectivist feminine prose: Silvia Molina. In novels like her classic *La mañana debe seguir gris* (*The Morning Must Continue to Be Gray*, 1977), Molina adopts a subjectivist tone that is nonetheless self-reflective and tends toward problematization.[95] Molina's influence shows in certain aspects of *El umbral*. In 1990, Molina published *Imagen de Héctor* (*Image of Héctor*), a type of biographical novel on scholar Héctor Pérez Martínez.[96] The central trait of this novel is the inability to apprehend her subject; it provides the narration of a life that, paradoxically, is re-created in a self-referential world but never captures its protagonist's subjectivity. Something similar could be said of *El umbral*: García Bergua's procedures focus on the world created by Julius rather than on Julius himself, and his full personality remains a mystery throughout the book. While García Bergua believes that novels capture whole words, this totalizing gesture is not inherently related to exhaustive or proliferating forms of narration. On the contrary, the fiction authors in her generation to whom she feels an affinity (Adriana Díaz Enciso, Verónica Murguía, the Domínguez Michael of *William Pescador*) all share the ability to pack their narrative worlds into concise, economical forms of writing.

In their readings of *El umbral* and other early works, critics have frequently noted that the general idea of the Mexican woman writer grows problematic when approaching García Bergua. Above, I mentioned Niamh Thornton's insight that García Bergua does not fit into the categories imposed by the *Boom femenino*; Thornton further notes that, insofar as the idea of a boom implies "aesthetic commonalities," the "cross-generational sweep" prompts the notion that she is "unclassifiable."[97] Yet, Thornton continues, it is important to understand that García Bergua is younger than Mastretta and Esquivel (and even Boullosa by a few years) and as such has a different experience of the challenges faced by women writers. If Esquivel and Mastretta's successes blazed trails and Boullosa has been able to occupy a more ambiguous space between the literary field and the market, then García Bergua is able to shake off the more constrained role of the woman writer and thus "play with gender roles in her narratives."[98] In a similar vein, Anadeli Bencomo notes that García Bergua is in a strange position, because, as a woman writer, she belongs to a category that is read first and foremost through categories of the feminine; at the same time, early reviews praised her for *not* fitting the feminine mold and generally compared her to her brother Jordi. According to Bencomo, this left García Bergua's work in a sort of double orphanhood: not only was she affiliated with her lost sibling, but she was also essentially left without a literary tradition of her own.[99] Bencomo reads both *El umbral* and *El imaginador* as early anomalies that do not represent her later turn to realism—a turn that is problematic in itself, because *Rosas negras* is in fact premised on a fantasy. Still, Bencomo's characterization of the stories in *El imaginador* as "calisthenics" in which one can identify echoes of some of the twentieth century's most important fantasy writers (Fuentes, Arreola, Rulfo) is relevant.[100] The short stories of *El imaginador*, along with some of her better-known narratives, like "Los conservadores" ("The Conservatives"), illustrate García Bergua's economy in full.[101] Her precise narrations are never hyperbolic; their richness lies in the layers of the stories she tells.

A significant aspect of García Bergua's experience as a writer stems from her relationship to the Spanish exile community. Mads Rosendahl Thomsen reminds us that migration and exile are essential components of world literature, given that the nation becomes "less of a project" and writers in that condition bring "a certain strangeness to something familiar."[102] Although Thomsen's focus is on writers who reach international recognition, García Bergua's case certainly reveals a worldliness operating in her connection to different networks that define her style and intellectual identity. In a text on her intellectual identity, García Bergua claims her belonging to the "Hispano-Mexican generation," which refers to children of Spanish exiles who were educated as if they were going to return to Spain; thus, their roots in both their family's homeland and their country of birth became problematic.[103] She describes *El Umbral* in terms of these experiences:

> I suppose this is the novel which tells something about my life and background. It tells a fantastic story of angels, messengers and sects in the middle of a world of Spanish refugees which was, for want of a better phrase, my own paradox. Within a few months of starting to write it, I realized that I had not abandoned it, as I had done with so many others, and that the destiny of Julius—the main character—had become something of considerable importance to me.[104]

García Bergua's dislocated presence in the "Hispano-Mexican" interstitial identity produces the estrangement of the roles of both the Mexican writer in general and the Mexican woman writer in particular; her narratives interrupt the very possibility of the family and bildung sagas that inform more properly nationalist narratives like Esquivel's *Como agua para chocolate*. This is also why García Bergua emphasizes, in the few spaces where she writes about her own poetics, the idea of the modern novel as journey and observation. In reference to her novel-writing process, she states: "I feel as if I am setting off on a journey without a destination. The meaning of any journey lies, precisely, in the things we find along the way. For that reason, I think novels and travel narratives are very similar."[105] The meaning of her world literary canon lies not so much in the choice of authors who would renew a local tradition (as Pitol's translations would do) or the ability to break with genre conventions (as is true of Padilla or Boullosa). Rather, García Bergua identifies with a medular tradition of the novel, a tradition with which her prose is not obviously connected (due to the brevity of her own work). Ultimately, the point of that tradition is how it accounts for human experience rather than establishing a blueprint for a novel's structure or style:

> Gustave Flaubert, Marcel Proust, James Joyce, Kafka, Thomas Mann, the great inventors of our modern novel, created rich and complex, true worlds, authentic in their revelations about the human condition and the mysterious reality surrounding us. So that the novel can unveil a world, the novelist must listen to and watch it without prejudice. Many years ago, I read an interview with Juan Carlos Onetti, where the great Uruguayan writer described how he shared his home with his characters, who became part of the family. I remember thinking that his statement suggested he was a little mad, but, over time, I have come to understand what he was saying.[106]

Although García Bergua is not reluctant, when interviewed, to mention affinities to Mexican literature, it is clear that her attachment to ideas of universality—"true worlds, authentic in their revelations about the human condition"—are ways to formulate a theory of the novel that has more faith in literature itself than in literature's role in the construction of identity. The fact that her only autobiographical novel delves into the fantastic, rather than into her own experience or genealogy, is telling. In her work, strategic Occidentalism works to avoid identitarian rootedness, a trait that defined world literature written by women such as Mourad, Allende, Morrison, and Esquivel in the late 1980s and early 1990s.

Thomsen has argued that contemporary literature offers a particularly effective approach to the migrant experience not only because it embodies globalizing processes, but also because it generates "a formal quality that creates the opportunity to create a particular narrative voice," which in turn fosters "the writing of a world wherein the ideas of place, nation and identity are more complex than ever, and as such reveal how the strange and the familiar can and will mix in people's lives."[107] This phenomenon is crucial in the context of 1990s Mexican literature, because it allows authors like García Bergua (and to some degree Boullosa) to contest the role of the woman writer as an author of the national, the feminine, and the private. In the fiction of Esquivel, Mastretta, and other women writers, the predominance of the role of the wife, the space of the kitchen, and even the idea of the "private side" of history is displaced in García Bergua's work by constructing a sense of identity based not on gender, but on the condition of exile embedded in the "Hispano-Mexican" experience. The lack of rootedness allows García Bergua to resist imperatives that the editorial and critical establishment imposes on the woman writer. Here is the answer to Hind's point about the male narrators: the "particular narrative voice" described by Thomsen is not so much a suspension of García Bergua as a woman writer; rather, it is a suspension of the natural correlation between writing by women and the imperative to narrate the self. In describing her process with respect to *El umbral*—the idea of a journey, the narration of a world—García Bergua emphasizes that the point is not that her writing is "unfeminine," but that her concept of identity emerges from the narrated world rather than the narrated self. And insofar as this world is not predicated on nation but on space constructed through a long-term process of exile (she was born more than two decades after the start of Spanish exile), in which a return to the homeland was more an imagined persistence than a realistic choice, attachment to the nation was always met with estrangement, given that full acculturation was unacceptable. In these terms, we should not validate the type of judgment, cited by Bencomo, that praises García Bergua for not writing as "a woman."[108] Rather, what must be said is that García Bergua's worldliness, just like Boullosa's, expands the repertoires and aesthetic elections available to Mexican woman writers in the early 1990s, given that market conditions and commercial presses favored a narrower understanding of such of works. We must take care to refrain from attributing value judgments to literature on the basis of whether or not it participates in commercial venues: as we saw in Boullosa's case, this attitude impedes a fair reading of a woman writer. Instead, we should understand that writers create symbolic capital in terms of how much they accept or reject a habitus defined by a literary tradition that, due to processes affiliated with neoliberalization, has in itself become more and more commercial. In this sense, then, García Bergua is much closer to the Crack writers than any other woman writer. Although she does not participate in any group dynamics or militant manifestos, as Crack writers do, she seeks to change the terms of the literature that the market expects from a woman writer.

In recent years, García Bergua has established herself as one of the most important figures in Mexican fiction. I disagree with Bencomo's assessment that her two earlier books would cede to other styles. I would say, rather, that the elements I have described ultimately foreground a narrative style that develops many rich elements that she would continue to unfold in subsequent books. Even if her later works have come closer to exploring the history of Mexico, her experience of migrancy and her ideas of the cartography and the imagination remain at the core of her narrative. Her great comic novel *La bomba de San José* (*The Bomb of San José*, 2012) clearly configures and employs humor within the same experience of exile as shown in *El umbral*, while her more recent novel, *Fuego 20* (*Fire 20*, 2017) uses the protagonist's self-fictionalization as a central narrative device.[109] García Bergua, like the Crack writers, embodies the ways in which Occidentalism allows Mexican authors of the 1990s to be faithful to their cultural ideologies and aesthetic practices as the literary market began to trump the autonomous literary field as a source of cultural capital and imperatives. Her later development as a novelist shows that the books she wrote in her formative period ("calisthenics," as Bencomo called them) created the conditions of possibility for her to become one of the most unique and exciting novelists at work in Mexican fiction today.

Cristina Rivera Garza: World Literature in Late Book Culture

Cristina Rivera Garza is the last writer I will discuss, because, as I will argue in the remainder of this chapter, her work connects the problems discussed in the book so far—strategic Occidentalism, editorial neoliberalization, and the idea of the "Mexican" and the "woman" writer in new world literature—with the most important developments in the evolution of literary practice and the world literary market in the twenty-first century. Her first novel, *Nadie me verá llorar*, rapidly made her a household name in Mexican literature. However, one of the reasons for its success is that, as I mentioned above, the book follows some elements in the scripts of the *Boom femenino* related to gender and the historical novel. Unsurprisingly, she has elicited readings that place her squarely within the canons of women writers representing the U.S.-Mexico border—she is originally from the border state of Tamaulipas—and her portrayal of madness has helped rethink and problematize the relationship between gender, history, and patriarchy.[110] Many of these critical readings show that Rivera Garza's importance in redefining the representation of women in Mexico is not unwarranted: her character Matilde Burgos is among the most significant fictional women in Mexican literary history. As various critics discuss, Rivera Garza's use of Foucauldian ideas of madness, and her particular approach to cultural history (the novel was derived from a doctoral dissertation in history on discourses of madness), is a paradigm shift in the representation of both Mexican history and the history of women in Mexican fiction.[111] However, her contributions to the representation of women are underpinned by a constellation of intellectual engagements, in which her openly self-reflexive positions on being a woman writer, and on studying women in the archive, cut across avant-garde conceptions of literature as well as her dialogue with both idiosyncratic fiction writers and a sophisticated canon of continental theory. What I will suggest in the remainder of this chapter is that Rivera Garza's strategic Occidentalism, openly affiliated with new forms of conceiving the narrative and the book, short-circuits the concerns about neoliberalization expressed both by Crack writers and by women authors like Boullosa and García Bergua. In doing so, she ultimately puts forward a literary praxis and a system of ideas meant to engage with the transformations undergone by the material practices of literature in the early twentieth century.

In reference to the Argentine case, Craig Epplin has identified the emergence in Latin America of a "late book culture" in which the book merges with digital technologies (such as the blog) and marginal practices (such as *cartoneras*, publishers that issue handmade books fashioned with discarded cardboard and paper) to create a new material practice of literature.[112] Rivera Garza does not quite engage in a full-fledged late book culture, but her writing is certainly attentive to the role of digital media in writers' work. Rivera Garza's blog *No hay tal lugar*, active since January 2004, is among the most influential blogs in shaping Mexican literature's relationship to the internet.[113] As Betina Keizman explains in the most comprehensive exploration of the blog's diverse materials, the format allows her to publish writings-in-progress, organize performance practices, and engage in intermedial pursuits that connect literature to other arts through more flexible means than the book alone.[114] For my purposes, three aspects of Rivera Garza's interventions in electronic and late book culture are important to highlight. First, as Epplin discusses in regard to the Argentine case, late book culture emerges as a response both to the legacies of the military dictatorship and to economic neoliberalization.[115] To be sure, Mexico has been more impervious to these radical transformations, partly because the level of suppression and censorship conducted by the PRI regime never reached that of a military dictatorship, and partly because the 1994 Mexican crisis did not have as devastating an effect on literary institutions and the overall public sphere as the 2001 crisis had in Argentina. However, we should not overlook the challenges posed by technological development and their important consequences in Mexican literature. Many writers today have influential blogs that are essential complements to, or even replacements of, their book production. One example is the highly active blog run by Alberto Chimal, which, besides sharing his own texts, features means of contact with readers through short story contests and reading recommendations; another is the work of Heriberto Yépez, a pioneer of Mexican literature in the blogosphere who now publishes most of his work electronically.[116] As I will discuss momentarily, although Rivera Garza very much participates in the mainstream book market, she has also developed a reflective stance on late book culture that directly engages with the challenges of editorial neoliberalization and helps construct a world literature of her own—one that operates in distinct institutional and symbolic channels.

The second point is that the neoliberal era in Latin America has brought about important changes in the social function of literature and in the ideologies that connect literature with politics and society. Until 1980s, Latin American literature was articulated by the paradigm that Ángel Rama studied in his landmark book *The Lettered City*, and literary intellectuals, regardless of their changing nature, maintained positions as public intellectuals that are no longer viable today.[117] As Jean Franco has shown, contemporary literature in Latin America is at the end of a *longue durée* process in which the lettered city's symbolic power has gradually declined and the rise of "commercial patronage" radically reconfigures the politics of literature.[118] Complicating things further, the various economic crises across the continent, the political instability generated by neoliberal political regimes, and the rise of political and criminal violence have exacerbated this process, and although literary intellectuals continue to engage with the public sphere, there is an increasing sense that literature no longer has an epistemological privilege to make sense of contemporaneity. As Patrick Dove argues in a book on this subject, "An important social consequence of the societal transformation that accompanies neoliberal globalization is that literature has now relinquished the position it occupied during much of the nineteenth and twentieth century in Western society."[119] This, in turn challenges the praxis of literary writers: Dove points out (following Fredric Jameson), "It would seem that literature and aesthetic experience are no longer able to sustain this claim to autonomy as fields capable of assigning themselves their own laws. Under the 'cultural logic' of late capitalism (Jameson), and the shift from industry to service economy, aesthetic experience can no longer lay claim to being removed from the demands and constrains of other spheres."[120] At this juncture, contemporary Mexican writers operate in a realm with specific challenges, because the decline of the lettered city and of literature's social capital is accompanied by the persistence of a highly institutionalized book culture, in which high levels of state subsidy go hand in hand with the neoliberal editorial market—in the form of fellowships and awards to writers and publishers, as well as government interventions in publication and distribution structures.[121] In the cases discussed so far, we can see that most writers react against this phenomenon.

While the Crack movement is cognizant of the rise of editorial neoliberal-ization, the manifestos and public interventions very much argue that the writer should take over—and should certainly define what the market ought to be publishing through their criteria of intellectual autonomy. They also are explicit about the preservation of the role of public intellectual, as is par-ticularly clear in Palou and Volpi's work in the public sector and the opinion sections of various media sources. The language deployed by Boullosa and García Bergua on the value of writing and imagination in literature implicitly suggests that the autonomy of literature is essential in preserving aesthetic engagement in the market context and in resisting the commercial imper-atives imposed on the figure of the Mexican woman writer. Rivera Garza blunts those approaches; her literature openly addresses the idea that the contemporary writer cannot simply resist the onslaught of editorial neoliber-alization and the challenges to literature's social and symbolic capital.

Third, the potential of world literature and strategic Occidentalism at this juncture is necessarily revised; it is undeniable that world literature from the 1990s onward no longer holds the possibility for resistance and democratiza-tion on which authors like Pitol and García Bergua construct their respective cultural ethos. On the contrary, as the editors of the journal *n+1* noted in their controversial essay "World Lite," "The progress of World Literature since the '90s has accompanied that of global capitalism."[122] The economy of "networks, scouts and book fairs" described by the article is absolutely a component of the Mexican writer's experience; a case in point is Mexi-co's participation in circuits like the Hay Festival and the myriad book fairs and events that accompany corporate editorial consolidation. Writers from Pitol to the Crack group employed strategies to sidestep the mechanisms of world literature distribution by exercising erudition as an alternative—either through active translation, as in Pitol's case, or by tracing genealogies to rare literary traditions, as Padilla did with Kakanian authors. Latin American writers directly participate in the local and global dynamics of "World Lite." For instance, the editors of *n+1* note that many authors in world literature have university appointments or participate in the M.F.A. network, which is true of writers like Pedro Ángel Palou (tenured at Tufts) or Yuri Herrera (in a tenure-track position at Tulane after earning an M.F.A. from the University of Texas in El Paso and a Ph.D. from UC Berkeley). Rivera Garza is among the most notable cases: she recently moved to an endowed professorship at the University of Houston to create the U.S. academy's very first doctoral program in Spanish-language creative writing. I depart from the perspective of the "World Lite" piece because I find merit in reflexivity, and Rivera Garza shows, whether or not one approves of her particular strategies, that there is a way to think through neoliberalization beyond nostalgia or denuncia-tion. I recognize the existence of what the *n+1* editors call "Global Lit": that is, the set of institutions that "treats literature as a self-evident autonomous good" but ultimately validates "the tastes of an international middlebrow audience." Nonetheless, Rivera Garza, without openly projecting herself onto the notion of world literature, would claim that the path forward is found in understanding the materiality of literary writing and assuming it in its frictional, paradoxical relationship to neoliberalism.

Rivera Garza embodies a changing landscape in Mexican culture, one directly related to the process by which she has detached from the mode of gendered historical writing she practiced in *Nadie me verá llorar*. Rivera Garza's trajectory has gradually moved away from traditional forms of the novel and adopted a form of prose writing that employs different forms of engaging the literary in the present day. Her theoretical and literary work explores the contradictory expectations that writers and artists must face in the changing landscapes described by scholars like Dove. As Irmgard Emmelhainz explains in relation to the visual arts, today's cultural practice emerges from imperatives of cultural democratization, seeking to provide wider access to audiences, contribute to the alleviation of phenomena like violence, and foster symbolic bonds across communities.[123] The problem, Emmelhainz elaborates, is that such imperatives can be subsumed into private schemes of cultural production in which democratization, while it may expand access through neoliberal forms of consumption, may also produce masks of purported social reconciliation and self-help to cover up the inoperative nature of neoliberal regimes.[124] Over the past fifteen years, Rivera Garza's literary thinking has evolved to gradually engage with questions of democratization, the commons, technology, and the status of literary writing. This process has been informed by her development of a new strategic Occidentalism. In this Occidentalism, her world literature is not created, like Pitol's, from the common experience of authoritarianism that joined Mexico to Eastern Europe, or through the claim of novelistic freedom that enabled Crack writers or García Bergua to defend their personal aesthetics and ideologies of the novel from commercial imperatives. Instead, Rivera Garza's quest appeals to forms of literary writing that directly address the challenges outlined in the previous paragraphs: the emergence of technology, the changing role of literature as a structure of thinking and feeling, and the demand that literature engage with forms of democratization tied generally to ideologies affiliated with the global neoliberal era and more concretely with the dictates of democratization in post-PRI Mexico.

For Rivera Garza to move in that direction, she had to confront the question of her position as a Mexican woman writer. As an author and critic, Rivera Garza has a keen sense of this position. In a column published in *El Universal* that subsequently appeared on her blog, she recognizes the role of the Diana Morán workshop in developing criticism attentive to women's literature:

> Las actividades intelectuales del grupo Diana Morán nos recuerdan que la historia de la literatura no es necesariamente la historia de la literatura escrita por varones, es decir, que la historia de la literatura

no tiene porque ser sexista, sino que esta historia incluye a partici-
pantes de variados géneros. Al hacer esto, las investigadoras del Diana
Morán también ponen de manifiesto—y a las pruebas se remiten—
que tanto nuestras historias como nuestros presentes literarios son
territorios amplios, flexibles, lúdicos, inesperados. En suma, cada uno
de los libros editados por el grupo Diana Morán—y ya llevan cinco—
nos recuerda que la literatura es en realidad *las* literaturas y que así,
en plural, esas literaturas resultan más complejas y, por lo tanto, más
interesantes.[125]

The intellectual activities of the Diana Morán group remind us that
the history of literature is not necessarily the history of literature
written by men; that is, that the history of literature does not have
to be sexist, but rather that this history includes participants of various genders. By doing this, the researchers of the Diana Morán also
show—and they stand to proof—that our histories, just like our literary presents, are vast, flexible, playful, and surprising territories. In
sum, each of the books edited by the Diana Morán group—five so
far—reminds us that literature is actually *literatures*, and that in this
way, plurally, they are more complex and, therefore more interesting.

This piece comments on a daring book by the Diana Morán scholars, *Escrituras en contraste*, in which each individual critic in the group (all are women)
contribute a piece comparing a male and a female writer based on a shared
trope or theme.[126] Rivera Garza's remarks are meaningful for my discussion
in various ways. First, they show how Rivera Garza, even in her uncollected
writings such as columns and the like, enunciates from a locus of reflexivity regarding the challenges faced by women in literature. Unlike Boullosa
and García Bergua, who respond to this issue by refusing to identify with
notions of feminist reading and feminine writing, Rivera Garza embraces
these readings (which the Diana Morán workshop produces as a collective)
and redirects her strategies toward efforts of critical engagement, both with
the imperatives imposed on women writers and the critical silence receiving them. By celebrating the efforts of the Diana Morán scholars, she also
highlights the relevance of feminist critique in understanding Mexican literature as such, and in embracing the idea that criticism must proactively
embrace its role in cultural democratization rather than defending twentieth-
century ideas of autonomous literary value that do not correspond to the
nature of literature in the twenty-first century. Finally, and notably, this is just
one instance in which Rivera Garza, herself a scholar, shapes her intellectual
practice both through open debate and within the academy, breaking from
the resistance to the university that a significant part of the Mexican literary
field performs to this day. In one of her most memorable interventions in this
regard, Rivera Garza organized an event in 2006 called "La Internacional

Semana de la Mujer Invisible," in which she invited artists and friends to bring works of art and examples of the invisibilization of women. Maricruz Castro Ricalde, a member of the Diana Morán collective, brought the covers of all anthologies of Latin American literature that include no women writers, demonstrating the way in which the canon excludes even the handful of women renowned by the critical establishment.[127] The organization of such an event, and Castro Ricalde's intervention, illustrates how Rivera Garza no longer shares the sense that led Boullosa and García Bergua, a decade and a half prior, to distance themselves from the *Boom femenino*. Instead, she embraces the notion that proactive feminist interventions, and proactive readings of women writers, are indispensable strategies in the cultural politics of the neoliberal era.

Rivera Garza's early novels trace a path in which gender-based reflections gradually shift their genealogies from the bounds of national tradition to the realm of a world literature constructed along paths different from those laid by the Mexican commercial market. After *Nadie me verá llorar*, Rivera Garza went further in claiming her role as a woman writer and published *La cresta de Ilón* (*Ilón's Crest*, 2002), a fictional tribute to cult Mexican writer Ámparo Dávila, famous for the haunting books of fantastical fiction she published in the mid-twentieth century.[128] In choosing Dávila, it becomes clear that, rather than distancing herself from the underground women writers of the midcentury who never reached canonical notoriety, she sees it as essential for a twenty-first-century writer to claim a direct lineage back to them. Dávila is significant because her uncanny narratives went against the grain of dominant tendencies in Mexican narrative (represented by authors like the then-young Carlos Fuentes), which were rooted in strong allegorizations of the national. By tracing her genealogy to Dávila, Rivera Garza implicitly engages in a series of refusals: the refusal to recognize a lineage with nationalist and magical realist modes of writing, the refusal to define her personal canons in terms of the market, and the refusal to deny the importance that women writers and feminism have had in making her own work possible. I must be clear: I do not mean to argue that this strategy is better than the one followed by Boullosa or García Bergua. Rather, it illustrates how much happened in a single decade—changing the very idea of literature written by women from something that had to be discreetly disavowed to something that had to be embraced. Boullosa and García Bergua obtained recognition thanks to their skillful deployment of the former strategy; Rivera Garza did so by embracing the latter. The difference is relational: in the context of a literary field grappling with the success of writers like Esquivel and Allende, women writers had to distinguish themselves to acquire symbolic capital. In the early twenty-first century, when that success had eroded and writers from an all-male group, the Crack movement, were representing Mexican fiction transnationally, it became newly meaningful and symbolically effective to emphasize the value of women writers.

Beneath Rivera Garza's revival of Dávila's work there was a gesture regarding literary writing itself that would gradually move to the center of her fiction. In a provocative article, Emily Hind argues that part of the motivation in recovering Dávila came from Rivera Garza's will to construct a "nonconsumable" literature that would resist "la memoria y el dominio de los lectores."[129] In Hind's reading, the novel represents the act of reading Dávila precisely by re-creating an experience that is not for consumption (tied, of course, to neoliberal literary commercialism) that *La cresta de Ilón* itself sought to elicit in its own readers. Yet, as Eugenia Berenice Reza Dávila underscores, Rivera Garza focuses on Davila's stories about the relationship between literature and femininity, which is central to the connection between gender and transgression that Rivera Garza had already explored in *Nadie me verá llorar* and would further develop in her metaphysical noir novel *La muerte me da* (*Death Hits Me*, 2007).[130] Both *La cresta de Ilón* and *Nadie me verá llorar* are the early stages of an approach to the relationship between history and literature that Rivera Garza would develop throughout the 2000s and ultimately theorize in her 2013 book *Los muertos indóciles* (*The Restless Dead*).[131] In this book, Rivera Garza argues that there is a distinction between "historical novels," which she sees as commercial literary products sought by readers to learn about the past, and "documentary fiction," which problematizes both the past and the present-day reader's ability to access it.[132] The difference is parallactic: Rivera Garza argues that the historical novelist builds her book by taking information in documents at face value, viewing them as objective and ahistorical, while documentary fiction is concerned with the historicity of the materials. In the context of my discussion, we can see that Rivera Garza's approach to the past roots itself in nonconsumable, transgressive genealogies accessed through problematized and historicized documents, ultimately contesting the ways in which both female and male authors deal with history. While gendered commercial historical novels like *Como agua para chocolate* and *Arráncame la vida* read the archive against the grain by imagining female worlds in the hidden side of history, their approach to archives of domesticity and emotion (cookbooks, *boleros*) are not in themselves problematized; rather, they are represented as if they contained a historical truth to be unveiled. Similarly, Rivera Garza's take evolves out of Boullosa's work with fictionalization. Boullosa constructs her narratives in the gaps of stories like Exquemelin's, or, as in *El libro de Ana*, she supplements Tolstoy's narrative by fictionalizing parts of the story that a male writer had overlooked.

Rivera Garza takes this approach to a more radical conclusion: she enacts a reading of historical sources in which the narrated silences must be accompanied by a disclosure of the documents' material nature and internal gaps. In *Nadie me verá llorar*, for instance, the female character retrieved from the archive and out of historical oblivion, Matilde, is narrated alongside the photographer who registered her images, problematizing the historicity of the visual and archival record.[133] In *La cresta de Ilón*, Rivera Garza furthers this theoretical exploration by portraying Dávila's texts as something not to be merely recovered, but also to be problematized in their spectral existence within the literary canon; in their formal rarity and material absence, these texts can never be grasped. In this case, Rivera Garza elusively and deconstructively fictionalizes what she calls, following Nathalie Piégay-Gros, the "future anterior" of the archive—that is, the small, forgotten, irrelevant documents that push literature to resist historical totalization and instead account for the appropriated archive's becomings.[134] This procedure serves to account for the transformation of the role and rules of literature in the neoliberal era, as discussed above. While writers like García Bergua or the signatories of the Crack manifesto could still postulate the autonomy of literature and operate with a perception of the novel as a self-contained, monadic object, Rivera Garza's earlier novels and literary theories suggest that a proper engagement with the consequences of neoliberalization involves puncturing the procedures of autonomous literature and showing the ideological seams of the novelist's materials. This approach, then, is entirely the opposite of García Bergua's; the latter, as we have seen, does not write about her sources, and beyond general statements on the history of the novel, she rarely discloses the references for her fiction. Cécile Quintana studies the totality of Rivera Garza's work as an *écriture-mouvement*, or writing-movement, that rejects ideas of truth or signification as structuring principles and works with the consistent displacement of the meanings associated with categories such as language or the body.[135] Quintana's extensive, suggestive reading shows that Rivera Garza's fiction operates in the unwillingness to establish fixed meanings—which, in my view, is an attempt to distance herself from the philosophies of narration predominant both in the Crack movement and among fellow women writers of the 1990s, all of whom defend some variant of the thesis of literature's special powers and epistemological specificity. Rivera Garza embraces the opposite response to the decline of literature's epistemological privilege: she appeals to a paradigmatic reframing of literature itself. The conceptual coordinates of *Los muertos indóciles* are predicated on the very transformations I identified earlier: Rivera Garza devotes chapters to writing in an age of violence, writers who no longer assume literature as a self-evident pursuit, and the changes that technology brings to the writer's trade and craft.

Rivera Garza's system of thinking is based on the gradual construction of a world literature that radically departs from the canons built by Mexicans writers from the middle of the twentieth century onward. Her work contains hardly any traces of the canons established by Pitol or claimed by the Crack group. She also has no meaningful relationship to the core tradition of the Western novel, while both Boullosa and García Bergua appeal to authors like Cervantes and Tolstoy. Instead, Rivera Garza develops a personal world literature in which she creates readerly and intellectual bonds to writers and theorists united by the concern about the exhaustion of twentieth-century literary paradigms. Her sources include the trends in Anglo-American poetry that have sought reflexive positions on language and representation. *La cresta de Ilón,* for example, opens with an epigraph from Canadian writer Steve McCaffery's *Panopticon* (1984), a highly experimental novel that inverts Jeremy Bentham's concept to create a narrated space in which nothing, rather than everything, can be seen.[136] This text belongs to the nonconsumable category as defined by Hind: it is a highly reflexive book with little interest in constructing any kind of semantic or affective closure. As Marjorie Perloff explains in her study of the novel, McCaffery operates by presenting familiar signifiers that get estranged by the text's questioning of the institution of language.[137] Rivera Garza becomes the most important reader in Mexico of trends such as Language poetry (as represented by Charles Bernstein), conceptualism (Kenneth Goldsmith, Vanessa Place), and other forms of writing concerned with ideas of authorship, signification, and linguistic expression. She has been central to the introduction of these ideas into the Mexican tradition—quite a feat in itself if one considers that, until the 1990s, the core traditions of Mexican poetry were still firmly rooted in traditions favored by poets like Octavio Paz and Gerardo Deniz, and that even South American poets who had been experimenting with the visual and the semantic as early as the 1970s (like Chilean Raúl Zurita or Argentine Héctor Viel Temperley) were not published in Mexican editions until the mid-2000s. Rivera Garza translated Robert Fitterman and Vanessa Place's *Notes on Conceptualisms,* a theoretical work seeking to account for new forms of writing and reading in the contemporary era.[138] Another source is experimental novelist David Markson, whose work questions ideas of authorship and identity as constructed entities in fiction. Rivera Garza devotes a whole section of *Los muertos indóciles* to Markson's novel *Wittgenstein's Mistress,* which she characterizes as a text that explores questions of autobiography, identity, and the body in the context of forms of writing performed not with language, but against it.[139] Without delving too deeply into the complexity of Rivera Garza's theoretical archive, the point to highlight is that her literature does not refuse to engage with the question of gender representation (Markson's book is about a female character). Rather, she opts to construct a new tradition for writing gender, language, and the body, because she draws from the premise that modernist representations of the female experience—such as the one enacted by the archives used in *Nadie me verá llorar*—can no longer be operative. The canon of reflexive terminology developed by Rivera Garza as based on her readings of Anglo-American poetry—disappropriation, conceptualism, and so on—is an attempt to systematize the experience of writing in a language that is no longer understood as a vehicle capable of conveying truth, which was the case in Mexican fiction until the 1990s.

The consequence of this politics of language is that Rivera Garza's work eventually becomes the site of struggle between stories that need to be narrated (generally the stories of women defined by identities that never actually crystallize in subjectivity) and the reflexive deployment of text theories (such as the one discussed above) and poststructuralist readings of the subject (derived from Jacques Derrida, Michel Foucault, Gilles Deleuze, and Jacques Lacan). The result is a literary work that unfolds in a resistance to the fixation of meaning and which questions the very premises of the Occidentalist traditions on which Mexican fiction has been constructed. This is clear in the texts that Rivera Garza has written after *La cresta de Ilón*, such as the novel *Verde Shangai* (*Shangai Green,* 2011), in which the protagonist has two distinct identities and a subjectivity problematized by the encounter between them.[140] The novel is intensely metatextual: it incorporates the short stories Rivera Garza published in a much earlier book, *La guerra no importa* (*The War Doesn't Matter,* 1991); weaves a representation of Mexico's problematic history with Chinese immigration into the protagonist's alter ego; and incorporates excerpts from dozens of other writers into its literary discourse, marked in italics and credited only in the book's acknowledgments.[141]

Rivera Garza's strategic Occidentalism no longer believes in the centrality of the European modernist tradition as the paradigmatic location of emancipating literary devices—a faith that Pitol, the Crack writers, and García Bergua have evidently sustained. Rivera Garza identifies with forms of literary writing in English—the predominant imperial language in the neoliberal era—but focuses on the traditions seeking to undermine that very power. This happens, for instance, in her most recent poetry collection, *La imaginación pública* (*The Public Imagination,* 2016), in which she appropriates descriptions of medical conditions available on Wikipedia and lays them out to perform the (in)capacity of language to represent the body.[142] Rivera Garza is the first major twentieth-century writer in Mexico, because she is the first to theorize what a literary genealogy that can no longer self-fashion as modernist would look like. Rivera Garza creates a world literature out of negative cosmopolitanism, no longer predicated on the belief in a universal subject made conceivable through the common bonds of the Western imaginary. Rivera Garza argues that, in the twenty-first century, we can only write out of the sense that the history of this imaginary is the history of silences and suppressions. She argues, too, that our inherited literary language is not an ally for our cultural identities, but a problematic obstacle that we can overcome only if we are aware of its material and historical underpinnings and pitfalls. In this way, Rivera Garza is among the writers setting the terms of Mexican literature today. If a twenty-first-century Mexican world literature is to emerge, it may be the one that, rather than participating in late neoliberal sensoria, begins to write against them.

Conclusion

✦

Mexican World Literature and "World Literature" Theory circa 2017

The persistent force of strategic Occidentalism as a strategy for confronting the aesthetic and institutional challenges posed by fiction writing in Mexico remains palpable even in the most recent books. The novel most recently published in Mexico before writing this conclusion, Liliana Blum's *El monstruo pentápodo* (*The Pentapod Monster*, 2017), a bone-chilling rewriting of *Lolita* with a more brutal focus on the violence of abuse than in Nabokov's narrative, provides an excellent example of the ways in which literary innovation and publication in the new commercial landscape can be bolstered through engagement with strategic Occidentalism.[1] The novel tells the story of an architect, sexually obsessed with girls under the age of nine, as he chases, kidnaps, tortures, and rapes a victim. Blum is one of Mexico's leading short story writers, and her work in the genre is characterized by subtle but powerful strokes used to narrate nuances in gender identities and relationships. More recently, Blum has begun a trajectory as a novelist, first in a novella called *Residuos de espanto* (*Residues of Horror*, 2013), on the experience of two elderly Holocaust survivors, and later in a novel as such, *Pandora* (2015), in which she explores the everyday horrors of paraphilia.[2] As a novelist, Blum has gained recognition for her ability to give narrative form to unspeakable stories and plots, from those plaguing memory (like the marks left by the Shoah) to the violence at work in extreme desire. It is hardly surprising, then, that in *El monstruo pentápodo*, which tackles subject matters with little to no precedent in Mexican fiction, she uses multiple epigraphs to invoke a mostly Anglophone tradition concerned with the abuse of children, sexual violence, and the trauma caused by kidnapping. The novel's epigraph is the quotation from *Lolita* that lends Blum the title for her own book: "I was a pentapod monster, but I loved you," Humbert Humbert pleads near the end of the novel.[3] This particular passage in itself activates a long Western literary tradition of narrating innocence. As Ellen Pifer argues, Nabokov's use of the term "pentapod monster" is tied to a long-standing Romantic and Victorian conception of childhood innocence as an all-or-nothing concept, as well as the idea of the monster as someone who defiles his offspring, which dates back to Shelley's *Frankenstein*.[4] From there, Blum's novel establishes a dialectical relationship between the horror of her own narrative and the parallel savagery that marks various other works of literature. Her sources include Joyce Carol Oates's harrowing *Daddy Love* (2013), in which a boy is persuaded that he is the son of a priest who regularly abuses children and is tortured every time he disobeys his abuser; Hanya Yanahigara's *The People in Trees* (2013), on the abuse of aboriginal children by an anthropologist; and Emma Donoghue's *Room* (2010), the famous novel about a five-year-old boy and his mother who are held captive by the woman's rapist.[5]

El *monstruo pentápodo* is the most recent instance of the processes I have tried to engage in this book. At the formal and aesthetic level, Blum activates a tradition heavily grounded in Anglophone fiction (although with interesting departures, such as a line of dialogue from Lars von Trier's film *Nymphomaniac*) to search for means of approaching a topic that, while largely unprecedented in Mexico, has become prominent in U.S. literature of the last decade. In many passages, *El monstruo pentápodo* clearly responds to particular moments and narrative strategies invoked by the epigraphs, making Blum's book as much a story about the unmediated horrors of pedophilia and child abuse as it is a self-reflective work on literature's very capacity to engage with extreme topics. Beyond the formal realm, however, we should note that the legibility of Blum's work is built on the reorientation toward the United States that Hispanophone publishing in general, and literary readership in Mexico in particular, has undergone. Mexican world literature in the late twentieth century, thanks in part to Pitol's translation efforts and to the interest of writers like the Crack group in creating their own hyperliterary genealogies so as to counter editorial neoliberalism, favored Central and Eastern European fiction as a point of reference for their own aesthetic self-fashioning, using erudition and rarity as criteria for accruing symbolic capital. This status quo has undoubtedly changed since then. U.S. literature became more prominent as Anagrama began translating writers such as Richard Ford and Paul Auster, who have a significant following in Mexico, and as poets and experimental writers like Cristina Rivera Garza began dialoguing with the U.S. Language poets. The success of books like Jonathan Franzen's *The Corrections* and Donna Tartt's *The Goldfinch* in both the commercial world and in literary circles—as well as the emergence of novelists like Blum and Jaime Mesa, who are clearly influenced by U.S. fiction—have broken with the predominance of rare European fiction. It is equally important to note that a woman writer like Blum can move toward the aesthetics of horror that characterize her novels thanks in part to the role played by precursors like Boullosa and García Bergua in shattering the imperatives tied to the idea of the woman writer. Indeed, without denying the important gender components of her works (*El monstruo pentápodo* is partially narrated by the letters and diaries of a woman who fell in love with the abuser and helped him conduct the kidnapping), Blum also belongs to one of the most diverse and ample generations of women writers in Mexican literary history. Finally, Blum's editorial trajectory, from the independent and government presses that published her short story collections to nationwide distribution in Tusquets (now an imprint of the mighty Grupo Planeta), provides yet another example of how building a literary tradition to upend or overcome the limits of Mexican literary legacies also contributes to the publication not of alternative literature, but of commercial literature partly defined by writers who resist pressures from the editorial market. In short, Blum is among the most recent examples of the way in which writing in Mexico remains shaped by the various processes discussed in the preceding chapters.

In this book, I have studied how world literature in general and strategic Occidentalism in particular were essential factors in framing literary writing and writers' means of self-positioning throughout the rise and consolidation of neoliberal publishing institutions. I sought to understand this question by studying three processes that unfolded simultaneously from the early 1970s to the mid-2000s. First, I used the category of "strategic Occidentalism" to name the concrete engagements that Mexican writers constructed with Western literature—insofar as Mexican world literature remains firmly grounded in the European and the transatlantic. In doing so, I argued that to understand the development of a national world literature, as well as the aesthetics of fiction prevalent in a specific tradition, we must understand the material and concrete practices at work in the construction of worldly canons. I do think Rebecca Walkowitz is right that contemporary literature contains a vast array of works being born in various languages and countries and that the idea of national literature must be problematized accordingly.[6] I would add, however, that these new manifestations of the literary, even those that fall under Epplin's definition of "late capitalist book culture" as described in the previous chapter, have not by any means replaced the national and the regional as sites of construction of world literature. My study of Sergio Pitol's career as a translator and novelist, and as a founding figure in two of the most influential publishing houses in the Spanish language, shows that canons cannot be reliably understood from the sole perspective of global cartographies; practices like his cause entire national world literatures to depart from the norm of what is generally understood to be world literature. World literature canons in a specific context are constructed through an aggregate of practices in the context of a given literary field. The invisibility of these aggregates in world literature theory, which generally defines the canon as built either by a hegemonic model (solely replicating the literature that global conglomerates produce) or by academic models (highlighting the personal preferences of the critic describing them), is essential, because, as far as I can see as a Latin Americanist, there is no critical work that properly accounts for the practice of world literary canonicity in concrete times and spaces. In my view, the study of translations, publishers, and individual figures is the starting point for any account of world literature; it is essential for disputing diffusionist theories that see countries like those comprising Latin America as mere receptacles for waves of European modernism, as semiperipheries that intermittently innovate the conception of what the global is, or as purveyors of cultural authenticities that counterpoint the European universal. The writers studied in this book show that Mexican literature is none of those three.

My second point is that canons can only be understood in engagement with the material institutions that construct them, and, in the case of the works studied here, with the seismic changes undergone by literary publishing in the neoliberal era. The existence of a specific literary tradition as a world literature cannot be understood at all if we do not understand the material structures enabling both that tradition's contact with the world and the frameworks in which writers must operate. The authors studied here have all had to navigate a changing landscape of literary publishing in the postauthoritarian societies of Latin America and Spain. Pitol's centrality is due in part to Anagrama and Tusquets's ultimate influence on the writing of Latin American literature, and on world literature canons—which was difficult to foresee during the period when Pitol was advocating for heterodoxy in the 1970s. The very existence of the Crack group as a movement resulted from the increasing power of corporate publishers in defining what kind of Mexican literature could be published, upending the literary establishment's control over its own aesthetics. And the rise of women writers in the 1990s could certainly not be explained without understanding that one of the effects of corporate publishers' subversion of the literary field was a new economy of gender in literary writing. Future studies of literary cosmopolitanism in Mexico could indeed go further in analyzing how the state, independent presses, and digital publication are all contenders in processes of canon formation, or in studying the ultimate impact of the duopoly of Spanish-language literary publishing on the formation of a Latin American literature that remains very much marked by the diversifications of the 1990s.

Finally, the third process I sought to describe was the way in which the construction of personal canons and practices under the aegis of strategic Occidentalism allowed writers to self-fashion as authors and intellectuals in tension (and sometimes in outright conflict) with the imperatives created in the neoliberal literary landscape: from the role of the "Latin American writer" as a trafficker of commodified exoticism at the service of the "postcolonial exotic" described by Graham Huggan to the idea of the woman writer as constructed by literary markets. If we are to be consistent in believing that literature must be read in the context of practices and institutions, we should advocate not so much for close reading in the old philological sense (which, readers may have noted, is not a method I use in this book) as for a focus on specificity and concreteness, even when discussing networks and macrostructures. The Eurocentric inclination of world literature theory partly ensues from some models' disinterest in the concrete and the specific. Writers like Pitol, Palou, or Boullosa—authors of complex world literatures, both as writers and as actors in other roles within the literary field—are unreadable when we conflate the world literature produced by hegemonic global institutions with world literature as such; when we advocate for outsourcing the work of attentive reading to specialists in national literature (as Moretti does in *Distant Reading*); or when we think the only authors of world literature are those available in wide translation.

My interest throughout the book has been to understand world literature from the perspective of one Latin American country, Mexico, as functioning differently from both planetary and globalist readings of world literature, which define it exclusively in terms of works that circulate across international boundaries. As I hope is evident in my analysis, world literature is neither a self-evident category nor a literature that cleanly corresponds to idealistic notions of the world. Rather, world literature, for me, is always the result of material practices and cultural ideologies that ground the category in diverse contexts that cannot be reduced to a single process. While my analysis does not seek to contradict the study of world literature either as an ideal of internationalism or as a manifestation of unequal economic relations across regions (from the "world system" invoked by Franco Moretti to the concept of "unequal and combined development" activated by the Warwick Research Collective), my aim has been to demonstrate that Latin America's woefully inadequate representation in most transnationalist models of world literature derives from a one-dimensional portrayal of its role in the international division of intellectual labor—a portrayal that generally sidesteps and ignores the material workings of worldliness within Latin American nations themselves. The provocation underlying the claim of the existence of a "Mexican world literature," one much richer than the relatively small number of works of Mexican fiction in international circulation, is meant to show that national literary traditions (existing insofar as there are still literary institutions, national in nature, that foster them) involve concrete practices and institutions that imagine the "world" in world literature in concrete and identifiable ways. World literature, as constructed and imagined in Mexico's national institutions and in the overlapping institutional structures of the Hispanophone publishing world, sometimes bears little resemblance to the object of study that has emerged and expanded in comparative programs in the United States and Western Europe. Moreover, its contributions and subtleties are usually ignored by the paltry symbolic capital possessed by Spanish as language of critique in the Anglophone and Francophone academies; with a handful of exceptions, non–Latin Americanist comparatists demonstrate little interest in Latin America.

In the process of writing this book, I became convinced that the idea of world literature is limited not only by the fact that its models and cartographies usually reproduce the very structures of cultural coloniality and Eurocentrism that it claims to critique (a phenomenon I discuss in the collection I edited in 2006 on this matter), but also the way in which world literature theory is shaped by anxieties about the increasing precarization of comparative literature and English literature as disciplines, not to mention the literary humanities at large, in the neoliberal university. Not surprisingly, from the perspective of someone like me, a scholar with no institutional investment in the survival of comparative literature as a department or in the crisis of the English Department—beyond, of course, the solidarity necessary to defend critique and its spaces from neoliberal threats—many landmark books of world literature theory (understandably) spend an inordinate amount of time on the state of the discipline, and their understanding of world literature often unproblematically reflects the impact of such anxieties when they become paradigms or methodologies. At the same time, in reading works of theory and historiography written by scholars outside my field and comfort zone, I have grown able to think about Mexican literature in ways that engage—I hope—in dialogues that are not at all unique to Mexicanists and Latin Americanists. My discipline certainly needs more of these dialogues. All of us literary critics are aware that the national and linguistic divisions of literary disciplines do not correspond to the fluid circulation of languages, works, and aesthetics that has always characterized literary writing. However, cosmopolitanism also depends on the eye of the beholder. Insofar as no writer or critic can have a totalizing view of world literature (if such a thing even exists), we cannot understand the limitations, partialities, and specificities of every world literature—of every manifestation of a category that we must start thinking about in the plural—if we are not attentive to the specific structures producing it.

If we start seeing world literatures as the product of overlapping sets of institutions constructed in a diversity of spaces, I think we can start overcoming the intellectual limitations and academic anxieties embedded in overarching notions of world literature as a single object. For instance, I can imagine how a vision of Mexican world literature, a conception formed by scholars and critics like myself and others, will be able to join the views from other regions and countries of Latin America, and that this aggregate of views will help us more expansively study Latin American world literatures. This process, in turn, may result in a discussion of world literatures from hemispheric, Western, transatlantic, transpacific, Southern, global, or planetary spaces—none of which is necessarily better than the other, and all of which contain frictions, limits, ideologies, and institutions that remain to be identified and examined. And even though I speak of Mexican world literature here, there are smaller units to be studied as well: state and local world literatures, individual world literatures as constructed by specific authors or critics, and so on. This approach is different from the idea of "distant reading" that Franco Moretti has productively and polemically put forward. I do not believe that world literature is "one and unequal."[7] Rather, I think that world literature, in the singular and in lowercase, constitutes a large number of world literatures that exist to varying degrees—from individual writers to the entire planet—and in uneven and unequal networks that con-nect them to each other. This is why Moretti's methodological proposition of "distant reading," in which a comparatist reads only what individual experts in national literatures produce, is insufficient. I do not mean that the method is invalid; I myself use it often in this book. But I think that Moretti's advocacy for distance can be dangerous: in addressing the inability to be attentive to everything, he suggests not being attentive to hardly anything. The range of flattening methods that Moretti favors in his theoretical writ-ings, from big-data approaches to the "great unread" to the use of evolution theory to understand literary form, run the risk of taking the system's inher-ent inequalities—which even he acknowledges—for granted. Indeed, there is inequality at work in the selection of criticism for translation (most U.S. university presses show little interest in translating theory and criticism from Latin America, while the complete works of many French philosophers *du jour* are made meticulously available) and in the construction of data sets in the digital humanities (you could not begin to conduct the kind of analy-sis he promotes with Hispanophone writing, because works in Spanish are rarely digitized and there are no resources to do so on the scale that has been enacted in English). Specificity and close attention to concrete sites—which, paradoxically, Moretti himself practices in *The Bourgeois*, a true masterwork of comparative critique—are necessary to counter the naturalization of Euro-centrism, the inequalities in cultural capital, and the uneven translation and distribution that plague the study of Global Southern literatures in U.S. and Western European academic debate. Even if one disagrees with the concept of world literatures in the plural, as I present here, one thing is undeniable: no model of world literature should stand if it does not account for the mate-rial practices of world literature in diverse world sites, rather than reifying, as "the" world literature, models that inherently and unreflexively reproduce the very provincialisms and inequalities they seek to overcome.

Encouragingly, recent approaches to the study of world literature account for the need to study world literature in terms of concrete sites, and I think this book already exists within a network of parallel efforts. The most nota-ble is the series Literature as World Literature, published by Bloomsbury. This series includes volumes on national literatures as world literature—including Danish, Romanian, German, and American—as well as volumes on individual authors (Roberto Bolaño), movements (surrealism), and genres (crime fic-tion).[8] Although these works do not go as far into the claims of specific world literatures as I do here, the series clearly illustrates the usefulness of local-ized and plural ideas of world literature when the problem is examined from the perspective of literatures in languages with less symbolic capital on the global scene (like Romanian) or through the emergence of individual figures that embody world literature in peculiar ways (like Roberto Bolaño). What we can certainly say is that, as world literature theory and debates expand beyond the Anglophone and Francophone academies, the shortcomings of a single, centralized model become more evident. It is not surprising, for instance, that a leading theorist of world literature based in Denmark, Mads Rosendahl Thomsen, proposed the concept of the "constellation" in mapping world literature—a concept that allows for the identification of patterns and commonalities without defining a single world literature.[9] This book, then, seeks to show that world literature is not a self-evident object, but an object constructed and practiced within specific institutional contexts and with particular aesthetics, ideologies, and position-takings that must be accounted for.

My approach also calls for a reconception of the ways in which Latin America participates in world literature without conforming to the stereotypes at work in world literature theories with respect to particular regions. It also requires moving beyond the thesis of Latin America's desire to participate in Western culture—a thesis as old as Latin America itself. The two books in English that have dealt with the question of Latin America and world literature in a prominent way, Mariano Siskind's *Cosmopolitan Desires* and Héctor Hoyos's *Beyond Bolaño*, suffer from this limitation, even if they are otherwise compelling works of scholarship.[10] Even as they seek to account for Latin American nuances in the process of literary globalization and cosmopolitanism, both Hoyos and Siskind operate with an axiomatic acceptance of a hegemonic world literary order, in conjunction with which Latin Americans build relations of aspiration and resistance. In a critical argument addressing both works, Oswaldo Zavala contends that they accept hegemonic theories of world literature as a "discourse of power" enunciated from "the hegemonic academic centers of Ivy-League universities," which is demonstrated in part by the fact that Hoyos and Siskind work in the same institutions as Franco Moretti and David Damrosch, respectively.[11] Zavala's critique is foregrounded by his presentation of Bolaño as an author who "brings to the fore this shift of literary modernity by politically opposing a Latin American intellectual singularity not so much against, but in tension with, the global hegemony of Western cultural capital"—meaning, in turn, that an author like Bolaño cannot be studied through prevailing theories of world literature, because "such models are constructed on inevitable lacunae resulting from historical and political erasures of literatures not entirely belonging to the symbolic coordinates of literary fields of Europe and the US."[12] In this way, Zavala diagnoses the limitations of a top-down approach to world literary theory, one in which global connections are the starting point and then proceed to overdetermine the reading of literatures that play lesser roles in the global cultural hegemony. As a response to these limitations, the concept of "Mexican world literature" is based on the idea of reconstructing world literature theory from the bottom up; that is, on an understanding of its material operations in diverse contexts as a necessary step to foregrounding macro claims. The goal, then, is to avoid the problem that Zavala diagnoses in works like Hoyos's and Siskind's: namely, taking for granted the existence of a world literature that reflects only the perspective of an academic establishment in a small group of universities. Avoiding this problem is not easy; indeed, the resources offered by elite research institutions (like the one I work for) are useful in producing the wide-ranging research that world literature theory requires. In my first foray into world literature theory back in 2006, almost a decade before Siskind and Hoyos, I decided to name the book *América Latina en la "literatura mundial,"* placing world literature in quotations marks, to emphasize the fact that I was referring to a construction and not to a materially existing object.[13] I think such a gesture can be claimed to be pointless today, because the academy has so thoroughly naturalized the term that it is now a recognizable element of contemporary critical vocabulary. That said, the thinking that prompted the gesture is still present, which is why I still occasionally use the quotation marks. Moreover, in my case, it has advanced to the level of methodology: to speak of world literature is only possible only when we speak of it as a construction of concrete fields and practices. Both Hoyos and Siskind wrote their books after the concept of world literature had been further institutionalized, while my book was originally conceived when the debate still focused on interventions by Moretti and Casanova. Consequently, Hoyos and Siskind sidestep various discussions that occurred in my edited volume regarding Eurocentrism and the concept's constructed nature (neither of their books mentions the articles in that work more than in passing). I think, however, that it is time to revisit some of those problems. As I suggested in the introduction, we need to reclaim the idea of "world literature"—lowercase, in quotations, never taken for granted—to reflect the plurality of literary practices on the ground, rather than the top-down notions of cosmopolitanism or the underlying concern over academic disciplines that still plague many interventions in the field.

We need to create approaches like the one I have engaged throughout this book because literatures keep being written, translated, and distributed in ways that exert constant tension between the fluid circulation of works and the friction that impedes it. Mexican world literature in 2017, as I write this conclusion, has already evolved in significant ways—not only from the point when this book was first conceived, in 2006, but even as of mid-2016, when I wrote the introduction. In the introduction, I mentioned that Valeria Luiselli had emerged as a major figure in Mexican literature in translation. She is spearheading a growing trend in the translation of Mexican literature, a trend that enjoys increasing critical and readerly attention. Independent publishers like Coffee House Press and Deep Vellum Publishing, along with committed translators like George Henson, Lisa Dillman, and Christina McSweeney, have created what seems to be a steady stream of Mexican literary works available to readers in the U.S. and the U.K. Among them, I would highlight works like Laia Jufresa's *Umami* (2015), a beautiful novel about memory and loss, or Daniel Saldaña París's *En medio de extrañas víctimas* (*Among Strange Victims*, 2013), an enjoyable comic novel involving a satire of Mexico's intellectual class.[14] More auspiciously still, Mexican writers seem to be breaking into the corporate English-language public world for the first time in many years. Álvaro Enrigue's *Muerte súbita* (*Sudden Death*, 2013), a highly cosmopolitan novel that imagines a tennis match between Caravaggio and Francisco de Quevedo as the basis for narrating a history of the world, was released by Riverhead Books, a Penguin imprint, in 2016, in Natasha Wimmer's translation.[15] More notably, the playful *Campeón gabacho* (*The Gringo Champion*, 2015), written by then-nineteen-year-old prodigy Aura Xilonen, was released in 2016 by Europa Books, an independent publisher distributed by Penguin Random House, where she shares the catalog with two of the most important women writers in the world today, Amélie Nothomb and Elena Ferrante.[16] This internationalization is rooted in the authors studied here: Carmen Boullosa, Jorge Volpi, and Cristina Rivera Garza were all translated in a more timid wave of translations that took place in the early 2000s, and the diversity of their poetics, as well as their intervention in the idea of Mexican literature, has allowed younger writers like Luiselli, Jufresa, and Xilonen to write in ways that differ substantially from each other while still attaining internationalization.

The authors studied in the preceding chapters remain central figures in contemporary Mexican literature, and one of my aims, in terms of the Mexicanist debate, was to acknowledge their rightful place in the construction of Mexican fiction as we know it today. Sergio Pitol's translations are being released as an exclusive series by the press of Universidad Veracruzana, the public university of his home state, recognizing his decisive influence in shaping Mexico's cosmopolitan readings. His two main trilogies are in the process of being translated by Deep Vellum in Dallas; hopefully, thus, more English-language readers will discover this indispensable writer in translation, which would do some justice to his own role in making so many writers known in the Spanish-language world. The Crack group remains active; in 2016, they celebrated the twentieth anniversary of their manifesto with renewed calls in favor of the novel and gratifyingly complex writing. Jorge Volpi released a remarkable book in 2016, *Examen de mi padre* (*Examination of My Father*), an erudite memoir interweaving family recollections, political reflections, and literary thinking.[17] Pedro Ángel Palou has become a leading writer of historical fiction, and his 2016 work of biographical fiction on the life of Lázaro Cárdenas, *Tierra roja* (*Red Land*), embodies the same faith in the novel as a genre that the Crack movement has defended for twenty years.[18] Ignacio Padilla passed away in a tragic accident in 2016, but his legacy as one of Mexican fiction's most imaginative writers has left many admirers who carry on his ideals, including authors such as Alberto Chimal. Even if few young writers willingly claim the Crack group as an influence, Mexican fiction has undeniably experienced a process of "crackificación," as Heriberto Yépez calls it. While Yépez sees this as a negative outcome—the predominance of a cosmopolitan literature that dares not break down symbolic and political walls in Mexico—even he, a detractor, recognizes that the

Crack movement was central influence on Mexican literature as it is written today.[19] Carmen Boullosa remains an active and prolific writer, and many of her major works are finally reaching English translation thanks to Deep Vellum, which is advancing the work that Grove Press initiated a few years back. Ana García Bergua, though still untranslated into English, is still a leading figure in Mexican fiction. And Cristina Rivera Garza, who has won a flurry of awards and recognitions, is perhaps one of the two most influential writers in Mexico today (the other being Juan Villoro), and her literary experiments and creative approach to the canon are all progressing: she recently founded the first doctoral program in creative writing in Spanish in the U.S., at the University of Houston, where she works alongside another Mexican writer with a very unique style, José Ramón Ruisánchez. Taken together, the writers studied here have been essential in shaping the editorial, intellectual, and aesthetic processes that defined Mexican literature in the early twenty-first century, and I hope that this study, besides contributing to the recognition of their crucial involvement, also helps garner them readers and translators of the many important works that remain unavailable in English.

Mexican literature faces various critical junctures in 2017. In a sense, this already means that the process studied here is nearly complete and must make way for new forms of writing. If Mexican literature has become worldly in many contexts, it has insufficiently engaged with the violence and political turmoil of the past few years—with notable exceptions, of course, such as Sara Uribe, Yuri Herrera, and Antonio Ortuño. This reluctance to write about politics was inherited from the twentieth-century resistance to participation in official nationalism; perhaps, too, it has been fostered by Mexican literature's ongoing dependence on government funds and corporate publishing. If a Mexican world literature is to continue to develop, and if it is to stay relevant in the future, I believe it will need to use worldly language to reengage the present. What's more, with President Trump in office, bolstered by a discourse that demonized Mexican immigrants, Mexican literature will invariably play an important role in countering stereotypes against Mexicans and showing the cultural diversity of Mexican society. In any case, the Mexican world literature that has been built over the past thirty years provides a much fuller and more fruitful context than the one available in the 1990s for Mexican literature to be written and read, both at home and abroad. Today, circa 2017, we can afford to hope that literary writing and its institutions will face these challenges in the years to come.

NOTES

Introduction

1. Valeria Luiselli, *La historia de mis dientes* (Mexico City: Sexto Piso, 2013). Translated by Christina MacSweeney as *The Story of My Teeth* (Minneapolis: Coffee House, 2015).

2. Aaron Bady, "Bolaño's Teeth: Valeria Luiselli and the Renaissance of Mexican Literature," *Los Angeles Review of Books*, December 4, 2015, http://lareviewofbooks.org.

3. Ignacio M. Sánchez Prado, *Screening Neoliberalism: Transforming Mexican Cinema 1988–2012* (Nashville: Vanderbilt University Press, 2014).

4. Valeria Luiselli, *Papeles falsos* (Mexico City: Sexto Piso, 2010). Translated by Christina MacSweeney as *Sidewalks* (Minneapolis: Coffee House, 2014).

5. Sergio Pitol, *El arte de la fuga* (Mexico City: Era, 1996). Translated by George Henson as *The Art of Flight* (Dallas: Deep Vellum, 2015).

6. Valeria Luiselli, "Best Untranslated Writers: Sergio Pitol," *Granta*, January 8, 2013, http://granta.com.

7. Valeria Luiselli, *Los ingrávidos* (Mexico City: Sexto Piso, 2011). Translated by Christina MacSweeney as *Faces in the Crowd* (Minneapolis: Coffee House, 2012).

8. Jorge Volpi, *A pesar del oscuro silencio* (Mexico City: Joaquín Mortz, 1922); translated by Olivia Maciel as *In Spite of the Dark Silence* (Chicago: Swan Isle, 2010). Pedro Ángel Palou, *En la alcoba de un mundo* (Mexico City: Fondo de Cultura Económica, 1992). For a discussion of the role of the Contemporáneos in both novels, see Tamara Williams, "The *Contemporáneos* as a Holy Grail: Towards a Genealogy of the Poet as Quest in the Mexican Novel," *Cuaderno Internacional de Estudios Humanísticos y Literature: CIEHL* 14 (2010): 35–44; and Tomás Regalado López, "De Contemporáneos al Crack: Jorge Cuesta y Xaviel Villaurrutia en la novela mexicana de fin de siglo," *Lectura y signo* 10 (2015): 45–67.

9. For a concise discussion of this subject, see Margo Glantz, "Vigencia de Nellie Campobello," in *El salto de Minerva: Intelectuales, género y Estado en América Latina*, ed. Mabel Moraña and María Rosa Olivera Williams (Madrid: Vervuert, 2005), 121–26. For a broader discussion of the role of women in literary writing, see Nuala Finnegan, "Women Writers in the Land of 'Virile' Literature," in *A History of Mexican Literature*, ed. Ignacio M. Sánchez Prado, Anna M. Nogar, and José Ramón Ruisánchez Serra (New York: Cambridge University Press, 2016), 338–49.

10. Nuala Finnegan and Jane Lavery, eds., *The Boom Femenino in Mexico: Reading Contemporary Women's Writing* (Newcastle upon Tyne: Cambridge Scholars, 2010).

11. *Mexico20: New Voices, Old Traditions* (London: Pushkin Press, 2015).

12. Mabel Moraña, *Inscripciones críticas: Ensayos sobre cultura latinoamericana* (Santiago de Chile: Cuarto Propio, 2014), 183–212.

13. Charles Hatfield, *The Limits of Identity: Politics and Poetics in Latin America* (Austin: University of Texas Press, 2015).

14. Ignacio M. Sánchez Prado, "Poscolonialismo *avant la lettre:* El pensamiento mexicano y la crítica de la razón colonial," in *La tradición teórico-crítica en América Latina: Mapas y perspectivas*, ed. Rodrigo García de la Sienra, Mónica Quijano, and Irene Fenoglio Limón (Mexico City: Bonilla Artigas / Universidad Veracruzana, 2013), 73–90.

15. For a counter to this tradition, see the compilation of Latin American postcolonial thought in Mabel Moraña, Enrique Dussel, and Carlos A. Jáuregui, eds., *Coloniality at Large: Latin America and the Postcolonial Debate* (Durham, N.C.: Duke University Press, 2008).

16. David Damrosch, *What Is World Literature?* (Princeton, N.J.: Princeton University Press, 2003).

17. Franco Moretti, *Distant Reading* (London: Verso, 2013); Pascale Casanova, *The World Republic of Letters*, trans. M. B. Debevoise (Cambridge, Mass.: Harvard University Press, 2004).

18. Unsurprisingly, this history can be found in these very books. For a history of the notion, see Theo D'Haen, *The Routledge Concise History of World Literature* (London: Routledge, 2012). A compilation of the texts that have most centrally contributed to the definition of the concept can be found in Theo D'Haen, César Domínguez, and Mads Rosendahl Thomsen, eds., *World Literature: A Reader* (London: Routledge, 2013). A comprehensive discussion of the contemporary debate appears in Theo D'Haen, David Damrosch, and Djelal Kadir, *The Routledge Companion to World Literature* (London: Routledge, 2012). The direct critique of the notion's rise in comparative literature is articulated by Emily Apter in *Against World Literature: On the Politics of Untranslatability* (London: Verso, 2013).

19. Gayatri Chakravorty Spivak, *An Aesthetic Education in the Era of Globalization* (Cambridge, Mass.: Harvard University Press, 2012), 468.

20. Ignacio M. Sánchez Prado, ed., *América Latina en la "literatura mundial"* (Pittsburgh: Instituto Internacional de Literatura Iberoamericana, 2006).

21. Juan de Castro, *The Spaces of Latin American Literature: Tradition, Globalization and Cultural Production* (New York: Palgrave Macmillan, 2008); Mariano Siskind, *Cosmopolitan Desires: Global Modernity and World Literature in Latin America* (Evanston, Ill.: Northwestern University Press, 2014); *Beyond Bolaño: The Global Latin American Novel* (New York: Columbia University Press, 2015).

22. Guillermina de Ferrari, ed., *Utopías críticas: La literatura mundial en América Latina*, in *1616: Anuario de literatura comparada* 2 (2012): 15–144; Gesine Müller and Dunia Gras Miravet, eds., *América Latina en la literatura mundial: Mercado editorial, redes globales y la invención de un continente* (Madrid: Iberoamericana Vervuert, 2015).

23. De Ferrari, *Utopías críticas*, 32.

24. Wai Chee Dimock and Lawrence Buell, eds., *Shades of the Planet: American Literature as World Literature* (Princeton, N.J.: Princeton University Press, 2007). See also the books in Bloomsbury's Literature as World Literature series.

25. Peter Hallward, *Absolutely Postcolonial: Writing Between the Singular and the Specific* (Manchester: Manchester University Press, 2001).

26. Stefan Helgeson and Pieter Vermeulen, eds., *Institutions of World Literature: Writing, Translation, Markets* (London: Routledge, 2016).

27. Sarah Brouillette, "World Literature and Market Dynamics," in Helgeson and Vermeulen, *Institutions of World Literature*, 104.

28. Pheng Cheah, *What Is a World? On Postcolonial Literature as World Literature* (Durham, N.C.: Duke University Press, 2016).

29. Cheah, *What Is a World?*, 89.

30. Aamir R. Mufti, *Forget English! Orientalism and World Literatures* (Cambridge, Mass.: Harvard University Press, 2016).

31. Mufti, *Forget English!*, 33.

32. Mufti, *Forget English!*, 11.

33. Mufti, *Forget English!*, 9.

34. Combing academic databases, I found only one other place in which the term "strategic Occidentalism" is defined and used. James A. Ketelaar derives a notion of strategic Occidentalism from Edward Said's opposition of Occidentalism to Orientalism to describe the way in which Japanese Meiji Buddhists "stage" the Occident and appropriate some of these elements. Although it is the title of the article, the term only appears once in Ketelaar's argument, which does not make any reference to Spivak. Although the part where he describes appropriation for local political uses is similar to my notion here, the focus in my work is different: not so much the staging of the Occident as such but rather the construction of a cosmopolitan cultural persona. See James A. Ketelaar, "Strategic Occidentalism: Meiji Buddhists and the World Parliament of Religions," *Buddhist-Christian Studies* 11 (1991): 37–56. Also, as the discussion below illustrates, my notion is derived from postcolonial discussions of Occidentalism that bear no relation to the Japanese case and that were fully elaborated after the writing of this particular article.

35. Ignacio M. Sánchez Prado, *Naciones intelectuales: Las fundaciones de la modernidad literaria mexicana (1917–1959)* (West Lafayette, Ind.: Purdue University Press, 2009), 150–55.

36. Couze Venn, *Occidentalism: Modernism and Subjectivity* (London: Sage, 2000), 15; Walter Mignolo, *Local Histories / Global Designs: Coloniality, Subaltern Knowledges, and Border Thinking* (Princeton, N.J.: Princeton University Press, 2000), 59. Mignolo derives this notion from precursor studies by Aníbal Quijano and Roberto Fernández Retamar, as well as a concurrent definition of the concept by Fernando Coronil.

Chapter 1

1. Sergio Pitol, *Obras reunidas IV: Escritos autobiográficos* (Mexico City: Fondo de Económica, 2006). For the sake of consistency, I will cite from this five-volume edition of Pitol's collected works whenever the cited text is available as part of it. All translations of Pitol's work are mine. An English edition of *El viaje* just became available: *The Journey*, trans. George Henson (Dallas: Deep Vellum, 2015). Other works by Pitol are in the process of being translated by Henson.

2. For a very fine reading of *El viaje* in terms of Pitol's literary discoveries, see Jorge Bustamante García, *El viaje y los sueños: Un ensayo vagabundo* (Mexico City: UNAM / Ediciones Sin Nombre, 2013).

3. Sergio Pitol, *Adicción a los ingleses*, included in *Obras reunidas V: Ensayos* (Mexico City: Fondo de Cultura Económica, 2008), 21–84.

4. Alexander Beecroft, *An Ecology of World Literature* (London: Verso, 2015).

5. There are a few exceptions to this statement, of course, but most are limited to listing Pitol's influences rather than drawing meaningful connections. The most useful essay for getting a general sense of Pitol's cosmopolitanism is Hans-Otto Dill, "El cosmopolitismo literario de Sergio Pitol," in *La modernidad revis(it)ada: Literatura y cultura latinoamericanas de los siglo XIX y XX*, ed. Inke Gunia, Katharina Niemeyer, Sabine Schlickers, and Hans Paschen (Berlin: Edition Tranvia / Verlag Walter Frey, 2000), 405–15.

6. Luz Fernández de Alba, *Del tañido al arte de la fuga: Una lectura crítica de Sergio Pitol* (Mexico City: Universidad Nacional Autónoma de México, 1998); Jesús Salas-Elorza, *La narrativa dialógica de Sergio Pitol* (Providence, R.I.: Inti, 1999); Maricruz Castro Ricalde, *Ficción, narración y polifonía* (Toluca: Universidad Autónoma del Estado de México, 2000); Genaro J. Pérez, *Rabelais, Bajtin y formalismo en la narrativa de Sergio Pitol* (Newark, Del.: Juan de la Cuesta, 2011).

7. Alfonso Montelongo, *Vientres troqueles: La narrativa de Sergio Pitol* (Xalapa: Universidad Veracruzana, 1998); Teresa García Díaz, *Del Tajín a Venecia: Un regreso a ninguna parte* (Xalapa: Universidad Veracruzana, 2002); Laura Cázares Hernández, *El caldero fáustico: La narrativa de Sergio Pitol* (Mexico City: Universidad Autónoma Metropolitana, 2006); Karim Benmiloud, *Sergio Pitol ou le carnaval des vanités: El desfile del amor* (Paris: CNED / PUF, 2012); Alejandro Hermosilla Sánchez, *Sergio Pitol, las máscaras del viajero: Caleidoscopios, lentes fractales y territorios asimétricos de la literatura mexicana. La danza en el laberinto* (Xalapa: Universidad Veracruzana, 2012); Elizabeth Corral, *La escritura insumisa: Correspondencia en la obra de Sergio Pitol* (San Luis Potosí: El Colegio de San Luis, 2013). Notable studies on Pitol's short fiction include Renato Prada Oropeza, *La narrativa de Sergio Pitol: Los cuentos* (Xalapa: Universidad Veracruzana, 1996), and Hugo Valdés Manríquez, *El laberinto cuentístico de Sergio Pitol* (Monterrey: Fondo Estatal para la Cultura y las Artes de Nuevo León, 1998). For more on Pitol's essays, see Luz Fernández de Alba, *Sergio Pitol, ensayista* (Xalapa: Universidad Veracruzana, 2010).

8. The most notable are Eduardo Serrato, comp., *Tiempo abierto, tiempo cerrado: Sergio Pitol ante la crítica* (Mexico City: Era/UNAM, 1994); José Brú, comp., *Acercamientos a Sergio Pitol: Premio Juan Rulfo 1999* (Mexico City: Universidad de Guadalajara, 1999), and *Sergio Pitol, los territorios del viajero* (Mexico City: Era, 2000); Teresa García Díaz, coord., *Victorio Ferri se hizo mago en Viena* (Xalapa: Universidad Veracruzana, 2007); and Karim Benmiloud and Raphaël Estève, *El planeta Pitol* (Bourdeaux: Presses Universitaires de Bourdeaux, 2013). Among the journals devoted to Pitol are special issues of *Batarro* (38–40 [2002]); *La palabra y el hombre* (2006); and *Casa de las Américas* (255 [2009]).

9. Sergio Pitol, *El tercer personaje* (Mexico City: Era, 2013).

10. Pitol's memoir was recently reissued with minor modifications as *Memoria 1933–1966* (Mexico City: Era, 2011). I will nonetheless follow the text of *Obras reunidas IV*. The reason behind the title change may be that the name *Autobiografía precoz* was shared by a series of memoirs written by young Mexican

writers, Pitol included, in the 1960s; the new title, generic as it is, allows for the text's republication outside the original series.

11. Diana Lary, *China's Civil War: A Social History, 1945–1949* (Cambridge: Cambridge University Press, 2015), 206.

12. *Obras reunidas IV*, 36–37. This was not Pitol's only experience in China. For a chronicle of his relationship to the country, see Pilar Jiménez, "Sergio Pitol en China: Un viajero en su fuga," *Revista de la Universidad de México* 90 (August 2011): 25–30.

13. Austin Jersild, *The Sino-Soviet Alliance: An International History* (Chapel Hill: University of North Carolina Press, 2014), 224.

14. Matthew D. Rothwell documents this period in *Transpacific Revolutionaries: The Chinese Revolution in Latin America* (London: Routledge, 2012), 28–47.

15. Jiménez, "Sergio Pitol en China," 26–27.

16. Pitol, *Obras reunidas IV*, 35.

17. Pitol, *Obras reunidas IV*, 35. The books he references are Simone de Beauvoir, *La longue marche: Essai sur la Chine* (Paris: Gallimard, 1958); Claude Roy, *Clefs sur la Chine* (Paris: Gallimard, 1953); and Vercors, *Les divagations d'un français en Chine* (Paris: Albin Michel, 1956).

18. Pitol, *Obras reunidas V*, 257. The English translation of this book will be published by Deep Vellum in 2016.

19. For a discussion of Lao She (or Lao Che, as Pitol transliterates his name), see David Wang, *Fictional Realism in Twentieth-Century China: Mao Dun, Lao She, Shen Congwen* (New York: Columbia University Press, 1992), 111–200.

20. In the interests of consistency with the editions used and with Pitol's own writing, I will use the standard Spanish transliteration. The writer is typically known in English as Lu Xun.

21. The original edition was published in 1971 by the Heterodoxos series that Pitol directed at the Spanish press Tusquets. I will cite the following edition here: Lu Hsun, *Diario de un loco*, trans. Sergio Pitol (Xalapa: Universidad Veracruzana, 2007).

22. Huang Sung-K'uang, *Lu Hsun and the New Culture Movement of Modern China* (Amsterdam: Djambatan, 1957), 37.

23. Sung K'uang, *Lu Hsun*, 55. For a study on the complex uses of Lu Hsun in the Cultural Revolution, see Merle Goldman, "The Political Use of Lu Hsun in the Revolution and After," in Leo Ou-Fan Lee, *Lu Hsun and His Legacy* (Berkeley: University of California Press, 1971), 180–96.

24. Lu Hsun, *Diario*, 7.

25. Lu Hsun, *Diario*, 7.

26. Lu Hsun, *Diario*, 7–8.

27. Lu Hsun, *Diario*, 9–10.

28. Oswaldo Zavala, "La síntesis y su trascendencia: Sergio Pitol, la escritura autobiográfica y el fin del occidentalismo," *RILCE* 28.1 (2012): 257–72.

29. Beecroft, *An Ecology of World Literature*, 269. Beecroft develops this category earlier and more concisely in his article "World Literature without a Hyphen: Towards a Typology of Literary Systems," *New Left Review* 54 (2008); https://newleftreview.org/II/54/alexander-beecroft-world-literature-without-a-hyphen.

30. See Pascale Casanova, *The World Republic of Letters* (Cambridge, Mass.: Harvard University Press, 2004), 96–97. For a less simplistic account of the

politics of the Spanish language in *modernismo*, one that does not reify French as the sole determining factor, see Alejandro Mejías-López, *The Inverted Conquest: The Myth of Modernity and the Transatlantic Onset of Modernism* (Nashville: Vanderbilt University Press, 2009).

31. See Moretti, *Distant Reading* (London: Verso, 2013), 50–51. To his credit, though, Moretti does recognize in a note that Spanish and Portuguese are the kinds of languages for which "extra-European" exchanges might be more relevant than "intra-European" ones (42), although such a statement implicitly defines Spain and Portugal as the core of those language traditions (which, historically, is not always the case).

32. For further discussion on the historical status of Spanish within Latin American literature, see Roberto Ignacio Díaz, *Unhomely Rooms: Foreign Tongues and Spanish American Literature* (Lewisburg, Pa.: Bucknell University Press, 2002).

33. Michael Cronin, *Translation and Globalization* (London: Routledge, 2003), 121.

34. For a useful description and critique of systemic theories of world literature, see Theo D'haen, *The Routledge Concise History of World Literature* (London: Routledge, 2011), 96–116.

35. Moretti, *Distant Reading*, 63.

36. Casanova, *The World Republic of Letters*, 108.

37. See Mario Santana, *Foreigners in the Homeland: The Spanish American New Novel in Spain, 1962–1974* (Lewisburg, Pa.: Bucknell University Press, 2000), 33–63, and Alejandro Herrero-Olaizola, *The Censorship Files: Latin American Writers and Franco's Spain* (Albany: State University of New York Press, 2007), 1–36. We should note these works do not offer a detailed study of Tusquets, which was not a major outlet for Latin American Boom writers.

38. This information is cited by Santana, *Foreigners in the Homeland*, 47, from data provided by UNESCO.

39. Juan Cruz Ruiz, *Por el gusto de leer: Beatriz de Moura, editora por vocación* (Barcelona: Tusquets, 2014), 46–47.

40. Cruz Ruiz, *Por el gusto de leer*, 45.

41. Herrero-Olaizola, *The Censorship Files*, 19.

42. Pitol, *El tercer personaje*, 137.

43. Jerzy Grotowski, *Teatro Laboratorio* (Barcelona: Tusquets, 1970).

44. Sergio Pitol, ed., *Cuatro dramaturgos polacos* (Xalapa: Universidad Veracruzana, 1970). Another relevant book from this period is Pitol's celebrated *Antología del cuento polaco contemporáneo* (*Anthology of Contemporary Polish Short Fiction* [Mexico City: Era, 1967]). It includes seventeen short stories translated by Pitol, including works by authors he would translate extensively in later years (like Gombrowicz, Andrzejewski, and Kasimierz Brandys), as well as authors who would later become references in Mexican literary circles, including Bruno Schulz and Leszek Kolakowski.

45. For a historical account of Pitol's time in Barcelona and his general involvement with the literary world and the Latin American Boom, see Xavi Ayén, *Aquellos años del boom: García Márquez, Vargas Llosa y el grupo de amigos que lo cambiaron todo* (Barcelona: RBA, 2014), 455–65.

46. Jerzy Lukowski and Hubert Zawadzki, *A Concise History of Poland*, 2nd ed. (Cambridge: Cambridge University Press, 2006), 299.

47. To be sure, Pitol does engage meaningfully with both traditions. He is a champion of Spanish writers like Benito Pérez Galdós, and, among his most important translations, one may recall Elio Vittorini's *Las ciudades del mundo* (*The Cities of the World* [Barcelona: Barral, 1971]); Luigi Malerba's *Salto mortal* (*Deadly Leap* [Barcelona: Barral, 1971]); and Giorgio Bassani's *Lida Mantovani y otras historias de Ferrara* (*Lida Mantovani and Other Stories from Ferrara* [Barcelona: Barral, 1971]). These were intended for a larger commercial market than the text published by Heterodoxos, but Pitol did translate all of these works in Barcelona during the same period.

48. Pitol, *El tercer personaje*, 216–17.

49. Jerzy Andrzejewski, *Las puertas del paraíso* (Mexico City: Joaquín Mortiz, 1965; Xalapa: Universidad Veracruzana, 1966). My citations are from Universidad Veracruzana edition.

50. Andrzejewski, *Las puertas del paraíso*, 17.

51. Mariano Siskind, *Cosmopolitan Desires: Global Modernity and World Literature in Latin America* (Evanston, Ill.: Northwestern University Press, 2014), 19; Casanova, *The World Republic of Letters*, 177.

52. For a detailed study of Joaquín Mortiz in this period, see Danny J. Anderson, "Creating Cultural Prestige: Editorial Joaquín Mortiz," *Latin American Research Review* 31.2 (1996): 3–41.

53. Pitol refers to his literary ideas from this period in *Obras reunidas V*, 355–58.

54. Pitol, *Obras reunidas IV*, 99.

55. Pitol, *Obras reunidas V*, 115.

56. Pitol, *Obras reunidas V*, 115–16.

57. Mark Slonim, *Soviet Russian Literature: Writers and Problems, 1917–1977*, 2nd rev. ed. (New York: Oxford University Press, 1977). The first edition of Slonim's book was published in 1967 and already included the essay on Pilniak. Due to the dates of Pitol's essay and his translations of the Russian author, he was probably consulting the 1977 edition, but the earlier one contains the exact same text on Pilniak.

58. Slonim, *Soviet Russian Literature*, 64.

59. Slonim, *Soviet Russian Literature*, 67.

60. Robert A. Maguire, *Red Virgin Soil: Soviet Literature in the 1920s* (Princeton, N.J.: Princeton University Press, 1968), 101.

61. Pitol, *Obras reunidas V*, 116.

62. While I will not elaborate on the memoirs, the nature of Pitol's time in Moscow is central to understanding this contention. For an excellent study comparing Walter Benjamin's Moscow with Pitol's, see Raúl Rodríguez-Hernández, "Seduction, Constellation, Illumination: The Afterlife of Walter Benjamin in the Writings of Sergio Pitol," *Discourse* 32.1 (2010): 117–37.

63. T. N. R. Edwards, *Three Russian Writers and the Irrational: Zamyatin, Pil'Nyak, and Bulgakov* (Cambridge: Cambridge University Press, 1982), 99–100.

64. Pitol, *Obras reunidas V*, 120.

65. See Boris Pilniak, *Caoba*, trans. Sergio Pitol (Mexico City: Universidad Nacional Autónoma de México, 1980; Barcelona: Anagrama, 1987). Editor Jorge Herralde refers to this translation as an important work in the Panorama series; see Herralde, *Opiniones mohicanas*, 72. Pitol introduced Mexican readers

to Pilniak in a piece published in the UNAM magazine, accompanied by a translation of one of his short stories. See Pitol, "Del modo en que Pilniak cuenta un cuento," *Revista de la Universidad de México* (September 1980): 2.

66. Pitol, *El tercer personaje*, 142.

67. Jorge Herralde, *El optimismo de la voluntad: Experiencias editoriales en América Latina* (Mexico City: Fondo de Cultura Económica, 2009), 34; *Por orden alfabético: Escritores, editores, amigos* (Barcelona: Anagrama, 2006), 249. See also Witold Gombrowicz, *Transtlántico* (Barcelona: Anagrama, 1986).

68. Pitol, *El tercer personaje*, 143.

69. Kazimierz Brandys, *Rondó*, trans. Sergio Pitol (Barcelona: Anagrama, 1991). The Mexican election of 1988, in which former president Carlos Salinas de Gortari beat left-wing candidate Cuauhtémoc Cárdenas, was considered an electoral fraud by large sectors of Mexican society and a setback to the country's early efforts to establish a multiparty democracy.

70. Kazimiers Brandys, *Cartas a la señora Z* (Xalapa: Universidad Veracruzana, 1966); *Madre de Reyes* (Mexico City: Era, 1968); "Cómo ser amada," in Pitol, *Antología del cuento polaco contemporáneo*, 208–35.

71. An English edition of *Rondó* is available (New York: Europa, 2011).

72. Aleksandar Flaker, "A Polemics with History: Kazimierz Brandys's *Rondó*," in *History: Another Text; Essays on Kazimierz Brandys, Danilo Kis, György Konrad and Christa Wolf* (Ann Arbor: Michigan Studies in the Humanities, 1988), 8–9.

73. Lawrence Venuti, *The Translator's Invisibility: A History of Translation* (London: Routledge, 1995), 18.

74. Venuti, *The Translator's Invisibility*, 19.

75. Venuti, *The Translator's Invisibility*, 20.

76. See Henry James, *Las bostonianas* (Barcelona: Seix Barral, 1966); *Washington Square* (Barcelona: Seix Barral, 1970); *Lo que Maisie sabía* (Barcelona: Seix Barral, 1971); *Otra vuelta de tuerca* (Barcelona: Salvat, 1971); *Daisy Miller y los papeles de Aspern* (Mexico: UNAM, 1984).

77. Jane Austen, *Emma* (Barcelona: Salvat, 1972); Joseph Conrad, *El corazón de las tinieblas* (Barcelona: Lumen, 1974). It is indeed important to note that Conrad has Polish origins, although Pitol does not discuss him as a Polish writer.

78. Sergio Pitol, *De Jane Austen a Virginia Woolf: Seis novelistas en sus textos* (Mexico: SepSetentas, 1975). The book was later retitled, first as *Una adicción a la novela inglesa* (Mexico City: Biblioteca del ISSSTE, 1999) and finally as its current *Adicción a los ingleses: Vida y obra de diez novelistas* (Mexico City: Lectorum, 2002), which includes the original essays (on Emily Brontë, Jane Austen, Robert Louis Stevenson, Joseph Conrad, and Virginia Woolf), plus the essays on Ivy Compton-Burnett, Evelyn Waush, Ronald Firbank, and Flann O'Brien from other collections. Here I use the version from *Obras reunidas*, which for some reason omits the Stevenson essay.

79. Given space limitations, I will not focus on formal matters in Pitol's essays here, but readers interested in this question will find a good study in Fernández de Alba, *Sergio Pitol, ensayista*. Further elaborations on Pitol's work in the essay genre may be found in María del Pilar Vila, "La alquimia de un género: Sergio Pitol y el ensayo literario," *Revista Iberoamericana* 240 (2013): 605–21. This latter essay makes contentions similar to mine regarding Pitol's use of the essay to position himself in the literary field.

80. Michael Goddard, *Gombrowicz, Polish Modernism and the Subversion of Form* (West Lafayette, Ind.: Purdue University Press, 2010), 28–29.

81. Goddard, *Gombrowicz*, 10.

82. Anita Starosta, *Form and Instability: Eastern Europe, Literature, Postimperial Difference* (Evanston, Ill.: Northwestern University Press, 2016).

83. Starosta, *Form and Instability*, 125.

84. Starosta, *Form and Instability*, 129.

85. Pitol, *Obras reunidas V*, 38.

86. Pitol, *Obras reunidas V*, 63.

87. Starosta, *Form and Instability*, 175–200.

88. Pitol, *Obras reunidas V*, 125.

89. Jorge Herralde, *Opiniones mohicanas* (Barcelona: El Acantilado, 2001), 115–18.

90. Jane Bowles, *Dos damas muy serias* (Barcelona: Anagrama, 1981). A recent English edition is available (New York: Ecco, 2014).

91. Jorge Herralde, *Flashes sobre escritores y otros textos editoriales* (Mexico: El Ermitaño, 2003), 100.

92. Italo Calvino, *Six Memos for the New Millennium* (Cambridge, Mass.: Harvard University Press, 1988); Milan Kundera, *The Art of the Novel*, trans. Linda Asher (New York: Grove, 1988); *Testaments Betrayed: An Essay in Nine Parts*, trans. Linda Asher (New York: HarperCollins, 1995).

93. For more on Kundera's engagement with Tusquets, see Cruz Ruiz, *Por el gusto de leer*, 100–103.

94. Kundera, *The Art of the Novel*, 13–20; Jaroslav Hašek, *Las aventuras del buen soldado Schveik durante la segunda guerra mundial*, trans. Sergio Pitol (Mexico City: Conaculta, 1992); Pitol, *Obras reunidas IV*, 229–38.

95. Kundera, *Testaments Betrayed*, 1–35.

96. Kundera, *The Art of the Novel*, 18.

97. For various examples of critics making this point, see Montelongo, *Vientres troqueles*, 60–61.

98. Readers interested in this question should read Salas-Elorza, *La narrativa dialógica de Sergio Pitol*, and Genaro J. Pérez, *Rabelais, Bajtín y formalismo en la narrativa de Sergio Pitol* (Newark, Del.: Juan de la Cuesta, 2011).

99. For more on Joyce's influence in Mexico, see Brian L. Price, "Non Serviam: James Joyce and Mexico," *Comparative Literature* 64.2 (2012): 192–206.

100. For a discussion of Fuentes and James, see Ricardo López Landeira, "*Aura, The Aspern Papers*, 'A Rose for Emily': A Literary Relationship," *Journal of Spanish Studies* 3 (1975): 125–43, and Djelal Kadir, "Another Sense of the Past: Henry James' *The Aspern Papers* and Carlos Fuentes' *Aura*," *Revue de Littérature Comparée* 50 (1976): 448–54.

101. Ryan F. Long, *Fictions of Totality: The Mexican Novel, 1968 and the National-Popular State* (West Lafayette, Ind.: Purdue University Press, 2008).

102. Pitol, *Obras reunidas IV*, 186.

103. Viktor Shklovsky, *Theory of Prose*, trans. Benjamin Sher (Normal, Ill.: Dalkey Archive, 1991), 6.

104. Pitol, *Obras reunidas V*, 185.

105. Rebecca L. Walkowitz, *Cosmopolitan Style: Modernism beyond the Nation* (New York: Columbia University Press, 2006), 4.

106. Walkowitz, *Cosmopolitan Style*, 12.

107. Nicholas Brown, *Utopian Generations: The Political Horizon of Twentieth-Century Literature* (Princeton, N.J.: Princeton University Press, 2005), 187; Franco Moretti, *Modern Epic: The World System from Goethe to García Márquez* (London: Verso, 2006), 50.

108. Robert F. Kiernan, *Frivolity Unbound: Six Masters of the Camp Novel* (New York: Continuum, 1990), 142.

109. Ignacio M. Sánchez Prado, "Sergio Pitol y sus afinidades electivas: El affaire Compton-Burnett," in *Línea de sombra: Ensayos sobre Sergio Pitol*, ed. José Homerao (Mexico City: Conaculta, 2009), 87–100.

110. Ángel Rama, *Transculturación narrativa en América Latina* (Mexico: Siglo XXI Editores, 1982).

111. Sergio Pitol, *Obras reunidas I: El tañido de una flauta; juegos florales* (Mexico City: Fondo de Cultura Económica, 2003), 12–13.

112. Pitol, *Obras reunidas I*, 19.

113. Cynthia Steele, *Politics, Gender and the Mexican Novel, 1968–1988: Beyond the Pyramid* (Austin: University of Texas Press, 1992).

114. Carol Clark D'Lugo, *The Fragmented Novel in Mexico: The Politics of Form* (Austin: University of Texas Press, 1997).

115. Quoted in Sara Sefchovich, *México: País de ideas, país de novelas. Una sociología de la literatura mexicana* (Mexico City: Grijalbo, 1987).

116. Long, *Fictions of Totality*. Long's study of Del Paso focuses on *José Trigo*, not on *Palinuro de México*.

117. Long, *Fictions of Totality*, 183.

118. For a study on this phenomenon, see Ignacio M. Sánchez Prado, "The Democratic Dogma: Héctor Aguilar Camín, Jorge G. Castañeda and Enrique Krauze in the Neoliberal Crucible," in *Mexican Public Intellectuals*, ed. Debra A. Castilo and Stuart A. Day (New York: Palgrave Macmillan, 2014), 15–44.

119. For a study of this decline, see Ángel Rama, "El boom en perspectiva," in *La crítica de la cultura en América Latina* (Caracas: Ayacucho, 1985).

120. Neige Sinno, *Lectores entre líneas: Roberto Bolaño, Ricardo Piglia y Sergio Pitol* (Mexico City: Aldus/Conaculta, 2011).

121. A discussion of these two authors would exceed the purposes of this book, and the fact that both have elicited numerous critical studies testifies to the complexity of this question. For additional references, I would point, for Piglia, to Jorge Fornet, *El escritor y la tradición: Ricardo Piglia y la literatura argentina* (Buenos Aires: Fondo de Cultura Económica, 2007). It is more difficult to name a good reference for Bolaño, given the proliferation of studies accompanying his growing literary fame, but I believe the one that best discusses the questions raised here is Oswaldo Zavala, *La modernidad insufrible: Roberto Bolaño en los límites de la literatura latinoamericana contemporánea* (Chapel Hill: North Carolina Studies in the Romance Languages and Literatures, 2016).

122. Sinno, *Lectores entre líneas*, 217.

123. Pitol, *Obras reunidas III*, 29.

124. Pitol, *Obras reunidas III*, 31–35; César Rodríguez Chicharro, "Infierno de todos," in *Tiempo cerrado, tiempo abierto: Sergio Pitol ante la crítica*, comp. Eduardo Serrato (Mexico City: Era/UNAM, 1994), 81–83.

125. Pitol, *Obras reunidas III*, 81.

126. Pitol, *Obras reunidas I*, 92.

127. Pitol, *Obras reunidas III*, 250.

128. Fernández de Alba, *Del tañido al arte de la fuga*, 56.

129. This description comes from Sarah Crangle, "Ivy Compton-Burnett and Risibility," in *British Fiction after Modernism: The Novel at Mid-Century*, ed. Marina MacKay and Lyndsey Stonebridge (New York: Palgrave Macmillan, 2007), 99–117.

130. Pitol, *Obras reunidas V*, 132.

131. Pitol, *Obras reunidas V*, 117.

132. This is not the only boundary questioned by the story. For a discussion of the division between fiction and reality, see Cázares Hernández, *El caldero fáustico*, 65–78.

133. Pitol, *Obras reunidas III*, 261.

134. Pitol, *Obras reunidas III*, 261.

135. Pitol, *Obras reunidas III*, 261.

136. Moretti, *Modern Epic*, 233–50.

137. Sarah Pollack, "Latin America Translated (Again): Roberto Bolaño's *The Savage Detectives* in the United States," *Comparative Literature* 61.3 (2009): 346–65.

138. Roberto Bolaño, *Entre paréntesis* (Barcelona: Anagrama, 2004), 135–37, 342.

139. Enrique Vila-Matas, *El viento ligero en Parma* (Madrid: Sexto Piso, 2008), 190.

140. Sylvia Molloy, "Latin America in the US Imaginary: Postcolonialism, Translation and the Magical Realist Imperative," in *Ideologies of Hispanism* (Nashville: Vanderbilt University Press, 2005), 189–200.

141. Hector Hoyos, *Beyond Bolaño: The Global Latin American Novel* (New York: Columbia University Press, 2015).

142. See notes 4, 5, and 6 to this chapter.

143. Renato Prada Oropeza, *La narrativa de Sergio Pitol: Los cuentos* (Xalapa: Universidad Veracruzana, 70–71).

144. Sergio Pitol, *Obras reunidas III*, 260; emphasis in the original. I have taken the Kott quote from Jan Kott, *Theatre Notebooks 1947–1967*, trans. Boleslaw Taborski (Garden City, N.Y.: Doubleday, 1968).

145. Pitol, *Obras reunidas III*, 238.

146. Pitol, *Obras reunidas II*, 214.

147. Brian L. Price, *Cult of Defeat in Mexico's Historical Fiction: Failure, Trauma and Loss* (New York: Palgrave Macmillan, 2012).

148. Elisabeth Guerrero, *Confronting History and Modernity in Mexican Narrative* (New York: Palgrave Macmillan, 2008).

149. For a reading of *Noticias del imperio* in these terms, see María Cristina Pons, *Memorias del olvido: La novela histórica de fines del siglo XX* (Mexico City: Siglo XXI, 1996), 110–60.

150. Pitol, *Obras reunidas V*, 178–85. See Jorge Ibargüengoitia, *Los relámpagos de agosto* (Mexico City: Joaquín Mortiz, 1964).

151. Pitol, *Obras reunidas V*, 324.

152. Karim Benmiloud, *Sergio Pitol ou le carnival des vanités* (Paris: PUF, 2013). A chapter-by-chapter description of the book according to Bakhtin's

theory can be found in Pérez, *Rabelais, Bajtín y formalismo en la narrativa de Sergio Pitol*, 75–99. Finally, a close reading of the book can be found in José Eduardo Serrato Córdova, *Las tramas de la parodia* (Mexico City: Universidad Nacional Autónoma de México, 2013).

153. Pitol, *Obras reunidas II*, 28.

154. Benmiloud, *Sergio Pitol ou le carnival des vanités*, 59.

155. Pitol, *Obras reunidas II*, 55.

156. Pitol, *Obras reunidas II*, 75.

157. For alternative accounts of how historical layers are constructed in this book, see Benmiloud, *Sergio Pitol ou le carnival des vanités*, and Marie-José Hanaï, "*El desfile del amor*: Un juego de pistas históricas," in Benmiloud and Estève, *El planeta Pitol*, 173–87.

158. For each historical period, see, respectively, Gareth Williams, *The Mexican Exception: Sovereignty, Police and Democracy* (New York: Palgrave Macmillan, 2011), 49; Gilbert M. Joseph and Jürgen Buchenau, *Mexico's Once and Future Revolution: Social Upheaval and the Challenge of Rule since the Late Nineteenth Century* (Durham, N.C.: Duke University Press, 2013), 144–45; Joseph and Buchenau, *Mexico's Once and Future Revolution*, 172.

159. Pitol, *Obras reunidas II*, 205–6.

160. Friedrich E. Schuler, "Alemania, México y los Estados Unidos durante la Segunda Guerra Mundial," *Secuencias* 7 (1987): 173–86. See also Friedrich E. Schuler, *Mexico between Hitler and Roosevelt: Mexican Foreign Relations in the Age of Lázaro Cárdenas* (Albuquerque: University of New Mexico Press, 1998).

161. For a description of this period, see María Elena Paz, *Strategy, Security and Spies: Mexico and the US as Allies in World War II* (University Park: Pennsylvania State University Press, 1997), 123–32.

162. See Kazimierz Brandys, *Madre de Reyes*, trans. Sergio Pitol (Xalapa: Universidad Veracruzana, 2008), and *Rondó*. We should bear in mind that other books translated by Pitol were centered on the two world wars. See, for example, Robert Graves, *Adiós a todo eso*, trans. Sergio Pitol (Barcelona: Seix Barral, 1971), a translation of *Good-Bye to All That* (New York: Vintage, 1991). The book is a 1929 autobiography focused on a soldier in World War I and the loss of innocence in the conflict. Graves's narrative relies heavily on comedy, and one could certainly make the case that the style and perspective of this book may have influenced the tone of *El desfile del amor*.

163. Vicente Alfonso, "El enigma, el mago y el desfile," in Homerao, *Línea de sombra*, 103–11. A more detailed reading of *El desfile del amor* as a detective fiction may be found in Gerardo Hurtado, "*El desfile del amor* de Sergio Pitol: Una tragicomedia policial en tres actos," in *Bang! Bang! Pesquisas sobre narrativa policiaca mexicana* (Mexico City: UNAM, 2005), 91–113.

164. Corral, *La escritura insumisa*, 75.

165. Sharon Lubkemann Allen, *EccentriCities: Writing in the Margins of Modernism. St. Petersburg to Rio de Janeiro* (Manchester: Manchester University Press, 2013), 199.

166. Sergio Pitol, *Obras reunidas V*, 104.

167. Rafael Gutiérrez Girardot, "*Poeta doctus*: Sergio Pitol o la transgresión en los géneros literarios," in García Díaz, *Victorio Ferri se hizo mago en Viena*, 193–202.

168. Saikat Majumdar, *Prose of the World: Modernism and the Banality of Empire* (New York: Columbia University Press, 2013), 12.

169. Majumdar, *Prose of the World*, 4.

170. José Eduardo Serrato Córdova, "Algunas fuentes literarias en *El desfile del amor*," in García Díaz, *Victorio Ferri se hizo mago en Viena*, 225–34.

171. For a study of elements relevant to this question, see Lisa Coletta, *Dark Humor and Social Satire in the Modern British Novel* (New York: Palgrave Macmillan, 2003). In particular, Coletta's reading of Compton-Burnett and Waugh illustrates elements that Pitol would incorporate into Mexican fiction.

172. Castro Ricalde, *Ficción, narración y polifonía*, 1.

173. Sinno, *Lectores entre líneas*, 207. For readers interested in detailed explorations of Pitol's work, see Hermosilla Sánchez, *Sergio Pitol, Las máscaras del viajero*, and Hugo Valdés, *El dueño y el creador: Un acercamiento al dédalo narrativo de Sergio Pitol* (Monterrey: Conarte/Conaculta, 2014). Both books are extensive nonacademic essays that provide wonderful and in-depth personal explorations of Pitol's work, sometimes weaving even fiction and memoir into their analyses. Both books respond well to Pitol's reader-writer aesthetic and provide a view of his work from a "creative reader's" perspective.

Chapter 2

1. Sergio Pitol, *El arte de la fuga* (Mexico City: Era, 1996).

2. Pedro Ángel Palou, *Memoria de los días* (Mexico City: Joaquín Mortiz, 1995); Jorge Volpi, *El temperamento melancólico* (Mexico City: Nueva Imagen, 1996); Ignacio Padilla, *Si volviesen sus majestades* (Mexico City: Nueva Imagen, 1996); Eloy Urroz, *Las rémoras* (Mexico City: Nueva Imagen, 1996); Ricardo Chávez Castañeda, *La conspiración idiota* (Mexico City: Alfaguara, 2003). Chávez Castañeda's book was forthcoming at the time of the presentation, but he ultimately published another work first, *El día del hurón* (Mexico City: Nueva Imagen, 1997). The novel was not published until 2003. For Chávez Castañeda's account of this matter, see Sandra Licona, "Entrar al mundo editorial implica una conspiración idiota: Ricardo Chávez Castañeda, escritor," in *La Crónica de Hoy* (Mexico City), June 10, 2006. The only one of these novels currently available in English translation is *Las rémoras*. See Eloy Urroz, *The Obstacles*, trans. Ezra Fitz (Normal, Ill.: Dalkey Archive, 2006). The manifesto was originally published in the independent magazine *Descrituras*; it was later released in Spain in the magazine *Lateral* in 2000. I am citing the version included in Chávez Castañeda et al., *Crack: Instrucciones de uso* (Mexico City: Mondadori, 2004).

3. Chávez Castañeda et al., *Crack: Instrucciones de uso*, includes not only the manifesto, but also texts by each member, written in 2004, on their respective experiences, as well as an annotated bibliography by Regalado. Padilla wrote his take on the movement in *Si hace crack es boom* (Barcelona: Umbriel, 2007). More recently, Eloy Urroz wrote an extensive autobiographical roman à clef that fictionalizes the group's formation and development. See Eloy Urroz, *La mujer del novelista* (Mexico City: Alfaguara, 2014). See also Tomás Regalado López, *La novedad del antiguo: La novela de Jorge Volpi (1992–1999) y la tradición de la ruptura* (Salamanca: Universidad de Salamanca, 2009); "Del Boom al Crack: Anotaciones críticas sobre la narrativa hispanoamericana del nuevo milenio," in *Tendencias de la narrativa mexicana actual*, ed. José Carlos González Boixo (Madrid: Iberoamericana Vervuert,

2009), 143–68; "The Crack and Contemporary Latin American Literature: An Introductory Study," in *New Trends in Contemporary Latin American Narrative: Post-National Literatures and the Canon*, ed. Timothy R. Robbins and José Eduardo González (New York: Palgrave Macmillan, 2014), 54–83; and Ramón Alvarado, *Literatura del Crack* (Mexico City: Arlequín, 2016). For a comparison between the Crack and McOndo groups in South America, see Brent Carbajal, "The Packaging of Contemporary Latin American Literature: 'La generación del Crack' and 'McOndo,'" *Confluencia* 20.2 (2005): 122–32.

4. "Variaciones sobre un tema de Faulkner," in Chávez Castañeda et al., *Crack: Instrucciones de uso*, 15–123.

5. Jorge Volpi, Eloy Urroz, and Ignacio Padilla, *Tres bosquejos del mal* (Mexico City: Siglo XXI, 1994).

6. See Eloy Urroz, *Herir tu fiera carne* (Mexico City: Nueva Imagen, 1998); Jorge Volpi, *Sanar tu piel amarga* (Mexico City: Nueva Imagen, 1998); Pedro Ángel Palou, *Bolero* (Mexico City: Nueva Imagen, 1998).

7. On the role of this award in the history of Latin American literature, see Fabio Espósito, "Seix Barral y el *boom* de la nueva narrativa hispanoamericana: Las mediaciones culturales de la edición española," *Orbis Tertius* 15 (2009); http://www.orbistertius.unlp.edu.ar/article/view/OTv14n15d03/5009.

8. Ignacio Padilla passed away in a tragic accident during the revision of this book, thus marking the Crack group's twentieth-anniversary celebration with an unexpected and sad conclusion of their trajectory.

9. For a short discussion of Urroz's work, see Ignacio M. Sánchez Prado, "Eloy Urroz (Mexico City, 1967)," in *The Contemporary Spanish-American Novel Bolaño and After*, ed. Will H. Corral, Juan E. de Castro, and Nicholas Birns (New York: Bloomsbury, 2013), 81–83. For a discussion of Chávez Castañeda, see Ignacio M. Sánchez Prado, "Ricardo Chávez Castañeda: The Limits of Fiction," in *The Crack Group*, ed. Héctor Jaimes (New York: Palgrave, 2017), forthcoming.

10. I must disclose that my own interest is not altogether objective. I was a college student of both Palou and Padilla in Mexico, and I now closely collaborate with Palou, who teaches at Tufts University. I will say, however, that the group's importance is beyond question, as I will document in this chapter, particularly since Volpi was granted the Biblioteca Breve Award in 1999. My personal contact with these writers has allowed me to document issues necessary for a full comprehension of their work, given the lack of critical studies available (far less than the materials accessible for Del Paso, Pitol, and Rivera Garza). I am very grateful to Volpi, Palou, and Padilla for answering my questions about their work, as well as to Sandro Cohen, the editor who supported the release of the first Crack novels and the group manifesto, for helping me with this chapter.

11. Padilla, *Si hace crack es boom*, 41–52.

12. Ángel Rama, *La novela latinoamericana 1920–1980* (Bogotá: Instituto Colombiano de Cultura, 1982), 235–93.

13. For a reading of Del Paso's *Palinuro de México* in terms of its strategic Occidentalism, see Ignacio M. Sánchez Prado, "Dying Mirrors, Medieval Moralists and Tristram Shandies: The Literary Traditions of Fernando del Paso's *Palinuro de México*," *Comparative Literature* 60.2 (2008): 142–63.

14. The overall topic of Joaquín Mortiz exceeds my purposes here, but one can consult Danny J. Anderson's superb study of Mortiz's role in the construction of

Mexican literature. See Danny J. Anderson, "Creating Cultural Prestige: Editorial Joaquín Mortiz," *Latin American Research Review* 31.2 (1996): 3–41.

15. The authors who would lead Anagrama's push into Latin America (Bolaño, Piglia, Villoro) would not be fully part of the catalog until the 2000s.

16. I will not discuss the book market in detail here, but a full-length analysis may be found in Ignacio M. Sánchez Prado, "Más allá del Mercado: Los usos de la literatura latinoamericana en la era neoliberal," in *Libro mercado: Literatura y neoliberalismo,* ed. José Ramón Ruisánchez Serra (Mexico City: Universidad Iberoamericana, 2015), 15–40.

17. Sandro Cohen, email to the author, December 27, 2015.

18. Graham Huggan, *The Postcolonial Exotic: Marketing the Margins* (London: Routledge, 2001).

19. Huggan, *The Postcolonial Exotic,* 19–20.

20. Huggan, *The Postcolonial Exotic,* 71–72.

21. As a counterexample, see Emilio Sauri's brilliant study of Faulkner's derivations in García Márquez and Fuentes and how they relate to emerging neoliberalism: Emilio Sauri, "Faulkner and His Brothers," *Studies in American Fiction* 40.2 (2013): 259–83. Another good example is Kumkum Sangari's excellent study of the comparison between García Márquez and Rushdie in *Politics of the Possible: Essays on Gender, History, Narratives, Colonial English* (New Delhi: Tulika, 1999), 1–28.

22. Mariano Siskind, *Cosmopolitan Desires: Global Modernity and World Literature in Latin America* (Evanston, Ill.: Northwestern University Press, 2014), 88.

23. Siskind, *Cosmopolitan Desires,* 97.

24. Warwick Research Collective, *Combined and Uneven Development: Towards a New Theory of World Literature* (Liverpool: Liverpool University Press, 2015), 50.

25. Warwick Research Collective, *Combined and Uneven Development,* 68.

26. Warwick Research Collective, *Combined and Uneven Development,* 80.

27. Sylvia Molloy, "Latin America in the US Imaginary: Postcolonialism, Translation and the Magical Realist Imperative," in *Ideologies of Hispanism,* ed. Mabel Moraña (Nashville: Vanderbilt University Press, 2005), 189–200.

28. Gesine Müller, "Las novelas del 'Boom' como provocación canónica: Interacciones literarias entre 'La Onda,' el 'Crack' y Carlos Fuentes," *Revista de crítica literaria latinoamericana* 59 (2004): 43–52; Regalado López, "The Crack and Contemporary Latin American Narrative."

29. Laura Esquivel, *Como agua para chocolate* (Mexico City: Planeta, 1989); English version, *Like Water for Chocolate,* trans. Carol and Thomas Christensen (New York: Doubleday, 1992). See also Claire Taylor, "Laura Esquivel and the *Boom Femenino*: Popular Genres and Double Encoding," in *The Boom Femenino in Mexico: Reading Contemporary Women's Writing,* ed. Nuala Finnegan and Jane Lavery (Newcastle upon Tyne: Cambridge Scholars, 2010), 199–216.

30. Victoria Martínez, "*Como agua para chocolate*: A Recipe for Neoliberalism," *Chasqui* 33.1 (2004): 28–41.

31. Italo Calvino, *Six Memos for the New Millennium,* trans. Patrick Creagh (Cambridge, Mass.: Harvard University Press, 1988). I discuss this book's importance to Pitol's project in chapter 2.

32. Chávez Castañeda et al., *Crack: Instrucciones de uso,* 210–11.

33. Chávez Castañeda et al., *Crack: Instrucciones de uso*, 212–13.

34. Eric Hayot, *On Literary Worlds* (Oxford: Oxford University Press, 2012), 122–23.

35. Chávez Castañeda et al., *Crack: Instrucciones de uso*, 213.

36. Pedro Ángel Palou, *Paraíso clausurado* (Barcelona: Muchnik, 2000).

37. Chávez Castañeda et al., *Crack: Instrucciones de uso*, 213. The reference is to John S. Brushwood, *Mexico in Its Novel: A Nation and Its Search for Identity* (Austin: University of Texas Press, 1966).

38. Chávez Castañeda et al., *Crack: Instrucciones de uso*, 219.

39. Chávez Castañeda et al., *Crack: Instrucciones de uso*, 219.

40. Regalado López, "The Crack and Contemporary Latin American Literature," 67.

41. Gullermo J. Fadanelli, "La literatura del frac," *Sábado* (August 16, 1996): 14.

42. Sarah Brouillette, *Postcolonial Writers in the Global Literary Marketplace* (New York: Palgrave Macmillan, 2007), 174–76.

43. Brouillette, *Postcolonial Writers in the Global Literary Marketplace*, 79–80. Referenced texts are Pascale Casanova, *The World Republic of Letters*, trans. M. V. DeBevoise (Cambridge, Mass.: Harvard University Press, 2004), and James F. English, *The Economy of Prestige, Prizes, Awards and the Circulation of Cultural Value* (Cambridge, Mass.: Harvard University Press, 2005).

44. This is masterfully developed by Brouillette in her second monograph, *Literature and the Creative Economy* (Stanford, Calif.: Stanford University Press, 2014), where she rigorously tracks literature's growing relationship with neoliberal ideologies of the "creative economy."

45. Sarah Brouillette and Christopher Doody, "The Literary as Cultural Industry," in *The Routledge Companion to Cultural Industries*, ed. Kate Oakley and Justin O' Connor (London: Routledge, 2015), 107.

46. Brouillette, *Postcolonial Writers in the Global Literary Marketplace*, 80.

47. Pierre Bourdieu, *The Rules of Art: Genesis and Structure of the Literary Field*, trans. Susan Emanuel (Stanford, Calif.: Stanford University Press, 1996), 225–31.

48. Pedro Ángel Palou, *La casa del silencio: Aproximación en tres tiempos a Contemporáneos* (Zamora: El Colegio de Michoacán, 1997). For a history of the group and its debates, see Guillermo Sheridan, *Los Contemporáneos ayer* (Mexico City: Fondo de Cultura Económica, 1985).

49. Beyond Palou, I have developed this contention to describe the Mexican postrevolutionary literary field at large. See Ignacio M. Sánchez Prado, *Naciones intelectuales: Las fundaciones de la modernidad literaria mexicana (1917–1959)* (West Lafayette, Ind.: Purdue University Press, 2009).

50. Mabel Moraña, *Bourdieu en la periferia: Capital simbólico y campo cultural en América Latina* (Santiago de Chile: Cuarto Propio, 2014), 100–101.

51. Jorge Volpi, *A pesar del oscuro silencio* (Mexico City: Joaquín Mortiz, 1992); English version, *In Spite of Dark Silence* (Chicago: Swan Isle, 2011).

52. Volpi interprets Cuesta's work as a critic in "El magisterio de Jorge Cuesta," *Plural* 234 (1989): 26–40.

53. Danny J. Anderson, "The Novels of Jorge Volpi and the Possiblity of Knowledge," *Studies in the Literary Imagination* 33.1 (2000): 2–4.

54. Christopher Domínguez Michael, *Tiros en el concierto: Literatura mexicana del siglo V* (Mexico City: Era, 1997), 233.

55. Pedro Ángel Palou, "En la alcoba de un mundo," *La palabra y el hombre* 138 (2006): 183–89.

56. Tamara Williams, "The *Contemporáneos* as Holy Grail: Towards a Genealogy of the Poet as Quest in the Mexican Novel," *Cuaderno International de Estudiso Humanísticos y de Literatura: CIEHL* 14 (2010): 36.

57. Valeria Luiselli, *Los ingrávidos* (Mexico City: Sexto Piso, 2011); English version, *Faces in the Crowd*, trans. Christina MacSweeney (Minneapolis: Coffee House, 2014).

58. Jorge Volpi, *La imaginación y el poder: Una historia intelectual de 1968* (Mexico City: Era, 1998); *La guerra y las palabras: Una historia intelectual de 1994* (Mexico City: Era, 1994).

59. Samuel Steinberg, *Photopoetics at Tlatelolco: Afterimages of Mexico, 1968* (Austin: University of Texas Press, 2015), 164.

60. Ignacio Padilla, *Arte y olvido del terremoto* (Oaxaca: Almadía, 2010). For an account of this historical event, see Carlos Monsiváis, *Entrada libre: Crónicas de una sociedad que se organiza* (Mexico City: Era, 1987).

61. The thesis was published in an edited and abridged version as *El diablo y Cervantes* (Mexico City: Fondo de Cultura Económica, 1995); see also the essays in *Digestivos cervantinos* (Mexico City: Universidad Iberoamericana, 2011) and *Los demonios de Cervantes* (Mexico City: Fondo de Cultura Económica, 2016).

62. Eloy Urroz, *La silenciosa herejía: Forma y contrautopía en las novelas de Jorge Volpi* (Mexico City: Aldus, 2000).

63. Ricardo Chávez Castañeda and Celso Santajuliana, *La generación de los enterradores: Una expedición a la narrativa mexicana del tercer milenio* (Mexico City: Nueva Imagen, 2000); *La generación de los enterradores II: Una nueva expedición a la narrativa mexicana del tercer milenio* (Mexico City: Nueva Imagen, 2003).

64. Leonardo da Jandra and Roberto Max, comps., *Dispersión multitudinaria* (Mexico City: Joaquín Mortiz, 1997).

65. Jorge Volpi, *En busca de Klingsor* (Barcelona: Seix Barral, 1999); English version, *In Search of Klingsor*, trans. Kristina Cordero (New York: Scribner, 2002).

66. Jorge Volpi, "Narrativa hispanoamericana, Inc.," in *Entre lo local y lo global: La narrativa latinoamericana en el cambio de siglo (1990–2006)*, ed. Jesús Montoya Juárez and Ángel Esteban (Madrid: Iberoamericana Vervuert, 2008), 98–112.

67. Volpi, "Narrativa hispanoamericana, Inc.," 107–8.

68. Héctor Hoyos, *Beyond Bolaño: The Global Latin American Novel* (New York: Columbia University Press, 2015), 190. See also Fredric Jameson, "Third World Literature in the Era of Multinational Capitalism," *Social Text* 15 (1986): 65–88.

69. Jorge Volpi, *Mentiras contagiosas: Ensayos* (Madrid: Páginas de Espuma, 2008), 236.

70. Volpi, "Narrativa hispanoamericana, Inc.," 111.

71. Jorge Volpi, *El insomnio de Bolívar: Cuatro consideraciones intempestivas sobre América Latina en el siglo XXI* (Mexico City: Debate, 2009).

72. For a further development of Volpi's ideas in this regard, see Cristóbal Pera, "¿Nación? ¿Qué nación? La idea de América Latina en Volpi y Bolaño," *Revista de Estudios Hispánicos* 46 (2012): 99–113.

73. Volpi, *Mentiras contagiosas*, 224.

74. Roger Bartra, *Blood, Ink, and Culture: Miseries and Splendors of the Post-Mexican Condition*, trans. Mark Alan Healey (Durham, N.C.: Duke University Press, 2002), 47.

75. Brian Whitener, "Ontology and Crisis of State and Finance in Jorge Volpi's *En busca de Klingsor*," *Journal of Latin American Cultural Studies* 24.1 (2015): 56.

76. Volpi, *Mentiras contagiosas*, 230.

77. Volpi, *Mentiras contagiosas*, 230.

78. Jorge Volpi, "Días de ira," in Volpi, Urroz, and Padilla, *Tres bosquejos del mal*, 179–229.

79. Ana Pellicer López, "*Días de ira*: Texto inicial e iniciático," in *En busca de Jorge Volpi: Ensayos sobre su obra*, ed. Juan Manuel López de Abiada, Félix Jiménez Ramírez, and Augusta López Bernasocchi (Madrid: Verbum, 2004), 220–33.

80. See Regalado López, "The Crack and Latin American Narrative," 61–64.

81. Carlos Fuentes, *La gran novela latinoamericana* (Mexico City: Alfaguara, 2011); Miguel Ángel de Villena, "*En busca de Klingsor*, de Jorge Volpi, será traducida a siete idiomas," *El País* (Madrid, Spain), November 13, 1999.

82. See, for example, Oliver Morton, "Problem Solved," *The Guardian* (London, England), May 9, 2003.

83. Christopher Domínguez Michael, "La patología de la recepción," *Letras Libres* 63 (March 2004): 48–51.

84. Hoyos, *Beyond Bolaño*, 55.

85. José Emilio Pacheco, *Morirás lejos* (Mexico City: Joaquín Mortiz, 1967); English version, *You Will Die in a Distant Land*, trans. Elizabeth Umlas (Coral Gables, Fla.: North-South Center University of Miami, 1991).

86. Sarah Pollack, "Latin America Translated (Again): Roberto Bolaño's *The Savage Detectives* in the United States," *Comparative Literature* 61.3 (2009): 352–53.

87. José Manuel López de Abiada and Daniel Leuenbergo, "La recepción de *En busca de Klingsor* en el ámbito de la cultura alemana," in López de Abiada, Jiménez Ramírez, and López Bernasocchi, *En busca de Jorge Volpi*, 355–70.

88. For readings on Nazism, see Hoyos, *Beyond Bolaño*, 33–64; González, "Klingsor/Schmitt: Sobre el dilema estético de la novela contaminada de historia," in López de Abiada, Jiménez Ramírez, and López Bernasocchi, *En busca de Jorge Volpi*, 123–44. The science readings are far more numerous, so I will single out a couple: Joaquín Lahsen, "Transposición científica de *En busca de Klingsor* Jorge Volpi: Teoría del todo," *Latin Americanist* 58.2 (2014): 75–95; Gioconda Marún, "El teorema de Gödel y la literatura latinoamericana," *Hispania* 92.4 (2009): 696–704.

89. This is best developed in Marcie Paul, "The Search for Identity: The Return to Analytic Detective Fiction in Mexico," in *Hispanic and Luso-Brazilian Detective Fiction: Essays on the Género Negro Tradition*, ed. Renée W. Craig-Odders, Jacky Collins, and Glen S. Close (Jefferson, N.C.: McFarland, 2006), 185–91.

90. Umberto Eco, *The Name of the Rose*, trans. William Weaver (San Diego: Harcourt Brace Jovanovich, 1983). The reference to Eco was raised by Susana

Fortes. See Domínguez Michael, "Jorge Volpi o el horro al vacío," in López de Abiada, Jiménez Ramírez, and López Bernasocchi, *En busca de Jorge Volpi*, 101. For Eco's Borgesian genealogy, see Deborah Parker, "The Literature of Appropriation: Eco's Use of Borges in *Il Nome della Rosa*," *Modern Literature Review* 95 (1990): 842–49.

91. Glen S. Close, *Contemporary Hispanic Crime Fiction: A Transatlantic Discourse on Urban Violence* (New York: Palgrave Macmillan, 2008), 178.

92. Volpi, *En busca de Klingsor*, 23–26; *In Search of Klingsor*, 23–26.

93. Volpi, *En busca de Klingsor*, 177–81; *In Search of Klingsor*, 165–69.

94. For a general introduction to the concepts used by Volpi, I recommend the entries in the *Stanford Encyclopedia of Philosophy*, https://plato.stanford.edu/, which provide sophisticated yet accessible explanations. For Erwin Schrödinger, see Bruce Weber, "Life," *Stanford Encyclopedia of Philosophy* (Spring 2015 ed.), ed. Edward N. Zalta. For Gödel's incompleteness theorems, see Panu Raatikainen, "Gödel's Incompleteness Theorems," *Stanford Encyclopedia of Philosophy* (Spring 2015 ed.), ed. Edward N. Zalta. For Eisenberg's Uncertainty Principle, see Jan Hilgevoord and Jos Uffink, "The Uncertainty Principle," *Stanford Encyclopedia of Philosophy* (Spring 2014 ed.), ed. Edward N. Zalta.

95. This is a fragment of the epigraph, which comes from Schrödinger's papers and is cited by Walter Moore, *Schrödinger: Life and Thought* (Cambridge: Cambridge University Press, 1989), 348. Volpi himself references this source in his acknowledgments.

96. Ingrid Simson, "El principio de la paradoja en la literatura latinoamericana: De Jorge Luis Borges a Jorge Volpi," in *La narración paradójica: "Normas narrativas" y el principio de la "transgresión,"* ed. Nina Grabe, Sabine Lang, and Klaus Meyer-Minnemann (Madrid: Iberoamericana Vervuert, 2006), 113–20.

97. Félix Jiménez Ramírez, "*En busca de Klingsor*, Jorge Volpi y el lenguaje científico," in López de Abiada, Jiménez Ramírez, and López Bernasocchi, *En busca de Jorge Volpi*, 184–85.

98. Volpi, *En busca de Klingsor*, 437; *In Search of Klingsor*, 408. Here I would point out Sara Calderón's study of ambiguity in Volpi. See Sara Calderón, *Jorge Volpi ou l'esthétique de l'ambigüeté* (Paris: L'Harmattan, 2010).

99. Sergio Ricardo Arenas Martínez, *Volpi-Links-Klingsor: Autores inciertos* (Villahermosa: Universidad Juárez Autónoma de Tabasco, 2007), 158.

100. Douglas R. Hofstadter, *Gödel, Escher, Bach: An Eternal Golden Braid* (New York: Vintage, 1980). Volpi, *En busca de Klingsor*, 442; *In Search of Klingsor*, 413. For Volpi's theorization on Hofstadter, see *Leer la mente: El cerebro y el arte de la ficción* (Mexico City: Alfaguara, 2011), 51–74. For a further discussion of this connection, see Marún, "El teorema de Gödel y la literatura latinoamericana," 699–700.

101. Brian McHale, *Postmodernist Fiction* (London: Routledge, 1987), 113.

102. McHale, *Postmodernist Fiction*, 213.

103. A parallel reading is proposed by Héctor Fernández L'Hoeste, who suggests that the overarching point would be to say that the object of the novel's uncertainty principle is ultimately Mexicanness; i.e., that the book's recourse to science is a way to comment allegorically on the impossibility of understanding any identity, including the Mexican identity. As I have made clear in this chapter, I do not share this reading; nonetheless, I find it worth considering. See Héctor

D. Fernández L'Hoeste, "On Science and Mexican Nationalism: The Politics of Identity in Jorge Volpi's *In Search of Klingsor*," in *Science, Literature and Film in the Hispanic World*, ed. Jerry Hoeg and Kevin S. Larsen (New York: Palgrave Macmillan, 2006), 107–28.

104. Jodi Melamed, *Represent and Destroy: Rationalizing Violence in the New Racial Capitalism* (Minneapolis: University of Minnesota Press, 2011); Alberto Fuguet, "Magical Neoliberalism," *Foreign Policy* 125 (2001): 66–73.

105. Jorge Volpi, *Leer la mente: El cerebro y el arte de la ficción* (Madrid: Alfaguara, 2011).

106. David Gascoigne, "Elucidating Uncertainties: Michel Rio and the Science of Fiction," *Nottingham French Studies* 41.1 (2002): 19–27. It is worth mentioning that Rio has based one of his books on Heisenberg's ideas: Michel Rio, *Le prince d'incertitude Roman* (Paris: Seuil, 1993).

107. Henry Sussman, "The Calculable, the Incalculable and the Rest: Kafka's Virtual Environment," *MLN* 127.5 (2012): 1147; emphasis in the original.

108. Hoyos, *Beyond Bolaño*, 55.

109. Michael Frayn, *Copenhagen* (New York: Anchor, 2000).

110. Jorge Volpi, "Encuentro en Copenhague," *Letras Libres* 27 (2001): 60.

111. Jorge Fornet, *Los nuevos paradigmas: Prólogo narrativo al siglo XXI* (Havana: Letras Cubanas, 2006), 30; Volpi, *En busca de Klingsor*, 19; Volpi, *In Search of Klingsor*, 19.

112. Jorge Volpi, *No será la tierra* (Madrid: Alfaguara, 2006); English version, *Season of Ash: A Novel in Three Acts*, trans. Alfred J. MacAdam (Rochester, N.Y.: Open Letter Books, 2009). For a good study of this book, see Eduardo Íñiguez, "Tiempo de declive: Continuidad y ruptura con las formas del mito en *No será la tierra* de Jorge Volpi," *Bulletin of Hispanic Studies* 89.5 (2012): 531–41.

113. Fornet, *Los nuevos paradigmas*, 34.

114. Lidia Santos, "El cosmopolitismo de mercado: Del fin de las literaturas nacionales a la cultura de las celebridades (Brasil, Mexico y Chile)," *Revista de crítica literaria latinoamericana* 69 (2009): 153–65.

115. Eduardo Becerra, "La narrativa hispanoamericana en España: En busca de un nuevo lector," *Letras Libres España* 7 (April 2002): 34–37.

116. The Crack romance novels are Pedro Ángel Palou's *Bolero* (Mexico City: Nueva Imagen, 1997) and a diptych of novels, Eloy Urroz's *Herir tu fiera carne* (*Hurting Your Fierce Flesh*) and Volpi's *Sanar tu piel amarga* (*Healing Your Bitter Skin*), also published in 1997. These last two were republished as a single volume: Jorge Volpi and Eloy Urroz, *Dos novelitas poco edificantes* (Cádiz: Algaida / Ayuntamiento de Cádiz, 2008).

117. Jorge Volpi, email to author, December 28, 2015.

118. Rebecca Walkowitz, *Born Translated: The Contemporary Novel in the Age of World Literary Translation* (New York: Columbia University Press, 2015).

119. Jorge Volpi, *El jardín devastado* (Mexico City: Alfaguara, 2008).

120. José Enrique Navarro, "You'll Never Write Alone: Online Sharing Economy and the New Role of the Reader," *Hispanic Issues On Line* 9 (2012): 123–37.

121. Ramón Alvarado Ruiz, "Escribir en la era digital desde un *jardín devastado*," *Espéculo* 54 (2015): 35.

122. Sergio Gutiérrez Negrón, "Ética cosmopolita en *El jardín devastado y Oscuro bosque oscuro* de Jorge Volpi," *Confluencia* 28.2 (2013): 111.

123. For *A Thousand and One Nights* as world literature, see Richard van Leuween, "The Canonization of the *Thousand and One Nights* in World Literature," in *Foundational Texts of World Literature*, ed. Dominique Jullien (New York: Peter Lang, 2011), 101–18.

124. See Salma K. Jayussi, "Umayyad Poetry," in *The Cambridge History of Arabic Literature: Arabic Literature to the End of the Umayyad Period*, ed. A. F. L. Beeston, T. M. Johnstone, R. B. Serjeant, and G. R. Smith (Cambridge: Cambridge University Press, 1983). For the popularization of the Nizami version, see Ali Asghar Seyed Gohrab, *Layli and Majnun: Love, Madness and Mystic Longing in Nizami's Epic Romance* (Leiden: Brill, 2003).

125. Volpi, *El jardín devastado*, 36.

126. David Palumbo-Liu, *The Deliverance of Others: Reading Literature in a Global Age* (Durham, N.C.: Duke University Press, 2012), xii.

127. Palumbo-Liu, *The Deliverance of Others*, 40.

128. Jorge Volpi, *Oscuro bosque oscuro* (Oaxaca: Almadía, 2009).

129. Jorge Volpi, *Memorial del engaño* (Madrid: Alfaguara, 2013).

130. George Steiner, *Grammars of Creation: Originating in the Guifford Lectures for 1990* (New Haven, Conn.: Yale University Press, 2001), 257.

131. Steiner, *Grammars of Creation*, 6.

132. Ignacio Padilla, *Amphytrion* (Madrid: Espasa-Calpe, 2000); English version, *Shadow without a Name*, trans. Peter Bush and Anne McLean (New York: Farrar, Straus and Giroux, 2003). Ignacio Padilla, *La gruta del Toscano* (Mexico City: Alfaguara, 2006).

133. *Amadís de Gaula: Versión de Garci Rodríguez de Montalvo*, 2 vols., ed. Juan Manuel Cacho Blecua (Madrid: Cátedra, 1987–88). For a discussion on the question of time and myth in *Amadís* and *Don Quixote*, see Luis Murillo, "The Summer of Myth: *Don Quijote de la Mancha* and *Amadís de Gaula*," in *Hispanic Studies in Honor of Edward de Chasca* (Iowa City: University of Iowa Press, 1972), 145–57.

134. Linda Hutcheon, *A Poetics of Postmodernism: History, Theory, Fiction* (London: Routledge, 1988).

135. Chávez Castañeda et al., *Crack: Instrucciones de uso*, 35; Christoph Ransmayr, *The Last World*, trans. John E. Woods (New York: Grove Weidenfeld, 1990).

136. Amanda Holmes, "Transformations of the Magical Real: Ransmayr and García Márquez," *Canadian Review of Comparative Literature* 29.4 (2002): 537–51.

137. Lynne Cooke, "The Novels of Christoph Ransmary: Towards a Final Myth," *Modern Austrian Literature* 31.3–4 (1998): 22. For Blumenberg's reflections on myth and absolute reality, see Hans Blumenberg, *Work on Myth*, trans. Robert Wallace (Cambridge, Mass.: MIT Press, 1990).

138. Robin MacKenzie, "Center and Periphery in Lawrence Norfolk's *The Pope's Rhynoceros* and Christoph Ransmayr's *Die Ietzet Welt*," *Orbis Litterarum* 67.5 (2016): 416–36. See also Franco Moretti, *Atlas of the European Model 1800–1900* (London: Verso, 1998), 40.

139. Juan García Ponce, *La errancia sin fin: Musil, Borges, Klossowski* (Barcelona: Anagrama, 1981); *Ante los demonios: A propósito de una novela excepcional; Los demonios de Heimito Von Doderer* (Mexico City: Universidad Nacional Autónoma de Mexico / El equilibrista, 1993).

140. José María Pérez Gay, *El imperio perdido* (Mexico City: Cal y Arena, 1991).

141. Claudio Magris, *El mito habsbúrgico de la literatura austriaca moderna*, trans. Guillermo Fernández (Mexico City: Universidad Nacional Autónoma de México, 1998).

142. Ignacio Padilla, email to the author, December 15, 2015. Kakanian is the name that authors like Musil give to the Habsburg culture of the Austro-Hungarian Empire.

143. Claudia Macías Rodríguez, "Memoria y olvido en torno al problema de la identidad en *Amphytrion* de Ignacio Padilla," *Revista de Literatura Mexicana Contemporánea* 42 (2009): 27–37.

144. Paul, "The Search for Identity," 192–98; Ezequiel de Rosso, "Huellas de sentido: *Amphytrion*," in *La fugitiva contemporaneidad: Narrativa latinoamericana 1990–2000*, ed. Celina Manzoni (Buenos Aires: Corregidor, 2003), 167–84.

145. Anne Marie Stachura, "Transnational Injustice: The Subversion of Myth in Ignacio Padilla's *Amphytrion*," in *Myth and Subversion in the Contemporary Novel*, ed. José Manuel Losada-Goya and Marta Guirao Ochoa (Newcastle upon Tyne: Cambridge Scholars, 2012), 285.

146. William Collins Donohue, *The End of Modernism: Elias Canetti's Auto-da-Fé* (Chapel Hill: University of North Carolina Press, 2001), 187–89.

147. Kathleen L. Komar, "Inscriptions of Power: Broch's Narratives of History in *Die Schlafwandler*," in *Hermann Broch, Visionary in Exile: The 2001 Yale Symposium*, ed. Paul Michael Lützeler (Rochester, N.Y.: Camden House, 2003), 109.

148. For accounts of the earthquake and its consequences in Mexican politics and civil society, see Carlos Monsiváis, *Entrada libre, crónicas de una sociedad que se organiza* (Mexico City: Era, 1987), and Elena Poniatowska, *Nada, nadie* (Mexico City: Era, 1988).

149. Ignacio Padilla, *Arte y olvido del terremoto* (Oaxaca: Almadía, 2010).

150. Padilla, *Arte y olvido del terremoto*, 132.

151. Padilla, *Arte y olvido del terremoto*, 133.

152. Marianne Hirsch, *The Generation of Postmemory: Writing and Visual Culture after the Holocaust* (New York: Columbia University Press, 2012).

153. Ignacio Padilla, *La catedral de los ahogados* (Mexico City: Universidad Autónoma Metropolitana, 1995) and *Si volviesen sus majestades* (Mexico City: Nueva Imagen, 1996).

154. Ignacio Padilla, *La vida íntima de los encendedores: Animismo en la sociedad ultramoderna* (Madrid: Páginas de Espuma, 2009).

155. Ignacio Padilla, *El legado de los monstruos: Tratado sorbe el miedo y lo terrible* (Mexico City: Taurus, 2013) and *Las fauces del abismo* (Mexico City: Océano, 2014).

156. Ignacio Padilla, email to the author, December 15, 2015.

157. Rosario Hubert, "Rewriting Travel Literature: A Cosmopolitan Critique of Exoticism in Contemporary Latin American Fiction," in *Peripheral Transmodernities: South-to-South Intercultural Dialogues between the Luso-Hispanic World and "the Orient,"* ed. Ignacio López-Calvo (Newcastle upon Tyne: Cambridge Scholars, 2012), 49–50.

158. Vesna Goldsworthy, *Inventing Ruritania: The Imperialism of the Imagination* (London: Hurst and Company, 2012).

159. Cristina della Coletta, *World's Fairs Italian Style: The Great Exhibitions in Turin and Their Narratives 1860–1915* (Toronto: University of Toronto Press, 2006), 140–41.

160. Ignacio Padilla, *El peso de las cosas* (Puebla: Universidad de las Américas–Puebla, 2006).

161. Ignacio Padilla, *Crónicas africanas: Espejismo y utopía en el reino de Swazilandia* (Mexico City: Colibrí / Secretaría de Cultura–Puebla, 2001).

162. Richard F. Patteson, *A World Outside: The Fiction of Paul Bowles* (Austin: University of Texas Press, 1987), 60.

163. Padilla, *El peso de las cosas*, 94–95.

164. Padilla, *El peso de las cosas*, 94.

165. Laura Chrisman, *Rereading the Imperial Romance: British Imperialism and South African Resistance in Haggard, Schreiner and Plaatje* (Oxford: Clarendon, 2000).

166. Elleke Boehmer, "The Worlding of the Jingo Poem," *Yearbook of English Studies* 41.2 (2011): 41–57.

167. Thomas Richards, *The Imperial Archive: Knowledge and the Fantasy of Empire* (London: Verso, 1993).

168. Aaron Worth, *Imperial Media: Colonial Networks and Information Technologies in the British Literary Imagination, 1857–1918* (Columbus: Ohio State University Press, 2014), 7.

169. Padilla, *El diablo y Cervantes*.

170. Padilla, *La gruta del Toscano*, 16.

171. Pedro Ángel Palou, *Paraíso clausurado* (Barcelona: Muchnik, 2000).

172. Pedro Ángel Palou, *Malheridos* (Mexico City: Joaquín Mortiz, 2003).

173. Pedro Ángel Palou, *Demasiadas vidas* (Mexico City: Plaza y Janés, 2001); *Qliphoth* (Buenos Aires: Sudamericana, 2003); *Casa de la magnolia* (Mexico City: Sudamericana, 2004). These books were recently collected in *Mar fantasma* (Mexico City: Seix Barral, 2016).

174. Pedro Ángel Palou, *Con la muerte en los puños* (Mexico City: Alfaguara, 2003).

175. See, respectively, Pedro Ángel Palou, *Zapata* (Mexico City: Planeta, 2006); *No me dejen morir así* (Mexico City: Planeta, 2014); and *Pobre patria mía: La novela de Porfirio Díaz* (Mexico City: Planeta, 2010).

176. Pedro Ángel Palou, *El impostor* (Mexico City: Planeta, 2012); *El dinero del diablo* (Mexico City: Planeta, 2009); *La amante del ghetto* (Mexico City: Planeta, 2013).

177. For this reading, see Mattias Devrient, Diana Castilleja, and Eugenia Houvenaghel, "Pedro Ángel Palou (La generación del Crack): ¿Un escritor posmoderno?," *Bulletin of Hispanic Studies* 89.7 (2012): 737–50. This text is probably the most serious attempt at an academic reading of Palou's fiction. Unfortunately, some of its contentions are problematic due to factual imprecisions. It claims, for instance, that the characters in *Paraíso clausurado* are influenced by Palou's tenure in a high-ranking university position, but Palou assumed the presidency of the University of the Américas–Puebla (where he was a faculty member at the time) many years after writing the novel. It also claims that *Memoria de los días* contains a reference to a book by José Saramago that was published after Palou's novel and that Gavito is a stand-in for García Márquez (given its resemblance to

the word "Gabo," the Colombian writer's nickname), an assertion with no basis in the character's trajectory or Palou's literary ideas.

178. Pedro Ángel Palou, *Resistencia de materiales* (Mexico City: Instituto Politécnico Nacional, 2000), 45.

179. Volpi, Urroz, and Padilla, *Tres bosquejos del mal*; Vicente F. Herrasti, *Diorama* (Barcelona: Muchnik, 2000).

180. Pedro Ángel Palou, *Paraíso clausurado* (Mexico City: Tusquets, 2016). All subsequent citations of the novel refer to the Muchnik edition, not this one.

181. Palou, *Paraíso clausurado*, 7; Ted Hughes, *Birthday Letters* (New York: Farrar, Straus and Giroux, 1998).

182. Palou, *Paraíso clausurado*, 7; Eugenio Montale, *Satura 1962–1970*, trans. Willam Arrowsmith (New York: Norton, 1998), 191.

183. Rebecca J. West, *Eugenio Montale: Poet on the Edge* (Cambridge, Mass.: Harvard University Press, 1981), 95.

184. Palou, *Paraíso clausurado*, 12.

185. Daniel Sada, "Museo de la melancolía," *Letras libres* 28 (2001): 83.

186. Chávez Castañeda et al., *Crack: Instrucciones de uso*, 203.

187. Edward W. Said, *On Late Style* (New York: Vintage, 2007), 17.

188. West, *Eugenio Montale*, 120–21.

189. Jonathan Boulter, *Melancholy and the Archive: Trauma, History and Memory in the Contemporary Novel* (London: Continuum, 2011), 184–85.

190. Raymond Klibansky, Erwin Panofsky, and Fritz Saxl, *Saturn and Melancholy: Studies in the History of Natural Philosophy, Religion and Art* (London: Thomas Nelson and Sons, 1964). These references were shared with me by Jorge Volpi. For a further study of this tradition, see Margot and Rudolf Wittkower, *Born under Saturn: The Character and Conduct of Artists* (New York: New York Review Books, 2007).

191. Robert Burton, *The Anatomy of Melancholy* (New York: New York Review Books, 2001).

192. Stephanie Shirilan, *Robert Burton and the Transformative Powers of Melancholy* (Farnham, U.K.: Ashgate, 2015).

193. Palou, *Paraíso clausurado*, 105–11.

194. Kyra Giorgi, *Emotions, Language and Identity on the Margins of Europe* (New York: Palgrave Macmillan, 2014), 29–76.

195. Palou, *Paraíso clausurado*, 23.

196. Palou, *Paraíso clausurado*, 293.

197. Eloy Urroz, *Siete ensayos capitales* (Mexico City: Taurus/UNAM, 2004), 143.

Chapter 3

1. Nuala Finnegan and Jane Lavery, *The Boom Femenino in Mexico: Reading Contemporary Women's Writing* (Newcastle upon Tyne: Cambridge Scholars, 2010).

2. Nuala Finnegan, "Women Writers in the Land of 'Virile' Literature," in *A History of Mexican Literature*, ed. Ignacio M. Sánchez Prado, Anna M. Nogar, and José Ramón Ruisánchez Serra (Cambridge: Cambridge University Press, 2016), 338–49.

3. Emily Hind, *Feminism and the Mexican Woman Intellectual from Sor Juana to Poniatowska: Boob Lit* (New York: Palgrave Macmillan, 2010); Oswaldo Estrada, *Ser mujer y estar presente: Disidencias de género en la literatura mexicana contemporánea* (Mexico City: Universidad Nacional Autónoma de México, 2014).

4. Pierre Bourdieu, *Masculine Domination*, trans. Richard Nice (Stanford, Calif.: Stanford University Press, 1998), 93; emphasis in original.

5. Bourdieu, *Masculine Domination*, 93.

6. Sarah E. L. Bowskill, *Gender, Nation and the Formation of the Twentieth-Century Mexican Literary Canon* (London: Legenda, 2011).

7. Among these books, I would call attention to Ana Rosa Domenella, coord., *Territorio de leonas: Cartografía de narradoras mexicanas de los noventa* (Mexico City: Juan Pablos / UAM, 2001), as well as the series Desbordar el Canon, in which various members of the group contribute to books on individual women writers who have generally been ignored by critics. Of the authors in the series, one could highlight Elena Garro, Josefina Vicens, Ámparo Dávila, and Guadalupe Dueñas.

8. Jean Franco, *Plotting Women: Gender and Representation in Mexico* (New York: Columbia University Press, 1991); Claudia Schaefer, *Textured Lives: Women, Art and Representation in Modern Mexico* (Tucson: University of Arizona Press, 1992); Debra A. Castillo, *Easy Women: Sex and Gender in Modern Mexican Fiction* (Minneapolis: University of Minnesota Press, 1998); María Elena de Valdés, *The Shattered Mirror: Representations of Women in Mexican Literature* (Austin: University of Texas Press, 1998).

9. For the original formulation of the concept, see Hélène Cixous, "The Laugh of the Medusa," in *The Portable Cixous*, ed. Marta Segarra (New York: Columbia University Press, 2010), 27–39.

10. Sarah E. L. Bowskill, "The Origins of the Mexican *Boom Femenino*," in Finnegan and Lavery, *The Boom Femenino en Mexico*, 75–76.

11. Bowskill, "The Origins of the Mexican *Boom Femenino*," 83.

12. For more on the "economy of symbolic goods" and the concept of autonomy, see Pierre Bourdieu, *The Rules of Art: Genesis and Structure of the Literary Field*, trans. Susan Emanuel (Stanford, Calif.: Stanford University Press, 1996), 141–73.

13. See Janice A. Radway, *Reading the Romance: Women, Patriarchy and Popular Literature* (Chapel Hill: University of North Carolina Press, 1984); Tania Modleski, *Loving with a Vengeance: Mass Fantasies Produced for Women* (London: Routledge, 1982).

14. Debra A. Castillo, "Gender and Sexuality in World Literature," in *The Routledge Companion to World Literature*, ed. Theo D'haen, David Damrosch, and Djelal Kadir (London: Routledge, 2012), 393–403.

15. Marguerite Duras, *The Lover*, trans. Barbara Bray (New York: Pantheon, 1985); Amy Tan, *The Joy Luck Club* (New York: Putnam, 1989); *Regards from the Dead Princess*, trans. Sabine Destree and Anna Williams (New York: Arcade, 1989).

16. Graham Huggan, *The Postcolonial Exotic: Marketing the Margins* (London: Routledge, 2001), 155–76; Rebecca L. Walkowitz, *Born Translated: The*

Contemporary Novel in the Age of World Literature (New York: Columbia University Press, 2017).

17. Shu-Mei Shih, "Global Literatures and the Technologies of Recognition," in *World Literature: A Reader*, ed. Theo D'Haen, César Domínguez, and Mads Rosendahl Thomsen (London: Routledge, 2013), 260.

18. Bourdieu, *Rules of Art*, 231–34.

19. Cited in Niamh Thornton, "Ana García Bergua's *Púrpura*: Gay Narrative and the *Boom Femenino* in Mexico," in Finnegan and Lavery, *The Boom Femenino in Mexico*, 221; Ana Garcia Bergua, *Púrpura* (Mexico City: Era, 1999).

20. Thornton, "Ana García Bergua's *Púrpura*," 218. See also García Bergua, *Púrpura*.

21. Thornton, "Ana García Bergua's *Púrpura*," 235–36.

22. Emily Hind, "Six Authors of the Conservative Side of the *Boom Femenino*, 1985–2003: Boullosa, Esquivel, Loaeza, Mastretta, Nissán, Sefchovich," in Finnegan and Lavery, *The Boom Femenino in Mexico*, 51–53.

23. Carmen Boullosa, *Mejor desaparece* (Mexico City: Océano, 1987); English version, *Better Disappear*, trans. Christy Rodgers (Saarbuken: VDM Verlag, 2009). Carmen Boullosa, *Antes* (Mexico City: Vuelta, 1989); English version, *Before*, trans. Peter R. Bush (Dallas: Deep Vellum, 2016).

24. Carmen Boullosa, *Llanto: Novelas imposibles* (Mexico City: Era, 1992); *Duerme* (Madrid: Alfaguara, 1994).

25. Cristina Rivera Garza, *Nadie me verá llorar* (Mexico City: Tusquets / Conaculta, 1999); English version, *No One Will See Me Cry*, trans. Andrew Hurley (Willimantic, Conn.: Curbstone, 2003).

26. The historical saga and family narrations are such important topics at the time that Jean Franco devotes three chapters to these questions. See Franco, *Plotting Women*, 129–87.

27. See Carmen Boullosa, *Son vacas somos puercos* (Mexico City: Era, 1991); English version, *They're Cows, We're Pigs*, trans. Leland H. Chambers (New York: Grove, 1997). Carmen Boullosa, *El medico de los piratas* (Madrid: Siruela, 1992).

28. For examples of her early-period poetry, see Boullosa, *La salvaja* (Mexico City: Fondo de Cultura Económica, 1989). For a rare, fine study of her poetry, see Jacobo Sefamí, "Las camaleónicas huidizas en la poesía de Carmen Boullosa," in *Acercamientos a Carmen Boullosa: Actas del simposio "Conjugarse en infinitivo"; Carmen Boullosa*, ed. Barbara Dröscher and Carlos Rincón (Berlin: Tranvía / Walter Frey, 1997), 245–54.

29. See Carmen Boullosa, *Cielos de la tierra* (Madrid: Alfaguara, 1997); English version, *Heavens on Earth*, trans. Shelby Vincent (Dallas: Deep Vellum, 2016). I will not attempt to encompass the whole of this massive critical output; I limit myself to the secondary bibliography relevant to my contentions. But it is worth noting that there is more scholarly output on Boullosa than on any other author in this book (perhaps with the exception of Pitol).

30. Sarah Brouillette, "World Literature and Market Dynamics," in *Institutions of World Literature: Writers, Translation, Markets*, ed. Stefan Helgesson and Pieter Vermeulen (London: Routledge, 2016), 103. On the question of subsumption of the contemporary artwork and the problematization of the notion of autonomy, see Nicholas Brown, "The Work of Art in the Age of Its

Real Subsumption," *Nonsite* (March 13, 2012), http://nonsite.org/editorial/the-work-of-art-in-the-age-of-its-real-subsumption-under-capital.

31. Emily Hind, *Entrevistas con quince autoras mexicanas* (Madrid: Iberoamericana Vervuert, 2003), 34.

32. Ellen Spielman, "Entrevista con Carmen Boullosa," in Dröscher and Rincón, *Acercamientos a Carmen Boullosa*, 261.

33. Guadalupe Gómez del Campo, "Una defeña en Brooklin: Entrevista con Carmen Boullosa," *Literal* 2 (April 2, 2012), http://literalmagazine.com/una-defena-en-brooklin-entrevista-con-carmen-boullosa/.

34. Spielman, "Entrevista con Carmen Boullosa," 262.

35. Inés Ferrero Cárdenas, "Entrevista a Carmen Boullosa," *Grafemas*, December 2007, http://people.wku.edu/inma.pertusa/encuentros/grafemas/diciembre_07/ferrero.html.

36. Ferrero Cárdenas, "Entrevista a Carmen Boullosa."

37. Ferrero Cárdenas, "Entrevista a Carmen Boullosa."

38. Carmen Boullosa, *De un salto descabalga la reina* (Madrid: Debate, 2002); English version, *Cleopatra Dismounts*, trans. Geoff Hargreaves (New York: Grove, 2003).

39. Pedro Ángel Palou, *En la alcoba de un mundo* (Madrid: Debate, 2002); Ana García Bergua, *La confianza en los extraños* (Madrid: Debate, 2002); Sergio Pitol, comp., *Los cuentos de una vida: Antología del cuento universal* (Madrid: Debate, 2002). The series also included landmark books by Guillermo Fadanelli and other writers, as well as a major anthology of Daniel Sada, who was on the rise as a key figure in Mexican literature.

40. Carmen Boullosa, *Treinta años* (Madrid: Alfaguara, 1999); English version, *Leaving Tabasco*, trans. Geoff Hargreaves (New York: Grove, 2003).

41. Víctor Barrera Enderle, "Entradas y salidas del fenómeno literario actual o la 'alfaguarización' de la literatura hispanoamericana," *Sincronías* 1 (2002); http://sincronia.cucsh.udg.mx/alfaguar.htm.

42. Carmen Boullosa, *La otra mano de Lepanto* (Mexico City: Fondo de Cultura Económica, 2005).

43. Carmen Boullosa, *Salto de mantarraya (y otros dos)* (Mexico City: Fondo de Cultura Económica, 2004).

44. Sergio Pitol, *El mago de Viena* (Mexico City: Fondo de Cultura Económica, 2006); English version, *The Magician of Vienna*, trans. George Henson (Dallas: Deep Vellum, 2017). Álvaro Uribe, *La linterna de los muertos (y otros cuentos fantásticos)* (Mexico City: Fondo de Cultura Económica, 2006).

45. Boullosa, *La otra mano de Lepanto*, 435.

46. Carmen Boullosa, *La milagrosa* (Mexico City: Era, 1994). For the positive reviews, see Christopher Domínguez Michael, "Son vacas, somos puercos de Carmen Boullosa," *Vuelta* 182 (January 1992): 48; Adriana Díaz Enciso, "El médico de los piratas de Carmen Boullosa," *Vuelta* 192 (November 1992): 41–42; Domínguez Michael, "Profecía, sueño," *Vuelta* 193 (December 1992): 41–42; Adolfo Castañón, "La milagrosa de Carmen Boullosa," *Vuelta* 207 (February 1994): 44–46.

47. Christopher Domínguez Michael, "La civilización sin alma," *Vuelta* 220 (March 1995): 40. It is worth noting that the review also trashes another historical novel: Ignacio Solares, *Nen, la inútil* (Mexico City: Alfaguara, 1994).

48. Domínguez Michael, "La civilización sin alma," 40–41.

49. Estrada, *Ser mujer y estar presente*, 123–24; Ute Seydel, *Narrar historia(s): La ficcionalización de temas históricos por las escritoras Elena Garro, Rosa Beltrán y Carmen Boullosa* (Madrid: Iberoamericana Vervuert, 2007), 442.

50. Seydel, *Narrar historia(s)*, 447.

51. Hind, *Feminism and the Mexican Woman Intellectual*, 10.

52. Seydel, *Narrar historia(s)*, 446. Seydel refers to a review by Tomás Granados Salinas comparing Boullosa to the spiritual writer Antonio Velasco Piña, founder of an ultra-Mexicanist group with esoteric approaches to pre-Columbian culture.

53. Lucía Melgar, "El horror de cerca," *Letras Libres* 83 (2005): 74–75. See also Carmen Boullosa, "Cielos de Tierra," *Vuelta* 245 (April 1997): 27–29.

54. Melgar, "El horror de cerca," 75. See also Carmen Boullosa, *El complot de los románticos* (Madrid: Siruela, 2009).

55. Christopher Domínguez Michael, "El gato y el garabato," *Letras Libres* 126 (June 2009): 81.

56. Carmen Boullosa, *La novela perfecta* (Mexico City: Alfaguara, 2006). Carmen Boullosa, *Texas: La gran ladronería en el lejano Norte* (Mexico City; Alfaguara, 2012); English version, *Texas: The Great Theft*, trans. Samantha Schnee (Dallas: Deep Vellum, 2014).

57. Carmen Boullosa, *El Velázquez de París* (Madrid: Siruela, 2007); *La virgen y el violin* (Madrid: Siruela, 2008); *El complot de los románticos* (Siruela, 2009); and *Las paredes hablan* (Madrid: Siruela, 2010).

58. Hind, *Feminism and the Mexican Woman Intellectual*, 40.

59. Hind, *Feminism and the Mexican Woman Intellectual*, 41, 142, 160.

60. Cristina Santos, *Bending the Rules in the Quest for an Authentic Female Identity: Clarice Lispector and Carmen Boullosa* (New York: Peter Lang, 2004), 142.

61. Yolanda Melgar Pernías, *Los Bildungsromane femeninos de Carmen Boullosa y Sandra Cisneros: Mexicanidades, Fronteras, Puentes* (Woodbridge: Támesis, 2008).

62. Alessandra Luiselli, *Letras mexicanas: Ensayos críticos sobre escritores mexicanos de la segunda mitad del siglo XX* (Mexico City: Universidad Nacional Autónoma de México, 2006), 136. Anna Forné correctly points out that Menton places Boullosa in the traditional category of the historical novel, not in the new one. See *La piratería textual: Un estudio hipertextual de Son vacas, somos puercos y El médico de los piratas de Carmen Boullosa* (Lund: Romanska Institutiones / Lunds Universitet, 2001), 39.

63. Cynthia Margarita Tompkins, *Latin American Postmodernisms: Women Writers and Experimentation* (Gainesville: University Press of Florida, 2006).

64. Alexander O. Exquemelin, *The Buccaneers of America*, trans. Alexis Brown (Mineola, N.Y.: Dover, 2000). For a detailed comparison between Boullosa's work and the source, see Andreas Gooses, "Utopía, violencia y la relación entre los géneros en el mundo de los piratas," in Dröscher and Rincón, *Acercamientos a Carmen Boullosa*, 133–44. Further considerations on the questions of memory and narrative can be found in Michaela Peters, "Narrar la memoria colectiva: *Son vacas, somos puercos*," in Dröscher and Rincón, *Acercamientos a Carmen Boullosa*, 120–32.

65. Peter Hallward, *Absolutely Postcolonial: Writing between the Singular and the Specific* (Manchester: Manchester University Press, 2001), 331–32.

66. Hallward, *Absolutely Postcolonial*, 334.

67. Díaz Enciso, "El médico de los piratas," 54–55.

68. See note 9.

69. Boullosa openly discusses this question in an interview; she justifies publishing both novels on the basis of their different narrative perspectives. Interestingly, in this interview she also emphasizes the instability of the narrative "I," which contradicts readings of her books as bildungsromans. See Erna Pfeiffer, *Exiliadas, emigrantes, viajeras: Encuentros con diez escritoras latinoamericanas* (Madrid: Iberoamericana Vervuert, 1993), 43.

70. Pfeiffer, *Exiliadas, emigrantes, viajeras*, 41.

71. Gabriella de Beer, *Contemporary Mexican Women Writers: Five Voices* (Austin: University of Texas Press, 1996), 178.

72. Carmen Boullosa, *Cuando me volví mortal* (Mexico City: Cal y Arena, 2010), 144.

73. See, for instance, Jessica Burke, "Consuming the Other: Cannibals and Vampires in Carmen Boullosa's Fiction," *Romance Notes* 49.2 (2009): 177–84. See also Cornelia Ruhe, "El pirata devorado: Piratería literaria en la novela de Carmen Boullosa *Son vacas, somos puercos*," *Iberoromania* 66 (2009): 61–79.

74. Tompkins, *Latin American Postmodernisms*, 148.

75. Estrada, *Ser mujer y estar presente*, 117.

76. Karim Benmiloud, "Le modèle du roman d'aventures revisité par Carmen Boullosa: *Son vacas, somos puercos*," *América—Cahiers du CRICCAL* 34 (2006): 57–67.

77. Forné, *La piratería textual*, 161–62. Tompkins underscores a similar point when she explains that "Boullosa complements thematic kernels and figures of excess with rhetorical devices such as hyperbole, metonymy, intertextuality and self-reflexivity." See Tompkins, *Latin American Postmodernisms*, 136.

78. Ana García Bergua, *Isla de bobos* (Mexico City: Seix Barral, 2007).

79. Laura Restrepo, *Isla de la pasión* (Bogotá: Planeta, 1989); Pablo Raphael, *Clipperton* (Mexico City: Random House, 2014).

80. Ana García Bergua, *Rosas negras* (Mexico City: Plaza y Janés, 2004).

81. Hind, *Entrevistas con quince autoras mexicanas*, 72.

82. Milagros Ezquerro, "*Isla de bobos*: Primer asedio," in *Tres escritoras mexicanas: Elena Poniatowska, Ana García Bergua, Cristina Rivera Garza*, ed. Karim Benmiloud and Alba Lara-Alengrin (Rennes: Presses Universitaires de Rennes, 2014), 170.

83. Davy Desmas, "Indagando los márgenes de la historia: La imaginación femenina en *Isla de bobos* de Ana García Bergua," in Benmiloud and Lara-Alengrin, *Tres escritoras mexicanas*, 103.

84. Hind, *Entrevistas con quince autoras mexicanas*, 67.

85. Hind, *Entrevistas con quince autoras mexicanas*, 67.

86. Ana García Bergua, *El umbral: Travels and Adventures* (Mexico City: Era, 1993); *El imaginador* (Mexico City: Era, 1996).

87. Ana García Bergua, "Los grandes dones de Ignacio Padilla," *Laberinto* 689 (August 27, 2016): 8.

88. See Efrén Hernández, *Tachas y otros cuentos*, intro. by Ana García Bergua (Mexico City: UNAM, 2002).

89. Jordi García Bergua, *Karpus Minthej* (Mexico City: Fondo de Cultura Económica, 1981).

90. Mauricio Carrera and Betina Keizman, *El minotauro y la sirena: Entrevistas-ensayos con nuevos narradores mexicanos* (Mexico: Lectorum, 2001), 218.

91. Carrera and Keizman, *El minotauro y la sirena*, 208.

92. García Bergua, *El umbral*, 79.

93. Ana García Bergua, "Un mundo paralelo," in *La novela según los novelistas*, coord. Cristina Rivera Garza (Mexico City: Fondo de Cultura Económica, 2007), 59.

94. García Bergua, "Un mundo paralelo," 61.

95. Silvia Molina, *La mañana debe seguir gris* (Mexico City: Joaquín Mortiz, 1977).

96. Silvia Molina, *Imagen de Héctor* (Mexico City: Cal y Arena, 1990).

97. Thornton, "Ana García Bergua's *Púrpura*," 220.

98. Thornton, "Ana García Bergua's *Púrpura*," 222.

99. Anadeli Bencomo, "La imaginadora: El arte narrativo de Ana García Bergua," *Explicación de textos literarios* 36.1–2 (2007–8): 78–79.

100. Bencomo, "La imaginadora," 80.

101. Most of her short stories can be found compiled in Ana García Bergua, *El limbo bajo la lluvia* (Mexico City: Textofilia, 2013).

102. Mads Rosendahl Thomsen, *Mapping World Literature: International Canonization and Transnational Literature* (London: Continuum, 2008), 74–75.

103. Ana García Bergua, "The Inverted Room," in *Transcultural Encounters amongst Women: Redrawing Boundaries in Hispanic and Lusophone Art, Literature and Film*, ed. Patricia O'Byrne, Gabrielle Carty, and Niamh Thornton (Newcastle upon Tyne: Cambridge Scholars, 2010), 103.

104. García Bergua, "The Inverted Room," 106–7.

105. García Bergua, "The Inverted Room," 107.

106. García Bergua, "The Inverted Room," 107–8.

107. Thomsen, *Mapping World Literature*, 99–100.

108. In particular, Bencomo cites Christopher Domínguez Michael's assertion that García Bergua "vacía a la autora" (preempts the woman author). See Bencomo, "La imaginadora," 79.

109. Ana García Bergua, *La bomba de San José* (Mexico City: Era/UNAM, 2012); *Fuego 20* (Mexico City: Era/UNAM, 2017).

110. For an example of Rivera Garza's alignment with ideas of the northern Mexican writer, see Graciela Silva Rodríguez, *La frontera norteña femenina: Transgresión y resistencia identitaria en Esalí, Conde y Rivera Garza* (Mexico City: Eón, 2010). While a reading of Rivera Garza as a border writer has merit—she is a binational author hovering between Texas, California, and Tamaulipas—I think that this approach flattens important dimensions of Rivera Garza's work and puts her on the same plane as writers like Rosina Conde, who writes in radically different ways. A more suggestive approach to questions of the border and gender in Rivera Garza can be found in Lila McDowell Carlsen, "'Te conozco de cuando eras árbol': Gender, Utopianism and the Border in Cristina Rivera Garza's *La cresta de Ilón*," *Symposium* 64.4 (2010): 229–42.

111. As a topic that departs from the themes discussed here, I do not elaborate further on this question, but excellent work has been done in this regard. For extensive discussions, see Laura Kanost, "Pasillos sin luz: Reading the Asylum in *Nadie me verá llorar* by Cristina Rivera Garza," *Hispanic Review* 76.3 (2008): 299–316; Rebecca Garoznik, "Deconstructing Psychiatric Discourse and Idealized Madness in Cristina Rivera Garza's *Nadie me verá llorar*," *Chasqui* 43.1 (2014): 3–14.

112. Craig Epplin, *Late Book Culture in Argentina* (London: Bloomsbury, 2014).

113. See Cristina Rivera Garza, *No hay tal lugar: U-tópicos contemporáneos*, http://cristinariveragarza.blogspot.com.

114. Betina Keizman, "El blog de Cristina Rivera Garza. Experiencia literaria y terreno de contienda," *Chasqui* 42.1 (2013): 3–15.

115. Epplin, *Late Book Culture in Argentina*, 18–19.

116. See Alberto Chimal, *Las historias*, http://www.lashistorias.com.mx. See also Heriberto Yépez, *Archivo Hache*, http://archivohache.blogspot.com, and *Border Destroyer*, https://borderdestroyer.com. Previous iterations of Yépez's blogs do not seem to be online at the time of this writing, but he has maintained an active internet presence since the late 1990s.

117. See Ángel Rama, *The Lettered City*, trans. John Charles Chasteen (Durham, N.C.: Duke University Press, 1996).

118. Jean Franco, *The Decline and Fall of the Lettered City: Latin America in the Cold War* (Cambridge, Mass.: Harvard University Press, 2002), 260–61. See also Josefina Ludmer, *Aquí América Latina: Una especulación* (Buenos Aires: Eterna Cadencia, 2010). For a discussion on the role of the market under these circumstances, see José Ramón Ruisánchez Serra, coord., *Libro Mercado: Literatura y neoliberalismo* (Mexico City: Universidad Iberoamericana, 2015).

119. Patrick Dove, *Literature and "Interregnum": Globalization, War, and the Crisis of Sovereignty in Latin America* (Albany: State University of New York, 2016), 11.

120. Dove, *Literature and "Interregnum,"* 13. Dove discusses the concept of "postautonomous literature" posed by Ludmer in *Aquí América Latina* and implicitly dialogues with the same phenomena discussed by Epplin in *Late Book Culture in Argentina*.

121. For a discussion of this topic with data on the nature of the subsidies, see Ignacio M. Sánchez Prado, "The Public Economy of Prestige: Mexican Literature and the Paradox of State-Funded Capital," in *Pierre Bourdieu and Hispanic Studies* (New York: Palgrave, forthcoming in 2018).

122. "World Lite," *n+1* 17 (2013); https://nplusonemag.com/issue-17/the-intellectual-situation/world-lite/.

123. Irmgard Emmelhainz, *La tiranía del sentido común: La reconversión neoliberal en México* (Mexico City: Paradiso, 2016), 134–35.

124. Emmelhainz, *La tiranía del sentido común*, 144.

125. Cristina Rivera Garza, "Chocar, diferir, dialogar," in *No hay tal lugar*, December 12, 2004.

126. Maricruz Castro, Laura Cázares, and Gloria Prado, eds., *Escrituras en contraste: Femenino/Masculino en la literatura mexicana del siglo XX* (Mexico City: Aldus/UAM, 2004).

127. For a chronicle of this event, see Eve Gil, "¡No me hallo! ¡no me veo!," *All about Eve* (blog), May 28, 2006, http://evegil.blogspot.com/2006/05/no-me -hallo-no-me-veo.html.

128. Cristina Rivera Garza, *La cresta de Ilón* (Mexico City: Tusquets, 2002). As part of a revival of Dávila's work, to which Rivera Garza's novel contributed, a definitive edition of her short stories now exists. See Ámparo Dávila, *Cuentos reunidos* (Mexico City: Fondo de Cultura Económica, 2009).

129. Emily Hind, "El consumo textual y *La cresta de Ilón* de Cristina Rivera Garza," in *Filología y Lingüística* 31.1 (2005): 36.

130. Eugenia Berenice Reza Dávila, "Transgresión y fronteras en *La cresta de Ilón* de Cristina Rivera Garza," in Benmiloud and Lara-Alengrin, *Tres escritoras mexicanas*, 244; Cristina Rivera Garza, *La muerte me da* (Mexico: Tusquets, 2007).

131. Cristina Rivera Garza, *Los muertos indóciles: Necroescritura y desapropiación* (Mexico City: Tusquets, 2013).

132. Rivera Garza, *Los muertos indóciles*, 113–14.

133. On this matter, see Marta Sierra, "Memento Mori: Photography and Narrative in Cristina Rivera Garza's *Nadie me verá llorar*," in *Espectros: Ghostly Hauntings in Contemporary Transhispanic Narratives*, ed. Alberto Ribas-Casasayas and Amanda L. Petersen (Lewisburg, Pa.: Bucknell University Press, 2016), 151–64.

134. Rivera Garza, *Los muertos indóciles*, 99; Nathalie Piégay-Gros, *Le futur antérieur de l'archive* (Quebec: Tangence, 2012), 20.

135. Cécile Quintana, *Cristina Rivera Garza: Une écriture-mouvement* (Rennes: Presses Universitaires de Rennes, 2016).

136. Steve McCaffery, *Panopticon* (Toronto: Blueointment, 1984).

137. Marjorie Perloff, *Poetic License: Essays on Modernist and Post-Modernist Lyric* (Evanston, Ill.: Northwestern University Press, 1990), 287–89.

138. Robert Fitterman and Vanessa Place, *Notes on Conceptualisms* (New York: Ugly Duckling, 2009); Spanish version, *Notas sobre conceptualismos* (Mexico City: Conaculta, 2013).

139. Rivera Garza, *Los muertos indóciles*, 53–78; David Markson, *Wittgenstein's Mistress* (Normal, Ill.: Dalkey Archive, 2005).

140. Cristina Rivera Garza, *Verde Shangai* (Mexico City: Tusquets, 2011).

141. Cristina Rivera Garza, *La guerra no importa* (Mexico City: Joaquín Mortz, 1991). The explanations of the novel's sources are found in Rivera Garza, *Verde Shangai*, 317–19.

142. Cristina Rivera Garza, *La imaginación pública* (Mexico City: Conaculta, 2013).

Conclusion

1. Liliana Blum, *El monstruo pentápodo* (Mexico City: Tusquets, 2017).

2. Liliana V. Blum, *Residuos de espanto* (Mexico City: Ficticia, 2013); *Pandora* (Mexico City: Tusquets, 2015).

3. Blum, *El monstruo pentápodo*, 11; Vladimir Nabokov, *Lolita* (New York: Vintage, 1997), 284.

4. Ellen Pifer, "Nabokov's Novel Offspring: Lolita and Her Kin," in *Vladimir Nabokov's Lolita: A Casebook*, ed. Ellen Pifer (Oxford: Oxford University Press, 2003), 83–110.

5. Joyce Carol Oates, *Daddy Love* (New York: Mysterious Press, 2013); Hanya Yanagihara, *The People in Trees* (New York: Doubleday, 2013); Emma Donoghue, *Room* (New York: Picador, 2010).

6. Rebecca Walkowitz, *Born Translated: The Contemporary Novel in the Age of World Literature* (New York: Columbia University Press, 2015), 30.

7. For all of the contentions discussed here, see Franco Moretti, *Distant Reading* (London: Verso, 2013), 42–62.

8. For information on books in the series, see http://www.bloomsbury.com/uk /series/literatures-as-world-literature/?pg=1.

9. Mads Rosendhal Thomsen, *Mapping World Literature: International Canonization and Transnational Literatures* (London: Continuum, 2008).

10. Mariano Siskind, *Cosmopolitan Desires: Global Modernity and World Literature in Latin America* (Evanston, Ill.: Northwestern University Press, 2014); Héctor Hoyos, *Beyond Bolaño: The Global Latin American Novel* (New York: Columbia University Press, 2015).

11. Oswaldo Zavala, "The Repoliticization of the Latin American Shore: Roberto Bolaño and the Dispersion of 'World Literature,' " in *Roberto Bolaño as World Literature*, ed. Nicholas Birns and Juan E. De Castro (London: Bloomsbury, 2017), 93.

12. Zavala, "The Repoliticization of the Latin American Shore," 81.

13. Ignacio M. Sánchez Prado, ed., *América Latina en la "literatura mundial"* (Pittsburgh: Instituto Internacional de Literatura Iberoamericana, 2006).

14. Daniel Saldaña París, *En medio de extrañas víctimas* (Mexico City: Sexto Piso, 2013); English version, *Among Strange Victims*, trans. Christina McSweeney (Minneapolis: Coffee House, 2016). Laia Jufresa, *Umami* (Mexico City: Literatura Random House, 2015); English version, *Umami*, trans. Sophie Hughes (London: Oneworld, 2016).

15. Álvaro Enrigue, *Muerte súbita* (Barcelona: Anagrama, 2013); English version, *Sudden Death*, trans. Natasha Wimmer (New York: Riverhead Books, 2016).

16. Aura Xilonen, *Campeón gabacho* (Mexico City: Literatura Random House, 2015); English version, *The Gringo Champion*, trans. Andrea Rosenberg (New York: Europa Books, 2016).

17. Jorge Volpi, *Anatomía de mi padre* (Mexico City: Alfaguara, 2016).

18. Pedro Ángel Palou, *Tierra roja* (Mexico City: Planeta, 2016).

19. Heriberto Yépez, "La crackificación," *Laberinto 585* (August 30, 2014): 12.

INDEX